The Little Rock & Fort Smith Railway:
History Through the Miles

Barton Jennings

Arkansas Valley Route, Volume 1

The Little Rock & Fort Smith Railway: History Through the Miles
Copyright © 2026 by Barton Jennings

Publisher's Cataloging-in-Publication Data
Jennings, Barton

The Little Rock & Fort Smith Railway: History Through the Miles
556p.; 23cm.
ISBN: 979-8-9904307-3-0
Library of Congress Control Number: 2026934408

Front cover photos by Barton Jennings: Clarksville, Morrilton, and Russellville depots.
Back cover photo by Sarah Jennings
All interior photos by Barton Jennings unless otherwise noted.

Please send comments or corrections to sarah@techscribes.com

TechScribes, Inc.
PO Box 2199
Alma, AR 72921
www.techscribes.com

Printed in the United States of America

Contents

Other books by Barton Jennings

<u>History Through the Miles</u>

Arkansas & Missouri Railroad: History Through the Miles

Alaska Railroad: History Through the Miles

Iowa Interstate Railroad: History Through the Miles

Everett Railroad: History Through the Miles

Tennessee Central Railway: History Through the Miles

Whitewater Valley Railroad: History Through the Miles

Oregon's Joseph Branch: History Through the Miles

Missouri & North Arkansas Railroad: History Through the Miles

Hennepin Canal Parkway: History Through the Miles

Idaho's Payette River Railroads: History Through the Miles

*Delta Heritage Trail (Missouri Pacific's Wynne Subdivision):
History Through the Miles*

The Choctaw Route: History Through the Miles

The Railroads of U.S. Sugar: History Through the Miles

The Heavener Sub: History Through the Miles

The Little Rock: History Through the Miles

Iowa Northern Railway: History Through the Miles

The DeQueen & Eastern Railroad: History Through the Miles

<u>Textbook</u>

*The Basics of Transportation: Policies, Practices and Pricing –
An Applied Perspective*

<u>History</u>

The Solgohachia Murders: A Fryer Family Tragedy

Acknowledgments

Having once worked for Union Pacific, the author has been fortunate enough to know some of the employees who worked for the railroad over the last several decades. Additionally, he has had the pleasure to get to know a number of the people who have researched the railroad. These contacts are all thanked for their help.

David Hoge is a master of newspaper research, and his collection of more than 3000 pages of railroad-related newspaper articles from Arkansas is a masterful source of information. He deserves thanks for sharing this resource. Articles written by Clifton E. "Gene" Hull, Bill Pollard, and others provided a good start on the histories of the railroad over multiple decades. Dr. Pollard's continued work through the Arkansas Railroad History website is much appreciated. The late Mike Condren developed what is certainly the most detailed web page about the history of the railroads in the Fort Smith area. The Missouri Pacific Historical Society has also made available substantial amounts of information about the various lines once operated by the company.

A number of documents were also used in writing this book. It is amazing what can be found on the internet these days. Copies of the *Official Guide*, the annual reports of various state railroad and corporation commissions, Interstate Commerce Commission reports, and other such documents were great resources. The St. Louis, Iron Mountain & Southern, as well as Missouri Pacific, produced numerous documents that are still available. These include timetables, track charts, lists of stations, contracts, annual reports, and even its own company magazine. Related sources such as the *Arkansas Marketing and Industrial Guide*, *The Coal Dealers Blue Book*, local histories published by the Goodspeed Publishing Company, Sanborn Insurance Maps, and others were a great aid. Newspapers also reported heavily on the construction and operations of the Little Rock & Fort Smith. Many of these are available through the Library of Congress.

The author has had the pleasure of riding across the route between Little Rock, Van Buren and Fort Smith numerous times. Visits to the Faulkner County Museum in Conway, the Ozark Area Depot Museum, the Morrilton Depot Museum, the Altus Heritage House Museum, the offices of Main Street Russellville, and the visitors center at Van Buren have also aided in the research.

Finally, the author has a house with several rooms full of books, timetables, and other documents about this and other railroads. All of these and more were used in producing this volume.

Thanks to everyone who has helped in digging into the history of the Little Rock & Fort Smith Railway.

What Was the Arkansas Valley Route?

When Union Pacific transferred me from Oregon to McGehee, Arkansas, I started hearing a great deal about the Valley Route, or the line from Little Rock to McGehee. I had previously heard the term growing up in Arkansas, but never understood it. As I began to research the name, I found that it was created in the 1870s when the Little Rock & Fort Smith Railway and the Little Rock, Mississippi River & Texas Railway came under control of the same Boston bondholders. This led to the idea of a through railroad route parallel to the Arkansas River which became known as the Arkansas Valley Route, or simply the Valley Route. In reality, it was the centerpiece of a planned Kansas City to New Orleans rail system, with connections to places like St. Louis, Denver, Houston, and elsewhere.

During the late 1800s, the term Arkansas Valley Route was heavily promoted as the coordinated services of the Little Rock & Fort Smith Railway and the Little Rock, Mississippi River & Texas Railway.

The name Arkansas Valley Route came from the plan for the railroad to essentially replace the steamboats that operated on the Arkansas River. The rail route connected the Arkansas River at Fort Smith, on the western border of Arkansas, to Arkansas City, located on the Mississippi River in the southeast corner of Arkansas. The Arkansas Valley, up to forty miles wide, lies between the Ozark Mountains to the north and the Ouachita Mountains to the south. South of Little Rock, the route passes into the Arkansas Delta region. Both provided room for the railroad, and the communities, farms and businesses that would grow up alongside the tracks.

The Arkansas Valley Route was initially built as two separate projects. The track from Little Rock westward to Fort Smith was built by the appropriately named Little Rock & Fort Smith Railway. The route to the southeast of Little Rock was completed by the Little Rock, Mississippi River & Texas Railway. The route was further extended towards Kansas City with the construction of a third railroad, the Kansas & Arkansas Valley. All of these lines became controlled by the St. Louis, Iron Mountain & Southern, then Missouri Pacific. Today, they are part of Union Pacific.

What Was the Little Rock & Fort Smith Railway?

The Little Rock & Fort Smith Railway was a rail line built from the Little Rock area in Arkansas, westward to what was then Indian Territory in what became Oklahoma. The line later connected with the Kansas & Arkansas Valley Railway as part of a line that stretched on north to Coffeyville, Kansas, and eventually Kansas City. With its partner line, the Little Rock, Mississippi River & Texas Railway, this created a rail route on south towards the Gulf of Mexico. While planning for the Little Rock to western Arkansas line started with the Arkansas incorporation of the "Little Rock and Fort Smith Branch of the Cairo and Fulton Railroad Company" on November 25, 1853, the approximately 160-mile-long rail line wasn't completed to Van Buren until July 11, 1876, and to Fort Smith on January 30, 1879. During this time, several corporate names under various ownership groups worked to build a line along the north side of the Arkansas River, opening up large tracts of land and creating a number of new towns and cities. The railroad then went through the ownership of the St. Louis, Iron Mountain & Southern Railway, and then Missouri Pacific Railroad. Today, the route is the Van Buren Subdivision of Union Pacific Railroad.

Construction was not a steady process as there were several failed starts and then a number of stops. Multiple reorganizations took place between the initial proposal and the work's completion, but the goals were reached. The line's construction included 50.1 miles of track built in 1871, 15.0 miles in 1872, 35.0 miles in 1873, 20.0 miles in 1875, and 45.0 miles in 1876. About 5 miles of construction in 1879 finished the original route. An early report also stated that there were 7.25 miles of sidings when the line was completed. Four parts of the railroad were improved with significant new construction during 1902-04, with the older parts eventually abandoned.

Since that time, the route built by the Little Rock & Fort Smith has been organized a number of ways by its owners. The first major changes took place by the St. Louis, Iron Mountain & Southern Railway.

During November 1890, the Iron Mountain concentrated its properties and divided the system into three divisions. The Arkansas Valley Lines – Little Rock & Fort Smith; Little Rock, Mississippi River & Texas; and Kansas & Arkansas Valley – were all united as part of the Central Division with headquarters in Little Rock.

Next, Missouri Pacific Railroad made some changes, but generally kept the Little Rock & Fort Smith as part of their Central Division. Initially, the track between North Little Rock and Van Buren was the Van Buren District of the Central Division, then it became the Van Buren Subdivision. Starting during the 1980s after the Union Pacific-Missouri Pacific merger, a number of reorganizations not only changed the end points of the subdivision, but also what division the line was assigned to. These included:

> 1984 – North Little Rock to Van Buren as Van Buren Subdivision of Arkansas Division
>
> 1986 – North Little Rock to Coffeyville as Van Buren Subdivision of Kansas Division
>
> 1988 – North Little Rock to Coffeyville as Van Buren Subdivision of Van Buren Division
>
> 1992 – North Little Rock to Leeds Junction as Coffeyville Subdivision of Van Buren Division
>
> 1995 – North Little Rock to Leeds Junction as Coffeyville Subdivision of Central Service Unit
>
> 1998 – North Little Rock to Van Buren as Van Buren Subdivision of North Little Rock Area

The entire line has been modernized with new CTC signals, heavier bridges and new sidings, and today sees approximately 20 freight trains a day. The line still connects Kansas City and routes to the west and north with the Gulf Coast and the southeast. The founders and builders of the Little Rock & Fort Smith Railway would be proud.

This is part of a map published in 1873 by G. W. & C. B. Colton & Co. of New York. It shows the route of the Little Rock & Fort Smith from Little Rock to Van Buren, and then further west into Indian Territory. *Map showing the connections of the Little Rock and Fort Smith Railroad and its land grant.* G. W. & C. B. Colton & Co, and Little Rock & Fort Smith R.R. Co. New York, 1873. Map. Retrieved from the Library of Congress, https://www.loc.gov/item/98688694/.

Development of the Little Rock & Fort Smith Railway

Like most railroads, it took several efforts and several companies to actually build the tracks between Little Rock and Fort Smith, both located in Arkansas. Some of this was due to a lack of local financing, some was due to the Civil War, and much of this was due to the enormous expenses involved with building a railroad through a countryside where little revenue freight or passengers could be obtained. Essentially, the railroad developed the farms and towns that it served. This meant that construction would often start and stop as funding was available. It also meant that the bonds and stock of the railroad would go through cycles of being valuable and then being worthless. Bondholders would reorganize the railroad, or even create a new company to take over the assets in attempts to preserve their investments. However, as with many such railroads, the Little Rock & Fort Smith wasn't stabilized until investors with deep enough pockets took an interest, and combined the property with a larger and better financed rail system. The more than half-dozen firms involved in this process are covered here, along with their individual roles in creating today's Van Buren Subdivision.

Little Rock and Fort Smith Branch of the Cairo and Fulton Railroad

As with many railroads, the rail line from Little Rock to Fort Smith began with several false starts. During the 1850s, several proposals were being made to build railroads across Arkansas, both north to south and east to west. As a part of these plans, the United States Congress prepared land grants that could be used by designated railroads along specific routes. The first general survey took place in late 1850 when Captain Joshua K. Barney of the U.S. Topographical Engineers passed through Little Rock looking for a route to the Pacific Ocean.

Barney was later involved with the Cairo & Fulton and the Little Rock & Fort Smith railroads.

Initially, the general consensus was that the Cairo & Fulton Railroad Company would be the primary rail route. It would cross Arkansas from northeast to southwest, and would have branches from Little Rock eastward to Memphis, and westward to Fort Smith. On February 1, 1853, Congress passed *An act granting the right of way and making a grant of lands to the States of Arkansas and Missouri, to aid in the construction of a railroad from a point on the Mississippi river, opposite the mouth of the Ohio, via Little Rock, to the Texas boundary, near Fulton, in Arkansas, with branches, one to Fort Smith and one to a point on the Mississippi river.*

Despite the plan, the two branches were actually built by separate companies. To the east was the Memphis & Little Rock Railroad Company, organized by a Special Act of the Arkansas General Assembly that was approved January 11, 1853. This line eventually became part of the Choctaw Route of the Chicago, Rock Island & Pacific, a part of the line westward from Memphis, Tennessee, to Tucumcari, New Mexico. Details on this line can be found in the book *The Choctaw Route: History Through the Miles*, written by the author of this book.

To the west of Little Rock, the first railroad approved by the general laws of Arkansas (November 25, 1853) was the Little Rock and Fort Smith Branch of the Cairo and Fulton Railroad Company, backed by a number of Boston capitalists and Arkansas politicians. The railroad was created this way so it could apply for the land grants originally created for the Cairo & Fulton Railroad. However, it wasn't actually associated with the other corporation. The Little Rock and Fort Smith Branch never built any track, but on January 19, 1855, the United States Congress officially transferred the land grant rights to the company with *An Act fixing the line of the Little Rock and Fort Smith branch of the Cairo and Fulton railroad and granting the lands donated by Congress to the State in aid thereof.*

As was typical at the time, a series of meetings were held along the general route of the proposed railroad to spark interest in the project and to raise capital for the construction. Stock and bond purchases, donations, and gifts of free right-of-ways were all encouraged. Those who subscribed to the stock sale were regularly called upon to make payments, including a 5 per cent payment on November 9, 1853, and a 1.5 per cent payment on June 8, 1854.

Little Rock & Fort Smith Railroad Company

With the sales of stock and the transfer of the land grants, the Little Rock and Fort Smith Branch of the Cairo and Fulton Railroad Company changed its name to the Little Rock & Fort Smith Railroad Company on January 22, 1855, although both names, or versions of both names, were used for years. The Arkansas General Assembly transferred the land grants adjacent to the Little Rock to Fort Smith route to the new company on November 26, 1856. Several surveys were made and a plan to build the line along the north side of the Arkansas River was chosen. Thomas A. Hendricks, United States Land Commissioner, reported in early 1858 that 550,525 acres of federal granted lands had been provided to Arkansas as aid for construction of the Little Rock & Fort Smith Railroad.

Two surveys were made for what would eventually be the Little Rock & Fort Smith Railway. Both were made in 1854, with Captain R. L. Hunter making a survey for the Arkansas Pacific Railroad, organized at Fort Smith during the first few years of the 1850s. Captain Joshua Barney made a survey for the backers of the Little Rock & Fort Smith Branch. Both surveys followed the north side of the Arkansas River west of Russellville, with Barney's survey actually connecting to the Cairo & Fulton about 20 or 25 miles north of Little Rock, with a line from Cadron Mountain southward to Little Rock. Joshua Barney estimated the cost of construction to be $2,460,778 for 153.75 miles of railroad. He also provided a cost of depots and rolling stock, which was estimated at an additional $360,000. Hunter's survey crossed the Arkansas River at Dardanelle and stayed south of the Arkansas River on to Little Rock at an estimated cost of $2,422,965. The board of the Little Rock & Fort Smith would accept and use parts of each survey.

In 1857, the Little Rock & Fort Smith tried to start construction on the line. The first contractor hired was John J. Shoemaker of Pennsylvania, who was later described as an "irresponsible" party "united to great energy of character and plausibility of address, the audacity and the deceit of an accomplished scoundrel." Shoemaker was issued a contract to grade 25 miles of right-of-way or build 10 miles of railroad, but he disappeared after only doing some minor work. As published in the *Reports of the Several Railroads in the State of Arkansas Made to The Governor* (1858), "Mr. Shoemaker went to work with seemingly great drive and earnestness, to fulfill his contract, and, in the midst of it, he left ostensibly for the purpose of bringing on the necessary means to prosecute the work, and I believe, has scarcely been heard of since." Unfortunately, the railroad had an obligation to do this work by November 25, 1858, as set forth by the United States Congress in its land grant.

Because of the construction issues experienced in 1857, the Arkansas General Assembly removed the November 25, 1858, requirement. Changes were also made to allow the railroads east and west of Little Rock to consolidate as the Central Pacific Railroad on February 8, 1859, although this never took place. Several detailed surveys were made in 1859 and plans were made to sell off some of the land grants to pay for construction, although little was actually sold. In October 1859, the railroad (still using the Little Rock and Fort Smith Branch of the Cairo and Fulton Railroad name) advertised for bids to build 20 miles of railroad east from Van Buren. In reality, the railroad divided the job into smaller one-mile sections, and bidders could make offers on any or all of the sections. The railroad stated that it would prefer to make payment with company stock or lands instead of cash.

On December 3, 1859, Waddell, Black & Company of Ohio was awarded a contract for grading, grubbing and timber work on a 32-mile section from Van Buren to Ozark. The western end of the line was the first project since many of the railroad's directors and officers lived in Van Buren. Also, low water levels on the Arkansas River often prevented boat service on this stretch of the river, making the railroad more important here. Unfortunately, only about 15 miles of the right-of-way were even worked on and none were completed, with the work halted in July 1860 due to a lack of funds. Attempts to borrow money from New York banks or obtain local investors failed. However, there was another source of funding – the revenue from the State of Arkansas Clarksville Swamp Land Fund. This was a sale of land owned by Arkansas in the Clarksville Swamp Land District, a sale which raised $38,000, which was paid to the railroad on March 28, 1861. Despite the call for contractors, the contract issued, and the efforts to raise funds, little was done until the Civil War ended all work on the railroad. During the war, the treasury of the railroad, which amounted to $31,304 in gold, was hidden from both the military and civil officers of the Union and Confederate States. This provided the company some funding to restart construction following the war.

The year 1866 was a busy and confusing one for the railroad. The *Annual Report of the President of the Little Rock and Fort Smith Railroad – 1866*, explained one of the major challenges facing the railroad after the Civil War. It stated that half of the stockholders and directors of the railroad had died, left Arkansas, or were ruined financially during the conflict. At the May 17, 1866, directors' meeting, not enough surviving directors attended to hold a quorum. Most of the railroad's documents were missing, including papers, maps, surveys, engineer's papers, and pretty much everything else except the records of the board of directors' meetings and some files found at the Arkansas Secretary of State's office. Meanwhile, the railroad lost its land grants because it failed to build 20 miles within ten years.

Little Rock & Fort Smith Railroad Company – The Reorganizations of the 1860s

Essentially, the effort to build the railroad would have to start over. To help with this, on July 28, 1866, the United States Congress renewed the railroad's land grants and even expanded them. About that time, an effort was made to reunite the Cairo & Fulton Railroad with the Little Rock & Fort Smith, something which didn't happen until several decades later when both became part of the St. Louis, Iron Mountain & Southern.

A big step was taken when on October 18, 1866, the Little Rock & Fort Smith was reorganized. New directors were selected to fill the seven empty board vacancies. The company also changed its charter in several ways, including removing the requirement of having Clarksville as the railroad's headquarters and the designation that the Little Rock & Fort Smith was a branch of the Cairo & Fulton. Despite all of these changes, both the Cairo & Fulton and the Memphis & Little Rock soon presented proposals to consolidate with the Little Rock & Fort Smith. On December 17, 1866, the stockholders of the Little Rock & Fort Smith had a meeting where they voted to form the Central Pacific Railroad by consolidating with the Memphis & Little Rock (M&LR),

if the M&LR board also agreed. The stockholders also elected a new board of directors and officers. Jesse Turner was elected president, A. J. Ward as vice-president, J. H. Haney as secretary, and P. Pennywit as treasurer.

Many of the early leaders of the Little Rock & Fort Smith Railway were buried in Fairview Cemetery at Van Buren, Arkansas. This small headstone marks the burial site of Jesse Turner. A much larger monument was added years later.

Jesse Turner was involved with the railroad almost from the start, and is often credited with holding it together until the proper funding was obtained. He was also heavily involved in Arkansas politics. Turner was born in North Carolina in 1805 and was admitted to the bar in North Carolina at the age of 20. He moved to Van Buren, Arkansas, in 1831. He was elected to represent Crawford County in the Arkansas House of Representatives in 1838, and in 1841 was appointed by the Secretary of War as a member of the examining board for cadets at West Point. Turner was then appointed District Attorney by President Fillmore in 1851 when the Western Federal District of Arkansas was created. Turner served as a member of the Arkansas Convention of 1861, voting against secession. After the Civil War, he represented both Crawford and Franklin counties in the Arkansas Senate, was a delegate at large at the National Democratic Convention in 1876, and was appointed Associate Supreme Court Judge in 1878. On the local Van Buren scene, he was one of the incorporators of the Crawford Institute in 1854, and the president of the Van Buren Board of Education for many years. Judge Turner was also the first president of the Little Rock & Fort Smith Railroad, serving 11 years. Later, he was made vice president and served 1880-1884 in that position. Jesse Turner passed away on November 22, 1894, while at an opera house listening to Colonel Robert Crockett lecture on the life of David Crockett. Turner was buried in Fairview Cemetery in Van Buren, Arkansas.

The other officers also had important roles in the railroad's creation. **Augustus Joseph Ward** was born in Connecticut in 1814 and moved to Arkansas and Indian Territory by the late 1830s. He brought supplies from back east and opened the Ward & Southmayd mercantile, and then formed other firms, being noted as one of the early merchants in Van Buren. Being a business leader in the county, Ward was Crawford County treasurer for more than 24 years (1846-1860, 1866-1868, and 1872-1882). He was also elected mayor of Van Buren three times – 1849, 1855, and 1859. His local leadership allowed him to raise support and funds for the Little Rock & Fort Smith Railroad, and also to obtain supplies at reasonable prices. He died in 1883 and was buried in Fairview Cemetery in Van Buren, Arkansas.

Joseph Hancock Haney was a young civil engineer from Ohio (born there on March 5, 1835) who came to Van Buren, Arkansas, shortly before the Civil War to work on the Little Rock & Fort Smith. He was involved with some of the initial railroad grading out of Van Buren, but little work was done before the war began. During the Civil War, Haney fought with different Confederate units, but began to be assigned to draw maps of various installations, troop placements, and battlefields. After the war, Captain Haney returned to the railroad as special agent and acting secretary, and soon led an eastern effort to raise funds and acquire supplies for the railroad. He wrote many of the early railroad documents, served as chief engineer of the company, and was elected to the railroad's board of directors in 1871. He also served on the board of directors of the Arkansas Western Railway Company in 1870 with Asa P. Robinson.

This tall stone monument marks the burial site of Augustus J. Ward, who was also buried in the Fairview Cemetery at Van Buren.

As new eastern owners took over the railroad, Haney's experience and advice was soon ignored and he went to work for Josiah Caldwell on his contract to complete the Little Rock & Fort Smith. He then resigned on January 20, 1873, after no work was done due to funding issues and management conflicts. J. H. Haney then got into the real estate business at Little Rock, operating out of Room 22 of the Denckla Block on Markham Street, today's Capital Hotel. He is known for being a member of the 1877 Mount Holly Cemetery Commission, a group of Little Rock businessmen who organized to improve the conditions at this historic cemetery. Haney was buried there when he passed away on August 12, 1904.

The Capital Hotel is a noted landmark in downtown Little Rock. It was actually created from the Denckla Block, a series of buildings which housed offices and living quarters. For a few years, Joseph Haney had an office in the Denckla Block, as did others involved with the Arkansas Valley Route.

Phillip Pennywit, born in Cincinnati in 1793, was an early pioneer navigator and operator of steamboats on western rivers, and is often cited as the first captain to sail up the White and upper Arkansas rivers in Arkansas, working boats up the rivers in the 1820s. A number of sources from the early 1800s state that Phillip (often spelled Philip) Pennywitt was "one of the most popular steam boat men of his day and his name is intertwined with navigation on the Ohio, Mississippi, and Arkansas Rivers." Captain Pennywit also invested in and created businesses across Arkansas, including a Van Buren riverfront storage warehouse, a busy flour mill, and a popular mineral bathhouse. He is famous as being the railroad's treasurer (with his "sagacity and fidelity") who hid $31,304.21 in company funds, mostly in gold, from both the Confederacy and the Union during the Civil War. Captain Philip Pennywitt died in Little Rock on January 9, 1868, and was buried in Fairview Cemetery in Van Buren, Arkansas.

This simple and very worn marker notes the final resting place of Philip Pennywitt. While the marker is simple, he was buried in the family section of John Drennen, co-founder of Van Buren.

Another reorganization of the Little Rock & Fort Smith took place on March 22, 1867, when the Arkansas General Assembly amended the railroad's charter that allowed it to change the number of officers and to determine the location of its corporate offices. A detailed survey for the railroad was approved for the fifty miles between Little Rock and Lewisburg (near today's Morrilton). Finally, the Memphis & Little Rock had by then chosen to not merge so J. H. Haney was appointed general agent and sent to New York City to find contractors to build the line. Within a year, it was announced that the railroad had made a contract with W. P. Denckla and D. W. C. Wheeler for the construction of the railroad. Despite this, several more years of fighting for financing and planning on how to pay contractors prevented any actual work from being conducted.

William P. Denckla was involved with the Little Rock & Fort Smith Railroad during the late 1860s, and was even elected a member of the board of directors in January 1868. William Paul Denckla was born in Germany in 1822 and came to Arkansas in 1855 as a mine engineer. He moved to California and then back to Arkansas to work as a railroad contractor. In 1868, Colonel William P. Denckla, "a man of wide experience in railroad matters" who possesses "a large influence among capitalists," received a contract to build the railroad. The agreement was for Denckla to receive all of the construction bonds, land bonds, and company stock in return for building the railroad. In May 1869, Denckla spent time back east to raise funds and was expected back "fully prepared for a vigorous prosecution of the work at several points where the road touches the river." While some work started later in the year, Denckla soon ended his direct relationship with the railroad, as well as the Cairo & Fulton and the Arkansas Western Railway Company.

Denckla was also involved with other Arkansas promotions, including co-authoring the book *Upon the Natural Resources of the Arkansas Valley, From Little Rock, Ark., to Fort Gibson, C. N.* However, he is probably best known in Arkansas for his Denckla Block on Markham Street in Little Rock. This large building contained offices, shops, and apartments that catered towards single and traveling businessmen. Denckla acquired the property from Supreme Court justice George C. Watkins and built the building in 1872. However, Watkins died late that year and the judge's heirs bought the property back. The

Metropolitan Hotel, located across the street and considered to be Little Rock's only upscale hotel, burned on December 14, 1876. Its manager then leased the Denckla Block and converted it into a hotel, soon with the name Capital Hotel. The hotel has had its ups and downs, and was listed on the National Register of Historic Places in 1974. It was renovated in the 1980s and then again in 2007, and brags about some of its famous guests such as Presidents Ulysses S. Grant, Jimmy Carter and George H. W. Bush.

This artwork (*"Arkansas" locomotive, Little Rock & Fort Smith Railroad, McKay & Aldus Iron Works*) was created for McKay & Aldus Iron Works, which built approximately 100 steam locomotives between 1864-1869. The firm originally built clipper and iron ships, as well as ship engines. It then expanded and built steam locomotives, mainly for the Central Pacific, which purchased 37 locomotives in 1866. Slow payments led to the company going bankrupt in December 1868. During the late 1860s, the Little Rock & Fort Smith Railroad was attempting to gain enough financial footing to build its railroad to Indian Territory, and the McKay & Aldus Iron Works was obviously hoping to sell several locomotives to the company. Source: DeGolyer Library, Southern Methodist University.

In 1868, the Arkansas General Assembly and voters approved a bill to provide $10,000 in bonds per mile of railroad for up to 150 miles (only bonds for 90 miles were ever collected). There were several requirements to obtain the bonds. First, Arkansas required the railroad to submit a map and estimated cost of construction. Second, the railroad had to demonstrate that it had the assets and means to grade 100 continuous miles of railroad and to have actually graded at least ten miles. Third, each railroad would be taxed equal to the amount of interest on the unpaid bonds held by the railroad. With this, there were numerous reports that the Little Rock & Fort Smith would begin construction "early in the coming year and be prosecuted vigorously." Several railroads in Arkansas obtained this aid, but the Little Rock & Fort Smith never even applied. However, the state still set aside the financial aid for the railroad, or any other railroad, that would build between Little Rock and Fort Smith. It was noted that at the time that three different railroads had announced plans to build along the general route. Meanwhile, the Unites States Congress granted an extension to April 28, 1870, for the Little Rock & Fort Smith to complete 20 miles. A final major change that took place in 1868 was the resignation of Jesse Turner and the appointment of Charles G. Scott as the company's new president.

Little Rock & Fort Smith Railroad Company – The 1869 Reorganization and Construction

In January, 1869, the stockholders led a change on the railroad, especially with much of the stock now in the hands of contractors. Later, Arkansas recognized that the Little Rock & Fort Smith was not simply a branch of the Cairo & Fulton Railroad and ensured that the land grants were available for this route independent of other proposed Arkansas railroads.

By early summer of 1869, newspapers and magazines were full of positive stories about the new management and the efforts to start construction of the railroad. One example published in the *American Railroad Journal* (May 1, 1869) was credited to the *Arkansas Gazette*.

> *Little Rock and Fort Smith Railroad. Col. W. P. Denckla, the energetic agent of the contractors, will return from the east in two or three weeks fully prepared for a vigorous prosecution of the work at several points where the road touches the river. This is, by far, the most promising enterprise which has been spoken of in connection with internal improvements west of the Mississippi river, and*

> south of the great Pacific; as it opens up a most magnif-
> icent country to railroad connection with the rest of the
> world, and will form the main chain of communication
> with the 35th parallel Pacific route, soon to assume a
> practical beginning. It is well known that this road has
> the finest grant of lands ever made to any railroad, lo-
> cated years ago, aid that our citizens are now daily add-
> ing to the public donation by thousands of acres, of the
> best selection, as private donations, and subscriptions of
> stock, over 50,000 acres having been subscribed in this
> city alone.

In June, reports were out that survey crews were about 8 miles west of the Illinois Bayou. Two routes were being surveyed between Carri-on Crow Mountain and Illinois Bayou, one via Dardanelle (south side of the Arkansas River) and one via Russellville (north side). An *Arkansas Gazette* article (June 25, 1869) stated that the "work of cutting out the timber, preparatory to throwing up the road-bed, is going on briskly – the axes having reached a point in Conway county, more than thirty miles from this city. The surveying party are in fine health and spirits, and were well received along the line."

With great fanfare and promise, on August 4, 1869, grading of the railroad began on the north shore of the Arkansas River at today's North Little Rock. Initially, 75 men were at work, with plans to in-crease the work force to 500, to 1000, to as many workers as could be hired. Contracts were being let for the first 80 miles of railroad and for a bridge across the Arkansas River at the foot of Rock Street in Little Rock. With all of the work underway, the railroad's stockholders met on September 1st to authorize new bonds, to mortgage the property of the railroad, and to increase the capital stock of the company to $6,000,000. The meeting also approved a motion to require all stock-holders to pay 10 per cent on the stock.

Work continued as fast as labor could be obtained. About this time, a battle began between Joseph H. Haney (railroad chief engineer) and Asa P. Robinson (in charge of contractor construction). Robinson was a Connecticut-born civil engineer who had worked for the Erie Railroad and the Missouri, Kansas & Texas Railroad. Robinson was backed by Boston financier Josiah Caldwell and he had a very negative opinion of black workers, calling them lazy, getting only half the work done as compared to a white worker. He ran off the local black workers hired by Haney and brought in Swedes, Norwegians, Danes and Irish workers from northern cities and directly from Europe.

Because of Robinson, during late 1869 work crews were being brought down the Mississippi River by steamboat to work on the Little Rock & Fort Smith. One of these crews was on the steamboat *Stonewall*, which on October 27, 1869, burned while passing Neely's Landing, located seventeen miles north of Cape Girardeau. The steamboat was carrying about 300 passengers, tons of cargo, and 200 head of livestock, and a fire of unknown origins started in a hay pile. The captain tried to beach the boat, but it struck a sandbar about 150 feet from the Missouri shoreline. The river's current then turned the boat and the north wind flamed the fire. More than 200 of the passengers died from the flames or drowned in the Mississippi River. Of the contractor's crew of 50 men, only two workers survived, finally arriving at Little Rock on November 12th.

By November, 10 miles of grade was completed and more than 2000 tons of rail, one locomotive, two passenger cars, and several platform cars had been ordered. The first 200 tons of rail arrived at Argenta (still known as Huntersville by many, later North Little Rock) at noon on December 3, 1869. The rail had been brought up from New Orleans on the steamboat *Utah*. The railroad had also advertised for 70,000 crossties, which would be accepted at a number of places along the Arkansas River or near the construction work on the railroad. Additional labor and supplies continued to arrive at Little Rock and then were sent up the grade to the head of construction. By the end of 1869, the railroad was also laying out the site of their depot in Huntersville/ Argenta.

James Gillespie Blaine and the Little Rock & Fort Smith Railroad Bonds

The majority of the bonds issued by the Little Rock & Fort Smith to pay for the railroad's construction wound up in the hands of Boston capitalists. After a few years and as work began on the railroad, the holders of the bonds wanted them sold so they could get their money out of them.

Eventually, U.S. Speaker of the House James G. Blaine was hired to sell these bonds. Blaine was a politician from Maine who served in the U.S. House of Representatives from 1863 to 1876, and later in the U. S. Senate (1876-1881). He was also Secretary of State (1881, 1889-1892), and ran for president several times, being narrowly defeated by Democrat Grover Cleveland in 1884.

James G. Blaine, a Maine politician who held numerous positions in the federal government, sold many of the LR&FS railroad bonds for their initial owners – Boston capitalists. His techniques to sell the bonds raised many questions which haunted his career for the rest of his life. *Hon. James G. Blaine of Maine.* Between 1870 and 1880. Photograph. Retrieved from the Library of Congress, https://www.loc.gov/item/2017893272/.

In November 1869, Blaine first attempted to sell $75 million in bonds to Jay Cooke, the first major investment banker in the United States. Cooke had been the major distributor of government debt during the Civil War and later financed the construction of the Northern Pacific Railway. After examining the property, Cooke declined the offer. Some of the bonds were then successfully sold to other railroad investors.

For much of his career, Blaine had to fight charges of corruption, especially related to railroads. He was accused of corruption in the awarding of railroad charters, of receiving bribes in the Crédit Mobilier scandal involving Union Pacific, and using the bonds of the Little Rock & Fort Smith as a way to receive illegal funds. There was little to prove any of these allegations, but they kept coming up every time Blaine ran for office. Some documents, what were called the Mulligan Letters, finally turned up in 1876 that indicated that Union Pacific had bought worthless LR&FS bonds from Blaine for $64,000 as a way to hide a bribe. James Mulligan was a Boston clerk who had been employed by Blaine's brother-in-law. He testified that he had arranged the transaction for James G. Blaine and had the letters to prove it. However, before they could be brought to the hearing, Blaine reportedly stole the letters from Mulligan and then refused to turn them over to the committee. Newspapers across the country reported on the matter, making the Little Rock & Fort Smith Railroad well known.

Arkansas Western Railway Company – 1870

Although little of the Little Rock & Fort Smith Railroad had been built, the stockholders and members of the board of directors were already planning new lines that would feed traffic to the primary route. During the first few days of May 1870, three additional railroads were incorporated in Arkansas, all with William P. Denckla and E. Wheeler as incorporators. None of these were ever built or even heard of after the early 1870s.

The **Arkansas Branch Railway Company** was incorporated on May 2, 1870 (some reports state May 27, 1870), but no clear route was ever announced and no construction took place. The incorporators were "Wm. P. Denckla, A. P. Robinson, E. Wheeler, J. H. Haney, and C. G. Scott." On May 6, 1870, the **Arkansas Eastern Railway Company** was incorporated by "Wm. P. Denckla, M. L. Rice, U. M. Rose, E. Wheeler, and M. W. Benjamin." Again, no specific route was announced and news about the railroad ended quickly.

The third railroad, the **Arkansas Western Railway Company**, was the only one that seemed to have been well-planned and heavily promoted. The Arkansas Western was incorporated on May 2, 1870, with the incorporators Wm. P. Denckla, A. P. Robinson, E. Wheeler, J. H. Haney, and C. G. Scott. The first reports about this railroad made it clear that it was tied to the Little Rock & Fort Smith Railroad. *The Railroad Record* (June 16, 1870) reported that the "Arkansas Western Railway Company has been organized to construct a railroad from some point on the line of the Little Rock and Fort Smith Railroad, near Van Buren, in a northerly direction through the counties of Crawford, Washington and Benton, passing through or near Cane Hill, Fayetteville and Bentonville, and intersecting the northern boundary of the state." The *American Railroad Journal* added that surveying and construction would be done after the Little Rock & Fort Smith had reached Van Buren, and that the Arkansas Western would be built by the LR&FS. The June 5, 1871, issue of the *Daily Arkansas Gazette* had a much more enthusiastic report.

> *The people of Van Buren, and all along the route of this proposed road, are thoroughly alive to its importance. A rousing convention is to be held at Bentonville on the 6th inst. [instant, in this case the next day] to mature a plan of operations looking toward securing the early building of the road. The road will run from Van Buren or Fort Smith, to the Missouri border, connecting with the Southwest Branch of the Pacific Railroad, now completed to Pierce City in Missouri, 27 miles this side of Springfield. By the 1st of July passenger trains will be run from St. Louis to Pierce City. A meeting was held at Bentonville on the 28th, appointed delegates to the Bentonville convention. The Press says: Our citizens have taken hold of the "Arkansas Western Railway Company" enterprise, with an enthusiasm, that is certainly commendable. In two days the commissioner received stock subscriptions*

to the amount of $100,000 and probably, the private sub-
scriptions of the county will amount to at least $150,000.

There were those who were against the planned railroad, or at least how it was being planned. There were public statements that there were really no plans to build the Arkansas Western Railway, but that the company "got the charter to prevent others from getting it and building the same." There were also claims that the charter was created to sell "to parties representing the South Pacific Railroad Company" (later the Frisco).

By October 1870, the *Fayetteville Democrat* was reporting that all the stock in the Arkansas Western had been subscribed with Benton County taking some $500,000. A meeting of the board of directors took place on October 25, 1870, with A. P. Robinson elected as chairman, president and chief engineer of the company. Leonard C. Southmayd was named secretary and treasurer. By November, Captain J. H. Haney had surveyed a route from Van Buren to the Missouri line.

However, no work was ever completed on the line, and a stockholders' meeting was held on February 28, 1872, to possibly sell, lease or consolidate with another company. The general route was used less than a decade later by the St. Louis, Arkansas & Texas Railway Company, which became the route of the St. Louis-San Francisco, or simply Frisco.

Little Rock & Fort Smith Railroad Company – The Early 1870s

Like many railroads, the Little Rock & Fort Smith Railroad experienced a boom in construction as funds became available, and then failed as the interest on bonds and other debts couldn't be paid. The first positive news about the railroad in January 1870 was that the railroad had built track down to the Arkansas River in what would become North Little Rock to be used for the arrival of a new locomotive, the railroad had laid about a mile of rail northward from the river, and that crossties were set out for several more miles. As published in several newspapers, "It will only be a few days now until the thunder of the hoofs of the Iron Horse, will be heard on the new track." Other good news was that the railroad had contracted for the entire 155 miles of the railroad, work had begun on 80 of these miles, and that 20 miles were graded and ready for track laying. An optimistic report stated that trains would begin to be running by March 15, 1870, and the rest of the railroad would be completed by the spring of 1871. To pay for this work, mortgage bonds were to be issued, as stated by the *American Railroad Journal* (January 29, 1870).

> *The Little Rock and Fort Smith Railroad Company have prepared $3,500,000 of first mortgage bonds, according to [an] agreement with Fisher & Co. Contractors, to be delivered to them as the work progresses. The bonds are of $1,000 each, principal and interest payable in gold. Interest six per cent., payable semi-annually in Boston, where the financial agency of the company has its office.*

On February 1, 1870, the railroad took a step back when its first steam locomotive sank into the Arkansas River, about 10 miles upstream of Pine Bluff, Arkansas. The barge that it was strapped to struck a sunken tree and sank, The steam locomotive, named *Pulaski*, was salvaged and delivered to the dock at Argenta on March 17th. It was cleaned up and repaired, making a trip northward about 3½ miles to what was known as Mountain Gap, the narrow valley between Big Rock Mountain and Park Hill near Levy. Besides the steam locomotive, 600 tons of rail, two box cars, and nine platform (flat) cars also arrived at the Argenta terminal. Newspapers then began an almost weekly report of new rail, freight car, and steam locomotive arrivals. By April, it was reported that 20 miles of track had been completed and the State of Arkansas had turned over $200,000 in aid.

With the railroad often being close to the Arkansas River, the Little Rock & Fort Smith purchased the steamboat *Colossal* in May 1870 to transport construction materials to different locations along the railroad route. This strategy allowed track to be built northward even before bridges were erected. One of the main concerns of the railroad owners was getting to the various cotton gins along the Arkansas River Valley. By the end of the year, the Arkansas governor produced a report about the Little Rock & Fort Smith.

It is now open to Lewisburg, fifty miles, and has been running regular trains to that point since November 21. Fifty miles more are already graded, and the ties are down ready for the iron. This second division will be open ready for travel in February, and the entire road from Little Rock to Fort Smith will be completed on or before the 1st of January 1872. The track, locomotive, passenger and freight cars are first class in every respect. Close connections are now made by stage from Lewisburg to all points from there to Fort Smith and Van Buren and points beyond.

The year 1871 was not a good one for the Little Rock & Fort Smith. Construction stopped due to a general strike, primarily blamed on contractors not paying their men. A battle between two boards also plagued the railroad. The "Old Board" had been accused of paying too much for the contractors and a new "Boston Board" took over. However, by August, investigations had determined that the payments were proper and the "Old Board" attempted to regain control of the railroad company. However, there may have been little to control as the company had been placed in receivership due to a failure to pay interest on bonds that were due on September 1, 1871. The railroad was also having problems with paying contractors and it was in the "custody of the law, having been attached by Messrs. Pierce, Steacey & Yorston" as security for payment for construction work on the railroad. Blame was pointed in many directions, but one of the most reported was a dispute between the Boston contractor and a sub-contractor. Until things could be settled, the State of Arkansas took possession of the railroad after making the payment on behalf of the railroad.

By December 1871, there were reports that the Little Rock & Fort Smith Railroad had been sold and consolidated with the Memphis & Little Rock through a lease held by the Southern Security Company. However, the sale was not completed and the railroad was back on its own, and construction continued past Lewisburg to the Point Remove bottoms. While construction continued slowly for the rest of the year, the railroad did experience its first significant derailment – near Palarm – on Christmas Day, 1872.

GENIAL CLIMATE,
FERTILE SOIL,
CHEAP LANDS,

—IN—

ARKANSAS!

The Little Rock & Fort Smith
RAILROAD

OFFERS FOR SALE

ONE MILLION ACRES OF LAND

In the rich valley of the Arkansas River, unsurpassed in the production of Cotton, Corn, Fruits, Vegetables, the Vine, and all cereals. The inexhaustible fertility of the soil, the climate (average annual temperature for December, January, February, and March, about 43° F.), permitting agricultural labor eleven months of the year; the unquestioned health of the valley; the various and abundant timber, and good water, with the rapid development of the State in Railroads, population, and general improvement, combine to render these lands the

GARDEN OF THE COUNTRY!

☞ UPLANDS from $2.50 to $6.00, and RIVER BOT. TOMS from $10.00 to $15.00 per acre, on long credit.

Exploring Tickets and Liberal Arrangements with Colonies.

Railroad and Steamboat Connection with St. Louis and Memphis.

For Maps and Pamphlets, free, address,

N. S. HOWE, LAND COMMISSIONER,

LITTLE ROCK, ARK.

Even as the Little Rock & Fort Smith Railroad approached financial failure, it continued to advertise that the railroad had one million acres of land for sale. This advertisement was placed in the *Mineral Point Tribune*, published in Mineral Point, Wisconsin, during April 1874. *Mineral Point Tribune*. (Mineral Point, WI) 2 Apr. 1874, p. 6. Retrieved from the Library of Congress, https://www.loc.gov/item/sn86086770/1874-04-02/ed-1/.

Good weather in early 1873 allowed construction to reach Russellville in March, and near Clarksville in May. However, construction stopped near here as an injunction was filed to keep a new board of directors from taking control of the railroad. It got even more serious than that on December 23rd when the Arkansas State Treasurer filed an application with the Pulaski County Chancery Court to place the railroad in receivership. This was done immediately, with Colonel S. B. Beaumont, the general manager of the Little Rock & Fort Smith, being appointed the receiver. A battle between the Boston Board, a local board, and several county circuit courts continued for a short time, but it was soon obvious that there was too much debt for the little funding that was available. For all practical purposes, 1874 was a year of no significant activity with no new construction, a few regular trains operating, and lots of court hearings. As the company was completing its reorganization, the Old Board could at least celebrate the fact that they had built 100.65 miles of track from Argenta (North Little Rock) to Clarksville.

The Little Rock & Fort Smith Railway

On December 10, 1874, the Little Rock & Fort Smith Railroad was sold at foreclosure in front of the United States courthouse at Main and Fourth streets in Little Rock. The railroad and its rolling stock, land grants, right-of-ways, and other assets were sold for $100,000 to "Messrs. Whitley, Shattuck and Wells," agents for the bondholders. On December 19th, the property was turned over to The Little Rock & Fort Smith Railroad, which changed its name to The Little Rock & Fort Smith Railway on June 12, 1875. About the same time, the Little Rock, Pine Bluff & New Orleans and the Mississippi, Ouachita & Red River railroads, which had consolidated as the Little Rock, Mississippi River & Texas, came under control of the same Boston bondholders who controlled the Little Rock & Fort Smith. This led to the idea of a through route which became known as the Arkansas Valley Route, or simply the Valley Route.

With the new corporation, a new board was created which almost immediately awarded a contract for 20 miles of track to J. N. Johnson and J. McCarthy, "old and experienced railroad contractors." One change in the operation of the contractors was that local labor would be used, giving people along the line a chance to earn some money. By March 1875, the railroad had reached Spadra, and then Altus by July when wheat began to move over the railroad from that location. Coal was also moving from the coal fields in Johnson County by September. Later that month, a contract was issued for the construction of the last 45 miles to Van Buren.

The railroad reached Ozark in February 1876, and heavy work using 8239 kegs of black powder was needed to build the track westward through a bluff alongside the Arkansas River. Newspaper reports from the time stated that twelve freight cars of rails were being shipped daily from Argenta to Ozark for the completion of the railroad. By April, the railroad reached 12 miles west of Ozark, and then reached Van Buren on July 11, 1876. The first through train, an excursion operation for company officials and dignitaries, reached Van Buren on July 24, 1876. With the railroad built, work to complete the details began. This included a number of depots, industry tracks, connections to adjacent coal mines, and stabilization of some locations along the line. One unexpected project was the actual removal of two miles of track that had been built west of Van Buren in the Cherokee Nation of Indian Territory.

Another project that the railroad had to face was improving its existing infrastructure. Many of the bridges were built quickly using timber, and with many components untreated, they didn't always last for long. This was especially true as traffic volumes increased and loads became heavier. An example of this issue is a wreck that occurred on July 30, 1878. In this case, a passing train had a bridge give way. Newspapers stated that the train was ditched and a number of persons were seriously hurt, some dangerously.

Van Buren was never the final objective of the railroad, and work began across the Arkansas River in January 1879 to build track on to downtown Fort Smith. The *Fort Smith Daily Herald* (January 22, 1879) reported on the kick-off of the work. "Work will be commenced this morning on the Fort Smith railway depot building, and all those who have volunteered labor for the railway are requested to report early on the ground – the site of the old Casper Reutzel building, opposite the St. Charles Hotel, where they will be put at work by the Superintendent."

As part of this work, the transfer boat *N. D. Munson* was moved to Van Buren to haul supplies, and then locomotives and freight cars, across the river. An incline track was built on each side of the river, with the one on the Fort Smith bank being named South Van Buren. Initially, all freight was transferred across the river and then shipped by wagon from the South Van Buren station to Fort Smith. However, by late January 1879, a mile of track had been laid and construction continued, with the last rail installed at 4pm on January 30, 1879. The first passenger train operated all the way to the new station at Fort Smith on the night of Thursday, January 30, 1879. This station was located north of Walnut Street, today's North A Street.

The railroad began to focus on the daily task of operating trains, but a lawsuit threw a wrench into the works. The legal case *Steacy et al. vs. Elisha Atkins et al.* brought to light some of the behind-the-scenes issues involved with building the railroad. The case showed that the railroad had contracted with Warren Fisher, of Boston, Massachusetts, to construct the road. Fisher was to receive in payment all the stock, bonds, and lands, becoming virtually the railroad's owner. Fisher then sub-contracted with Pierce, Steacy & Yorton to do the work. Before the work was completed, Fisher's organization failed and the railroad became insolvent. Steacy received a judgement for $1,000,000, but there was no one to pay it. He then sued Elisha Atkins, who had loaned Fisher money in return for control of the railroad's bonds. The court ruled that Atkins wasn't responsible for making the payment, and the case bounced through the courts for years as Steacy attempted to get paid for his work.

Elisha Atkins was involved with the Little Rock & Fort Smith starting in 1871 when he first loaned money to Fisher. For many years his leadership was quiet, but he was on the board of directors of the Little Rock & Fort Smith by 1880. Elisha Atkins had been involved with the founding of the Union Pacific Railroad through his connections with Oliver Ames, and served as the company's vice president for many years. He also served as the president of the Little Rock, Mississippi River & Texas Railroad, and the Little Rock & Fort Smith Railway.

In 1880, the U.S. Census included a census of transportation companies that provided a large amount of information about the various railroads. For the year ending June 30, 1880, the Little Rock & Fort Smith Railway (LR&FS) had invested $6,897,281.30 in the line's construction, plus $19,118.51 in building telegraph lines. The railroad had revenues of $408,330.59 during the previous year, as shown below.

$106,269.61 in local passenger service handling 58,527 passengers
$30,061.95 in through passenger service handling 5198 passengers
$9501.82 in express services
$9879.82 in handling mail
$899.98 in other passenger services
$182,969.89 in local freight service handling 58,540 tons of freight
$88,129.16 in through freight service handling 17,494 tons of freight

With the railroad established, the LR&FS was able to operate regular trains, using 10 steam locomotives, 5 passenger cars, 2 mail, baggage and express cars, 244 freight cars, and 6 other cars. At the time, the steam locomotives burned 1684 tons of coal a year and 4731 cords of wood. The freight volumes clearly represented the origins and destinations along the line. These included:

28,668 tons of cotton
25,287 tons of miscellaneous freight
10,371 tons of lumber and other forest products
4020 tons of coal
1858 tons of livestock
1807 tons of stone, brick, lime, cement, sands and clay
1473 tons of provisions
1369 tons of flour
1181 tons of grains

To handle the operations, the company had an annual payroll of $136,008.33 for the 231 employees. These employees included:

5 general officers
6 general office clerks
28 station men
9 locomotive engineers
6 conductors
25 other trainmen

3 machinists
5 carpenters
28 other shop men
70 track men
46 others

The census report also stated that the railroad had 172.35 miles of track, all with steel rail except for one mile of 60-pound iron rail. The company had bought 53,281 white oak ties at $0.27 each and they lasted about six years. The company had also built 3 boxcars, 3 flatcars and 2 cabooses in their own shops. One major issue for the railroad was that only 248,021.29 acres of their land grant property had been sold, and only for $1,043,885.86. An effort was made to sell more of the lands, and the year 1880 saw the most land ever sold in a single year – 73,590.08 acres for $288,406.03.

With what appeared to be a successful future, the stock and bonds of the Little Rock & Fort Smith were listed on the New York Stock Exchange in October 1880. Within two years, rumors began that several other railroads were attempting to buy the LR&FS, including railroad owners Jay Gould and C.P. Huntington. There was so much talk about the purchase that in November, company president Joseph H. Converse publicly denied the stories, and stated that he was trying to create a closer relationship with the Little Rock, Mississippi River & Texas by building a bridge over the Arkansas River at Little Rock. By this time, both railroads were controlled by many of the same stock and bond holders, with Joseph Converse, Elisha Atkins and F. Gordon Dexter serving as directors and/or officers on both railroads. To add some local representation, Jesse Turner was made vice president.

During the late 1800s, a regular report was published by the federal government about the growing railroad industry. *The Annual Report of the Commissioner of Railroads, Made to the Secretary of the Interior, for the Year Ending June 30, 1881*, had information on the Little Rock & Fort Smith Railway from an inspection made in September 1881.

> *This road extends from Argenta, opposite Little Rock, to Fort Smith, Arkansas, a distance of 165 miles. It passes up the Arkansas Valley on the north side of the river to Van Buren, thence south to Fort Smith.*
>
> *The location of the road is not beyond criticism, and at many points improvements might have been made with profit to the company.*

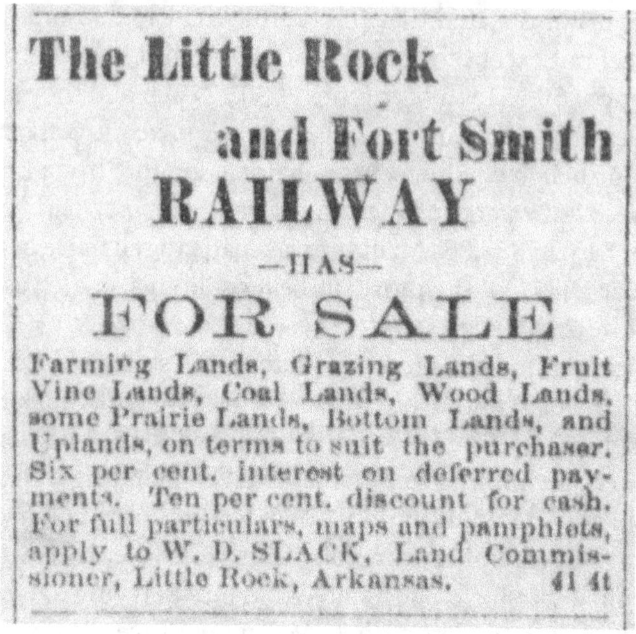

The Little Rock and Fort Smith RAILWAY

—HAS—

FOR SALE

Farming Lands, Grazing Lands, Fruit Vine Lands, Coal Lands, Wood Lands, some Prairie Lands, Bottom Lands, and Uplands, on terms to suit the purchaser. Six per cent. interest on deferred payments. Ten per cent. discount for cash. For full particulars, maps and pamphlets, apply to W. D. SLACK, Land Commissioner, Little Rock, Arkansas.   41 4t

CHEAP LANDS IN THE GREAT SOUTHWEST!

The Little Rock and Fort Smith Railway Company is selling, at exceptionally low prices and on terms to suit purchasers, over

ONE MILLION ACRES

of their magnificent grant on every side within twenty miles of their road. Admirably suited for production of Corn, Cotton, Grain, Grass, Fruits, and all other Northern crops. Winters are mild, permitting out-door labor for eleven months. Soil fertile beyond precedent. No grasshoppers, no drought. Special inducements for establishment of manufactories. For circulars, address W. D. SLACK, Land Commissioner, Little Rock, Arkansas.   41 4

These two advertisements were published in the April 4, 1877, issue of *The Forest Republican* newspaper of Tionesta, Pennsylvania. Such advertisements were generally found in rural newspapers where growing farmer families provided likely buyers of the railroad's land grants. *The Forest Republican*. (Tionesta, PA) 4 Apr. 1877. Retrieved from the Library of Congress, https://www.loc.gov/item/sn84026497/1877-04-04/ed-1/.

The crossing of the Arkansas River at Van Buren is made by means of a steam ferry-boat capable of carrying two passenger or four loaded freight cars, but the company proposes, at an early date, to erect a substantial iron bridge at this point.

The entire road is laid with iron rails of 56 pounds to the yard, but many of them are badly worn and require renewal. The cross-ties are 6 by 8 inches and 8-1/2 feet in length, and are laid 2,640 to the mile. There is very little broken stone or gravel ballast, earth being generally used. The switches are of the square stub pattern, with the exception of a few of the French split pattern.

The cuts and embankments require widening, and the ditches should be cleaned.

There are two combination bridges on the road, each of 200 feet span, one being of the Pratt and one of the Post patent, and ten covered Howe truss bridges of 75 to 150 span, each resting on first class masonry, all being in good condition. A Pratt iron bridge will be substituted this fall for the Post combination bridge. There are also about 200 open culverts ranging from 4 to 30 feet span, and 30 pieces of trestling from 30 to 100 feet in length. They are also in good condition, having had about 300,000 feet of timber put in them in renewals during the year.

During the year the company has erected 5 new depot buildings, all conveniently arranged for passengers and freight. The company also contemplates building a new passenger station at Fort Smith, where it is much needed, and a passenger and freight depot at Russell Station.

There are ten water-stations on the road, none of them being frost-proof, as that is unnecessary in this climate. Three are supplied by horse-power pumps, one by hot-air engine, and six by steam-power. All of the water is of good quality with the exception of that pumped from the Arkansas River, which is foul and muddy and clogs the boilers very badly.

Other reports from 1881 provided more information about the Little Rock & Fort Smith Railway. At the time, the board of directors was split between Boston, Massachusetts (4 members), Little Rock (3 members), Fort Smith (1 member), and Van Buren (1 member). The president was J. H. Converse of Boston, and the vice-president was Jesse Turner of Van Buren. Turner had been involved with the railroad since almost its founding, and Converse had been involved with the Boston & Chelsea Railway Company since the 1850s,

The railroad had received a total of 1,057,027.71 land-grant acres. The "old company" had sold 38,421.70 acres while the "new" company had sold 284,039.06 acres. This left 734,566.95 acres unsold. Some of this land had gone into farming, and the number of bales of cotton hauled September 1880-September 1881 totaled 115,059, up from 27,899 during September 1875-September 1876. The railroad was not heavily equipped and had only 12 steam locomotives. To move freight, the railroad had 163 flatcars, 158 boxcars, 20 stock cars, and 7 cabooses. Passengers could be moved in 11 passenger coaches, and there were 3 baggage cars.

On February 1, 1884, the railroad discontinued the use of wood as fuel for its locomotives, going fully to coal. Coal also played a part in the second 1884 action when the Coal Hill Branch of the Little Rock & Fort Smith Railway was chartered on December 26, 1884. This company was created to build the Coal Hill Branch towards Denning, and was sold to the Little Rock & Fort Smith Railway on January 12, 1885.

In 1886, two major projects took place. First, the last of the land grants, about 630,000 acres, were sold to The Homestead Company for $1.25 an acre. The Homestead Company was a New England firm that bought land from a number of railroads across the country and then attempted to create designed towns and worker communities. The second effort was a contract to use the Fort Smith & Van Buren Bridge Company's bridge over the Arkansas River at Van Buren. The 30-year agreement was made April 1, 1886, and it required the LR&FS to cover one-third of the annual maintenance, interest and tax costs on the bridge, or about $12,000 a year.

The Kansas & Arkansas Valley Railway

The Little Rock & Fort Smith only had authority to build to the Van Buren-Fort Smith area. The Kansas & Arkansas Valley Railway (K&AV) was incorporated in Arkansas on November 27, 1885, to build from Van Buren on to Coffeyville, Kansas, passing through Indian Territory in today's Oklahoma. This made it an extension of the Arkansas Valley Route, connecting southeast Arkansas with Kansas. The new railroad was owned and funded by the owners of the Little Rock & Fort Smith and the Little Rock, Mississippi River & Texas, and was essentially a subsidiary of the Little Rock & Fort Smith. Among those who incorporated the K&AV were Elisha Atkins and F. Gordon Dexter of Boston, and Jesse Turner of Van Buren.

Even before the railroad's incorporation, citizens of Van Buren had agreed to purchase the railroad's right-of-way from Van Buren to the Indian Territory line. The citizens had also agreed to provide 20 acres of land for a roundhouse, shops and yard. It was stated that the yard would be located between the yard of the Little Rock & Fort Smith "and the alley north of the Merrill House and the old tobacco factory, and taking the Hayman yard, north of his residence to the Little Rock and Fort Smith railway depot excepting Main and Lafayette streets."

Congressional approval to build across Indian Territory was received on June 1, 1886, and construction began within a year. By May 1, 1887, the Missouri Pacific Railway, through the St. Louis, Iron Mountain & Southern, was actually calling the shots and provided the funding and construction expertise to build the line. George J. Gould had also been elected president of the railroad.

A newspaper report on July 14, 1887, (*Daily Arkansas Gazette*) stated that the K&AV was laying track west of Lee's Creek, three miles from Van Buren. As track was built, the railroad was operated by the St. Louis, Iron Mountain & Southern Railway, with operations between Van Buren and Wagoner beginning on August 13, 1888. The line was extended to the Kansas state line south of Coffeyville in 1889. The Kansas & Arkansas Valley Railroad was created to build the last 2.41 miles of trackage in Kansas to reach Coffeyville. When finished, the railroad had a 164.63 mile single-track mainline.

On January 1, 1890, the K&AV was officially leased to the Little Rock & Fort Smith Railway, which then was leased to the St. Louis, Iron Mountain & Southern. In 1890, a 6.01-mile branch line was built from a place called Cherokee Junction, also called Greenwood Junction, located in Oklahoma, back to Fort Smith. This became the primary route to Fort Smith, replacing the trackage rights over the Frisco. On September 1, 1909, the Kansas & Arkansas Valley Railway was sold to the St. Louis, Iron Mountain & Southern Railway.

Further information about the route of the Kansas & Arkansas Valley Railway will be included in a later volume about the Arkansas Valley Route.

If you look around, you can still find signs of the land grants that the Little Rock & Fort Smith received, and then later sold or donated. This is the Trinity Lutheran Church at Wittenberg, located on Petit Jean Mountain near Morrilton. In 1887, the LR&FS sold 20 acres of land for $1 so that a church and cemetery counld be built in this German Lutheran community. Wittenberg was one of several similar German Lutheran communities along the railroad that received support from the LR&FS.

The Goulds Acquire the Little Rock & Fort Smith Railway

By the mid-1880s, New York millionaire Jay Gould already owned the Missouri Pacific and the St. Louis, Iron Mountain & Southern railroads, and he wanted to add more lines to control the Arkansas market. During December 1886, Jay Gould acquired the Little Rock, Mississippi River & Texas Railway (LRMR&T) at foreclosure. This was essentially the southern end of the Little Rock & Fort Smith and the reason the Little Rock Junction Railway was built. Without the traffic from the south that was delivered by the LRMR&T, the railroads of Jay Gould could cut off the Little Rock & Fort Smith from most area traffic.

With this issue, the owners of the Little Rock & Fort Smith and the Little Rock Junction sold out to Gould starting in February 1887. During 1887, Gould acquired enough stock that he had effective ownership of the Little Rock & Fort Smith, Kansas & Arkansas Valley, and Little Rock Junction Railway. This control made news across the country. For example, the *Salt Lake Evening Democrat* (Salt Lake City, Utah) reported in their April 1, 1887, issue on the purchase.

> *St. Louis, April 1. – A dispatch from Fort Smith, Arkansas, says: The Little Rock & Fort Smith Railway passes into the hands of Jay Gould today.*
>
> *The road is to be extended from Van Buren to Fort Gibson in the Cherokee nation and four miles of the track is now laid out from the first mentioned place. The Arkansas river will be crossed opposite this city and the Cantilever bridge is to be constructed at once.*

On April 28, 1887, the board of directors of each railroad elected a new board of directors with Jay and George Gould on each board. George J. Gould was elected president of each company, and it was stated that Missouri Pacific would take control of the companies on May 1, 1887. In reality, the Little Rock & Fort Smith remained as a separate company but was assigned to be operated by the St. Louis, Iron Mountain & Southern through purchase effective August 1, 1887.

During 1889, there was a complete resurvey of the Little Rock & Fort Smith Railway, and on January 1, 1890, the railroad was officially leased to the St. Louis, Iron Mountain & Southern for 50 years. By the end of the year, the LR&FS Argenta shops were closed and torn down, with all work being moved to the shops of the Iron Mountain. Other improvements were made by the St. Louis, Iron Mountain & Southern, such as new steel bridges, heavier rail, new stations, improved locomotives and equipment, and new operating strategies.

The Iron Mountain reported that "eighty-eight depots in Arkansas were remodeled or enlarged to provide separate waiting rooms for white and colored passengers, in compliance with the State law enacted in 1890. The cost of these changes aggregated $37,999." More money was soon spent on a branch line that was built into the coal fields from Coal Hill. One of the most important improvements was a series of new lines built 1902-1904 to eliminate a number of severe grades.

St. Louis, Iron Mountain & Southern Railway Company

The St. Louis, Iron Mountain & Southern Railway Company, generally known simply as the Iron Mountain, was created on April 30, 1874, with papers filed in Missouri on May 16, 1874, and in Arkansas on June 2, 1874. On April 13, 1906, the Little Rock & Fort Smith Railway was sold to the Iron Mountain after almost 20 years of being owned by the Gould family, and 16 years of being leased.

The Iron Mountain had operated the Little Rock & Fort Smith, so there were few noticeable changes when the acquisition occurred. Many structural improvements along the line had already been made and all the new owner had to do was to continue to modernize the property as needed. This included a number of new stations – Plumerville, Menifee, Conway, Montana, Clarksville, Marche, Ozark, and others – plus improvements like changes at the Van Buren shops and a new coal dock.

Between 1902 and 1904, the Iron Mountain rebuilt much of the Little Rock & Fort Smith with heavier rail and better ballast. Sections of the route were straightened and a number of grades were cut down. The work was big news across the state and reported on in many newspapers. The description of the work was generally like this one, found in the February 5, 1904, issue of *The Forrest City Times.*

Road Practically Rebuilt

The work of improving the Little Rock-Fort Smith line is approaching completion. This undertaking has cost about $2,500,000. It includes change of grade for 165 miles, with eleven detours and forty-two miles of track and the tunnel at Conway. Rock ballast has been placed on 120 miles and between Little Rock and Van Buren the track is laid with 85-pound steel rails. The grade work has been employing six to ten steam shovels per day and three rock crushers. The grade has been changed from 2 per cent to six-tenths of one per cent and the curves are reduced to four degrees. All bridges are renewed and stone and concrete used in construction, with stone for all the culverts.

In 1908, workers at the Van Buren shops went on strike and the Iron Mountain hired new workers to keep the shops working. The citizens of Van Buren generally supported the local workers against the thirty Italian strikebreakers who were lodged in bunk cars in the shops area. Because of the support and the lack of police protection for the railroad, officials announced that they were in talks with the elected officials of Fort Smith about moving the shops to Fort Smith. On Monday, June 29, 1908, a mob attacked the bunk cars, shooting several of the workers and a railroad guard. Two other guards were arrested for defending the property. Some of the strikers soon returned to work and nine others were indicted for the violence. The peace was short-lived and on May 2, 1910, over 1000 machinists and helpers walked off their jobs on the Missouri Pacific and the St. Louis, Iron Mountain & Southern. One of the issues was that the pay varied widely across the system, as did many of the work rules and contract agreements. The railroads had also proposed the use of more apprentices in the shops and the creation of mechanical teams working on staggered shifts. Again, local businessmen in Van Buren had sympathies with the strikers and often refused to sell goods and services to non-strikers. By December, most of the workers had returned to their jobs.

The St. Louis, Iron Mountain & Southern Railway entered receivership on August 19, 1915, being unable to pay its many bond obligations. Much of the blame was placed upon absentee management by the Goulds. Jay Gould served as president of the railroad from October 11, 1881, until his death on December 3, 1892. George Jay Gould, Jay Gould's son, retained control of the Iron Mountain until it entered receivership. The receiver of the railroad was Benjamin Franklin Bush, a long-time railroader. Bush started in the railroad industry as a rodman on the Northern Pacific, where he eventually was promoted to be a division engineer. He then worked for Union Pacific for two years as the engineer in charge of the Idaho and Oregon divisions. He then worked on a realty improvement project in Oregon and for the Northern Pacific Coal Company, which controlled the Northern Pacific's coal properties. In 1903, Bush became the fuel manager of the Missouri Pacific, heading up the coal properties of the Gould interests. Mr. Bush was president and then receiver of the Western Maryland Railroad (1907-1911). Bush became president of the Missouri Pacific and Iron Mountain railroads in 1911, and then the Denver & Rio Grande and the Western Pacific in 1913. He dropped his presidency of the Rio Grande and Western Pacific in 1915 to focus on the problems with the Missouri Pacific and Iron Mountain. Bush became receiver of the two railroads and held that position until the lines went out of the receivership on June 1, 1917. He then became president of the new Missouri Pacific Railroad. During World War I, he was made regional director of the Southwestern region of the government-run railroads, and then returned to Missouri Pacific when the government control ended. Mr. Bush was made chairman of the board of directors of the Missouri Pacific in April 1923, and retired a year later, staying on the board of directors until his death in 1927.

Missouri Pacific Railroad

On February 21, 1917, both the Missouri Pacific and the St. Louis, Iron Mountain & Southern were sold to Kuhn, Loeb & Company and the bondholder's Reorganization Committee. On May 12, 1917, the two railroads were merged into the new Missouri Pacific Railroad Company, incorporated in Missouri on March 5, 1917. For the next several decades, Missouri Pacific added trackage to fully connect the system together, and eliminated duplicate operations. It also reorganized its lines multiple times, creating and eliminating various divisions and extending and reducing the limits of subdivisions.

By the 1920s, the Little Rock & Fort Smith Railway route was known as the Van Buren District – North Little Rock to Van Buren. The route was actually a part of the line that connected Kansas City with Little Rock, and on south to the Gulf Coast. The mainline included the new lines built south of Clarksville and Altus, with the original mainline now operated as secondary routes through those communities. The 1930s saw the end of the Altus District, with all passenger and freight movements moved to the improved line through Alix. On April 27, 1933, Missouri Pacific also abandoned its 1.47 miles of trackage rights over the Frisco's Arkansas River Bridge at Van Buren, instead moving all trains over its own bridge on the branch out of Greenwood Junction, Oklahoma.

By the 1940s, the Kansas City to Coffeyville to Van Buren to North Little Rock route was the mainline of the South Kansas and Central Divisions. The mainline of the old LR&FS was now called the Van Buren Subdivision. The Clarksville Subdivision held on until the early 1960s when the trackage between Clarksville and AA Junction (Spadra Junction) was abandoned. The rest of the original mainline was removed during the late 1980s. The passenger trains that operated over the route didn't do well as Little Rock to Fort Smith passenger service ended operations in 1949, and the Little Rock to Kansas City passenger trains halted service in 1960.

During the early 1960s, many miles of the Van Buren Subdivision were rebuilt and improved as part of the Army Corps of Engineers work to make the Arkansas River navigable. A number of new bridges were built and miles of track were raised or moved to stay above the higher water levels. A major change was the abandonment of the Missouri Pacific bridge at Fort Smith and the move back to the Frisco bridge, a route and trackage rights abandoned in 1933.

The Van Buren Subdivision received ABS signaling during the 1940s and welded rail a few decades later. The traffic changed from local coal movements to national coal movements from the Powder River area of Wyoming, plus grains from the Midwest heading to the Gulf Coast or the growing poultry industry. In 1974, the railroad stated that an average of 8 trains per day moved over the line, hauling 13.84 million gross tons per year. This was increasing as western coal trains were being added to the route, and funds were being invested to extend some sidings. The stations along the line closed with the signal changes and the new radio communications. The next big change was the merger with Union Pacific.

Union Pacific Railroad

During the 1970s and 1980s, a series of railroad mergers across the country were taking place. One of these included Missouri Pacific, Union Pacific, and Western Pacific. On January 8, 1980, the Union Pacific Corporation announced an agreement to buy the Missouri Pacific Railroad. Approval was finally received on September 13, 1982, after a series of hearings and lawsuits. It finally took a Supreme Court ruling to allow the merger on December 22, 1982. A unique detail not known by many was that the Missouri Pacific had a number of outstanding bonds that prevented a full merger of the two companies. The bonds were finally closed during the mid-1990s, and the merger became final on January 1, 1997.

In the first fully combined timetable, *Union Pacific System Timetable No. 3*, dated April 27, 1986, the Van Buren Subdivision was part of the Arkansas Division of the Southeastern District. By *Timetable No. 4*, dated October 26, 1986, the Van Buren Subdivision had been extended northward to Coffeyville and made a part of the Kansas Division of the Central Region. In *Timetable No. 6*, dated May 15, 1988, the Van Buren Subdivision was a part of the Van Buren Division, based at Van Buren, Arkansas.

Changes continued as in *Timetable No. 9*, dated October 25, 1992, the Van Buren Subdivision was gone, replaced by the 319-mile-long Coffeyville Subdivision that connected North Little Rock with Leeds Junction, but it was still part of the Van Buren Division. The route was moved to the Central Service Unit in *Timetable No.1*, dated April 10, 1994. By October 25, 1998, *North Little Rock Area Timetable No. 1* had the line back to being the 155-mile-long Van Buren Subdivision. A few minor changes took place in the limits of the Van Buren Subdivision in *North Little Rock Area Timetable No. 3* (November 9, 2003) and *Timetable No. 5* (July 9, 2012). The biggest change during this time was moving the northern limits to Milepost 495.0, where the Wagoner Subdivision of the Kansas City Area began.

Another change involved the signaling over the route. The railroad had CTC signaling from the Van Buren Wye at North Little Rock northward to CP V355 – Marche at Milepost 355.4. Northward to Van Buren, the subdivision used Track Warrant Control/Absolute Block Signaling (TWC/ABS). In a 2011 report to the Surface Transportation Board, Union Pacific announced that the firm was planning on installing CTC over the entire Van Buren Subdivision. The CTC work was still in the planning stage when the 2015 Arkansas State Rail Plan was produced. Today, the entire route uses CTC signaling (PTC, or Positive Train Control, was not required on this route), and as many as 20 trains a day operate over the former Little Rock & Fort Smith Railway.

Passenger Trains on the Route of the Little Rock & Fort Smith Railway

The route built by the Little Rock & Fort Smith Railway was never a heavy passenger train route. At its peak, there were seldom more than two through passenger trains a day operating in each direction, and even these trains were never the most modern or heavily patronized. The first passenger excursion train operated out of Huntersville (Argenta, or today's North Little Rock) on April 28, 1870, basically a short trip with a passenger car or two to show that the railroad was being built. On November 21, 1870, the Little Rock & Fort Smith published a timetable showing passenger train service between Huntersville and Lewisburg (Morrilton), with a stage coach connection to Fort Smith. The train was noted as being a passenger and freight train, and the cars were described as being first class in every respect.

In little more than a year, the trains were running ten miles west of Lewisburg to a place called Perry. In June 1872, the daily train left Argenta at 8:15am and reached Perry at 12:30pm. It turned and left Perry at 1:00pm, arriving back at Argenta at 5:00pm. At the time, the Little Rock & Fort Smith Railroad heavily promoted its connections. At Argenta, the railroad listed "connections made with the Cairo & Fulton and the Memphis & Little Rock. Also, with steamers for all points on the Mississippi and Arkansas rivers. Stage coach connections made for Hot Springs, Camden, Washington and Pine Bluff." At Perry, there were "stage coach connections made for Russellville, Dardanelle, Clarksville, Ozark, Van Buren, Fort Smith and all points in the Indian Territory and Texas."

The passenger service was slowly extended northward as the line was completed, and the first passenger train, an excursion of officials and dignitaries, operated from Argenta to Van Buren on July 24, 1876. During this time, the railroad began to build some of its own passenger cars, and a trip for employees and their family members was operated in November using the first passenger and baggage car built at the company's shops in Argenta.

Little Rock and Fort Smith Railroad.

TIME CARD.

ON and after Monday, Nov. 21, 1870, a passenger and freight train will run as follows :

GOING WEST.

Leave—

Huntersville,	-	-	-	8.30 a. m.
Bartlett,	-	-	-	9.13 "
Palarm,	-	-	-	9.41 "
Gold Creek,	-	-	-	10.19 "
Conway,	-	-	-	10.40 "
Cadron,	-	-	-	11.16 "
Plummer's,	-	-	-	11.39 "

Arriving at Lewisburg 12.00 m.

GOING EAST.

Leave—

Lewisburg,	-	-	-	1.00 p. m.
Plummer's	-	-	-	1.21 "
Cadron,	-	-	-	1.44 "
Conway,	-	-	•	2.20 "
Gold Creek,	-	-	-	2.43 "
Palarm,	-	-	-	3.19 "
Bartlett,	-	-	-	3.47 "

Arriving at Huntersville 4.30 p. m.

☞ Stage connection between Lewisburg, Van Buren and Smith.

Coaches will also leave the principal hotels at Little Rock for transfer of passengers to and from the station at Huntersville.

For further information, inquire at the General Office of the Company, Real Estate Bank Building, corner of Markham and Commerce streets, up stairs.

D. W. C. BROWN, Gen'l Sup't.
LORING S. RICHARDSON, Gen'l Ticket Ag't.

nov. 22, '70tf

The Little Rock & Fort Smith posted its new November 21, 1870, timetable in newspapers across western Arkansas. *The Van Buren Press.* (Van Buren, AR) November 29, 1870. Retrieved from the Library of Congress, https://www.loc.gov/item/sn84022991/1870-11-29/ed-1/.

When the last of the planned route was built on to downtown Fort Smith, the first passenger train arrived the night of Thursday, January 30, 1879. In its 1880 report, the LR&FS stated that it had 7 passenger cars and 2 baggage cars to handle the traffic over its 165 miles of track. At the time, meal service was not available on the passenger trains and the railroad would make extended stops at Russellville so passengers could have a meal. In May 1881, the dinner stop was moved to Atkins, and then back to Russellville by the 1890s for local train No. 233. Food service was also available at Van Buren.

Pass.	Mi	Tick. fare.	May 28, 1877.	Pop.'70	Pass.
A. M.					P. M.
§7 00	0		ARGENTA		6 45
7 10	1		Cr. St.L.,I.M.&S.R.R		6 40
7 45	9		Warren	+	6 05
8 15	17		Palarm	+	5 40
8 50	25		Gold Creek	+	5 05
9 08	30		*Conway	100	4 45
9 27	35		Cadron	+	4 25
10 00	44		Plumerville	+	3 55
10 23	50		*MORRILTON	1275	3 30
10 40	55		Germantown	+	3 10
11 12	63		Atkins	+	2 37
11 35	69		Galla Creek	+	2 15
12 25	75		*Russellville	897	1 50
12 48	79		Mill Creek		1 10
1 06	83		Georgetown	+	12 52
1 20	87		Piney Bridge	+	12 35
1 38	90		Mayville	+	12 18
2 00	95		Cabin Creek	+	11 55
2 25	101		*Clarksville	466	11 30
3 05	111		Horsehead	+	10 50
3 40	120		Altus	+	10 15
4 00	125		Ozark	+	9 55
5 37	150		Alma	+	8 12
6 12	159		Van Buren	+	7 37
6 45	168		CHEROKEE		§7 00
P. M.			Arr	Lve	A. M.

(fare column, read vertically: "5 cents per mile.")

By early 1877, the Little Rock & Fort Smith was operating to Cherokee in the Cherokee Nation of Indian Territory. There, passengers and freight used a ferry to cross the Arkansas River and reach Fort Smith. Soon, legal issues forced the railroad back into Arkansas, where a ferry from near Van Buren was used. *Travelers Official Railway Guide for the United States and Canada, December 1877.*

LITTLE ROCK AND FORT SMITH RAILWAY.

J. H. CONVERSE, President, Boston, Mass.
THEO. HARTMAN, Gen. Supt.
J. W. GAY, Secretary and Auditor.
W. D. SLACK, Gen. Freight Agent.

R. S. CRAMPTON, Cashier.
P. J. BENNETT, Gen. Ticket Agent.
J. KAMPMAN, Treas., Boston, Mass.
W. D. SLACK, Land Commissioner.
General Offices— Little Rock, Ark.

† Daily, except Sunday; ‡ Meals; § Telegraph stations.

Mix	Exs.	Mls	January 30, 1882.	Mls	Exs.	Mix
A.M.	A.M.		(Jefferson City time.)		P.M.	P.M.
†4 00	†8 00		lve.**LittleRock**[1] § arr.		3 15	11 15
4 30	8 30	0	Argenta	165	2 45	10 45
5 25	9 05	10	Warren	155	2 12	9 45
6 05	9 30	17	Palarm	148	1 52	9 08
7 40	10 17	30	Conway §	135	1 10	7 50
8 15	10 37	35	Cadron	130	12 51	7 15
9 05	11 07	44	Plumerville	121	12 25	6 21
9 40	11 50	50	Morrilton ‡ §	115	12 05	6 45
11 00	12 35	63	Atkins	102	11 00	4 17
12 10	1 20	75	**Russellville**[2] §	90	10 25	3 00
12 45	1 37	80	Mill Creek	85	10 05	2 03
1 25	1 51	85	Georgetown	80	9 50	1 25
2 42	2 35	96	Cabin Creek	69	9 10	12 10
3 15	3 00	102	Clarksville	63	8 50	11 41
5 40	4 20	125	**Ozark**[3] ‡ §	40	7 30	9 35
7 45	5 42	150	**Alma**[4] §	15	5 35	7 20
8 30	6 15	159	Van Buren §	6	5 10	†6 30
P.M.	6 40	160	Gatlin	5	4 30	A.M.
	7 00	165	**Fort Smith**[5] §	0	†4 15	
	P.M.		ARRIVE] [LEAVE		A.M.	

Stop-over Checks issued on unlimited first-class coupon tickets only, good for 15 days.

CONNECTIONS.—[1] With Memphis & Little Rock R.R., and St. Louis, Iron Mountain & Southern Ry., and steamer lines. [2] With stages for Dardanelle. [3] With stages for Eureka Springs. [4] With stages for Fayetteville and Eureka Springs. [5] With stages for points in Indian Territory.

This timetable is dated January 30, 1882, and shows a mixed and express train in each direction. Note that Morrilton and Ozark were serving as the meal stops. *Travelers Official Railway Guide for the United States and Canada, April 1882.*

The June 23, 1883, issue of the *Arkansas Weekly Mansion* had a listing for the Little Rock & Fort Smith, a regular item in the newspaper. It listed W. D. Slack as the railroad's Land Commissioner, and stated that the railroad station and office was on the corner of Markham and Commerce in Little Rock. The newspaper also showed the Little Rock schedule of three LR&FS trains.

	Arrive	Leave
Pass and Express	2:40pm	12:45pm
Through Freight	12:30am	7:00pm
Ozark Local	6:45pm	6:30am

IMPROVED TRAIN SERVICE

Between Fort Smith, Little Rock and Memphis.

Commencing Sunday, November 4, 1888, and until further notice, double daily passenger trains over the Little Rock and Fort Smith railway will be run as follows:

GOING EAST.

	No. 632.	No. 634
Leave Fort Smith	9:50 a.m.	5:45 p.m.
Leave Van Buren	10:15 a.m.	6:03 p.m.
Leave Russellville	2:00 p.m.	9:40 p.m.
Arrive Little Rock	5:55 p.m.	1:00 a.m.

GOING WEST.

	No. 631.	No. 633.
Leave Little Rock	7:20 a.m.	2:45 p.m.
Arrive Russellville	11:05 a.m.	6:30 p.m.
Arrive Van Buren	2:57 p.m.	10:25 p.m.
Arrive Fort Smith	3:20 p.m.	10:50 p.m.

Trains 631 and 632 make close connection at Van Buren with trains on the Kansas and Arkansas Valley railway. Trains 632 and 634, carrying elegant reclining chair cars, make close connection at Union depot, Little Rock with trains to and from Memphis via Bald Knob.

On November 4, 1888, the Little Rock & Fort Smith Railway changed its passenger train schedules to ensure connections with those of the Kansas & Arkansas Valley at Van Buren. *The Russellville Democrat.* (Russellville, AR) 15 Nov. 1888, p. 3. Retrieved from the Library of Congress, https://www.loc.gov/item/sn84023017/1888-11-15/ed-1/.

During the late 1880s, the Kansas & Arkansas Valley Railway, backed by the Little Rock & Fort Smith, built a railroad between Van Buren and Coffeyville, providing a connection to Kansas City and western Kansas. Regular passenger service soon operated over the line connecting cities to the north and west with Little Rock and on south to the Gulf Coast.

While the passenger service stayed somewhat routine until it ended in 1960, the railroad did attempt several times to add special services or destinations. In June 1889, the Little Rock & Fort Smith Railway began to promote a special Little Rock to Mount Nebo train and rate. The train operated on Saturdays and the $5.30 round trip rate included a seat on the LR&FS train to Russellville, a seat on a train of the Dardanelle & Russellville, and then a stage coach from Dardanelle to the Summit Park Hotel at Mount Nebo. At the time, the Summit Park Hotel was a popular summer resort due to its cooler temperatures than found in Little Rock and the Arkansas River Valley. The dedicated train service didn't last long, ending in July. "The extra train on the Little Rock and Fort Smith railroad to Russellville for the convenience of visitors to Mount Nebo has been discontinued, but a special coach will be attached to the train each Saturday for the benefit of Mount Nebo passengers."

The Little Rock & Fort Smith also began to promote a Little Rock to Eureka Springs service in June 1893. "Passengers from Little Rock and all points on the Little Rock and Fort Smith Railway can reach Eureka Springs, Ark., the same day, via Van Buren and Frisco Line. Fast vestibule Columbian limited express leaves Van Buren daily at 4:38 p.m., landing passengers at Eureka Springs, (the) same evening at 9:08 p.m. Cheap Excursion tickets on sale all the year round. Inquire of nearest Ticket agent."

This Eureka Springs service involved a connection with LR&FS train No. 233, the daily northbound local from Little Rock to Van Buren. In 1893, the railroad operated a pair of daytime trains (Nos. 233 and 234) between Little Rock and Fort Smith. There was also a pair of overnight trains that connected Little Rock with Kansas City (Nos. 231 and 232). These trains featured a Pullman Buffet Sleeping Car between Kansas City and Little Rock, plus a through coach from Kansas City to Fort Smith and Little Rock. This service was via a connection at Coffeyville, Kansas, and was promoted as part of a "Memphis, Texarkana,

Hot Springs and Little Rock, and Fort Smith, Kansas City, Wichita, Pueblo, Denver and North-west" route.

April 24, 1893 – Condensed Schedule

#231	#233	Station	#234	#232
7:35pm	8:25am	Little Rock	1:20pm	7:45am
7:40pm	8:35am	Ft. Smith Xing	1:10pm	7:33am
8:55pm	9:43am	Conway	12:03pm	6:22am
10:35pm	11:40am*	Russellville	10:10am	4:25am
10:40pm	12:00noon	Russellville	10:10am	4:22am
12:38am	2:05pm	Altus	8:17am	2:20am
2:20am	3:50pm	Van Buren	6:50am	12:45am
2:35am	4:25pm	Fort Smith	6:15am	12:20am
2:40am		Fort Smith		12:15am
9:40am		Coffeyville		5:00pm
6:00pm		Kansas City		8:45am

*lunch stop

Improvements were made on the route during the first few years of the twentieth century, with new track built near Conway, Clarksville and Altus. The old line at Conway was immediately abandoned, but the lines through Clarksville and Altus were kept as secondary lines. The final schedule before the new lines were opened promoted the "Double Daily Service" provided on the line. By this time, all four trains had sleeping cars.

Train Nos. 55 and 56 featured "Pullman Sleeping Cars between Fort Smith and Kansas City; Day Coach. Train Nos. 53 and 54 – Pullman Sleeping Cars between Little Rock and Fort Smith, and Free Reclining Chair Car (seats free) between Little Rock, Fort Smith and Kansas City." At Little Rock, these trains had direct connections with passenger train service to the Louisiana destinations of Monroe, Alexandria, and New Orleans. At Russellville, all of the trains had connections with the Dardanelle & Russellville, with a daily stage line, except Sunday, providing service between Dardanelle and Mount Nebo.

April 25, 1904 – Condensed Schedule

#55	#53	Station	#54	#56
7:35am	8:45pm	Little Rock	7:00am	7:55pm
7:43am	8:53pm	Ft .Smith Xing	6:50am	7:47pm
8:52am	10:00pm	Conway	5:38am	6:44pm
10:40am	11:46pm	Russellville	3:50am	5:00pm
1:05pm	2:53am	Altus	1:53am	3:04pm
3:10pm	3:42am	Van Buren	12:05am	1:15pm
3:36pm	4:00am	Fort Smith	11:45pm	12:55pm
3:55pm	4:15am	Fort Smith	11:25pm	12:35pm
11:05pm	10:25am	Coffeyville	5:25pm	7:05am
11:20pm	10:35am	Coffeyville	4:55pm	6:45am
7:10am	5:50pm	Kansas City	9:55am	10:30pm

The passenger trains continued to use the older lines since the larger established cities were located on the original mainline. Despite the line improvements, the *Log Cabin Democrat* newspaper wasn't impressed. "A great deal has been said about the elegant service and fast time that would be put on his road when the reconstruction was completed, but the same old dirty, crowded, open-platform passenger cars and the same old easy-going, don't hurry time-card that we have enjoyed twenty years ago are ours again." At the time, the railroad showed that it owned a total of 10 passenger coaches and 2 baggage, mail and express coaches. However, a number of Iron Mountain and Missouri Pacific cars were used on the through Kansas City-Little Rock service.

On August 1, 1907, *The Log Cabin Democrat* of Conway, Arkansas, announced "Accommodation Train Put On" and that the "Long-Looked for Service Now a Reality."

> *The new service consists of two accommodation trains, each leaving Russellville early in the morning, one to Little Rock and one to Fort Smith, and each returning late in the afternoon. The train from Russellville to Little Rock leaves its initial station at 7:10 a.m., leaves Conway at 9:10 and arrives in Little Rock at 10:30. Returning it leaves Little Rock at 5 p.m., leaves Conway at 6:15 and arrives at Russellville at 8:15. The new time card for the*

six passenger trains between Russellville and Little Rock
is as follows:

> Southbound.
> No. 103 – Leave Russellville 4:51 p.m., Conway 6:44,
> arrive Little Rock 8:00.
> No. 105 – Leave Russellville 3:37 a.m., Conway 5:20,
> arrive Little Rock 6:40.
> No. 131, Accommodation – Leave Russellville 7:10
> a.m., Conway 9:10, arrive Little Rock 10:30.
>
> Northbound.
> No. 104 – Leave Little Rock 8:25 a.m., Conway 9:40,
> arrive Russellville 11:30.
> No. 106 – Leave Little Rock 9:30 p.m., Conway 10:35,
> arrive Russellville 12:10 a.m.
> No. 132, Accommodation – Leave Little Rock 5:00
> p.m., Conway 6:15, arrive Russellville 8:15.

The choice to operate all of the passenger trains on the old lines
became an issue as the railroad began to add premier, limited-stop
trains. The railroad moved these through trains to the new mainlines
and kept only the local passenger trains serving the old lines. Because
of this, in 1907, the Arkansas General Assembly passed a bill that required all passenger trains to operate over the old lines. About the
same time, there were a series of newspaper articles about the slow
passenger trains on the line between Little Rock and Fort Smith, often
with stories about slow track through the mountains and passenger
trains having to follow or meet freight trains, especially those that had
stalled and were having to double its train over the hill. At the time,
the southbound trains carried the names of *Texas & Louisiana Express*
(No. 105) and *Texas & Louisiana Mail and Express* (No. 103). Northbound, train No. 104 used the name *Kansas City Mail*, while No. 106
was assigned the name *Colorado and Kansas City Mail and Express*.

A bit of luxury was added to the line on January 29, 1912, when
the *Kansas City-Hot Springs Express* (Nos. 119 and 120) started operating plush service to the Arkansas resort city. The train handled
several drawing room sleepers, chair cars, coaches and a dining car.

There was even a Fort Smith-Hot Springs open-end cafe-observation car. To handle the market traffic between the many small towns along the line and the several larger cities, local passenger trains operated out of Russellville, Arkansas. This was in response to an Arkansas law passed in 1907 that required the railroad to establish a point halfway between Little Rock and Fort Smith as a terminal point for local passenger trains. The law was established to allow a local passenger train to operate between Little Rock and the halfway point all in one day. This established an eastern local that provided business to the retail businesses at Little Rock, and a western local that benefitted Van Buren and Fort Smith. These locals, called *Slickers*, provided morning arrivals at Little Rock and Fort Smith, with evening returns.

The Little Rock *Slicker* was soon extended westward to Spadra to allow the booming coal mine towns to have access to Little Rock. The *Kansas City-Hot Springs Express* wasn't the success that was hoped for and it was discontinued during August 1914. More cuts were made during World War I when the United States Railroad Administration assumed control of the railroad and cut the passenger service back to only two unnamed mainline trains until the railroads were returned to private control in March 1920.

As with many railroads, the passenger services and number of trains increased after the war, peaking during the 1920s. For the old LR&FS route, the two regular passenger trains were supplemented by the new *Rainbow Special*, train Nos. 117 and 118, inaugurated on July 17, 1921. By 1923, the line featured three through trains, two pairs of locals, and a daily except Sunday North Little Rock-Russellville morning mixed train ("Leaves North Little Rock 8:30am, arrives Russellville 4:00pm. Leaves Russellville 8:05am, arrives North Little Rock 3:35pm").

The two roundtrip local trains were operated to meet state government demands. Train No. 141 would depart Spadra at 6:15am and arrive at Little Rock at 10:25am. It would return as No. 142, departing Little Rock at 4:30pm and arrive at Spadra at 8:52pm. Meanwhile, train No. 144 would start its day at Russellville at 7:00am and arrive at Fort Smith at 11:00am. After spending a day at Fort Smith, passengers could catch No. 143 at 3:00pm and arrive back at Russellville at a scheduled 6:56pm.

Train Nos. 103 and 104 handled a 12-section drawing room sleeper (Fort Smith-Kansas City), a café parlor (Little Rock-Coffeyville), chair car (Little Rock-Kansas City), and coaches (Little Rock-Kansas City and Little Rock-Coffeyville). Train Nos. 105 and 106 handled a 16-section sleeper (Little Rock-Fort Smith), chair car (Little Rock-Osawatomie), and coaches (Little Rock-Osawatomie and Little Rock-Coffeyville). The trains also handled a Little Rock-Van Buren 12-section drawing room sleeper that was operated jointly with the Frisco to and from Monett, Missouri. Train Nos. 117 and 118, using the title *The Rainbow Special*, were Kansas City-Little Rock trains that provided service to Hot Springs, Arkansas. They handled chair cars, coaches, and combination baggage-coach cars that operated Kansas City-Little Rock. They also handled a number of 12-section drawing room sleepers. These included Omaha-Hot Springs, Denver-Little Rock, Kansas City-Fort Smith, Fort Smith-Little Rock, and Monett-Little Rock.

March 14, 1923 – Northbound Condensed Schedule

#104	#106	#118	Station
9:25am	9:00pm	8:30pm	Little Rock
9:35am	--------	--------	North Little Rock
10:33am	10:30pm	--------	Conway
12:10pm	12:35am	--------	Russellville
1:33pm	1:52am	--------	Spadra
4:10pm	4:15am	1:15am	Van Buren
4:35pm	4:45am	1:35am	Fort Smith
5:00pm	5:00am	1:50am	Fort Smith
11:15pm	10:50am	6:25am	Coffeyville
11:35pm	11:10am	6:40am	Coffeyville
7:30am	7:00pm	11:50am	Kansas City

March 14, 1923 – Southbound Condensed Schedule

Station	#117	#105	#103
Kansas City	4:00pm	8:30am	10:15pm
Coffeyville	8:28pm	4:45pm	5:25am
Coffeyville	8:43pm	5:05pm	5:45am
Fort Smith	2:30am	11:00pm	12:01pm
Fort Smith	2:40am	11:15pm	12:20pm
Van Buren	3:05am	11:55pm	12:50pm
Spadra	--------	2:38am	3:00pm
Russellville	--------	4:08am	4:16pm
Conway	--------	5:43am	6:09pm
North Little Rock	--------	--------	6:50pm
Little Rock	7:25am	7:00am	7:00pm

More improvements came in 1925 when on January 4th, train Nos. 105 and 106 became Nos. 115 and 116, then named the *Southerner* in July. These trains handled a number of sleepers, including Kansas City-New Orleans, Hot Springs-New Orleans, and Kansas City-Fort Smith. While the equipment on some trains had been expanded, the *Slicker* trains were down to using gasoline-powered motor cars. There were other trains that didn't show in Missouri Pacific Railroad Table 38 in *The Official Guide of the Railways*. A gas-electric motorcar made two roundtrips daily between Conway and Little Rock, but a turntable had to be installed at Conway before the service could begin. The service didn't last beyond January 31, 1927, as it didn't attract the passengers, mail and express that was hoped for. Mixed trains also operated daily except Sunday out of Russellville. The south end train would depart Russellville at 8:00am, and North Little Rock at 7:45am. The north end train departed Russellville at 8:20am, and Van Buren Yard at 7:00am.

The daily except Sunday mixed trains replaced local trains Nos. 103 and 104 in 1928, with a dedicated passenger train only operating on Sunday. The service was back to local daily passenger trains by the early 1930s, and the motor car locals out of Spadra and Russellville had been discontinued. As the Great Depression of the 1930s set in, the railroad cancelled more trains, leaving just the *Rainbow Special* (Nos. 117 and 118) and the *Southerner* (Nos. 115 and 116). The April 22, 1934, schedule was found in the Kansas City-Coffeyville-Fort Smith-Little Rock-Hot Springs-New Orleans timetable in Table 33 of the *Official Guide*, and the name *Southerner* wasn't even used. Supporting these trains were three pairs of Little Rock-Fort Smith buses, plus a single pair of Little Rock-Russellville buses. The bus company, Missouri Pacific Bus Lines, was created in 1928 as a subsidiary of Missouri Pacific Railroad. On January 1, 1929, the Missouri Pacific Transportation Company officially acquired and began operating the Smith-Arkansas Traveler Bus Company, plus several others, often on routes parallel to the railroad's existing passenger trains. The new bus company operated out of Little Rock in five directions, including Little Rock to Fort Smith. The bus company accepted train tickets, but bus tickets were not good on trains. In 1936 the Missouri Pacific Transportation Company joined Trailways and became Missouri Pacific Trailways, and then became independent in 1948. It was sold to Midwest Bus Lines in 1957, and then to Transcontinental Bus System/Continental Trailways in 1960.

During June 1937, the trains were reorganized system-wide, and the *Rainbow Special* became train Nos. 117 and 124, while the *Southerner* became train Nos. 116 and 125 and hauled a Denver-New Orleans sleeper. The services saw further drops before World War II, with diners replaced by grill coaches and sleeper routes shortened. With several military bases located along the line (Camp Robinson, Camp Jesse Turner, and Camp Chaffee), traffic boomed during World War II and full dining car service was added, along with additional coaches and sleeping cars. However, immediately after the war, passenger volumes dropped and services were removed, replaced by a half-dozen scheduled daily buses. By 1948, both trains had grill coaches to provide meal service, and the *Southerner* was simply a local train that was cut back to Monroe-Little Rock-Fort Smith during January 1949. The mail and express shipments were moved to Missouri Pacific's trucking subsidiary (Missouri Pacific Freight Transport Company, organized in April, 1938), and the railroad petitioned the Arkansas Public Service Commission for permission to discontinue money losing train Nos. 116 and 125. The Little Rock-Fort Smith segment of the *Southerner* was discontinued in July 1949.

November 11, 1945 – Condensed Schedule

#124	#116	Station	#117	#125
3:30pm	10:55am	Little Rock	1:00pm	11:00pm
4:15pm	11:48am	Conway	12:10pm	10:18pm
5:30pm	12:42pm	Russellville	10:49am	9:10pm
7:00pm	1:57pm	Ozark	9:28am	7:34pm
8:05pm	2:55pm	Van Buren	8:31am	6:33pm
8:25pm	3:15pm	Fort Smith	8:08am	6:12pm
8:37pm	3:27pm	Fort Smith	7:55am	5:57pm
1:20am	7:00pm	Coffeyville	4:00am	1:40pm
1:35am	7:15pm	Coffeyville	3:50am	1:30pm
7:00am	11:55pm	Kansas City	10:30pm	8:45am

Pullman service ended on the Little Rock-Kansas City route on March 6, 1954, and the *Rainbow Special* (Nos. 117 and 124) ended its named service on May 23, 1954. Daytime local passenger trains, Nos. 125 and 126, took over providing the service over the route. The grill coach service on the locals ended on April 30, 1956, and the trains started to make meal stops at Fort Smith and Coffeyville. To speed up the trains, grill service was reinstated on December 15, 1957, but discontinued again on January 31, 1959. This left a single passenger diesel locomotive (PA or E-7) pulling a heavyweight consist of a Railway Post Office-baggage car, baggage-passenger combination car, and a coach. On October 21, 1959, Missouri Pacific made public its plan to discontinue the train, and cities all along the route like Van Buren, Fort Smith, Clarksville, Conway and Russellville, protested Missouri Pacific's decision. However, the plan was approved by the Interstate Commerce Commission on March 21, 1960. A week later on March 28, 1960, the last Little Rock to Kansas City passenger trains operated over the former Little Rock & Fort Smith Railway.

Since 1960, passenger service over the Van Buren Subdivision has been limited to an occasional business train or special steam-power excursion train. These excursions and business trips have been extremely popular and have included all three major Union Pacific steam locomotives – #844 (4-8-4), #3985 (4-6-6-4 – *Challenger*), and #4014 (4-8-8-4 – *Big Boy*).

Creating a Little Rock & Fort Smith Railway Route Guide

This book is designed to provide a guide to the route of the old Little Rock & Fort Smith Railway, today's Van Buren Subdivision of Union Pacific, between the two cities found in the name of the railroad. Several false starts in the 1850s and early 1860s finally resulted in a railroad completed in 1879, but then substantially rebuilt during the first few years of the twentieth century. Additionally, the rail line has been improved numerous times over its more than 140 years. Hills have been cut down and bridges strengthened, stations and agents have been replaced by modern signals, and sidings have been installed and lengthened to handle the trains that pound across the line. Even with these changes, much of the line's history can still be found along its route. There are several museums along the line, a number of stations and bridges, and lots of trains that can still be photographed.

This work is based upon several earlier research projects on the railroad. This research has led to a collection of thousands of photographs and drawers full of railroad documents and company history. There is always the question about how much detail to provide in a book like this. While it cannot be the goal to include every detail about the line, there is an effort to explain the history of each community along the line, what shippers were located there, and what facilities the railroad had. Obviously, all of these changed over the more than one hundred and fifty years of the railroad's history, so the challenge is how much information to report. In writing this book, the author attempted to include information about the first few years of the railroad's existence, the improvements made by the St. Louis, Iron Mountain & Southern during the early 1900s, the peak of a community's activity, the railroad as it existed during the routine operations by Missouri Pacific, and what remains today as operated by Union Pacific. Not everything is reported, but enough history is provided to give the reader an idea of what happened at each location.

The railroad historically used north-south as the line's description, although in many areas it curves greatly from these directions. This north-south direction was based upon train traffic from the Kansas City area southward through Coffeyville to Little Rock and on south towards the Gulf Coast. However, much of the route north of Conway actually runs closer to east-west. The route description will use the north-south railroad directions, but will often use the real directions when describing certain features along the route.

The sidings, business and industry tracks were often described by their car-lengths. These car-lengths varied over the years, but were generally around 45 feet per car. Therefore, a track listed as being 20 cars in length could hold about 900 feet of train. Some of these tracks seemed to have had their length changed every few years. Examples of these lengths will often be provided.

Many of the bridges have also been lengthened, shortened, replaced or improved, so where timber trestles once stood, steel and concrete spans, and often large fills, can now be found. These changes continue even as this book goes to press.

An important help in following the railroad and knowing what was at many of the locations are the many maps available on the internet. County road maps, topographic (topo) maps, and many other maps from the era can be found. Comparing these older maps with newer maps can often make finding the railroad easier. The U.S. Geological Survey has been very active making their Historical Topographic Map Collection available through USGS TopoView. These maps are highly recommended and are far too numerous to reproduce in total in this book.

A final issue deals with all of the names that were used to represent parts of the railroad over its one-hundred-plus years. Some stations used several different names over the years while others moved around as customers moved. This was especially true in the coal fields of Johnson and Franklin counties.

The railroad also went through many names, especially during the 1800s as it was reorganized a number of times due to financial problems. To simplify the issue, the term Little Rock & Fort Smith or LR&FS will generally be used. Additionally, an ampersand (&) will be used in railroad company names to make them easier to identify. Especially with a company like the Little Rock & Fort Smith, mixing the railroad name and the cities that it served can get very confusing. Therefore, even if the firm did not use or always use an ampersand, one will be used in this book. Please forgive these simplifications.

Rock Street Branch
Little Rock to North Little Rock

This chapter covers the original mainline from the Arkansas River to the Fort Smith Crossing, plus the trackage built by the Little Rock Junction Railway to cross the Arkansas River to reach The Arkansas Valley passenger station in Little Rock. This short section of railroad consists of the first tracks built by the Little Rock & Fort Smith Railway, and also includes the railroad's Arkansas River dock where materials were delivered as well as the railroad's first shops.

Most of the route was built by the Little Rock & Fort Smith Railway, with its subsidiary Little Rock Junction Railway Company responsible for the bridge across the Arkansas River. This track between Rock Street Junction in Little Rock, and the old Fort Smith Crossing in North Little Rock, soon became part of the Pine Bluff Subdivision of the Louisiana Division of Missouri Pacific and was assigned to the North Little Rock Terminal. Thus, it is often more associated with the line of the former Little Rock, Mississippi River & Texas, the railroad from Little Rock south through Pine Bluff to McGehee, Arkansas. This route in the Little Rock area was replaced in 1984 and soon abandoned, with parts being used as trails.

Almost nothing of these two miles of track remain, but over the 100 years that they existed, stations were added and subtracted, shippers started up and shut down, and finally yards and shops were added, expanded and abandoned. Information about the various locations will be provided, generally quoted along with a date. The route guide provides information about each current and former station location, junctions and crossings, major bridges, and any unique train operations at that location.

Note that every location is identified by a milepost. None of the mileposts date back to the construction of the railroad. All have changed as the railroad was consolidated, purchased, and improved. After consolidation with the Missouri Pacific system, the mileposts were based upon the distance from St. Louis. The mileposts for each location included in this guide are based upon various timetables from the 1920s through today. Where they have changed, some comments may be included.

345.3 LITTLE ROCK VALLEY DEPOT – During the late 1800s and early 1900s, this was the south end of the Little Rock & Fort Smith Railway. However, the LR&FS technically didn't own the track here, but instead used the tracks of the Little Rock Junction Railway, which it owned and operated.

The track from North Little Rock (Argenta) to Little Rock was built to connect the Little Rock & Fort Smith and the Little Rock, Mississippi River & Texas railroads. A joint passenger station and office building was built in Little Rock to handle the business of the two railroads. This also required the creation of the Little Rock Junction Railway Company to build the Arkansas River bridge to connect the two rail lines.

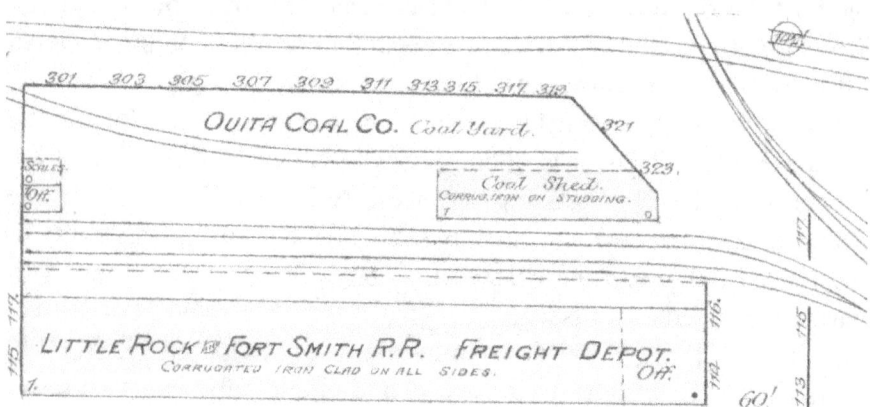

In 1886, the freight house of the Little Rock & Fort Smith was located just south of the Arkansas River between Cumberland and Rock Streets in Little Rock. *Sanborn Fire Insurance Map from Little Rock, Pulaski County, Arkansas.* Sanborn Map Company, July 1886. Map. Retrieved from the Library of Congress, https://www.loc.gov/item/sanborn00285_001/.

Just east of Rock Street Junction was the Little Rock station of the Little Rock & Fort Smith and the Little Rock, Mississippi River & Texas, often called the Arkansas Valley Railroads or Arkansas Valley Route. Located at 508 East Markham, the brick depot was built even before the Little Rock, Mississippi River & Texas was completed. Little Rock ordinances from December

24, 1879, and June 6, 1882, had authorized the construction of the Valley Depot on land provided by the city. Located between Sherman and Commerce Streets, the station featured the offices of the Little Rock & Fort Smith on the third floor. The east side of the building, shown as being at 510 East Markham, was an agricultural implements warehouse. The railroad's freight house was located just south of the Arkansas River between Cumberland and Rock Streets in Little Rock – west of the passenger station.

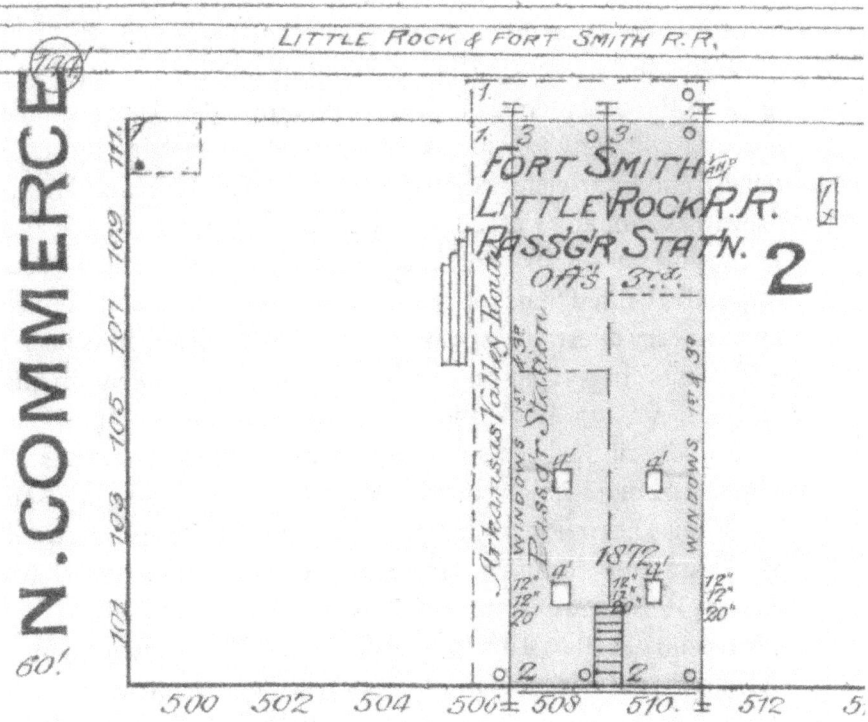

The station of the Arkansas Valley Railroads was located between Sherman and Commerce Streets, and north of Markham Street, in Little Rock. Mistakenly shown as the Fort Smith & Little Rock Railroad by Sanborn in 1886, the station building had the company offices located on the third floor. *Sanborn Fire Insurance Map from Little Rock, Pulaski County, Arkansas.* Sanborn Map Company, July 1886. Map. Retrieved from the Library of Congress, https://www.loc.gov/item/sanborn00285_001/.

By 1897, the Valley Depot in Little Rock was shown to be the East Little Rock Depot of the St. Louis, Iron Mountain & Southern. After the St. Louis, Iron Mountain & Southern acquired the two railroads that made up the Arkansas Valley Route, trains began to operate out of the Iron Mountain station on West Markham. Despite this, the Iron Mountain's land office reported that the Valley Depot was still in use as offices in 1903. However, within a few years, the passenger office was consolidated at the Iron Mountain station and other uses for the former Arkansas Valley station were sought after.

In 1909, it was announced that the Lemp Brewing Company of St. Louis was moving its cold storage plant and offices to the "old Valley depot." The company installed a refrigerating plant in the basement as ice was becoming a major part of the brewing company's business, and $10,000 was spent to make repairs and improvements to the building. The William J. Lemp Brewing Company was incorporated on November 1, 1892, and was soon a nationally known shipping brewery, serving markets across the United States. The company was considered to be the first brewery to establish coast-to-coast distribution of its beers, using 500 refrigerated railroad cars to make 10,000 shipments per year. At Little Rock, the firm operated a cold storage operation to distribute beer throughout the central Arkansas area.

The railroad's freight house was gone by 1913, and in 1921, the John Deere Plow Company bought vacant property at Markham and Commerce from the Little Rock Junction Railway. In 1925, a series of hearings were held in Little Rock due to Missouri Pacific plans to replace the old Valley Depot with a new depot at Markham and Main Streets, described as being at the foot of the Main Street Bridge. The old Valley Depot, which was located at Commerce and Markham, was being abandoned by the railroad and slated for demolition. Both the City of Little Rock and the Arkansas Railroad Commission approved the plan during September 1925, and some of the reports used the title Valley Passenger Station.

At the time, it was noted that only four passenger trains served the old Valley Depot daily. Most of the building was used for non-passenger purposes, with the upper levels used to store company records. The actual depot was in the lower rear of the building and was about 10 feet below street level. It was also noted that mostly black patrons used the depot due to its poor location and condition.

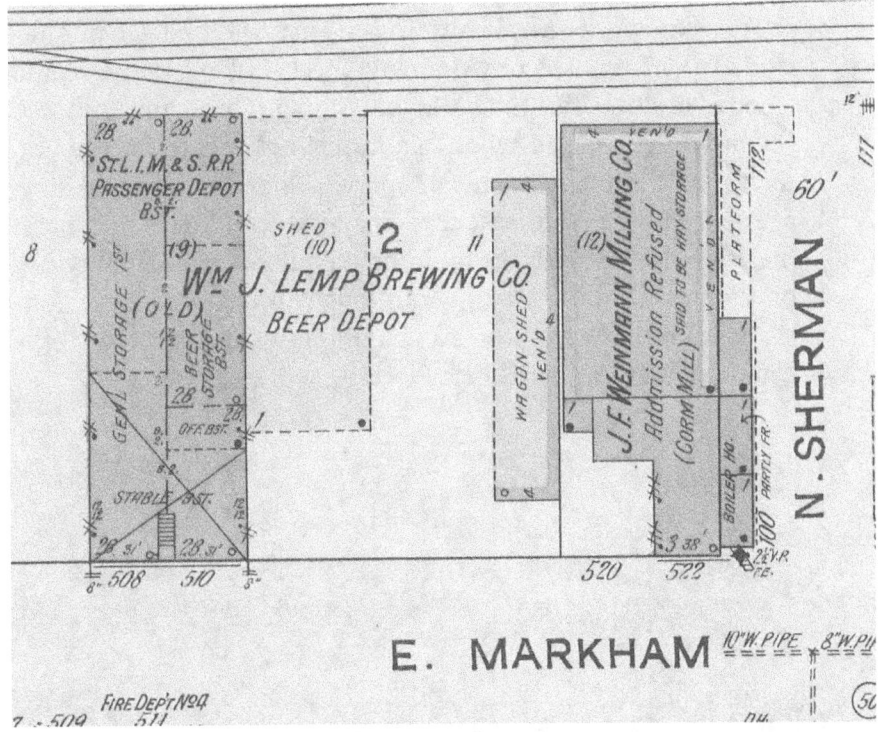

This Sanborn map from 1913 shows that the old Arkansas Valley Route station, generally called the Valley Depot, was being used by the William J. Lemp Brewing Company. *Sanborn Fire Insurance Map from Little Rock, Pulaski County, Arkansas.* Sanborn Map Company, Vol.1, 1913. Map. Retrieved from the Library of Congress, https://www.loc.gov/item/sanborn00285_005/.

Missouri Pacific sold the property to the Terminal Warehouse Company in August 1926 for $30,000. The old Valley Depot was torn down and a new warehouse was built on the property between Commerce and Sherman streets. Designed by architect Eugene Stern for developer Stonewall Jackson Beauchamp (Terminal Warehouse Company), the new Terminal Warehouse Building was built 1926-1927 to handle general merchandise storage. The four-story tall principal (south) elevation of the building faced East Markham Street and provided

180,000 square feet of storage space. It was proclaimed to be the largest building in Little Rock at the time of its construction and was famous for its 8-story tower located at the center bay. The design of the building is generally considered to be Venetian Gothic architecture.

Also known as Markham Tower East, the first tenants included the John Deere Company, food brokers Johnson and Cooper, and the Terminal Van and Storage Company. By 1939, the building featured wholesale farm implements storage and tractor and implements repair space, a coffee roaster and storage space in the southeast corner, and several floors of general merchandise storage. The building included a rail loading dock on the north side. Today, the building is mixed-use space consisting of restaurants, stores and a museum, and is listed on the National Register of Historic Places.

The Terminal Warehouse Building, proclaimed to be the largest building in Little Rock at the time of its construction in 1926-1927, stands where the Little Rock & Fort Smith station once stood in Little Rock.

345.2 ROCK STREET JUNCTION – This was the junction with the line to Little Rock Union Station to the west, the Valley Line of the Little Rock, Mississippi River & Texas Railroad to the east, and the Little Rock Junction Railway to the north. For trains heading west to Fort Smith, this was the start of the Little Rock Junction Railway Company, created by the Little Rock & Fort Smith Railway (LR&FS) and the Little Rock, Mississippi River & Texas Railroad (LRMR&T) to build a bridge across the Arkansas River. Located at Milepost 346.53 of the mainline from Little Rock Union Station, trains faced a 20-degree curve around the south leg of the wye as they headed towards the Junction Bridge.

In 1887, The Beck & Pauli Lithograph Company of Milwaukee produced this "Perspective Map of the City of Little Rock" for the Gazette Printing Company of Little Rock. It showed the Little Rock Junction Bridge, Rock Street Junction, the railroad's freight house, and the "Valley Route Depot" (marked as #2). *Perspective map of the city of Little Rock, Ark., State capital of Arkansas, county seat of Pulaski County.* Henry Wellge & Co, and Beck & Pauli. [Milwaukee, 1887] Map. Retrieved from the Library of Congress, https://www.loc.gov/item/75693083/.

The mileposts at Rock Street Junction, and along the entire Little Rock Junction line, have been changed a number of times over the years. Rock Street Junction was shown to be Milepost 345.16 during the 1960s, and Milepost 343.02 during the 1980s. It gets even more complicated when the line between Union Station and East Little Rock is included.

For decades, passenger trains arriving on the LRMR&T route from Monroe, Louisiana, would head around the south leg of the wye (Pine Bluff to North Little Rock mainline), and then back around the north leg of the wye and all the way to Little Rock Union Station. Meanwhile, Valley Line freight trains used the south leg as they arrived or left the large yard in North Little Rock.

The railroad also had a bridge tender house on the south end of Junction Bridge, located to the west of tracks. This office was used to house the operator of the turn span, and to collect tolls when the bridge was used by street traffic.

Little Rock Junction Railway Company

The Little Rock Junction Railway Company was chartered on December 8, 1883, and officially opened on December 9, 1884. The railroad and Arkansas River bridge was used as a connective link between the Little Rock & Fort Smith and Little Rock, Mississippi River & Texas railways. The company never had its own equipment and was instead operated by its owners. The Interstate Commerce Commission specifically noted that the Little Rock Junction Railway was operated by The Little Rock & Fort Smith Railway.

The stockholders of the two companies were "offered the right to purchase bonds and stock, which latter will be issued as full-paid stock in the Little Rock Junction Railway and Bridge Company." The railroad was described in a court hearing during the early 1900s as follows. "Little Rock Junction Railway from a point in Argenta about 1,000 feet from the river, thence across the Little Rock Junction Bridge, thence by the tracks of the Little Rock Junction Railway 1,088 feet farther on the Little Rock side of the river. The whole line of the Little Rock Junction Railway is about 4,100 feet, of which 2,014 feet is on the bridge mentioned, these figures being taken from drawings furnished by the Missouri Pacific Railway Company."

In April 1887, George J. Gould was elected president of the company as Missouri Pacific reportedly took control of the Little Rock Junction Railway on May 1, 1887. On January 1, 1890, the railroad was leased to the St. Louis, Iron Mountain & Southern for 50 years, under a rental of $26,100 per annum agreement (the interest on its mortgage at six per cent). In 1905, the Interstate Commerce Commission (ICC) stated that the railroad owned, but did not operate, 0.59 miles of track. At the time, it was a subsidiary of the St. Louis, Iron Mountain & Southern, which was a subsidiary of the Missouri Pacific. In 1910, the Little Rock Junction Railway was one of 23 shortline railroads in Arkansas and Louisiana that were consolidated into the St. Louis, Iron Mountain & Southern, but it was still shown by the ICC as a subsidiary of the Missouri Pacific.

For some reason, the ICC showed a reduction in tracks owned but not operated by the Little Rock Junction Railway between 1918 (0.59 miles) and 1919 (0.42 miles). On March 1, 1922, the Little Rock Junction Railway was conveyed by deed to the Missouri Pacific Railroad.

This route was an important line between North Little Rock and the Gulf Coast, especially the New Orleans area. However, because of its slow track and sharp curves, it was replaced in 1984 by a new route using the former Rock Island Railroad tracks around the south side of Little Rock. This left just a few trains using the line, all serving local customers. Eventually this work was assigned to Biddle Yard on the old Rock Island line, and the need for this route ended. During late 2001, the Union Pacific Railroad Company filed a request with the Surface Transportation Board to abandon "a 0.63-mile rail line over the Junction Bridge Line from milepost 343.65 to milepost 343.02." It was soon approved and the track was removed, with the bridge and some of the right-of-way being turned into part of a series of walking and biking trails.

345.0 ARKANSAS RIVER JUNCTION BRIDGE – This bridge was built as part of the creation of the Arkansas Valley Line, a partnership between the Little Rock, Mississippi River & Texas and the Little Rock & Fort Smith to build a rail route from the Gulf Coast to Indian Territory, now Oklahoma. Over the years, the bridge was referred to as the Junction Bridge, the Rock Street Bridge, and the Lower Bridge.

During the 1960s, this was shown in the employee timetables as Draw Bridge – Arkansas River, and was located at Milepost 345.05. After an effort to clean up some of the duplicate mileposts in the Little Rock Terminal, it became Milepost 343.20 by the 1980s.

The first reports about a bridge over the Arkansas River came out in 1869 when the Little Rock & Fort Smith sought bids on the construction of a bridge across the Arkansas River at the foot of Rock Street in Little Rock. As a part of the plan, both Little Rock and Pulaski County would subscribe to $100,000 in the stock and a deck would be added for foot and wagon traffic. No real action took place at the time. Almost a decade passed before surveys were made by the Little Rock, Mississippi River & Texas, with reports about the work coming out in May 1876.

Things again got serious in late 1883. On November 23, 1883, the stockholders of the Little Rock & Fort Smith and of the Mississippi River & Texas Railways were "offered the right to purchase bonds and stock, which latter will be issued as full-paid stock in the Little Rock Junction Railway and Bridge Company." On December 8, 1883, the Little Rock Junction Railway was organized to build a railroad bridge over the Arkansas River at Little Rock. The plan was to build a bridge at the "little rock" or point of rocks at the foot of Rock Street. Within a month, both the Little Rock & Fort Smith and the Little Rock Junction Railway submitted requests to the Secretary of War for approval of the bridge plans. It was stated at the time that the Little Rock & Fort Smith was given authority to build the bridge under the land grant approved by Congress on July 28, 1866, and that this authority was being transferred to the Little Rock Junction Railway. However, letters from the Office Chief of Engineers for the United States Army stated that no such authority existed, which conflicted with another decision by the Chief Engineer, General H. G. Wright, who stated that the authority was implied by the act of July 28, 1866, and that the Secretary of War simply could approve or deny the bridge's design.

With all of the indecision, Major T. E. Sickles, a Union Pacific consulting engineer hired to oversee construction of the bridge, began preparations to build piers for the structure on February 4, 1884. Anderson & Barr, the contractor for the bridge substructure, was also active by February 1884. This firm had built a number of bridges for the Iron Mountain and was described as being well qualified. Among the first work was removing some of the rock at the Little Rock end of the bridge, known as the Point of Rocks, La Petite Roche, or simply the Little Rock. This rock was the first outcropping along the riverbanks above its mouth on the south bank and was long a noted navigation landmark, and was used as the source of the name of today's capital of Arkansas.

The first load of timber for the bridge arrived on March 3rd, and Anderson & Barr began installing the piers in April. While the reports from the time stated that the piers were set on bedrock and filled with concrete, Piers 2, 3 and 4 began to lean soon after the bridge was completed, and repair work discovered that large volumes of stone and sand were used in the construction of the piers. As construction began, the Little Rock Junction Railway was chartered on May 14, 1884. Soon, the railroad petitioned Little Rock and received a right-of-way "over the alley, the extension on Elm street, between Rock and Sherman streets, for the purpose of laying its track."

One major change in the bridge's design took place in late spring as about 200 feet of the north shore was washed away during a series of floods. This required extending the bridge to cover this missing shoreline. After the piers were completed, an iron and steel superstructure built by the Union Bridge Company was being installed by summer. The Junction Bridge was completed on December 8, 1884, with the golden spike driven by Mrs. M. J. Grimes, wife of the contracting company's superintendent. The first train passed over the bridge soon after.

As described by various engineering reports, the "bridge consists of three 253 ft. 4-in., through truss spans, one 127 ft. 11-in., through truss span, and one 352 ft. 10-in., through truss swing draw-span, all single-track, resting on masonry piers and one abutment. Four of the piers are supported on pneumatic caissons and timber cribs. The pneumatic caissons are of ordinary timber construction, and rest on bed-rock, approximately 45 ft. below low water line." The bridge was 1258 feet long and cost about $400,000. Drawings of the structure showed Pier 1 on the south shore, with Pier 2 under the 352-foot through truss turn span. Between Pier 3 and Pier 4 was a 253-foot through truss span, with Pier 4 having repair caissons on each side to help support it. The next two spans were also 253-foot through truss spans, with a 128-foot through truss span between Pier 6 and Pier 7, which was on the north bank of the Arkansas River. Further north were a series of timber pile spans.

During January 1885, a wooden deck was added to the bridge to allow its use as a toll bridge for vehicles and pedestrians. Lights were added to the bridge for safety. This joint use by trains and roadway traffic required bridge tenders who were assigned at each end of the bridge to separate the traffic. This practice lasted until 1898 when the bridge returned to being used solely by trains when the Free Bridge opened. Within a few years, the old watch houses were closed and one was moved to Baring Cross and used in the yards. Another issue solved during the 1890s was the actual ownership of the land at the south end of the bridge. The land had originally been owned by William E. Woodruff, founder of the *Arkansas Gazette* newspaper. Woodruff also helped to determine the actual spelling of Arkansas, served as the state's first treasurer, and was the tenth postmaster of Little Rock. As stated in several reports, a snarled tale of sales, mortgages, liens, and auctions left the ownership undecided, but the owner(s) was due compensation from the railroad, and the businesses that quickly built in the area.

After the bridge opened, several engineering studies were conducted to determine the cause of the moving piers. As stated by one well-documented report, "the masonry piers were not located concentrically with the cribs, the timbers compressed unequally and caused the piers to lean, their tops moving in various directions. The piers were a constant source of trouble and expense from the date of construction in 1883 until recently when they were reconstructed." The first major work to stabilize piers took place in 1899. Pier 2 (the piers were numbered starting at Little Rock) under the turn span moved initially, followed by Pier 4, This helped to move Pier 3 and damage the top of Pier 5. Pier 4 was the most cited problem and there were many plans and efforts to end the movement and strengthen the bridge here. One of these took place during fall 1908 as the Missouri Valley Bridge and Iron Company made repairs to several piers and various parts of the bridge structure.

Because of problems with the bridge, a study was conducted in 1910 to determine if the Baring Cross Bridge could handle all of the rail business so that the Junction Bridge could be abandoned. Replacing Junction Bridge with a new double-track bridge was also considered. To measure the movements of the bridge, the railroad issued instructions on taking observations and measurements on the piers in 1910. In 1911, several floods caused sand to be washed away from Pier 3 and build up around Pier 4, with Pier 3 actually becoming straighter. In 1912, the Bates and Rogers Construction Company reinforced Pier 3 and reconstructed Pier 4. In 1913, the top of Pier 5 was reinforced by railroad forces.

During 1914, reports based upon a series of engineering studies began to be evaluated to determine what to do with the bridge. The engineering work found that the construction was not always what had been promised. "The south abutment is of masonry built on the rock that outcrops on the south bank. The pivot pier, commonly known as Pier 2, and Piers 3, 4, and 5, are rock-faced, concrete-filled, masonry piers, about 45 ft. high, resting on filled timber cribs and pneumatic caissons about 40 ft. high, the masonry of the draw-pier being annular, with a well down to the crib. Piers 6 and 7 are rock-faced, concrete-filled, masonry piers built on piles." Various small projects were conducted to strengthen, stiffen, and improve the bridge over the next several decades.

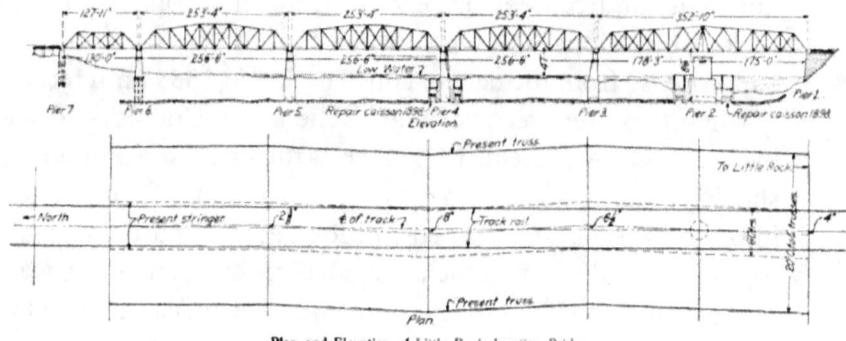

Plan and Elevation of Little Rock Junction Bridge

This drawing of Junction Bridge was included in the December 18, 1914, issue of *Railway Age Gazette* as a part of the explanation about construction on the structure.

In 1917, highway traffic returned to the bridge as the nearby Free Bridge was being repaired. Free Bridge was soon replaced by a new Main Street Bridge, and Broadway Bridge opened in 1922, ending the need for a highway deck on Junction Bridge. As the ownership of the bridge passed through the hands of the St. Louis, Iron Mountain & Southern and to Missouri Pacific, Junction Bridge became a key part of the line to the southeast from Little Rock. It was essentially the route of freight between the Gulf Coast at New Orleans, and northern cities like Kansas City and St. Louis.

While the bridge was built to open to allow tall river traffic to pass, it was seldom actually turned. For example, a newspaper article in January 1961 stated that the bridge was opened for the first time in 30 years to allow a pile driving barge to move up the river. During the 1960s, the bridge was inspected by the Corps of Engineers as part of the planning for the McClellan-Kerr Navigation Project on the Arkansas River. The project would allow larger barge tows to use the river, and larger openings were needed through all of the bridges at Little Rock. The plan announced in 1965 called for the Junction Bridge to have its turn span and Pier 2 removed, replaced by a lift span. This work was done in 1970 by Johnson Construction Company of Minneapolis (piers) and the American Bridge Division of U.S. Steel (lift span). American Bridge Company was founded in April 1900, as a J.P. Morgan-led consolidation of 28 of the largest United

States based steel fabricators and constructors. It immediately became one of the largest bridge builders in the world.

Missouri Pacific took advantage of the work to replace the rest of the spans, using the money paid to it for its bridge at Fort Smith, Arkansas. The first new span, which measured 205 feet long, was installed on June 11, 1970. The last span was installed in time to reopen the bridge in October 1970, with the 354-foot-long lift span, supported by two 90-foot towers, not being tested until February 1971. The last of the old piers were removed later that year. When completed, records indicated that the bridge consisted of a number of different types of spans. Starting on the Little Rock side, the new Junction Bridge included a 44-foot through truss open deck span, a 354-foot lift span, three through truss open deck spans that measured a total of 709 feet, a 128-foot through plate girder open deck span, 94 feet of reinforced concrete trestle, 94 feet of beam deck spans, and 19 feet of reinforced concrete trestle.

The work didn't get used for long, and this is an important part of the story of Missouri Pacific/Union Pacific acquiring parts of the Rock Island in the Little Rock area. Until 1984, MP/UP trains heading from North Little Rock to Pine Bluff and on to New Orleans (the Valley Route) faced a tough route out of town. Trains would curve south out of the North Little Rock yard, running just west of Interstate 30. They would then cross the Arkansas River on the Junction Bridge. Heading south off of the Little Rock Junction Bridge at Rock Street Junction, trains would curve east using a twenty degree curve, too sharp for some modern railroad equipment. Trains would then cross the Rock Island Railroad and curve around the east side of Little Rock, several blocks to the east of the Rock Island route. Near the Little Rock airport, the line headed south towards Pine Bluff.

This torturous route was replaced in early 1984 with a route using part of the Rock Island. Union Pacific made it a significant event by having their steam locomotive #8444 (4-8-4) inaugurate the new Valley Route through Little Rock. This route used the Baring Cross Bridge and Missouri Pacific's Texas mainline to a set of new crossovers and a switch to the former Rock Island mainline at 16th Street, named Little Rock Junction. From here, Union Pacific used the Rock Island to Biddle Yard. East of Biddle Yard, Union Pacific used the former Rock Island route to the Port of Little Rock to reach 25th Street, located near the airport runway. There, the tracks were realigned to connect to the southward Valley Route main. This left only local freight trains to use the bridge while serving nearby freight customers. Soon this work was moved to Biddle Yard in Little Rock, and trains no longer used Junction Bridge.

This photo of the Little Rock Junction Bridge was taken from the Little Rock bank of the Arkansas River. Visible are the raised lift span and the three modern through truss spans.

This photo from the deck of the Little Rock Junction Bridge shows the design of the various through truss spans.

On December 27, 2001, Union Pacific donated the bridge to the City of Little Rock, which transferred the bridge to the Pulaski County Bridge Facilities Board through a 99-year lease. The bridge was rebuilt for pedestrian use as part of the Arkansas River Trail, opening on May 17, 2008. To keep the river open for barge traffic, the lift span was raised and users of the bridge can use stairs or a glass-enclosed elevator to reach the span. The bridge is now known for its dynamic colored nighttime lighting. The entire project cost about $5.8 million.

Missouri Pacific rebuilt the Little Rock Junction Bridge in 1970 as part of the work on the McClellan-Kerr Navigation Project on the Arkansas River. This builder plate from the American Bridge Division of U.S. Steel can be found on the north end of the structure.

The former Little Rock Junction bridge over the Arkansas River is now a pedestrian walkway. This banner promotes the history of the structure.

The Arkansas River

The Arkansas River is a 1469-mile tributary of the Mississippi River, flowing from Lake County, Colorado, near Leadville, southeast across Kansas, Oklahoma and Arkansas until entering the Mississippi River at Napoleon, Arkansas. The river is the second-longest tributary of the Mississippi-Missouri River system, the sixth-longest river in the country, and the 45th longest river in the world. The Arkansas River was once the border between the United States and Mexico, as created by the Adams-Onís Treaty of 1821. This ended with the Texas Annexation, also known as the Treaty of Guadalupe Hidalgo.

The Arkansas River is now used by the McClellan-Kerr Arkansas River Navigation System. The commercial river system was named for Senators John L. McClellan of Arkansas, and Robert S. Kerr of Oklahoma. The work by the U.S. Corps of Engineers has made the river navigable from the Mississippi River as far west as the Tulsa Port of Catoosa. The McClellan-Kerr System officially opened on June 5, 1971, with President Richard M. Nixon attending the opening ceremony.

Arkansas River Trail

This series of trails connects parts of Little Rock and North Little Rock using a core trail alongside the Arkansas River. Much of the route generally parallels the former Rock Island Railroad westward to Pinnacle Mountain State Park. The original trail contained 16 miles of walkways from the Rock Island Bridge (Clinton Bridge) westward to the Two Rivers Park Bridge alongside the Rock Island line at Interstate 430. The trail has since been extended to Pinnacle Mountain State Park with many branches and plans for additional routes. In 2011, the American Automobile Association *Southern Traveler* magazine declared the Arkansas River Trail to be the "Best Bike Trail in the South."

The St. Louis Southwestern Railway

For many years, the St. Louis Southwestern Railway (SSW, or Cotton Belt) had a rail line that passed under the north end of the Junction Bridge, running down Arkansas Avenue. This Cotton Belt line operated under a number of different names, including the Little Rock Branch, the England Branch, and earlier as the Altheimer Branch. The rail line was built through the original charter of the Little Rock & Eastern Railway, incorporated on February 17, 1887. The purpose of the company was to build a railroad from Altheimer, on the mainline of the St. Louis, Arkansas & Texas Railway, to Argenta, (now North Little Rock), a bit more than forty miles away. On August 15, 1887, the rights and franchises of the Little Rock & Eastern (LR&E) were conveyed to the Arkansas & Southern Railway Company, which had created the LR&E to obtain permission to build the line.

On August 18, 1887, the Arkansas & Southern became an official part of the St. Louis, Arkansas & Texas Railway, and construction began, with the line being completed in 1888. While the line was built to connect the railroad with the Little Rock area, it mainly served as an agricultural line serving small farming towns. However, it did provide some competition to the Missouri Pacific (St. Louis, Iron Mountain & Southern) and Rock Island for some shippers in the North Little Rock area. For years, the railroad had their passenger station several blocks west of here.

In 1985, the Cotton Belt obtained trackage rights from Baldwin, near Pine Bluff, to North Little Rock over the former Missouri Pacific Pine Bluff Subdivision. These rights were part of a series of trackage rights created by the consolidation of railroad routes in the Pine Bluff area. The daily SSW Little Rock Local began to operate on the new route, and the Little Rock Branch was served by only an occasional train. This local service on the England Branch ended during April 1989 and 35.8 miles of the line were abandoned on July 1, 1991. Only a few miles of the line still remain in the Sherry, Rose City, and Broadway areas of North Little Rock. The Arkansas Midland Railroad operates what is left, 6.8 miles of track as far southeast as the Tarco Roofing Plant near Interstate 440, according to several Union Pacific sources. The tracks that once passed under the Junction Bridge have been removed as part of the city improvements along the Arkansas riverfront.

When the Little Rock Junction Bridge was rebuilt in 1970, the north end still included some timber trestles, soon replaced with several reinforced concrete trestle spans. Today, these spans are part of the walking trail that crosses the bridge.

344.8 NORTH SHORE – Until the Junction Bridge was completed, this was the south end of the Little Rock & Fort Smith. On August 4, 1869, grading began on the railroad, starting on the north shore of the Arkansas River near here. Several announcements were made that the railroad company was also seeking bids on a railroad bridge across the Arkansas River at the foot of Rock Street in Little Rock. The early plans for a bridge included the idea that Little Rock would purchase $100,000 in company stock to help finance its construction. No bridge was built until 1884.

By January 1870, the Little Rock & Fort Smith had laid about a mile of rail from the north shore of the Arkansas River, and a track had been built down to the river to connect to steamboats delivering company supplies and equipment.

344.7 WASHINGTON AVENUE – When the Junction Bridge was built, the railroad used a fill to reach the north end of the structure. This blocked a number of local streets, which were then raised to cross the tracks at grade. Over the years, several of these crossings were rebuilt to reduce the area's street congestion, adding both underpasses and overhead viaducts. For example, in May 1904, the City of North Little Rock lowered the grade of East Washington Avenue (Milepost 343.4 during the 1980s). Later that year in October, the St. Louis, Iron Mountain & Southern raised the track level and installed a bridge to provide clearance for vehicles underneath. By the 1980s, the overpass was a 60-foot-long through plate girder span. It was torn down as the tracks were removed in 2008-2009.

While the railroad bridge over the street is gone, the fill on either side of Washington Avenue remains. This street sign marks the general location.

344.6 SOUTH END SECOND MAINLINE – To the north of Washington Avenue, the railroad once had a second mainline, basically a place to meet trains entering and exiting the large yard at North Little Rock. Tracks also served a number of area rail shippers.

Over the years, this area had several names and was the junction between the Little Rock & Fort Smith Railway and the Little Rock Junction Railway. During the late 1800s, this was known as Argenta Junction, and then North Little Rock Junction during the 1900s.

Further north, the railroad had a 65-foot wooden viaduct, shown later by Union Pacific as being an open deck timber frame trestle, over East Second Street. During the 1800s, the Little Rock & Fort Smith had its Argenta freight house located here. For many years, the Memphis & Little Rock Railroad (Rock Island) also had its freight house along Second Street.

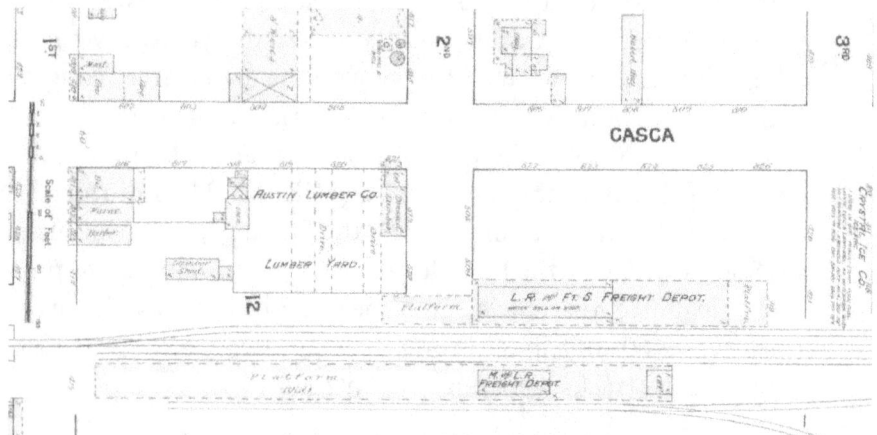

This Sanborn map from 1889 shows the Little Rock & Fort Smith, as well as the Memphis & Little Rock freight depots, in Argenta. The Memphis & Little Rock line changed names regularly until becoming the Chicago, Rock Island & Pacific Railroad. These freight depots were located near what today is Second and Poplar in North Little Rock. *Sanborn Fire Insurance Map from Little Rock, Pulaski County, Arkansas.* Sanborn Map Company, November 1889. Map. Retrieved from the Library of Congress, https://www.loc.gov/item/sanborn00285_002/.

344.6 NORTH LITTLE ROCK – The Broadway Street area has gone through multiple names, including Huntersville, Argenta, and now North Little Rock. For a number of years, it was even part of Little Rock. In this area was the station and freight house (30' x 196') of the Little Rock & Fort Smith. After the LR&FS was acquired by the St. Louis, Iron Mountain & Southern, its facilities were merged and the station closed. The freight house lasted into the 1950s.

Broadway has always been an important east-west street, and by the 1930s there was a concrete viaduct that crossed the street.

If you look carefully along Broadway Street in North Little Rock, you can still find the remains of the concrete headwalls that once supported the Little Rock & Fort Smith overpass. The earthen fill helps to identify the location.

Huntersville, Argenta, and North Little Rock

The area known as North Little Rock has gone through a number of names and organizations. At first, it was just a collection of homes, sheds and docks along the Arkansas River, across from the state capital of Little Rock. By 1838, several investors created the Town of D'Cantillon on the north side of the Arkansas River, "immediately opposite the State-house." However, much of the town soon washed away. With the Memphis & Little Rock Railroad reaching here, the area became very important during the Civil War. The Confederate States of America first developed the site as a supply depot, and when captured by

Union forces in 1863, the facilities were further expanded. These facilities included a large railroad terminal and roundhouse, ferry and ship docks, and a number of warehouses. During this time, the community became known as Huntersville, believed by some to be a kind of insult about how less sophisticated the residents were compared to the capital city. However, at least one newspaper report from early 1865 referred to a Mr. Hunter, "of railroad and stage office notoriety." Apparently, the Union military superintendent of the railroad was William Hunter, and some believe that his name was used for the community which grew up around the Union facilities.

By the early 1870s, Huntersville was the terminus of three railroads, causing the community to grow. A plat for the City of Argenta was created in March 1866, and a post office opened on April 18, 1871, using the name Argenta. The term argenta comes from the Latin word for silver, Argentum. The idea for the name Argenta came from Colonel Robert C. Newton, the son of Thomas Newton, a farmer and president of the Arkansas Mining Company. There were reports that the mining company had found some silver in their Kellogg Mine, located just north of Argenta. By Spring 1872, the Memphis & Little Rock Railroad was using the name Argenta for the community.

In 1890, an effort was made to incorporate the City of Argenta, but Little Rock annexed the area before the incorporation could take place. The case went to the Arkansas Supreme Court, but the annexation was found to be legal. In March 1903, the Hoxie-Walnut Ridge Bill was passed that allowed the annexation or consolidation of cities within one mile of each other as long as the residents of both cities approved. Land just north of Argenta was incorporated as North Little Rock, and efforts immediately began to annex the Argenta part of Little Rock. A July 1903 election resulted in the merger, and Little Rock was again located only south of the Arkansas River. The city on the north side of the Arkansas River became North Little Rock in 1904, back to Argenta in 1906, and then finally back to North Little Rock during October 1917.

Today, North Little Rock is the home of Union Pacific's Jenks Shops and the North Little Rock Hump Yard. It is also the home of about 70,000 residents, making it the seventh-most populous city in Arkansas. While mainly a residential city with plenty of shopping, it is an important transportation junction for rail and highway, with Interstates 30, 40 and 57 (U.S. Highway 67) meeting here. It is also the home of what is believed to be the last intact structure used in the movie *Gone With The Wind* – the Old Mill – now the site of more than 200 weddings and the destination of more than 100,000 visitors each year. There are few sources better for the entire history of North Little Rock than the book *North Little Rock: The Unique City* by Walter Adams.

344.5 CRIP CROSSING – Located at East Fourth Street, this was a grade crossing with the mainline of the Memphis & Little Rock Railroad (M&LR), later the Choctaw Route of the Chicago, Rock Island & Pacific. Before the Rock Island's Arkansas River bridge was built and the mainline turned south to cross it, the mainline continued west. This route connected to the St. Louis, Iron Mountain & Southern to get across the Arkansas River. During late 1873, the Memphis & Little Rock Railroad was encouraged by the Cairo & Fulton to extend their track to near the Fort Smith Crossing and use the Baring Cross Bridge across the Arkansas River. The plan became effective on January 5, 1874.

Almost immediately, the St. Louis, Iron Mountain & Southern attempted to prevent the M&LR from using the Baring Cross Bridge. However, in late 1877, the courts ruled against the Iron Mountain and forbade them from removing the connection between the two railroads.

In 1892, the Little Rock & Memphis Railroad (a reorganized M&LR) had two routes through North Little Rock, then known as Argenta. Both routes connected to the St. Louis, Iron Mountain & Southern to cross the Arkansas River to reach Little Rock. One route went through town between 4th (Bulah, later Madison) and 5th (Allen) to reach the Iron Mountain, and a depot was built at Newton Street, today's Main Street. The other route turned north up Newton and then curved west through the Little Rock Oil & Compress to connect to the Iron Mountain. At

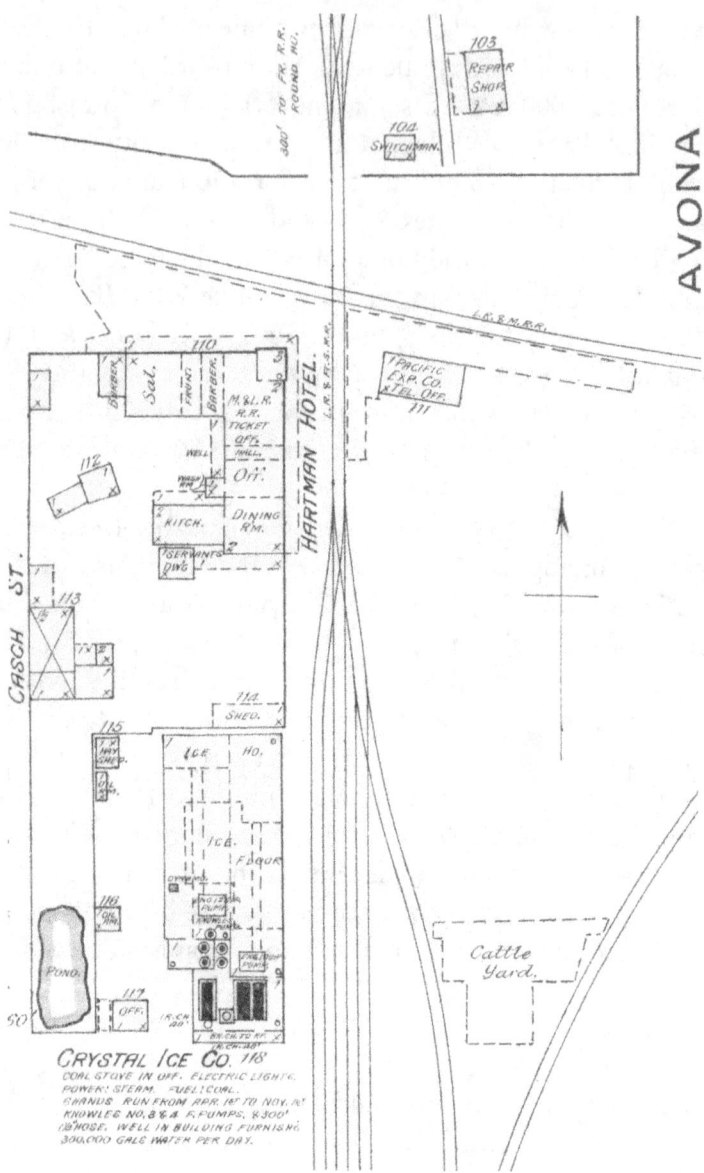

This Sanborn Fire Insurance Map from 1886 shows the crossing of the Little Rock & Fort Smith with the Little Rock & Memphis (LR&M – later Chicago, Rock Island & Pacific) at North Little Rock. This crossing was at today's Fourth and Magnolia. Note that the ticket office for the LR&M was in the adjacent Hartman Hotel, and the shops of the LR&FS were several hundred feet to the north. *Sanborn Fire Insurance Map from Little Rock, Pulaski County, Arkansas.* Sanborn Map Company, July 1886. Map. Retrieved from the Library of Congress, https://www.loc.gov/item/sanborn00285_001/.

the time, Little Rock Oil & Compress had both a cotton seed oil mill and stock yards. The cotton seed oil facility was where the Rock Region Metro offices and bus barns are today.

Until 1910, the locomotive and car shops of the Rock Island were located just east of here, land now used by Interstate 30. By 1914, the tracks no longer went west following 4th Street. The Rock Island Railroad continued to serve a feed mill, located a block east of Main Street. Their freight house was also in the area for many years. This required an industrial lead that crossed the Little Rock & Fort Smith line, thus this diamond. During the 1960s, a hand-operated gate was used to protect the train movements across the diamond, normally lined against Rock Island train movements.

Just north of the crossing was the large Cameron Feed Mills operation, a feed mill and elevator located to the west of the tracks. It was served by both railroads.

344.4 PRIME QUALITY FEEDS MILL – The track south of here was abandoned about 2001, with the track to the north abandoned in 2010. Located at 124 E. Fifth Street was the Prime Quality Feeds mill, a North Little Rock landmark since the 1920s. The facility was operated as the Mountaire Feed Mill, which was sold, along with the Prime Quality brand, to Minneapolis-based Cargill Animal Nutrition in early 2007. Cargill closed the mill in November 2007 after building a new production plant in Mississippi, and the complex was mostly torn down.

344.3 SEVENTH STREET – Known as Russell Street during the 1800s, this area was where the Little Rock & Fort Smith had their Little Rock yard, plus their locomotive and car shops. The initial shops were little more than a few wooden sheds. However, more modern shops were built during the early 1870s with the capacity to repair steam locomotives and to build new freight and passenger cars. In November 1876, a special passenger train was operated by the railroad using the first passenger and baggage car built at the company's shops.

This yard was known as Fort Smith Yard, Smith Yard, or Argenta Yard. The roundhouse once sat where Magnolia Street is now located. The railroad had a number of facilities in the area, and some reports state that the Little Rock & Fort Smith once owned about 25% of the entire town of Argenta.

A new nine-stall roundhouse with turntable opened during April 1879. The frame structure was built on a stone foundation, and the locomotive stalls were 62 feet deep. These shops handled the maintenance, repair and construction of equipment for the railroad for another decade, but were closed when the Iron Mountain took over the operations, and the work was moved to their nearby Baring Cross shops and roundhouse by late 1890. The old shop buildings were soon torn down, and the property was expanded as a yard with as many as ten tracks.

To handle the work moved from the Little Rock & Fort Smith shops to Baring Cross, a number of facilities were added or expanded at the Cairo & Fulton complex. Work on a new 25-stall fire-proof roundhouse began in 1889, a new coal chute was built at Baring Cross in 1891, and additional coal storage bins, a store house, and a one-story frame blacksmith shop (50' x 65') were built in 1893.

Around Seventh Street, a number of old foundations can still be found that once supported signals and buildings.

With the shops gone, Seventh Street was expanded through the property, and a wooden viaduct was built across the tracks. A small rail yard was created here to handle the business of local shippers. A 60' x 256' freight house was also built to the east of the tracks. Just south of the Seventh Street viaduct was Mechanics Lumber Company, located on the west side of the tracks.

To the west of the abandoned railroad grade between Sixth and Seventh streets is the River Rail Trolley Barn, home of the fleet of trolleys which serve downtown Little Rock and North Little Rock.

344.1 END OF TRACK – The current end of track is about Eighth Street. This leaves enough room for equipment to be turned on the wye off of the mainline.

343.9 MAIN STREET VIADUCT – With all of the rail lines passing through the area, there has long been an overhead bridge to carry Main Street across the tracks. The original viaduct featured a series of steel spans, with through truss spans over the main sets of tracks. As highway vehicles got heavier, the bridge was replaced in 1927 with a 1200-foot concrete structure between Eighth and 13th streets.

The August 28, 1926, issue of *Railway Age* reported on the construction, reportedly organized by the North Little Rock Viaduct District. "A contract has been awarded by this association to the Kelliher Construction Company, Little Rock, Ark., for the construction of a 1,857 ft reinforced concrete viaduct to carry Main street in North Little Rock over the tracks of the Missouri Pacific and the Chicago, Rock Island and Pacific. The cost is estimated at $305,997 and the railroads will share in the cost."

During the past few years, the city has made plans to replace the bridge with a more modern structure to handle the large increase in traffic.

This view of the Ninth Street Wye is from the nearby Main Street Viaduct. The former Little Rock & Fort Smith mainline once headed on south. However, today the wye can only handle a few locomotives at a time.

This is a view of the Ninth Street Wye as it passes under the Main Street Viaduct in North Little Rock, Arkansas. This was the route of the Little Rock & Fort Smith.

343.8 NORTH END SECOND MAINLINE – This location, shown as being at Milepost 344.23 during the 1980s, was the north end of a second track through the North Little Rock area.

343.6 NORTH LITTLE ROCK YARD – During the 1960s, this was the milepost cited for the connection to the Missouri Pacific rail yards in North Little Rock. Originally, the Little Rock & Fort Smith went straight across the St. Louis to Texas mainline. Later, this crossing was replaced by a pair of wyes since freight trains used the North Little Rock yard complex and seldom passed straight through the city.

By the 1980s, this was designated as Milepost 344.27, and was shown to be the end of the Junction Bridge Line. It was also shown to be Milepost 345.93 on the mainline from St. Louis.

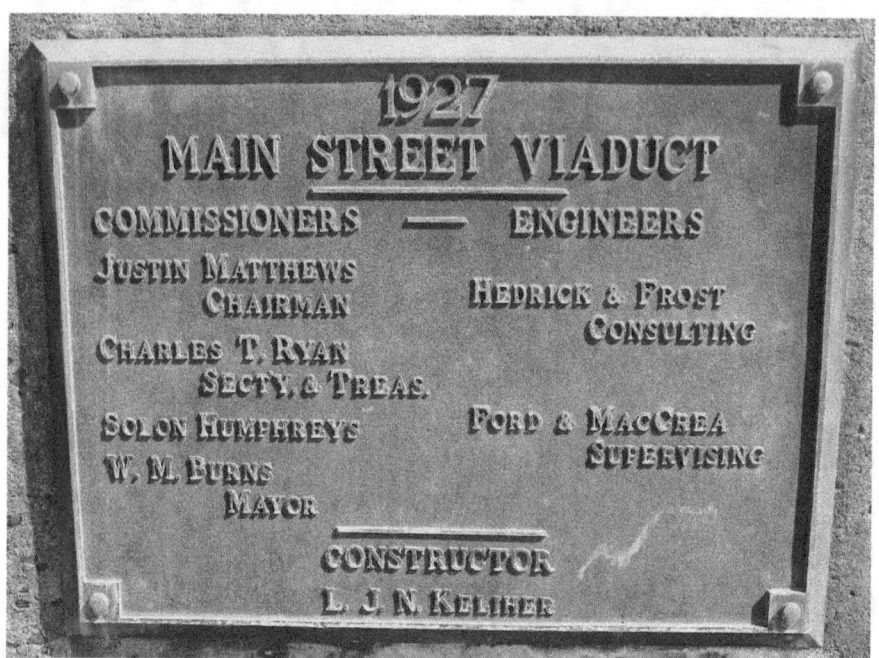

This marker on the Main Street Viaduct provides some basic information about who was involved with the bridge's construction.

343.5 FORT SMITH CROSSING – Once known as "Arkansas Division Crossing" and known today as "Begin Van Buren Line" in Union Pacific timetables and other documents, this was where the Little Rock & Fort Smith once crossed the St. Louis, Iron Mountain & Southern. During the late 1800s, this location also carried the name "St. Louis, Iron Mountain & Southern Crossing" and "St. Louis & Iron Mountain Crossing." The tracks were shown to be at an elevation of 259 feet, with grades of as much as 0.58% heading north towards Levy.

The Little Rock & Fort Smith was actually the first railroad here, having built a reported 24 miles of track from the Arkansas River to near Mayflower and Gold Creek. A newspaper report from December 29, 1869, stated that the railroad was laying out the site of their depot on the Newton estate in Argenta. The Cairo & Fulton (C&F) was grading through the area by late 1870, and reportedly began to use the yards, shops, turntable, water tanks, and buildings of the LR&FS. In January 1873, the Cairo & Fulton began construction towards Texas and had to cross the LR&FS. An injunction was obtained that prevented the crossing from being built, and any buildings on the LR&FS property from being removed. Apparently, there were several arguments over who owned which buildings and several C&F employees were arrested removing lumber and parts of several buildings. An independent committee was appointed to monitor the work and removal of property, and the Cairo & Fulton was soon building southward.

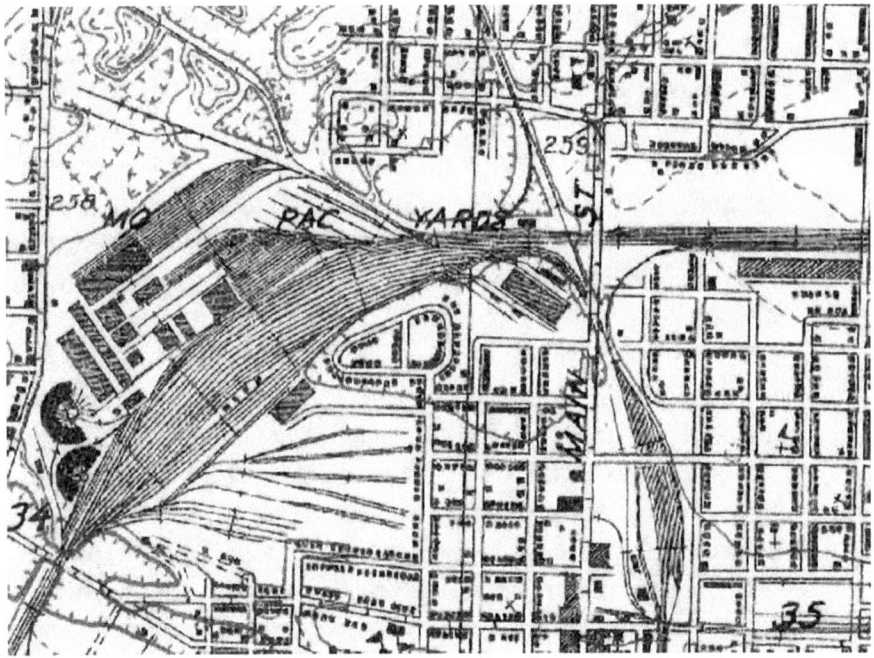

This topographic map from 1935 shows the area around Fort Smith Crossing. To the west were the Baring Cross Yard and Shops. To the east were a few yard and industry tracks. To the south was the yard of the Little Rock & Fort Smith, once the location of its shops. To the north is the mainline to Fort Smith. *North Little Rock (AR) Quadrangle, 1935.* U.S. Department of the Interior, U.S. Geological Survey.

Initially, the crossing involved a single track for each railroad, but soon each had several tracks in the area. For much of the life of Fort Smith Crossing, changed in the timetables to simply Argenta in 1904, there were five tracks or more on the Cairo & Fulton route. Being a busy junction between two important railroads, a number of facilities were built at Fort Smith Crossing.

One of the first was a depot, used as a transfer point for passengers from both railroads. Informally, the depot was known as the Fort Smith Crossing Union Station. After the merger of the railroads into the St. Louis, Iron Mountain & Southern, much of the passenger train service moved to stations in Little Rock or near downtown Argenta. During October 1893, the Fort Smith Crossing depot was moved to the south wye switch so that trains could stop there without making a reverse move. This location worked better as passenger trains typically headed to the Union Depot in Little Rock.

The plan apparently wasn't as successful as hoped as a new depot was opened on July 30, 1902. This new station contained both waiting rooms and a baggage room. The old depot was moved a short distance to Newton Street (today's Main Street) and became the yard office and base of operations for the Superintendent of Terminals. More work was done on the depot after the roof caught fire from a passing locomotive on October 25, 1909.

By the 1890s, the main route through Fort Smith Crossing was the Cairo & Fulton, and almost all trains off of the Little Rock & Fort Smith headed to the yards at Baring Cross, or the train station in Little Rock. Only a few LR&FS trains went directly through the crossing, generally to serve customers along the line in Argenta, or to connect with its Valley Line partner on the south side of Junction Bridge. To protect these moves, a guard gate across the LR&FS would be turned across the main lines of the Arkansas Division. This ended by the late 1940s when the crossing was removed, leaving just a wye on the west side of the Texas mainline. However, the 20' x 115' former depot continued in railroad use into the 1960s.

Cairo & Fulton Railroad

The railroad through North Little Rock south to Texarkana, now the Little Rock Subdivision of Union Pacific Railroad, was built by one of many railroads that eventually became part of Missouri Pacific Railroad. The Cairo & Fulton Railroad was part of a series of railroads designed to connect the upper Mississippi River area with Texas. As with many railroads, the corporation was divided into many smaller railroads, often established by state. For example, the Cairo & Fulton of Missouri was the part of the system north of Arkansas. It was reorganized as the Cairo, Arkansas & Texas Railroad on May 21, 1872.

Meanwhile in Arkansas, the Cairo & Fulton was initially chartered by the Arkansas General Assembly on January 12, 1853. Its charter stated that the railroad would be built from the Mississippi River opposite the mouth of the Ohio in Missouri, through Little Rock, and then to Fulton on the Texas border. The charter also allowed it to build a number of branch lines across Arkansas. Some work was done, but a lack of funding and then the Civil War halted the work throughout the 1860s.

With the aid of land grants, construction began during 1870, and by January 1871, the Cairo & Fulton had completed about 20 miles of track north from Argenta, with another 20 miles being graded. The land grants reportedly equaled 6400 acres per mile of track built, and the land was valued $5 to $10 per acre. By the end of the year, the tracks had been completed to near the Little Red River, and a special excursion using Little Rock & Fort Smith Railroad passenger cars was used to mark the event.

During early 1872, construction began south of the Arkansas River, and the railroad continued to build track north of Argenta. The tracks from Missouri were completed to Argenta on January 11, 1873. About the same time, the railroad announced that it was going to change its track gauge from 5' 6" to five feet. A third event in January was a legal battle between the Cairo & Fulton and the Little Rock & Fort Smith over the proposed crossing at what would become Fort Smith Crossing. This fight was over the lack of payment by the Cairo & Fulton for the use of tracks and facilities of the LR&FS, as well as issues about the ownership of lumber at the site. The fight didn't last long and the C&F opened the Baring Cross Bridge on Sunday, December 21, 1873, and started Little Rock-St. Louis passenger service two days later. The track was completed to Texarkana on January 15, 1874, and it was leased to the St. Louis, Iron Mountain & Southern on May 6, 1874. Different parts of the Iron Mountain had been built to different track gauges, and the line was rebuilt to standard gauge on June 28, 1879. On May 12, 1917, the St. Louis, Iron Mountain & Southern merged into Missouri Pacific, which became a part of Union Pacific in 1982.

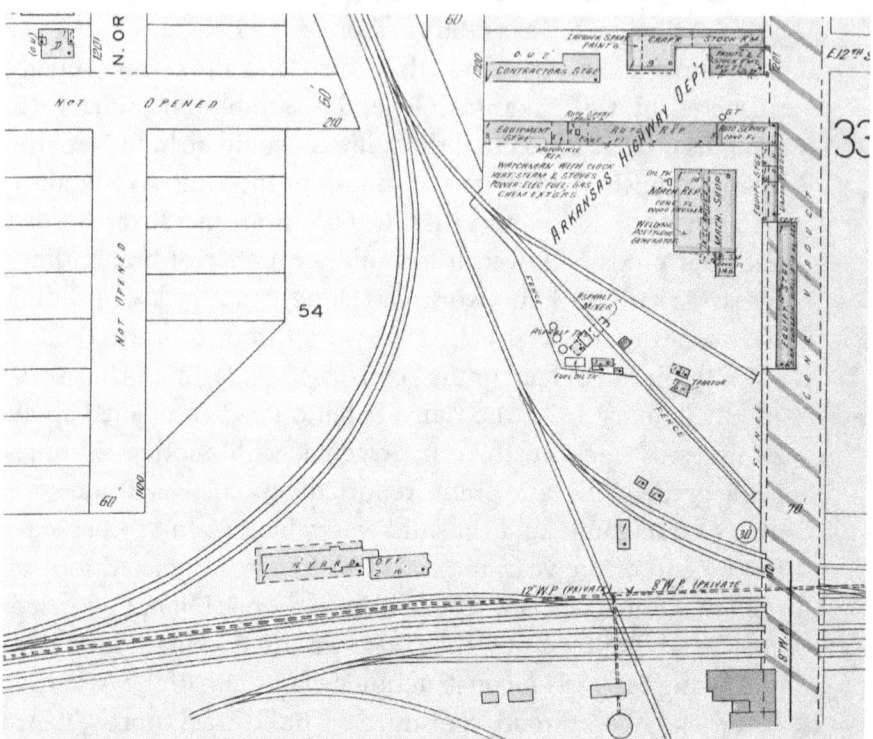

This Sanborn map from 1939 shows the Fort Smith Crossing area, with the former depot, then being used as a yard office, located inside the south wye switch. *Sanborn Fire Insurance Map from Little Rock, Pulaski County, Arkansas.* Sanborn Map Company, Vol. 3, 1939. Map. Retrieved from the Library of Congress, https://www.loc.gov/item/sanborn00285_009/.

North Little Rock

This location was also called Argenta, and then North Little Rock, in the railroad's timetables. However, because of the large yard complex, there were actually several locations that used these names. In 1907, the St. Louis, Iron Mountain & Southern called this Argenta and stated that there was a yard, scale, water station, coal station, wye, and turntable here. In 1944, the Van Buren Subdivision listed this as North Little Rock and showed a continuous train order office here. There was also still the yard, scale, water station, coal station, wye, and turntable in the terminal, plus a fuel oil facility.

Van Buren District
North Little Rock to Van Buren

This chapter covers the existing mainline that Union Pacific operates as their Van Buren Subdivision, and part of the Wagoner Subdivision. Parts of this route near Conway, Knoxville and Ozark use the improved lines built 1902-1904, with the original routes in these areas covered in other parts of this book. There are also a number of shorter "detours" which are detailed in this chapter.

Most of the route was built by the Little Rock & Fort Smith Railway, with significant realignments by the St. Louis, Iron Mountain & Southern, between Little Rock, Arkansas, and the Arkansas-Oklahoma border. Additional line changes have taken place along the route, mainly due to work on the Arkansas River. Name changes can also be found. In 1907, the St. Louis, Iron Mountain & Southern called this the Van Buren District. It later took on the name of the Van Buren Subdivision.

Railroads change over many years, and the lines of the Little Rock & Fort Smith are no different. Stations were added and subtracted, agencies were opened and closed, and shippers started up and shut down. Yards and shops were added, expanded and abandoned. Some of these have been gone for more than a century, with few reminders that they ever existed. This all leads to a complexity in describing a route. Because of the challenge of describing a railroad built and operated over more than a century, information about the various locations will be provided, generally quoted along with a date. The route guide provides information about each current and former station location, junctions and crossings, and major bridges. To explain some of the operations, it includes the current mileposts, office calls (telegraph call code) from 1925, and any unique train operations at that location.

Note that every location is identified by a milepost. Railroads identify locations along their routes by mileposts, much like highways do. None of the mileposts date back to the construction of the railroad. All have changed as the railroad was consolidated, purchased, and improved. The mileposts for each location included in this guide are based upon various timetables from the 1920s through today. By the 1920s,

Missouri Pacific was renumbering the miles based upon their distance from St. Louis. This created a great deal of confusion in the Little Rock area with multiple lines having the same mileposts. Comments will be made throughout this guide about these milepost changes.

343.6 NORTH LITTLE ROCK YARD – During the 1960s, this was the milepost cited for the connection to the Missouri Pacific rail yards in North Little Rock. Originally, the Little Rock & Fort Smith went straight across the St. Louis to Texas mainline. Later, this crossing was replaced by a pair of wyes since freight trains used the North Little Rock yard complex and seldom passed straight through the city. For many years, the yards were primarily to the south near the Baring Cross railroad shops. About 1960, Missouri Pacific built their hump yard to the north of the junction, causing many trains to head in that direction. Today, trains that are to be worked in the yard turn to the north, while through trains towards Louisiana and Texas turn to the south.

By the 1980s, this was designated as Milepost 344.27, and was shown to be the end of the Junction Bridge Line. It was also shown to be Milepost 345.93 on the mainline from St. Louis.

344.1 BEGIN VAN BUREN SUBDIVISION – In recent employee timetables, the switch to the St. Louis-Texas mainline was the south end of the Van Buren Subdivision. The route connects North Little Rock with Van Buren, both in Arkansas.

344.2 FORT SMITH CROSSING – This series of diamonds, removed long ago, was once known as Arkansas Division Crossing. Details about this crossing can be found on Page 104.

344.3 XO JUNCTION – This was a junction that was listed by the 1930s. It featured telephone communications by the 1940s. Missouri Pacific would use letters of the alphabet to identify junctions when no historical name existed for the location. Later, many of these locations would use names from nearby stations, or be named for officials of the railroad.

Recent timetables show this location to Van Buren Wye, or Control Point X343. Trains can turn east into the large North Little Rock yard, or west and then south on the mainline towards Texas. These tracks date back to the Cairo & Fulton Railroad.

During October 2023, Union Pacific 7801 was found heading south at Thirteenth Street, preparing to turn eastward towards the North Little Rock Yard. The train consisted of ETRX coal cars headed to Entergy's Independence Power Plant near Newport, Arkansas.

344.4 WEST FOURTEENTH STREET – As the twentieth century began, railroads and streets began to conflict with the growing traffic volumes. In Little Rock, the railroads were required to provide a crossing at every street. The residents in North Little Rock began to demand the same. During 1902, a wooden bridge was installed here to allow road traffic to cross from one embankment to the other, especially important as trains were often held here until space was available in the rail yards or there was an opportunity to cross the former Cairo & Fulton line. To assist with these train movements, automatic signals and a telephone booth were installed here in 1941.

This photo from the Historic American Engineering Record shows the general design of the now removed Fourteenth Street Bridge over the former Little Rock & Fort Smith tracks in North Little Rock. Historic American Engineering Record (HAER) photograph by Michael Swanda, September 1986. Retrieved from the Library of Congress, https://www.loc.gov/pictures/item/ar0100.photos.010461p/resource/.

By the 1920s, the Missouri Pacific was adding a second track through this area and a new bridge was built, using a pony Kingpost timber truss span over the tracks. Timber pile trestle spans were used on both approaches to the main span. The Kingpost, also known as the King post or crownpost truss, was used as far back as Roman times. It was generally used to support apex roofs. However, it was also used on lighter-capacity bridges like this one. The Historic American Engineering Record documented the bridge in 1988 and stated that the "bridge uses modified Kingpost timber trusses. All timber truss members are square in section. The top chord timbers are attached to the bottom chord with a butt joint and joined at the top of the peak with steel straps. Two timber vertical members are placed in the truss on either side of the center peak and are attached to the top and bottom chords with steel straps (the addition of these verticals modifies the basic Kingpost design)."

In May 1988, Union Pacific replaced the Kingpost span with a steel stringer span. This was apparently done to provide additional clearance for freight trains. At the time, the Fourteenth Street Bridge was the last timber Kingpost bridge in Arkansas. As of 2019, the bridge was still in place but closed, and there were plans to remove it, which occurred within a year. The railroad below it is now back to a single track.

Southbound trains on the LR&FS line were often held in this area until open tracks were available in North Little Rock. Because of this, a concrete pedestrian underpass was installed in 1944 at Milepost 344.8. Today, it is little used and seems to constantly be full of water and trash.

345.3 WEST PERSHING BOULEVARD BRIDGE – During the 1930s, the railroad through here had two main tracks, and a set of crossovers were located to the south that allowed trains to head in any direction at Fort Smith Crossing. Today, there is only a single mainline track.

This was formally 27th Street, now named Pershing Boulevard. The street was renamed to honor John Joseph Pershing, commander of the American Expeditionary Forces during World War I, and later the only person promoted in his own lifetime to General of the Armies, the highest possible rank in the United States Army.

Pershing Boulevard once ended at the tracks, but by the 1960s, it had been expanded to four lanes and there was talk about extending it westward under the railroad. The first detailed plans for this work were released in 1978, and Missouri Pacific hired an engineering firm to design an underpass, which would allow a series of area roads to be connected and expanded. An official ground breaking took place on June 25, 1981, and the through plate girder bridge was dedicated on November 17, 1982.

345.5 TOOL HOUSE – Historically, track crews walked or used hand cars to move over their assigned territories. To lessen their load, tool houses were located along the line with track parts and the tools to install them. During the early 1900s, a Missouri Pacific tool house stood here.

345.6 CAMP ROBINSON SPUR – Located immediately north of the grade crossing with Pike Avenue was once a switch for the branch to Camp Pike, now known as Camp Robinson. Railroad employee timetables from the 1940s show that the switch once used the name Military Junction. Part of this line is now used as a walking and biking trail.

The *First Annual Report of Missouri Pacific Railroad Company* (Seven Months Ended December 31, 1917) had details about this line. "A new line from Dalhoff, Ark., to Camp Pike, Ark., a distance of 4.05 miles was constructed for the purpose of transporting material for the construction of the National Army

Cantonment at that point and to afford facilities for the movement of troops and supplies. Minor changes due to remeasurements and reclassification, increased the mileage 0.94 miles."

As World War I started, the U.S. military developed facilities for the training of troops. During early 1917, the Little Rock Board of Commerce began work to attract a cantonment (a group of temporary billets for troops) for Central Arkansas. Land was found northwest of North Little Rock, and after a series of meetings and challenges to the location, plans were made for Camp Pike. Planners of the facility consulted with the Missouri Pacific Railroad on the lack of rail service and received assurance that the railroad could build the line in three weeks once confirmation of the plan was received. Construction on the camp began in June 1917, and Missouri Pacific had begun grading on the rail sidings in the warehouse section of the camp by late July. Missouri Pacific reports indicate that the railroad was essentially completed by August 1, 1917, and the camp itself was substantially complete by November 1917. The first troops began to arrive on September 5th, and on October 5, 1917, Missouri Pacific began operating a daily passenger train from Little Rock Union Station to Camp Pike. As many as 100,000 troops were here by the fall of 1918.

The camp was named for General Zebulon Montgomery Pike, an American brigadier general and explorer. Pike led two of the expeditions through the Louisiana Purchase territory under orders from President Thomas Jefferson. His first expedition (1805-1806) was through the upper northern reaches of the Mississippi River, while his second expedition (1806-1807) was through the southwest along the border with Spanish-colonial settlements. Colorado's Pikes Peak was named for him. Zebulon M. Pike was killed during the Battle of York in April 1813, a part of the War of 1812 campaign into Canada.

Camp Pike was initially the home and training camp for the 87th Division, made up of draftees from Alabama, Arkansas, Louisiana and Mississippi and activated here on August 25, 1917. Later it was used to train replacement troops. When the war ended, the camp became a demobilization station and home for the U.S. Third Infantry Division. It also became the headquarters of the Arkansas National Guard and the home of the Camp McRae Civilian Conservation Corps (CCC) camp (#3797). This CCC camp was used for initial processing and training, and then workers were assigned to their camps.

Camp Pike was built in late 1917, and was used initially as the home of the 87th Division of the U.S. Army. The 87th left Camp Pike for France in August, 1918 and an infantry training center was established here. This photo shows the freight yard at Camp Pike, heavily used to bring in materials to build the camp, and for the movement of troops in and out of the facility. "Freight Yards, Camp Pike, Arkansas." Signal Corps Photo #165-WW-528E-8. Records of the Office of the Chief Signal Officer (Record Group 111); National Archives at College Park, College Park, MD.

The branch track did see some passenger service for the military and the CCC after World War I. For example, on October 13, 1936, Missouri Pacific delivered a train of CCC workers from the Rock Island Transfer Track at Little Rock to North Little Rock and then to Camp Pike. The next day, another train of CCC workers was picked up in East Little Rock and moved to the camp. The moves were determined to be simple terminal moves as the Camp Pike switch was within the switching limits of the Little Rock terminal, located at "Mile Post 349-60."

The camp was renamed Camp Joseph T. Robinson in 1937. Joseph Taylor Robinson was a lifetime politician and attorney in Arkansas, serving as Arkansas state representative (1894-1898), U.S. House of Representatives (1902-1912), governor (1912-1913), and U.S. Senator (1913-1937). Robinson was Senate majority leader during the Great Depression and was even offered a seat on the Supreme Court if he could get the Senate to support a plan to add up to six new justices so that Franklin Roosevelt could control the courts system. Robinson died of a heart attack on July 14, 1937, delaying the proposal which later was dropped.

With war in Europe and Asia, the United States reclaimed the post and began to use it for the Thirty-fifth Division, a National Guard division being called to active duty for one year of training. After World War II began, Camp Robinson became a replacement training center, plus a training facility for army medics. It also served as a German prisoner of war facility, housing as many as 4000 enemy troops.

The camp was so big and important that President Franklin Delano Roosevelt visited the site on Palm Sunday, April 18, 1943. He came by train over the spur track, arriving early that morning. After he got off his private business car, President Roosevelt was driven through Camp Robinson on a route that was lined with soldiers who had not been told why they were formed up. He then attended religious services in the post's field house and left that afternoon.

President Franklin Roosevelt wasn't the first President Roosevelt to take a train across the Van Buren Subdivision. On April 20, 1912, former President Theodore Roosevelt (a fifth cousin) rode a special train from Fort Smith to Little Rock during his "Bull Moose Party" campaign. Teddy Roosevelt made speeches from the platform of the rear car at many of the stations along the line.

During World War II, Camp Robinson was the second largest city in Arkansas and had its own post office from 1939 until 1946. An estimated 750,000 soldiers were trained at Camp Robinson. In 1946, the 32,000 acres were handed back to Arkansas. Parts of the land were used for the new North Little Rock airport and a wildlife management area. Today, Camp Joseph T. Robinson is a training facility for the Army National Guard and serves as the headquarters for the Arkansas National Guard.

The 35th Infantry Division was mobilized for World War II on December 13, 1940, and sent to Camp Robinson for training. After the bombing of Pearl Harbor, the 35th Division was rushed to San Luis Obispo, California, in late December 1941, where it performed coastal defense duties. This photo shows troops loading onto a passenger train that was about to leave Camp Robinson. "Part of the 35th Division loading on railroad cars in preparation for leaving Camp Robinson, Ark. December 18, 1942 [sic]." Signal Corps Photo #162-244-41-188 by the 162nd Signal Photographic Company. Records of the Office of the Chief Signal Officer (Record Group 111); National Archives at College Park, College Park, MD.

Over the years, Camp Robinson was not the only customer on this line. Union Pacific showed that the mainline junction was at Milepost 345.64, and that there was a short spur track called Levy at Milepost 345.70. Other tracks were once located at Carbell Spur (Milepost 348.15) and Belmont (Milepost 349.45). The property line was at Milepost 349.68, and the railroad obtained trackage rights into Camp Pike on July 5, 1917. A large yard and a number of tracks to various warehouses were here, and the tracks ended at Milepost 351.02.

This photo shows equipment being loaded in International – Great Northern, Reading, and Texas & Pacific boxcars as the 35th Infantry Division was departing Camp Robinson for San Luis Obispo during December 1941. "Part of the 35th Division loading railroad cars in preparation for leaving Camp Robinson, Ark. December 18, 1941." Signal Corps Photo #162-244-41-536 by the 162nd Signal Photographic Company. Records of the Office of the Chief Signal Officer (Record Group 111); National Archives at College Park, College Park, MD.

The Station of Belmont

The station of Belmont had an interesting history, and was located just outside the gate to Camp Robinson. On July 1, 1907, Bishop John Baptist Morris purchased a 720-acre farm for the Catholic Diocese of Little Rock. The property, located on a hill with views of the Arkansas River Valley, was to be used for an orphanage. Using an Italian-style villa design, the complex soon featured a large brick and stone building with eighty rooms, a chapel, classrooms, a kitchen and dining room, a bakery, and a laundry. In 1917, the Belmont Hotel Company leased the complex for three years and used it as living quarters for officers, their wives, and friends. Meanwhile, the orphanage and school were moved to a Catholic church in Little Rock.

The area around the Belmont Hotel formed the Belmont business district, the home of a number of stores and other businesses. These included the Army Bank, a tailor who specialized in officer uniforms, at least three pool halls, several cafes and lunch counters, a cigar shop, a candy store, souvenir shops, a skating rink, a baseball field (where Babe Ruth played a spring-training game against the Brooklyn Dodgers in 1918), a branch of Pfeifer's Department Store, a watch store, a shoe store, a movie theater, a live action theater, an auto garage, a post office (1918-1919), and a photography studio where soldiers could create picture postcards to send home. Belmont was organized by the military to provide soldiers and their visiting families with safe, convenient, and wholesome pastimes.

Because of the Belmont Hotel Company and the local businesses, on March 18, 1918, the Arkansas Railroad Commission ordered Missouri Pacific to construct a depot at Belmont to serve the facility, as well as Camp Pike. On January 14, 1921, the railroad was ordered to close the Belmont Depot after the Belmont Hotel closed with the end of much of the activity at Camp Pike following the end of World War I.

Camp Robinson Spur Retirement

During both World Wars I and II, Missouri Pacific provided almost daily freight and passenger service over the spur track to the military camp. In 1990, the line was upgraded so that it could again handle heavy trains. In 1991, the Gulf War in Iraq led to carloads of military equipment being moved from Camp Robinson to ports and other military facilities.

However, by 2010, there had been no traffic over the line for several years and Union Pacific applied to abandon the line. On October 18, 2010, the Surface Transportation Board approved the abandonment of a "4.04-mile portion of its Camp Robinson Spur extending from milepost 345.64 to the end of the line at milepost 349.68." By the summer of 2011, the line was being dismantled, with the line gone by fall.

As with many old railroad grades, parts of the Camp Robinson Spur have been turned into a hiking and biking trail. Known as the Levy Spur Trail, about 2 miles of paved trail have been built from the Pike Avenue area northward through Levy.

Dalhoff, Arkansas

This area was called Mountain Gap during the early days of Arkansas, and the first few years of the railroad. Later, the switch to the mainline was known as Dalhoff, but was later changed to Levy. The station was originally named after Henry Dalhoff and his Dalhoff Construction Company, an Arkansas corporation that was involved with new railroad construction for three decades. The company built lines for Missouri Pacific; Rock Island; Louisiana & Arkansas; and many other railroads. As stated in the book *Historical Review of Arkansas* (1911), Dalhoff "was the contractor for the construction of the St. Louis, Iron Mountain & Southern Railroad from Helena to McGehee and south from the latter point, and he built the line of the Chicago & Rock Island system from Haskell to El Dorado and Crossett, as well as the line of the same system from Alexandria to Eunice, Louisiana. In the earlier years of his independent operations his first large contract was the building of the Choctaw Railroad west from Little Rock. He has constructed numerous small railroads for lumber companies and other private corporations."

This area was called Dalhoff Station because Henry Dalhoff owned and operated a large crusher plant for rock and cement work here. Dalhoff was credited as being the first to introduce cement construction in architectural work in the Little Rock area. The November 1, 1902, issue of *The Tradesman* had an article about the construction of the plant.

> *The new stone-crushing plant recently erected by the Dalhoff Construction Co., at Levy, on the line of the Little Rock & Fort Smith railroad, has about been completed and the trial tests are now being made for the output of the mill. The company has erected several buildings, including storehouse, barns, blacksmith*

shops, and dwellings for employes, and it is quite an addition to that extension to the city. They will work in all something more than a hundred men, and expect to be turning out ballast at the rate of 20 cars a day before many days. The output is used principally in railroad surfacing and concrete work in street paving.

The Dalhoff Construction Company entered receivership in late 1908 and it took the permission of a Little Rock bankruptcy court for them to complete a series of contracts that already existed. By late 1909, a sale of the company's assets was ordered. However, Dalhoff continued his work through partnerships with other operators until his death in June 1911.

Confusion with Train Orders

The September 4, 1911, issue of *The Log Cabin Democrat* newspaper reported the following head-on collision between two Iron Mountain trains.

Two engines came together in a head-on collision on the Central division of the St. Louis, Iron Mountain & Southern railroad, near the Dalhoff rock crusher, at Levy, two miles north of Argenta, yesterday morning about 11:30 o'clock. Engine No. 1811 was going west, with orders to make Palarm by 12 o'clock, having left Argenta at 11:15 o'clock. Engine No. 2322 was coming east, with orders to make Argenta by 11:30 o'clock, having come from Russellville.

Reviewing the orders, it is obvious that the two trains were given times that conflicted, with Engine #1811 departing Argenta 15 minutes before Engine #2322 was scheduled to arrive. This condition was noted for years by the Interstate Commerce Commission, which repeatedly suggested that signals be installed along the LR&FS route.

Engine #1811 was a 4-8-0 built by Brooks in 1901 as #1211. It was later rebuilt by the railroad and superheated. The 19 locomotives built in this series were generally used as helpers over the Gads Hill and Mineral Point grades in Missouri, and were considered to be too slow for most main-line freight service and were often used in switching service. The engineer of #1811 heard the whistle of the other train and had slowed to about 12 miles an hour before the collision.

Engine #2322 was running about 25 miles an hour when it struck the other engine and telescoped it. #2322 was part of the large fleet of 4-6-0 steam locomotives operating on the railroad. Missouri Pacific ordered 101 such locomotives that were built by Brooks in 1900.

The Log Cabin Democrat reported that the "wrecker arrived at the scene at 1:30 o'clock, and by 4 o'clock had the debris cleared away."

345.7 LEVY – Located at an elevation of 282 feet, the community of Levy was located north of the narrow valley between Big Rock Mountain to the west (over 500 feet in elevation), and Park Hill to the east (400 feet in elevation). The area was known for its water and grass prairies, and was a regular stop for farmers and drovers traveling the old road between Fort Smith and Little Rock. This activity attracted Ernest Stanley, who opened a general store near the campground in 1892. In 1901, a post office opened with Ernest Stanley serving as postmaster. He named the post office Levy, reportedly after dry-goods merchant Morris Levy, who had loaned Stanley $50 to start the store. Other members of the Stanley family also opened businesses at the start of Levy's history. Walter Stanley opened a grocery store, and William F. "Flake" Stanley and Oscar Stanley opened Stanley Hardware in 1901. The family always claimed the community would have been named Stanley if the name hadn't already been used elsewhere in the state.

A few other stores, like Dr. James F. Pairet's drugstore and Abraham B. Kyzer's grocery, added to the small community. The creation of nearby Camp Pike, later Camp Robinson, created a boom in the community as suddenly tens of thousands of troops were located next to Levy. Levy incorporated on May 7, 1917, with the first city elections held on August 7th, with Flake

Stanley elected as the first mayor. The town had only several hundred residents, but grew to 1400 by 1940, and then about 2000 in 1941 as military training for possible war escalated. With this growth came new businesses, but Levy has always traditionally been retail sales with little heavy industry. It was still on the main highway west towards Fort Smith, and gas stations and drive-in restaurants were found throughout the area. While the railroad didn't have many facilities at Levy, there was a mail crane that was used by passenger trains to pick up mail without stopping.

In 1946, Levy was annexed by North Little Rock, and the Levy post office closed in 1947, with service now being provided by the North Little Rock system. Being part of the larger city provided additional funding to help pave streets and make improvements in the water and sewer systems. The community remained mostly residential, and its population is currently about 12,000.

Because it was so close to North Little Rock, Levy never obtained its own depot or railroad agency. However, there was a 6' x 21' passenger shelter on the east side of the mainline. Heading north from here, trains face two short but steep grades. The first grade is as steep as 0.8% and is about a mile long, ending at an elevation of 305 feet at Milepost 347.7. The track then drops to 277 feet over the next mile before climbing again to 317 feet at Milepost 350.1. This second grade is a maximum of 0.7%. Southbound trains face similar grades over these two ridges.

345.8 INTERSTATE 40 – Located overhead is this 2555-mile-long highway which connects Wilmington, North Carolina, with Barstow, California. It is the third-longest Interstate Highway in the country, and the west end replaced Historic Route 66. The highway was established by the Federal Aid Highway Act of 1956, and construction was underway here by 1962. The construction moved many of the businesses a short distance to the north where the Levy Shopping Center opened in 1967.

On December 2, 2025, Union Pacific 7741 pulls an empty oil train northwards under the Interstate 40 bridges at Levy, Arkansas.

346.0 JK JUNCTION – By 1944, this was an important location on the former Little Rock & Fort Smith. Heading south, there were two main tracks, operated using ABS (Automatic Block Signal Indication) as far south as XO Junction. During 1945, ABS signals were installed all the way to Van Buren. Today, JK Junction no longer exists and there is only a single mainline track between here and North Little Rock.

JK Junction was located at the grade crossing with Doyle Venable Drive. This local street was named for Doyle Venable, who opened the Venable Lumber Company. Venable, who became known as Levy's unofficial mayor, created an annual paint sale event that included live music and other events. He was soon inviting political candidates to attend, which many did. This road is now a major connector between the Levy area and the westbound lanes of Interstate 40.

346.1 TERMINAL LIMITS – This location has historically been the dividing line between the Little Rock Terminal Division, the

Arkansas Division, the Central Division, or whatever divisions handled the Little Rock & Fort Smith route.

To the north is Edgewood Memorial Park, better known as Edgewood Cemetery, and the much smaller Thomas Cemetery. Edgewood cemetery was established on 60 acres of rolling hills in 1923 as a perpetual care cemetery.

To the east of Edgewood Cemetery is the Thomas Cemetery, established in 1876 with the first burial, and considered to be the oldest known cemetery in North Little Rock. The cemetery actually started when J. W. B. Thomas gave the 2-acre plot for a cemetery, to be managed by the Thomas Cemetery Association. The association disappeared during the 1920s and only one burial has taken place after the 1950s. In 2018, the abandoned cemetery was condemned and acquired by the City of North Little Rock. Later that year, the new Thomas Cemetery Association was formed to support and assist in the restoration and preservation of the area.

347.1 MACARTHUR DRIVE – The railroad passes under MacArthur Drive, also known as Arkansas Highway 365. MacArthur Drive is an extension of Pike Avenue that connects Levy with Maumelle. Arkansas Highway 365 replaced U.S. Highway 65 as it was rerouted onto various Interstate highways. It connects Pine Bluff and Conway, about 70 miles apart.

The current bridge was built in 2015 (some sources state 2017) and is a concrete structure set on steel beams and concrete bents. It consists of five long spans. It replaced the historic Amboy Overpass, a twelve-span structure built in 1941 for the Arkansas State Highway Commission and the Federal Works Agency Public Roads Administration. This bridge had a total length of 573 feet, with the longest span being 80 feet long. Most of the bridge was built of reinforced concrete by James P. McNulty, a contractor who built a number of bridges and roads across Arkansas. The highway bridge was listed on the National Register of Historic Places in 1995. However, the bridge was demolished and replaced by a new bridge due to structural and design issues.

MacArthur Drive is one of a number of Central Arkansas landmarks named for General Douglas MacArthur. MacArthur was born in the Arsenal Building in Little Rock on January 26, 1880, while his father (U.S. Army Captain Arthur MacArthur, Jr.) was stationed at the Little Rock Barracks. Douglas MacArthur had a long and decorated military career, and became one of only five men to rise to the rank of General of the Army.

This contractor plaque is located on the new MacArthur Drive bridge at Amboy. Note the 2015 date, although a number of sources state that the bridge opened in 2017.

347.1 AMBOY – Known by many as Amboy Switch, the siding and short house track was located at an elevation of 297 feet. In 1907, there was an 80-car siding at Amboy. In 1944, Missouri Pacific reported that the siding could hold 62 freight cars, and that there was a company telephone here. With the installation of ABS signaling in 1945, the siding was removed and Amboy wasn't even listed in company timetables by 1951.

After World War II, a few new housing subdivisions were built in the area, with many veterans who served at Camp Robinson moving here. Earlier, Amboy was shown to be a military passenger stop for Camp Pike and Camp Robinson.

In 1989, the Arkansas State Highway and Transportation Department described Amboy as part of the plans to enlarge

Interstate 40 and many of the area roads. "Amboy is bounded to the north by Camp Robinson, on the west by the Crystal Hill community, on the south by Burns Park and on the east by Alta Vista which is located adjacent to Camp Robinson. Most of this community is located within North Little Rock. Amboy is a sparsely populated community. Land use in Amboy is mixed residential and commercial with most of the commercial land use located along S.H. 365. Homes in Amboy are mostly one-story brick and frame."

The Head-On Collision of December 15, 1923

On December 15, 1923, Amboy was the scene of two passenger trains hitting head-on, resulting in the death of 2 employees and 1 trespasser, and the injury of 155 passengers, 8 employees, and 4 other persons. The Interstate Commerce Commission (ICC) conducted an investigation of the accident to determine the cause. The report produced provided a great deal of information about the Amboy area and the trains that were operating at the time.

The two trains involved were southbound passenger train No. 103, pulled by locomotive #5524 (4-4-2 built by Alco-Brooks in 1907) and consisting of 1 mail car, 1 baggage car, 2 coaches, 1 chair car, 1 dining car, and 1 business car, and northbound passenger train No. 106, pulled by locomotive #5508 (4-4-2 built by Alco-Brooks in 1904), consisting of 1 mail car, 1 baggage car, 1 coach, 1 chair car, and 2 Pullman sleeping cars.

The ICC also provided details about the track alignment at Amboy. "This accident occurred on the passing track at Amboy, at a point 314 feet south of the north switch; this is a facing-point switch for southbound trains and leads off the main track through a No. 10 turnout to the west. Approaching the point of accident from the north there is a 3 degree curve to the right 2,279 feet in length, followed by more than 4,000 feet of tangent, the accident occurring on this tangent at a point 979 feet from its northern end. The grade is descending for southbound trains, being 0.67 per cent at the point of accident. The switch-stand is located on the engineman's side of a southbound train; the night indications of the switch-light are red when the switch is lined for the passing track, and green when lined for the main track."

The two trains had orders to meet at Amboy, with northbound No. 106 using the siding. No. 106 stopped in the siding about 9:45pm. Southbound No. 103 was more than three hours late, requiring the special train order for the meet. As No. 103 approached the north switch at Amboy, the crew saw a green switch light and a proceed lantern signal indicating that the switch was lined for the mainline. Just before No. 103 reached the switch, the switch light changed to red, indicating that someone had just lined it. Train No. 103 went into the siding at a speed of about 25mph and crashed into the standing No. 106, with both locomotives severely damaged and all of the cars in both trains damaged by the force of the impact. The ICC determined that the switch had been lined purposely into the siding just before the train arrived, but no person could be positively proved to have done it, although an employee from train No. 106 was reportedly walking to the switch to line it after train No. 103 passed. The ICC felt that the cause was an employee who had the responsibility of lining the switch essentially becoming hypnotized and lining it before the train had passed. The inspectors could not prove it, but there were numerous such cases recorded, which explained the often quoted suggestion for signals and electric locks on switches to prevent them from being thrown when trains were approaching.

347.3 WEST MILITARY DRIVE – This road connects Interstate 40 (to the west) with the main gate to Camp Joseph T. Robinson (to the northeast). Heading towards Fort Smith, the railroad swings to the west and then back to the northwest.

348.4 CRYSTAL HILL ROAD – This is another busy grade crossing since it connects Arkansas Highway 365 with the unincorporated community of Crystal Hill. The name Crystal Hill is used for a hill on the north side of the Arkansas River, and for this community that is now partly in North Little Rock. The hill and bluff was a known landmark in the area. The bluff gave the area its name since it contained sandstone, shale and iron pyrite. This mixture would sparkle in the sun, creating the Crystal Hill name. Reportedly, at least one person mined the hill for silver, but no major success was reported.

At Milepost 348, just a short distance from the Crystal Hill Road crossing, is this large rocket, advertising a fireworks store. Train crews over the years have often warned the North Little Rock Terminal of their approach by broadcasting "passing the rocket."

The community of Crystal Hill can trace its history back to 1820 when Arkansas Governor James Miller bought land on the hill. At the time, the territorial capital was at Arkansas Post, but the territorial legislature had announced a search for a new site. Miller bought the land with the plan to make it the new center of government, but Little Rock and Cadron were the finalists, with Little Rock being selected. Miller built a home on Crystal Hill and insisted on doing much of his work there, but never platted a community. He later went to Salem, Massachusetts, after being appointed Collector of Customs by President James Monroe.

The Crystal Hill grade crossing is in the middle of a long curve. To the south, the railroad passes through a cut, while to the north, the railroad uses a high fill until Kelly Road at Milepost 349.7. Much of this grade came about due to a series of improvements made during the early 1900s.

349.0 SOUTH END OF DETOUR NO. 1 – During the early part of the twentieth century, both the St. Louis, Iron Mountain & Southern and Missouri Pacific made a number of line changes on the old Little Rock & Fort Smith to eliminate excessive grades and curves, and to move the tracks away from several waterways.

349.1 HAIG – This location was shown in a 1925 Missouri Pacific station listing, and simply consisted of a cinder platform to the west that was installed in 1918. The listing did say that no freight was handled at the location. Missouri Pacific records show that the station was previously known as Big Shanty, with the name changed on September 23, 1918.

There is more to this story than a simple name change. The mainline was moved westward between Mileposts 349.0 and 351.5 and was shown to be Detour No. 1. As the work was completed, several of the station locations were moved. For example, Big Shanty was moved from Milepost 349.9 to Milepost 349.1 during July 1918.

349.5 JEFFREY – There was a 65-car spur track here in 1964 known as Jeffrey Storage Track. In 1986, Union Pacific showed that there was a spur track to the east, and then a short siding (3479' during the early 1960s) to the west at Milepost 350. The elevation was shown to be 297 feet.

Looking to the east, several old quarries can be seen on the high ridge. Some maps show a community named Haig here (an early station at Milepost 349), but during the 1950s, Jeffrey Stone Company opened a quarry near the railroad. The railroad logically named the station Jeffrey after this rail customer. The quarry opened and closed as needed, and became known for the unique minerals found there. It was located "on a west-north-west-trending ridge whose crest, 500 to 550 feet in altitude, rises 300 feet above the adjacent valley to the south." The Jeffrey quarry was the only known source of abundant "needle" quartz in the Ouachita Mountains of Arkansas and Oklahoma; it is likewise the only major source of rectorite (an unusual clay material) and the only known occurrence of cookeite in Arkansas. Most of the quarry now creates two deep lakes. Some of the rock exposed by the quarry work is still explored by rock collectors, but only with permission from the owner of the site.

350.2 SECTION POST – During the first part of the twentieth century, signs marked the territories of the various track section gangs. This was one of those locations.

351.2 ATHABASCA SPUR – In 1925, Missouri Pacific listed Athabasca Spur as being located about where today's grade crossing with Oak Grove Road is. While inbound and outbound freight was handled, it was all prepaid as there was no freight agent here. The spur track to the east was removed during the summer of 1925.

351.3 NEWTON CREEK BRIDGE – This stream forms in the hills to the northeast and flows into White Oak Bayou several miles to the southwest. The railroad uses a 70-foot deck plate girder span to cross Newton Creek. Early records show that two 35-foot deck plate girder spans were used to form Bridge No. 24.

351.5 NORTH END OF DETOUR NO. 1 – This was the north end of where more than two miles of track were moved to the west to reduce curvature and grades in this area.

352.4 INTERSTATE 40 – Heading towards Fort Smith, this is the second time the rail line passes under I-40.

353.3 MARCHE (MC) – Marche (pronounced "Mar-Shay") has traditionally been the first major station outside Argenta (North

Little Rock). About 1870 as the railroad was being built, Judge Liberty Bartlett and a series of Chicago and New York investors acquired land here and attempted to establish a settlement, using the name Bartlett Springs. It was successful enough to be shown as Bartlett in the 1871 *Appletons' National Railway and Steam Navigation Guide for the United States and Canada*. However, the community failed and the Little Rock & Fort Smith Railroad acquired the property and plotted their own community, initially known as Warren Station. The *Official Guide* listed it as Warren in 1875. The community didn't grow and Captain Thomas J. Atkinson took the property with its two lakes and tried to turn it into a resort community. To do this, he built a 32' x 100' covered dancing pavilion, an ice cream and soda water stand, and a check room for picnic baskets and other items brought by visitors. Brush was cleared to create a rustic beach on one of the lakes and bands from Little Rock were brought in to provide entertainment. There were great hopes that the American centennial in 1876 would make the efforts profitable.

This plan also failed and Count Timothy von Choinski, a Polish nobleman, acquired 22,000 acres in March 1877 and created farms that he sold to Polish immigrants. The Count had seen the deplorable living conditions in large cities like New York and Chicago and wanted to provide a healthier and more profitable lifestyle for his countrymen who had moved to the United States. With the focus being on agriculture, he named the property Marche, a French word for marketplace. Some claim that the name is simply "marshy" spoken with a local accent.

The farms were not well accepted at first as most of the land had not been cleared, but almost 100 new residents settled in the community. By late 1878, the Holy Ghost Fathers, a congregation of Roman Catholic priests and brothers had arrived and built a small chapel named for the Immaculate Heart of Mary. The chapel was located on a low hill known as Jasna Góra, named after the important pilgrimage site in Częstochowa. A large chapel opened in 1896, which burned in 1932 and was replaced within a year.

In 1898, a post office opened at Marche in a small building attached to the local general store. With the post office using

Marche, the use of the name Warren essentially ended. Through the 1930s, Marche was still a rural community based upon farming, especially cotton, corn, hay, wood, milk, and livestock. The Hammond, Luens & Devore Lumber Company had a sawmill and there was at least one grocery store. At least four tornadoes hit the community during the first two decades of the twentieth century, a pattern that still continues today. Electricity reached the community during the Great Depression, but the post office closed in 1930.

During World War II, land in the area was used for Camp Robinson and also for one of the six new ordnance plants built in Arkansas. The Maumelle Ordnance Works was approved on June 6, 1941, to build a plant to produce picric acid, used in making explosives. Cities Services Defense Corporation of New York built the plant as a government-owned and contractor-operated facility, which started production on March 28, 1942. The plant employed fewer than 1000 workers, so no housing was built by the company, adding some residents to the Marche area. The plant closed in August 1945 and never operated again before being declared surplus and offered for sale in 1959. The property was acquired by North Little Rock as a planned industrial park, but it was sold in 1967 to Arkansas entrepreneur Jess P. Odom. Odom created the new town of Maumelle through the Maumelle Land Development Company.

Interstate 40 was built through the middle of Marche, separating the community into two parts. Marche is now heavily surrounded by the town of Maumelle. Despite this, Marche is still an unincorporated community with a generally rural population.

The Railroad at Marche

Bartlett, Warren (Warren Station), and then Marche have been listed as stations here alongside the Little Rock & Fort Smith since the line was built. A 440-foot business track was built at Marche in 1900. The 1903 *Missouri Pacific Annual Report* stated that the railroad had built a combination depot at Marche. A November 1907 news report stated that railroad had reopened their old depot, which had been "built some time before, but abandoned." There was a mail crane at Marche, as well as an 85-car siding.

In April 1909, the town of Marche petitioned the Arkansas Railroad Commission to force the St. Louis, Iron Mountain & Southern to construct a new depot and to open an agency. In July, the Arkansas Railroad Commission ordered the railroad to open a depot, but the request for an agency was denied. In 1910, a 14' x 38' board and batten depot was built on the west side of the mainline, replacing the old smaller building. During the early 1900s, there were also a section house, bunk house, and tool house at Marche. In 1925, there was a ticket and freight agency at the depot. The agency handled freight in volumes of carloads and less. The depot and train order signal were both retired and removed in July 1937. By the 1940s, the siding at Marche could handle 92 freight cars, and there was a telephone available. The switches for the siding were located at Mileposts 352.7 and 353.6. The siding has been moved northward and during the 1980s there was a spur to the east with the switch on the north end.

353.7 **CONTROL POINT V353** – This is the southern switch for the current Marche siding, which is located on the west side of the mainline. Trains often wait here for their turn into the North Little Rock yards. CP V353 stands for Control Point, Van Buren Subdivision, Mile 353. This is the terminology that Union Pacific has used for decades to identify locations along the railroad where Centralized Traffic Control (CTC) railway signaling is used. Modern signaling systems have created the need for more such facilities, many also called interlockings.

Basically, a Control Point (abbreviated as CP) is a designated location that is controlled by a remote operator or dispatcher. These locations can include a siding switch, a crossover between two parallel tracks, or a crossing of two or more tracks. On Union Pacific, the term dates to late 1979, when a bulletin was issued by the railroad's engineering department creating the new designation. On the Van Buren Subdivision, Control

Points are a relatively new feature, most being activated with the installation of CTC signaling about 2020.

353.9 WHITE OAK BAYOU BRIDGE – The mainline and siding cross White Oak Bayou, historically known as White Oak Creek, using a 119-foot-long, 6-span, reinforced concrete trestle. At one time this was an 8-panel frame and pile trestle that was replaced by a 10-panel pile trestle in 1926.

White Oak Bayou forms from several small streams within Camp Robinson to the northeast, and flows generally to the south before flowing into the Arkansas River at Burns Park. The stream is protected by the White Oak Bayou Wetlands Conservancy which states that the stream has a 42 square mile watershed and 1400 acres of wetland in Pulaski County. Much of the stream still flows through natural forests consisting of blackjack oak, bur oak, cherry bark oak, green ash, loblolly pine, overcup oak, post oak, shagbark hickory, short leaf pine, southern red oak, willow oak, bald cypress and water tupelo.

The first meeting of the first court ever held in Pulaski County was at the home of Judge Samuel McHenry, near where the White Oak Bayou flows into the Arkansas River.

355.3 MAUMELLE – The elevation here is 280 feet above sea level. There is an industrial spur track to the south into Maumelle.

During the 1800s, this was basically a scattering of small farms. The general region on both sides of the Arkansas River used the name Maumelle, believed to date from the early French explorers who traveled the Arkansas River. The French word mamelle means breast, and was a common term used to describe conical shaped mountains. Nearby Pinnacle Mountain was once known as Maumelle Mountain.

This area developed due to available land and Jacob Pyeatt's ferry across the Arkansas River, which operated by 1812. A small trading community formed that was known as Pyeattstown, and it had an estimated population of 150 by 1820. As the region was organized, the Pyeatte Township was formed in 1823, and then the Maumelle Township in 1842. The area remained a small farming town until 1941 when the land was acquired for the Maumelle Ordnance Works.

Today's Maumelle is essentially a planned community, developed on the property of the former Maumelle Ordinance Works Military Reservation, This picric acid (used in making explosives) plant was approved on June 6, 1941. It operated through World War II and then was closed, being sold to the Perry Equipment Company in 1959, and then North Little Rock in 1961. In 1967, the property was again sold, this time to Jess P. Odom and his Maumelle Land Development Company. A planned community was created on the property, along with an industrial park, retail shopping zone, and a series of parks. It was officially founded in 1974 and incorporated in 1985 with five distinct "villages" that could house as many as 60,000 residents. The population in the 1990 census was 6714, and has grown to 19,251 by the 2020 census. Maumelle currently has the highest median household income in the state of Arkansas.

These switches mark the end of the tracks that serve the Maumelle Industrial Park

Morgan Spur

Also once located at Milepost 355.3 was Morgan Spur, a track that headed off to the northeast. This was another early prepaid freight spur track used to serve local farmers. The source of the name Morgan is not clear, and the first land patents in the area went to George Day and David Martin in 1831 and 1832. The Little Rock & Fort Smith built its line about two miles west of Morgan, and a small platform and track were built here to serve the community. Unlike at a number of other places, the community of Morgan did not move to the tracks, creating a new town. The spur track was abandoned in 1936.

Exit 142 on Interstate 40 was originally known as the Morgan Interchange, but today it is generally called the Maumelle Exit. The interchange is now crowded with hotels, gas stations and restaurants. Despite this, Morgan is still an unincorporated community.

355.4 CONTROL POINT V355 – This is the northern switch for the current Marche siding, located on the west side of the mainline and described as being 7796 feet long. An industrial lead heads south from the very north end of the Marche Siding to serve the large and growing industrial park at Maumelle. The line serves Kimberly Clark and Cypress Cold Storage.

Automatic Block Signaling (ABS) was installed over the Van Buren Subdivision in 1945. The railroad's timetable released in April 1985 indicated that CTC signaling had just been installed between the Van Buren Wye (Fort Smith Crossing) and CP V355.

Arkansas Highway 100

Immediately north of CP V355, Arkansas Highway 100 (Maumelle Boulevard) bridges over the railroad. There have actually been two Highway 100 routes in Arkansas over the past few decades. One was what is today Riverfront Drive in North Little Rock. This road received the designation in 1965 but the road wasn't completed until the 1980s, with the designation becoming official on December 1, 1987, and it was decommissioned in 2019.

This segment was created on May 6, 1987, using parts of Maumelle Boulevard. It connects Arkansas Highway 365 with Maumelle and then on to Interstate 40, providing transportation routes for the booming community.

356.3 WEST MARCHE – For a short distance, the railroad is running east-west. During World War II, there was a wye to the south into the Maumelle Ordinance Works Military Reservation. The station of West Marche was created on October 4, 1941, in General Manager Circular No. 784. Construction of the tracks and a 9' x 30' depot, coal box, telephone booth, mail crane, and train order signals were approved in December 1941. A train order office was located here, but only during limited hours. The train order signal was removed by March 1949. By 1951, the train order office was closed and only a telephone was available.

During the late 1800s and early 1900s, there was a small community known as Wilder, located near where Palarm Creek enters the Arkansas River. The community was named for the Wilder family which arrived here during the 1800s. A Wilder post office was here 1914-1917 and the railroad had a station known as Wilder's Spur, Wilders Spur, and then simply Wilder's. The track at Wilder's Spur was retired in 1926.

357.5 SOUTH END OF DETOUR NO. 2 – The original mainline of the Little Rock & Fort Smith had a number of issues, and in numerous places the line was straightened or moved to better locations. Between Mileposts 357.5 and 359.0, the tracks were moved to the east and away from Palarm Creek and the Arkansas River. This work required a great deal of excavation of the ridges to the east. Part of this earlier grade is now known as Tracks Road.

357.8 CATORCE – This station from the late 1800s was located where the grade crossing is today for Thunder Mountain Road. The road to the west that follows the railroad is Tracks Road. In 1925, Missouri Pacific showed that there were two locations here named Catorce. The station sign of Catorce was located at Milepost 357.8, while Catorce Spur was located at Milepost 357.9. Catorce Spur was shown to be a prepaid freight station for both inbound and outbound moves. It was retired and removed in 1933.

The name Catorce is a Spanish word that means fourteen or fourteenth. This location is basically 14 miles from the Fort

Smith Crossing at North Little Rock. In this area, the railroad squeezes between a series of small hills and then around the west end of Clifton Mountain, a long narrow ridge running east-west along the line between Pulaski and Faulkner counties. Known earlier as Frenchman Mountain or Frenchmans Mountain, the peak of the mountain is at 571 feet, while the railroad is at an elevation of less than 300 feet.

The original grade of the Little Rock & Fort Smith was once located west of the current grade at Catorce. Tracks Road uses a short section of this old grade, replaced by Detour No. 2.

358.5 RECTOR SPUR – In this general area during the late 1800s was a spur track that served the nearby Rector Plantation. Locals also knew the location as Rector's Mill, described as being below Palarm.

The Rector family had a long history in Arkansas. Elias Rector held a New Madrid land claim entitling him to land in Hot Springs, which he passed along to Henry Massie Rector, Sr., in 1822. The land was caught up in the ownership controversies when the U.S. Department of the Interior created the Hot Springs Reservation, but some land remained with the Rector family to fight over for the next century.

This double box concrete culvert, with each box measuring 7' x 8', is used by the new grade to cross a small stream.

Near Palarm, the family had the Rector Plantation, which included farming, a sawmill, and a store at nearby Palarm. To the south of here along the Arkansas River, and on the west side of Maumelle, are Rector Brake and Rector Hill. These features are along a secondary channel of Palarm Creek, which once flowed south and entered the Arkansas River in this area.

Henry Massie Rector, Sr., served as Arkansas' sixth governor. His aunt was Ann Rector Conway, who was the mother of the first and fifth governors, James and Elias Conway, so he had political connections. Rector was known to be a skilled debater, but often described as being a poor planner and organizer. He had a reputation of being "a violent man who fights people," and was known to sue members of his own family, collect rents with a shotgun, and beat the teachers of his sons if they were disciplined at school.

William Field (Billy) Rector was born on the Rector Plantation in 1912, the great-grandson of Henry Massie Rector. Billy was a major developer in Central Arkansas, and founded the real estate firm Rector-Phillips-Morse. Billy Rector handled the sale of 1100 acres of farmland west of Little Rock for a development that became Pleasant Valley.

359.0 NORTH END OF DETOUR NO. 2 – Over the years, Palarm Creek and the Arkansas River both forced several realignments of the mainline through this area.

In 1990, Union Pacific 3340 was found heading north alongside Arkansas Highway 365 just north of the North End of Detour No. 2.

359.5 PALARM CREEK BRIDGE – Immediately next to Arkansas Highway 365 is the Palarm Creek Bridge, consisting of a 3-span reinforced concrete trestle (50 feet long), a 75-foot deck plate girder span, and then another 3-span reinforced concrete trestle (80 feet long). In this area, the tracks are squeezed between the Arkansas River and Highway 365.

Palarm Creek begins a mile north of Vilonia in Faulkner County, and then flows southwest into the Arkansas River. Because the stream passed through a relatively flat valley, it was an early area of settlement, despite having some areas described as being swampy and boggy. Palarm Creek was dammed in 1950 to form Lake Conway.

This was not the first railroad bridge over Palarm Creek, or even the first location. During 1902, the railroad was involved with a number of line relocations between North Little Rock and Van Buren. These included a line relocation at Palarm, a new bypass of Clarksville, and a new waterlevel track between Hartman and Ozark to avoid the grades at Coal Hill and Altus. The Dalhoff Construction Company had the primary contract for the project, and reports state that more than 1000 laborers were involved with the work, supported by as many as 30 work trains and 8 steam shovels.

Even when the track wasn't moved, the bridge over Palarm Creek, often called Palarm Bayou, did change. Known as Bridge No. 45, the older 120-foot through truss span that sat on masonry abutments was replaced with a 115-foot through plate girder span in 1923. The railroad also added a water tank, water column, pump house, and coal bin during late summer 1921, but removed them during the summer of 1929. During this time the railroad was running heavier trains and needed more water towers for the steam locomotives that hauled them. Later, steam locomotives with larger water tenders reduced the need for all of the water towers that had been installed and many were removed.

This wasn't the end of the track realignment at Palarm. To the west of the current span are several headwalls or abutments from an earlier bridge. During 1945, flooding impacted the bridge and Missouri Pacific parked a number of cars on the bridge to keep it from washing away. Instead, nine coal cars and boxcars were swept into the river. Soon, the railroad had plans to move the tracks to the east, requiring a rock cut through the end of Clifton Mountain. Land was needed for this move, and about seven acres was obtained from Ruth McKinney, Ruby Couch, Mary Adkisson, G.W. Adkisson, Jr., Mary Alice Adkisson and Mary Margaret Taylor. Some of the right-of-way of U.S. Highway 65 (now Arkansas Highway 365) was also required, and the highway was also moved to the east.

This is the north headwall of the old Palarm Creek Bridge, washed out in 1945. Notice how close the Arkansas River is now located to the old bridge location.

Union Pacific 2635 heads south across the Palarm Creek Bridge during April of 2023. It is pulling an ETRX coal train. A large increase in coal traffic during the 1970s and 1980s forced the railroad to upgrade the track and many of the bridges along the line.

Union Pacific 9093, in fresh yellow paint, shoves a southbound coal train across the Palarm Creek Bridge. Note the heavy concrete piles that hold up the bridge.

If you look carefully at different parts of the Palarm Creek Bridge, you will find several different dates on different parts of the structure. This 1976 date can be found on the north bridge approach, with a 1989 date on another nearby component.

Like many of the modern bridges along the Van Buren Subdivision, signs of the older structures can still be found at the Palarm Creek Bridge. These old timber piles show that at least part of the bridge once consisted of timber pile trestle spans.

The Palarm Creek bridge is a popular spot for rail enthusiasts, and Union Pacific 3059 is shown heading north across the stream. In the background is the Arkansas River, which this line closely follows all the way to Van Buren, Arkansas.

As a part of the new route, the new Palarm Creek bridge consisted of a 75-foot deck plate girder span. As the Arkansas River was made navigable, the bridge was lengthened using concrete spans.

At the north end of the current bridge is the Palarm Creek Park. The park features parking, trails, picnic tables, historical markers, and more. Parts of the original railroad grade and bridge abutments can be found in the park.

Battle of Palarm

One of the largest battles of the Brooks-Baxter War took place near the mouth of Palarm Creek. Forces supporting Elisha Baxter had obtained the steamboat *Hallie* and were heading to Little Rock with supplies and a few riflemen. Forces supporting Joseph Brooks lined the river and fired upon the boat, damaging its engine and leaving it adrift. The pilot and captain were killed and the boat was quickly captured.

The Civil War did not end the political and social conflicts within Arkansas, or even much of the country. During the late 1860s and early 1870s, the Republican Party had control of much of the state government and added new counties and opened up elections to former slaves, and in some areas, poor farmers and laborers from eastern and southern Europe. These efforts led to literal war in parts of the state as the Ku Klux Klan and other organizations attempted to regain control for the Democrat Party and plantation and business owners.

In Arkansas, this led to what was called the Brooks-Baxter War, resulting in several battles between forces numbering in the thousands, with several hundred killed. Most histories state that the war began with the ratification of the 1868 Arkansas Constitution, rewritten to allow Arkansas to rejoin the Union after the American Civil War. This led to the creation of two groups, one supported by "Minstrels" and "carpetbaggers" and the other by "scalawags" and "freedmen." Basically, it was a political war between those with a long history in Arkansas and those with strong connections outside the state, or more clearly, those who gained power from the new government and those who lost power. The 1872 election was close, and resulted in open warfare.

"Minstrel" Elisha Baxter narrowly won the vote, but "Scalawag" Joseph Brooks claimed fraud. and pointed out that to win, Baxter had brought former Confederates back into the government. A county judge declared Brooks the winner, but the federal government and President Ulysses S. Grant intervened and put Baxter back in the governor's office. A new Arkansas Constitution of 1874 was written, which ended the Reconstruction in Arkansas and put the governorship in control of the Democrat Party for the next 90 years.

County Line

The lower several miles of Palarm Creek serve as the boundary line between Pulaski and Faulkner Counties. **Pulaski County**, located to the south, is the crossroads of Arkansas, where the major north-south and east-west highways meet, and once where the major railroads also met. It is the most populous county in Arkansas with about 400,000 residents. Little Rock is the county seat, and is also the state capital and largest city in the state. Pulaski County was created on December 15, 1818, as the fifth county in Arkansas, and has been broken up several times to form other counties.

Trains heading south across Palarm Creek see these signs on the adjacent highway, announcing that they are entering Pulaski County.

Seven states (Arkansas, Georgia, Illinois, Indiana, Kentucky, Missouri and Virginia) have a county named after Casimir Pulaski, a Polish nobleman and military commander. Pulaski supported the idea of political freedom and came to North America to fight with the Continental Army in the American Revolutionary War. Having experience with calvary forces, he led a calvary charge at the Battle of Brandywine that was credited with saving the life of George Washington. He was soon promoted to Brigadier General, with the title of "Commander of the Horse." He taught calvary concepts to parts of the Continental Army and created his own Pulaski Cavalry Legion, which he led until his death in a calvary charge at the Battle of Savannah on October 11, 1779. He has since been one of the few people to be awarded honorary United States citizenship, and is one of several who have been called "the father of the American cavalry."

To the north is **Faulkner County**, created on April 12, 1873, as one of the last counties in the state. It was created by Republicans during the reconstruction era and was designed to break up the traditional power of the plantation owners. The county was named for Captain Sandford C. "Sandy" Faulkner (1803-1874), described as being a planter, raconteur (a person who tells anecdotes in a skillful and amusing way), and fiddle player. He has been given credit for writing the song *Arkansas Traveler*, the official historic song of the State of Arkansas since 1987. Faulkner was a unique choice as he actually served as an artillery officer assigned to the Trans-Mississippi Department of the Confederate States Army, managing supply depots at Little Rock and then Marshall, Texas.

Faulkner County was made up of small, rural farms and few towns of any size. Cotton, fruit and vegetables were the primary products grown. Construction of the LR&FS added some new residents, but the population was still only 12,786 in 1880. Conway, the county seat, grew due to its retail businesses, plus the three colleges that eventually located there. However, it wasn't until the 1960s that the population began to grow. The census in 1970 recorded 31,572 residents, and 46,192 in 1980. Much of this boom came about because of Interstate 40, which connected Faulkner County with the Little Rock area, where turmoil in the various school districts in Pulaski County led to a population movement to the surrounding counties. In the 2020 census, there were 123,498 citizens, making it the sixth-most-populous county in Arkansas.

359.8 PALARM (DI) – Palarm was an early station, listed in the *Official Guide* by 1875. The April 16, 1870, issue of the *American Railroad Journal* reported that 25 miles of railroad had been graded with ties laid, and bridges and culverts built. Track laying to Palarm was expected to be completed within 60 days. A 20' x 50' wood depot was built by the time the railroad arrived. Two section houses, 20' x 15' and 25' x 50', were built in 1884. The combination depot was remodeled in 1892, a cotton platform was built in 1901, and a standard one and one-half story frame section house and tool house were built in 1902. A water tank and pump house were built in 1904. A small depot was built here in 1910 to replace the original structure rebuilt in 1892. There was also a board and batten tool house and 2-story section house for track maintenance Section 62. For the steam locomotives used on the line, there was a 50,000-gallon water tank with Palarm Creek as the water source.

In 1907, Palarm had a day and night telegraph office, a mail crane, and an 80-car siding. There was also a 16' x 42' platform, a coal and oil house, a telephone booth, and a 9' x 13' tool house. In 1925, the depot, which was located on the east side of the tracks, had a ticket and freight agency. The station was located near the current private crossing, not far from the north end of the track realignment for the Palarm Creek Bridge. In 1928, the railroad retired and removed two carbodies that were used for housing and storage. The depot was removed in March 1937. In 1944, the depot was gone but there was a company telephone and 57-car siding. The siding was removed soon after the installation of ABS signaling in 1945.

A small community was located in the area, basically a trading center for a number of small farms scattered along Palarm Creek. A post office named Palarm opened in 1856, and finally closed for good in 1923. A nearby post office using the name Palarm Bayou was open 1870-1877. A cemetery, known as the

Palarm Bayou Pioneer Cemetery, was being used by the 1830s. One of the first buried there was Daniel E. Wilson, a local businessman and politician who was on the board of trustees for Little Rock and operated a toll bridge in Palarm. The cemetery was placed on the National Register of Historic Places in 2005 and is located south of the creek in the Mountain Crest Subdivision. The Palarm Bayou Pioneer Cemetery is possibly the oldest existing cemetery in Pulaski County.

There are ten identified graves in what was basically a family cemetery located on the family's farm. The families of Wilson, Boyle and Danley settled in the Palarm Creek area and intermarried. Despite the few identified burials, a number of early Arkansas leaders were buried here, including John N. Boyle (1835 Little Rock City Treasurer), Benjamin F. Danley (1848 Pulaski County Sheriff and Brigadier General and Chief of Staff under General Churchill in The Brooks-Baxter War), and Emzy Wilson (1831 Arkansas Territorial Auditor).

Today, this area has become a popular site for planned housing subdivisions. Many are located on the nearby Arkansas River and feature boat docks and terrific views. The railroad passes under Plantation Drive, an access road to one of these subdivisions, at Milepost 361.0. Not far to the north and to the east is a series of landfills.

360.4 SECTION HOUSE – A section house and toilet were once located to the east of the mainline. They were retired in 1933.

361.2 SECTION POST – This location was a dividing line between track section gangs during the early 1900s.

In this area was once a track known as McConnell Spur. In 1904, the Railroad Commission of Arkansas reported that the station was about one mile north of Palarm and three miles south of Mayflower.

362.3 AP&L SPUR NO. 2 – Located at an elevation of 298 feet, this is a switch for a spur track into an Arkansas Power & Light (AP&L) substation. AP&L was founded in 1913 by Harvey Crowley Couch, who later merged the Louisiana & Arkansas Railway, the Louisiana Navigation & Railway Company, and Kansas City Southern Railway into what was known as the K.C.S.-L.&A. System. Couch had gained information about the railroad and utility industries while working on various Railway Post Office routes across Arkansas and Louisiana. AP&L eventually became the primary electrical utility company for much of Arkansas. It became part of Middle South Utilities in 1949, and then Entergy Corporation in 1989. With this part of Arkansas growing quickly, the electric company has built a number of new electrical substations.

363.0 CONTROL POINT V363 – Historically, this switch has been known as South Mayflower. The siding is located on the west side of the mainline and is shown to be 10,691 feet long.

This sign marks the south switch of Mayflower Siding, now known as Control Point V363 – Mayflower.

363.6 MAYFLOWER – The Mayflower area has been settled for thousands of years, with the Quapaw, Osage, Choctaw, and other tribes living here when the first French explorers passed through the area. A few European settlers arrived during the late 1770s, fleeing the Revolutionary War to the east. They generally survived off of local farming and hunting, and some trading along the Arkansas River. However, no town developed at the time.

More settlers arrived in the area during the 1800s, and logging and farming became the main industries. The river bottoms were used for growing cotton into the mid-1900s, with a mix of crops still surviving between the growing number of subdivisions being built. The cotton led to the construction of a cotton gin, which attracted other businesses. Enough of a town was created that a school opened in the old Odd Fellows building. It was later replaced by the Woodmen of the World Order two-story building, which also served as a school, church, and a community center.

The name Mayflower came about when the railroad created Twenty Mile Camp a short distance east of the earlier community. A passenger car was spotted on a side track that was used as the headquarters of the railroad's construction superintendent. Most of the communications was via telegraph, and the telegraph call sign "Mayflower" was used by the construction superintendent, giving the name to the community in 1871. A small general store was opened soon after by a Mr. Lorentz.

A post office opened at Mayflower on November 9, 1880, the same year the first Methodist church and the first Church of Christ were established. The town started to grow as a trading center and the Wiley Mosley store opened in 1894, serving travelers and local farms. Within a few years of the arrival of the railroad, Mayflower was a main center for railroad ties, and several sawmills, a shingle mill, and a stave mill were operating here. A grist mill, wagon yard, and other businesses were open. A report about the area's cotton industry stated that several cotton gins were built at Mayflower due to a number of large area farms. Morrilton Cottonseed Oil Mill owned their gin in the late teens or early twenties and Al Enderlin owned it from the early 1930s until the early 1950s when it burned. Rose City Cottonseed Oil Mill of North Little Rock also had a gin on the south side of town.

1917 was an important year in the history of Mayflower as the Hays Realty Company bought up land and began residential development, starting on November 10th. Mayflower featured several hotels at the time to serve travelers heading to and from Little Rock, but this would end soon as roads were improved across the state. In 1926, Dr. J .R. Kitley arrived at Mayflower and quickly led an effort to incorporate the town, which happened on March 6, 1928.

By 1930, the Great Depression was hurting many local citizens, but Mayflower still featured three stores, one blacksmith shop, one garage, and two cotton gins. The census that year reported a population of 188. In 1931, a hard-surface Highway 65 was built, replacing the earlier dirt road. A number of local schools consolidated into the Mayflower schools, requiring the construction of larger and more modern buildings. Because of the lack of market for many area farm products, Gena Hathaway operated a canning kitchen to preserve food. The population dropped to 165 in the 1940 census, but was up to 293 by 1950.

In 1951, nearby Lake Conway was completed, bringing new businesses to Mayflower as it was soon known as a great place to fish. Interstate 40 was completed past Mayflower in 1965, and many of the businesses moved from alongside the tracks over to the freeway's exit, several blocks away. The highway also made Mayflower a home for those who worked in Little Rock and Conway. By 1970, the population was 469 and there were two banks, a drug store, two garages, a service station, four groceries, and a plumbing and electrical shop. It was bragged that Mayflower had a fire department with two trucks, and a police station with two cars and three policemen. The town grew 194.5% to 1381 residents during the 1970s, and today has a population of about 2000.

Looking at Mayflower, much of the town is new. This isn't just because of the growth over the past few decades. Mayflower is located on a path that has seen a number of tornadoes over the years. In particular, on April 27, 2014, an EF-5 tornado destroyed much of the town. The residents rebuilt and received numerous awards for their community efforts. New projects include an interchange on Interstate 40 that crosses the railroad and connects to the Conway Western Arterial Loop.

The Railroad at Mayflower

As previously stated, the name Mayflower came from the telegraph code used by the construction superintendent for the Little Rock & Fort Smith. Originally the railroad knew this location simply as Twenty Mile Camp, and it was a base for building the railroad, and later for obtaining crossties.

The first national news about the railroad at Mayflower was probably in late 1901 when an accident was reported in newspapers across the country. For example, *The Indianapolis Journal* (November 2, 1901) reported that on the previous day "Passenger train No. 321 on the Little Rock & Fort Smith Railroad, was telescoped at Mayflower today by a west-bound freight train. The rear coach of the passenger train was demolished and six passengers were injured."

In 1907, there was a 100-car siding and a mail crane at Mayflower. The railroad had a small combination depot, built in 1904, at Mayflower, sometimes spelled May Flower in early railroad documents. It was located north of the grade crossing with today's Miller Street, Arkansas Highway 89. The station was to the east in 1925, and it housed a ticket and freight agency. The freight agency was shown as handling carload and smaller shipments. There were also a tool house, coal house, and a toilet, also on the east side of the mainline. The train order signal was removed in February 1927, and then re-installed in August 1927. However, the nearby major station at Conway led the railroad to close the depot on July 21, 1931. Trains still stopped but tickets had to be bought on the train. Services apparently started and stopped before the depot and train order signal were removed during January 1938. A short siding located on the west side of the mainline was also at Mayflower.

This sign is for South Railroad Avenue, located on the east side of the tracks at Mayflower.

By 1944, the railroad showed that there was an 81-car siding, a telephone, and a mail crane at Mayflower. The cotton platform, located on the west side of the tracks, was removed that year. The siding was extended to 90 cars long as part of the 1945 installation of ABS signaling. Today, Mayflower is shown to be at an elevation of 288 feet and the 10,700-foot-long siding passes right through town. To the east of the tracks is Railroad Avenue, while to the west is Main Street. Heading north from May-flower, Arkansas Highway 365 follows the tracks to Conway.

The Van Buren Subdivision has been an important coal route since the 1980s. On the last day of 1990, Union Pacific 9297 is shown leading a coal train southward, meeting a northbound coal train at Mayflower.

365.2 CONTROL POINT V365 – Once known simply as North Switch Mayflower, the name changed with the installation of CTC signaling. For years, the north switch was located at Mile-post 364.

Like at the south switch, this sign marks the north switch of the Mayflower Siding, now known as Control Point V365 – Mayflower.

366.2 SECTION POST – This location was another dividing line between track section gangs during the early 1900s.

367.5 GOLD CREEK – Located where Crossover Road One crosses the tracks to connect Arkansas Highway 365 with Sturgis Road to the west was once the railroad station of Gold Creek. Also known as Gold Creek Switch, this was a railroad construction site in 1870, and there was a track by 1875 named for the nearby stream. Two section houses, measuring 10' x 14' and 18' x 36', were built in 1877. Two water tanks (16' diameter and 24' tall) were built in 1878. By 1907, there was a 92-car siding on the west side of the mainline, but it and the local telephone booth were removed in 1937.

A post office opened near here using the name Toram on May 15, 1878. A Gold Creek Post Office opened on April 17, 1879, and the Toram post office was moved to Gold Creek on September 17, 1879, and merged. However, the combined post office closed on February 18, 1880.

Gold Creek is credited as being the oldest black community in Faulkner Community, and it used the name Gold Lake initially. The community is still small, but growing with a number of new houses. It is often described simply as an unincorporated community on the western shore of Lake Conway.

367.8 BAKER-WILLS PARKWAY – The railroad passes under this new highway (opened in 2017) that connects Interstate 40 with the south and west sides of Conway. The idea of the highway started in 1994 as Conway saw enormous growth and its roads couldn't handle the traffic. As described by the builders, the "one-of-a-kind project includes bridges over an interstate, railroad, state highway, and a local road." This new highway has helped spur growth in the Gold Creek area, with both new homes and several businesses. To the east are several subdivisions built on the shore of Lake Conway.

368.4 GOLD CREEK BRIDGE – When built, this bridge (Bridge No. 80) was called "the most unsafe bridge I ever saw a train run over." Today, it is a well-photographed bridge consisting of two 55-foot deck plate girder spans with a center concrete pier. Gold Creek forms in the low hills to the west and is one of several streams that flow into Lake Conway. Not far to the west is one of several new communities built on the lake with homes having their own boat docks on the water.

Since the 1980s, the Van Buren Subdivision has seen a number of trains pulled by various Union Pacific steam locomotives. On November 15, 2019, UP Big Boy 4014 (4-8-8-4) pulled a special executive train northward across Gold Creek on the former Little Rock & Fort Smith.

Lake Conway is the largest man-made lake (6700 acres) ever created by a state wildlife commission in the United States, and it was the first to be created by the Arkansas Game and Fish Commission. Construction on the lake began in 1948, but the former swampy land that was once considered to be useless for farming suddenly grew in value, and it took several years to buy all of the land, especially with the several dozen court cases required.

The lake opened to great celebration on July 4, 1951, and was eight miles long with 52 miles of shoreline. It is never deep, with an average depth of six feet, and a maximum depth of 18 feet. The lake has a number of streams flowing into it, including Gold Creek, Little Cypress Creek, Palarm Creek, Panther Creek, and Stone Dam Creek. Lake Conway is popular for catfish, bream, bass and crappie fishing.

Lake Conway is actually larger than it was supposed to be. It was designed to dam Palarm Creek, but when the R. W. Hammock Construction Company started work, they found that it was too deep to reach bedrock at the original location. Therefore, the concrete spillway and dirt dam were built about a mile downstream from the original construction site.

368.6 PRESTON – Located on the north side of Gold Creek was once the community and railroad station of Preston, basically a twin community with Gold Creek. It too was an early Faulkner County "Negro community," claimed to be the second black community in the county. It is believed that the community had started years earlier and was named for an early white settler who lived along Gold Creek prior to 1860. The Preston post office opened on June 9, 1881, but it closed on July 14, 1906. A tool house was built at Preston in 1886, and a section house in 1896. In 1900, a water tank and pump house were installed. The railroad had a mail crane here during this time. This area is now essentially a rural suburb of nearby Conway, and its growing steadily.

The railroad once had a house track here, but it was removed in 1923. A 9' x 35' depot was made from a carbody and there was a 10' x 14' tool house. By the 1920s, the railroad stop at Preston was shown to handle LCL (less-than-carload) freight only, and it had to be prepaid. For trains heading north towards Conway and on to Fort Smith, they start to climb a series of hills as steep as 0.84% until they reach the Conway Tunnel.

370.0 NUCOR – To the west is the first of a number of industrial tracks in the Conway area, once the facility of Nucor Fastener. The facility opened in 1995, but closed within a decade, unable to compete against foreign manufacturers. It is now operated by Mercer Mass Timber, a firm that manufacturers customized wooden structural timbers. Structurlam opened the plant in 2021, and the company was acquired by Mercer in 2023. This plant produces both glued laminated timber (glulam) and cross-laminated timber (CLT), with a capacity of approximately 30 million board feet a year. The plant can produce CLT up to 12' wide and 60' long, and glulam beams 60' long, 4' tall and 20" wide. The company's Spokane plant produced the mass timbers used in 2025 for the construction of the new Theodore Roosevelt Presidential Library in Medora, North Dakota.

Conway was the first small city in Arkansas to develop their own series of industrial parks, and a number of the firms ship by rail.

370.4 STONE DAM CREEK BRIDGE – This 3-span reinforced concrete trestle (81 feet long) spans another stream that flows into Lake Conway. Stone Dam Creek (aka Stonedam Creek) had been used to dispose of Conway's sewage for decades, but with the construction of Lake Conway, improvements were made in the sewer system of the city. Today, a series of trails and parks line much of the stream, which forms on the northwest side of Conway and flows around the west side of downtown.

371.3 BRUMLEY – Built in January 1929, this private track to the east was extended in 1947 and connected with another track. The track is now gone and Brumley is considered to be a suburb of Conway and is located south of the grade crossing with Sturges Road.

371.5 ARKANSAS HIGHWAY 60 – Above the tracks is another major roadway built to provide access to parts of Conway from Interstate 40. Highway 60 heads west from here to Plainview, Arkansas, a distance of about 55 miles. Locally, the road carries the name of Dave Ward Drive, named for a local blacksmith from the 1930s. Dave Ward actually was involved with a number of businesses, including building the Toad Suck Ferry on the Arkansas River. When asked to make repairs and improvements to an early bus, he decided to get into the bus building business. His Ward Body Works company was at one time the largest school bus builder west of the Mississippi River. It was also the first school bus manufacturer to assemble buses on an assembly line. The company was reorganized in 1980 as American Transportation Corporation and was then acquired in 1991 by Navistar International.

About seven miles to the west is Toad Suck Park and the Toad Suck Lock and Dam on the Arkansas River. The unique name came from the days when low water on the Arkansas River would stop steamboats in the area. Legend has it that while waiting for higher water, the captains, crews and passengers would spend time in local taverns, and "They suck on the bottle 'til they swell up like toads." The name is famous in the area and led to the creation of Toad Suck Daze, an annual community music, arts, and food festival in Conway that attracts an estimated 160,000 visitors each year and has raised more than $1 million for local scholarships.

371.6 CONWAY INDUSTRIAL LEAD – To the east is a lead track into one of the industrial parks at Conway. It has historically served companies like International Paper and Kimberly-Clark. Because the line curves throughout the park, train crews have orders to hand-flag each crossing and to travel at a maximum speed of 5 miles per hour.

North of here at Milepost 371.8 is the south switch of the old Conway siding, now called the Conway Business Track.

This faded sign marks the south switch of the Conway Business Track.

372.5 DAVIES AVENUE FACILITIES – Davies Avenue has been renamed as Bruce Street. Missouri Pacific once had a number of facilities in this area. Immediately south of the grade crossing and to the west were once the Conway stock pens, relocated here from downtown in late 1926. Most of the pens were removed in 1943. In 1925-1926, the railroad moved many of its facilities out of downtown as part of a plan for improving the business district. A turntable was installed south of the stockpens in late 1925, but removed during the summer of 1926. There was also a turntable north of Davies Avenue that was removed in 1935.

These turntables were important due to a plan to operate twice-daily roundtrips (train Nos. 147 and 149 southbound and Nos. 146 and 148 northbound) between Little Rock and Conway. The trains would consist of gas-electric motorcars with mail and baggage sections, plus 45 seats. The service began on November 22, 1925, and the motorcar was turned on the turntable installed at the south end of the yard at Conway. The plan didn't work well and the service ended on January 31, 1927.

A Union Pacific local is generally based at Conway. On Sunday, June 15, 2025, it was parked in the Conway Business Track with a cut of boxcars.

372.7 NORTH SWITCH OF CONWAY BUSINESS TRACK – The siding that was here earlier went to Milepost 373.7, but the track was shortened to avoid blocking many of the downtown streets in Conway. This is now the location of the north switch for the Conway Business Track, located next to the St. Joseph Catholic Church.

The Little Rock & Fort Smith Railway played a large role in establishing this church. In 1878, Father Joseph Strub worked with the railroad to obtain land for Catholic emigrants fleeing persecution in Europe, especially in Germany where Prince Otto Von Bismarck created a number of laws that were aimed at the church. Father Strub wrote a guide book for Catholic emigrants called "The Guiding Star," providing information about the St. Joseph Colony near Conway. A number of European families moved into the communities along the railroad. Today, there are more than 5500 Catholics who are members of this parish.

373.0 PRAIRIE STREET – At one time, Prairie Street was the south end of the railroad's downtown facilities, many located where a large parking lot now sits. In 1886, a cotton platform and tool house were built at Conway, railroad stockyards were erected in 1896, and a sand house was installed in 1900. The railroad's stockpens were immediately north of Prairie Street until they were moved in 1926. A switch in the middle of the street allowed trains to access the stockyards and several industrial tracks to the west. The railroad's freight house was immediately north of the stockpens. The freight house once measured 213' x 20', but had the south sixty feet of the building removed in 1943. In 1947, its platform was shortened by 78 feet on the north end as trucks began to replace rail for the movement of small shipments. In 1925, a mail crane was installed on the east side of the mainline, across from the freight house and south of the passenger station.

373.1 CONWAY (CN) – For Union Pacific, and earlier Missouri Pacific and the Little Rock & Fort Smith, Conway was located at Main Street. It was appropriate as the railroad was responsible for the founding of Conway. Asa P. Robinson was a contractor and chief engineer for the Little Rock & Fort Smith. Part of his pay was one square mile of land in the area. He used part of this land as the site of a station that he named Conway Station.

The station was at an important location since there was a steep climb heading north to get over Cadron Ridge, using Cadron Gap. Conway was located at an elevation of 310 feet, while Cadron Gap was 80 feet higher and only about a mile away.

The former Little Rock & Fort Smith Railroad station at Conway was located in the middle of Main Street, to the east of the tracks in Front Street. The railroad used much of the right-of-way of Railroad Avenue, which often was immediately to the west of the tracks. By the 1880s, there was a siding to the west of the mainline, and there were several cotton platforms across the tracks from the depot. South of the platforms were an oil house and stock yards, while to the north was a cotton seed warehouse.

Located in Simon Park in Conway is Missouri Pacific caboose 13704. The location is appropriate as the Conway depot was located here.

Over the next several decades, additional rail shippers located at Conway, requiring the construction of more tracks. By 1892, these new shippers included J. M. Allinder's Cotton Gin & Grist Mill and the Robins & Carter Planing Mill. With cotton so important, additional seed houses were also built along the railroad. Some of these companies changed ownership, and Conway Roller Mills and the Allinder & McCullough Gin & Grist Mill were the primary businesses in town.

In 1909, there was a growing list of business using the railroad at Conway. North of Mill Street and west of the tracks was the Conway Cotton Oil Company, which later added a cotton gin south of Mill Street. A new track had been added to serve several shippers east of the depot, including Conway Roller Mills, a wholesale grocery warehouse south of Wright, and a fertilizer warehouse south of Prairie.

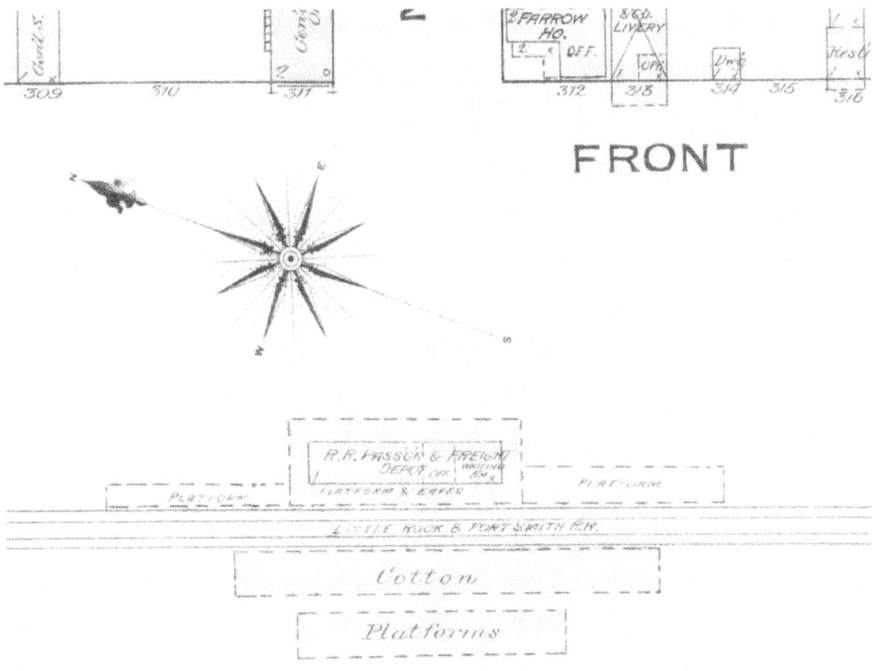

FRONT

The former Little Rock & Fort Smith Railway station at Conway was located in the middle of Main Street, to the east of the tracks, as shown by this July 1886 Sanborn map. Several cotton platforms were located across the tracks to the west. *Sanborn Fire Insurance Map from Conway, Faulkner County, Arkansas.* Sanborn Map Company, July 1886. Map. Retrieved from the Library of Congress, https://www.loc.gov/item/sanborn00221_001/.

In 1914, the wooden station was moved to the west side of the tracks and a new brick station was built in the same location in the middle of Main Street. The old station was rebuilt into a freight house and was then expanded by 1927. The new station was built with the passenger section to the north and an express building to the south. About this time the railroad had four stock pens with a capacity of five stock cars, plus water for the livestock.

With the changes, more tracks were added, including several house tracks for the freight house. A new spur track to the east and south of Mill Street served several shippers, including the Hill & Dawson Lumber Yard, the Plunkett & Jarrell Grocery Company, and several cotton seed warehouses. Another spur track to the east and south of Main Street served Cole's Grocery

Warehouse north of Elm, and Standard Oil Company of Louisiana south of Deer. By the mid-1920s, the Conway Cotton Oil Company was the Conway Oil & Ice Company, and the large Conway Cotton Compress Company was located east of the tracks and south of Sixth.

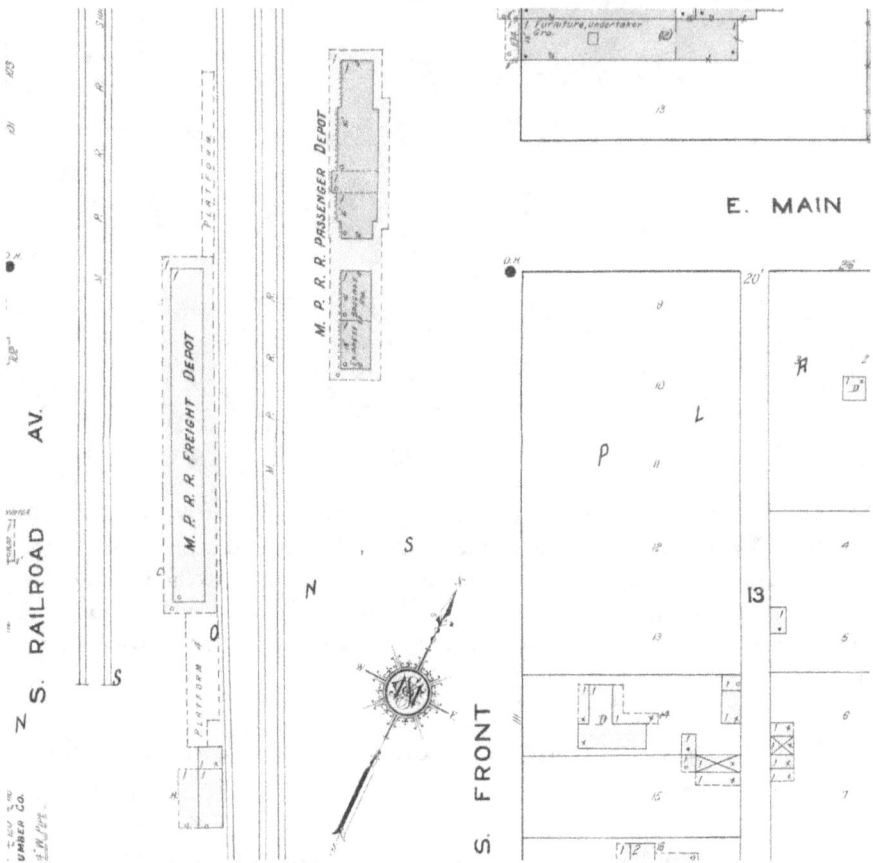

In 1914, Missouri Pacific built a new station at Conway, moving the old wooden depot across the tracks and turning it into a freight house. The railroad also moved a few tracks in the area and added two house tracks near the new freight house. As shown by the 1919 Sanborn map, the area around the Conway train station was getting busier. *Sanborn Fire Insurance Map from Conway, Faulkner County, Arkansas.* Sanborn Map Company, March 1919. Map. Retrieved from the Library of Congress, https://www.loc.gov/item/sanborn00221_007/.

As automobiles filled the streets of Conway, the location of the depot and freight house became an issue for the city. On March 19, 1925, Missouri Pacific offered to move the freight depot and stock pens to a location about one mile south of Main Street, but Conway had to purchase the land. The city estimated the cost of the land to be some $10,000, and the railroad began work converting the old downtown freight yard into a park during November 1926.

In 1944, the railroad had a continuous train order office at Conway, plus a siding that was 103 cars long. The siding had been extended to 144 car lengths by 1951. Missouri Pacific discontinued the station agent at Conway on July 13, 1970, but continued the telegrapher-clerk position. In July 1983, Missouri Pacific reported that Conway was protected by yard limits (Mileposts 371.0-374.0), and had a radio call-in system to the dispatcher, general order books, a standard clock, and a train order office. The siding was shown to be 7506 feet long. Much of this changed on December 22, 1983, when Union Pacific closed the Conway station, which had been moved into a small building at the south end of town. The siding was later turned into a business track, used to switch local shippers and to store freight cars and maintenance-of-way equipment.

A few other changes have happened at Conway that few citizens have probably noticed. First, in 1980, work was underway to replace the jointed rail between Little Rock and Kansas City with continuous welded rail (CWR). Missouri Pacific laid its first CWR in 1962, and almost half of the railroad's mainline used CWR by 1980. Near Conway in October of that year, Missouri Pacific installed the 5000th mile of CWR on the railroad. The second happened very recently when Centralized Traffic Control (CTC) railway signaling was installed through town, replacing the old ABS and track warrant system.

The Conway Depot

In 1869-1870, a combined passenger and freight depot (20' x 95') was built at Conway. The original wooden depot was of classic design, with large roof overhangs featuring lots of decorative eave brackets. The combination depot was remodeled in 1886 and 1903, with 60 feet added to the freight section during the latter work. However, by the early 1900s, it no longer could serve all the needs of the city and the railroad. The freight business was also growing and a separate freight house would benefit the operations. In fact, on October 11, 1907, the Railroad Commission of Arkansas ordered the St. Louis, Iron Mountain & Southern to "construct or provide and maintain a separate express office and agent at the town of Conway." The Commission did so by stating that Conway was "required to get along with the same service accorded to it when the depot was built some twenty years ago notwithstanding that the town has increased in size until it has become a considerable city." At the time, the railroad had a day and night telegraph office and an 80-car siding at Conway. In 1912, block signals were installed at every telegraph station between Little Rock and Fort Smith, including Conway. These signals allowed local operators to hand orders up to train crews as they passed.

Replacing the station was not a simple process. Meetings between the railroad and city leaders went on for several years until the St. Louis, Iron Mountain & Southern announced in February 1909 that it had agreed to build a new depot at Conway. However, in June, the Conway Board of Trade rejected the plan because it wanted the switching yard moved to another part of town. In June 1910, there was another announcement about an agreement with the city for the construction of a new depot. More public meetings were held where it was determined that some in the city wanted to create a public square on property needed for the railroad's improvements. Meanwhile, the Railroad Commission of Arkansas started hearings on the matter.

On October 3, 1910, the Railroad Commission held a meeting at Conway about a new station, needed because the existing depot had been in use for 35 years and was inadequate for the needs of the town. The frame depot was used for passenger, freight and express business and was described as being dilapidated. Everyone agreed that a new depot was needed, but the challenge seemed to be that the railroad needed a larger freight yard and no one could agree on the location. For example, in November 1911 there was a plan to build a new depot on the site of the existing depot. The old depot and yards would be moved about a quarter of a mile to the south. This plan led to a protest by the congregation of the St. Joseph's Catholic Church which claimed it would damage their school and church.

Public meetings and announcements seemed to end, but in the March 1, 1913, issue of *The Railway and Engineering Review*, there was a short announcement that the "St. Louis, Iron Mountain & Southern Ry. will build a passenger and freight station at Conway, Ark." Construction took place quickly and the new $40,000 brick depot (20' x 180') was dedicated on April 6, 1914. The dedication was attended by an estimated 500 citizens. The former wooden station was moved across the tracks and a number of new tracks were built to handle the freight and express business.

This photo of the Conway station, taken from the southwest, shows some of the tracks in the area, the train order signals, and the large design of the building. It also shows a Railway Express Agency truck and the many baggage wagons assigned to the station. Photo courtesy of the Faulkner County Museum, Conway, Arkansas.

For many years, Missouri Pacific had a large staff working at Conway. In 1925, Conway was shown to be a coupon ticket station, a ticket agency, and a freight agency for carload and less volumes. At the time, passengers were handled at the north end of the station while baggage and express were found at the south end.

On April 1, 1952, the freight office force was in the freight house across six tracks from the passenger station where the telegraphers worked. At the time, three Telegraphers (7:59am-3:59pm, 3:59pm-11:59pm, 11:59pm-7:59am) and an agent with no assigned hours (called an Exclusive Agent by the railroad) worked at the passenger station. At the freight house were a Bill Clerk (10:30am-2:30pm and 3:30pm-7:30pm), Check Clerk (7:00am-11:30am and 12:30pm-4:00pm), Cashier (8:00am-12noon and 1:00pm-5:00pm), and a Trucker (8:00am-12noon and 1:00pm-5:00pm). As the passenger, express and less-than-carload business declined, the Bill Clerk and Trucker positions were abolished later that year.

The last passenger train stopped at Conway on Monday, March 28, 1960. By this time, much of the express and mail business had been moved to trucks, and the station and freight house were mostly closed. By 1964, the station services were down to handling train orders for freight trains, and a freight agent to handle the needs of local customers. During the early 1970s, Missouri Pacific was replacing many of their old stations with smaller modern buildings, and Conway was interested in acquiring the land associated with their depot. In 1972, Conway purchased the abandoned Missouri Pacific depot and was planning to demolish the structure. The process took several years, and a part of the agreement stated that the depot was to be removed and Main Street extended from Front Street westwardly to Parkway Street. There was also a requirement that the city install fully automatic signals at the crossing. The Conway City Council approved an order to conduct the work on November 12, 1974, and the changes began within a year. Today, Main Street is open across the tracks as the station is now gone and little of the railroad remains downtown.

The City of Conway

The City of Conway was founded by Asa P. Robinson, who was the chief engineer for the Little Rock & Fort Smith Railroad. He laid out a town on property he had been given as pay for his work. He named the new town Conway Station after a powerful Arkansas family, and there was soon a depot, a few houses, a post office (opened 1871), two small stores, and two saloons.

The name Conway came from the Conway-Johnson family, often called "The Family" or "The Dynasty" in historical literature. Members of the family were politically powerful in other states, and continued to hold similar power after moving to Arkansas. Members of the family were in Arkansas by 1820, and several were deputy-surveyors under the patronage of their uncle, William Rector, Surveyor General of Missouri, Illinois, and Arkansas. James Sevier Conway (1798–1855) was the first member of the family to hold a state office, being Surveyor-General of Arkansas Territory (1832–1836), and then the first Governor of Arkansas (1836–1840). Elias Nelson Conway (1812–1892) was another holder of multiple offices. He was the Arkansas Auditor (1835–1849) and then the fifth Governor of Arkansas (1852–1860). Elias Conway was governor during the early days of the Little Rock & Fort Smith.

Conway was officially founded in 1872, and then named the county seat of Faulkner County when it was created in 1873. The town was incorporated on October 16, 1875. The population in the 1880 census was 1028. By this time, Conway served as a local trade center and market town, and local farm and timber products were shipped to markets on the railroad. At the same time, Father Joseph Strub, a priest in the Roman Catholic Holy Ghost Fathers, arrived in the area. His appearance would greatly benefit the railroad and the region. Strub founded the St. Joseph Colony and the St. Joseph Catholic Church of Conway, using 200,000 acres donated by the Little Rock & Fort Smith Railroad. As part of the agreement, Father Strub worked to attract German immigrants to the area, helping to sell them land owned by the railroad. Strub also handled things like transportation, education about Arkansas, farming techniques, and provided many other services to bring settlers to the lands of the LR&FS. More than 100 German families alone had settled in Conway by 1889, and German names were used for a number of streets and businesses. Examples include the Frauenthal Cotton Oil Company and Siebenmorgan Road.

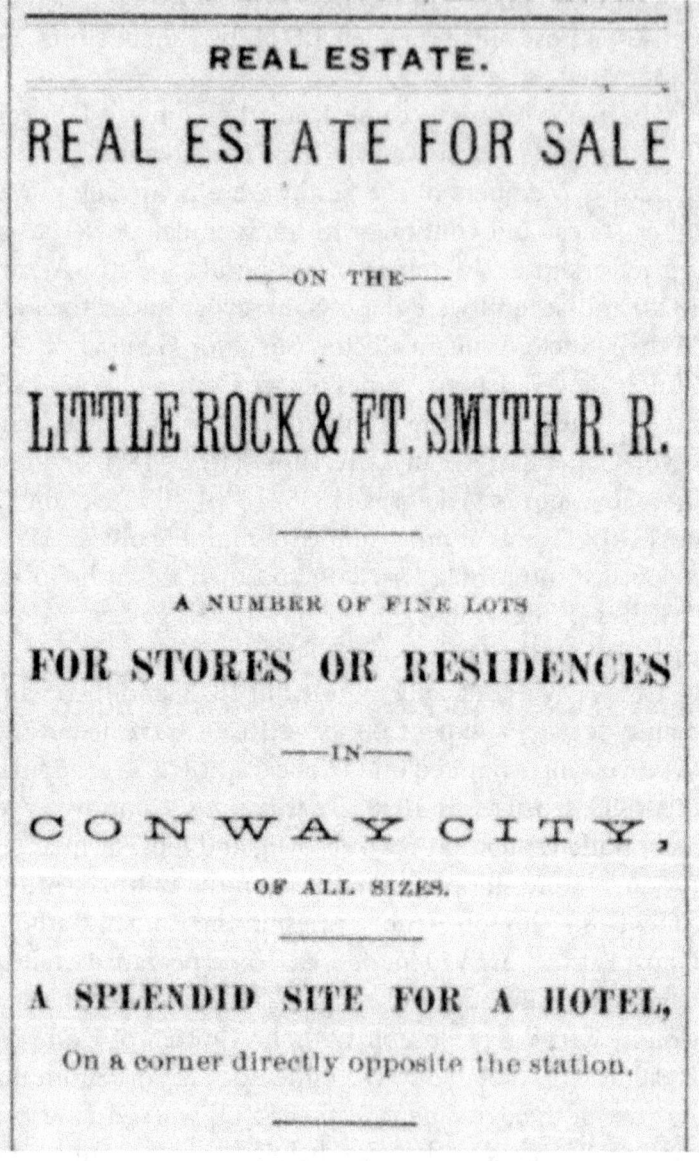

The land grants received by the Little Rock & Fort Smith were sold to pay for the railroad's construction. While the sales were slow, numerous advertisements were printed across the country. Some like this one in the *Little Rock Daily Republican* promoted a specific location – Conway. *Little Rock Daily Republican* (Little Rock, AR), August 22, 1872. Retrieved from the Library of Congress, https://www.loc.gov/item/sn82014368/1872-08-22/ed-1/.

Conway is unusual in that its population has grown with every census. In 1920, the population was 4564. The following year, the *1921 Arkansas Marketing and Industrial Guide* listed a large number of companies at Conway. These included the Conway Bottling Works and Gay-Ola Bottling Works; Central Broom Manufacturing Company; Miller & Opitz (cooperage works); Conway Cotton Oil & Gin Company; Conway Compress Company; and George Mobbs (hardwood).

Besides manufacturing and agriculture, Conway also developed the educational industry, with three schools of higher education in the city. In 1907, the Arkansas State Normal College was established in Conway. It became the Arkansas State Teachers College in 1925, and then the University of Central Arkansas in 1975. It has about 12,000 students, and was one of the first schools in the country to create an honor college. Hendrix College has an enrollment of more than 1300 students, and traces its history back to 1876 and the Central Institute at Altus, Arkansas. It became Hendrix College in 1889 and moved to Conway in 1890. The third school is Central Baptist College, a private Baptist college founded in 1952 as Conway Baptist College. It used the campus of Central College, which closed in 1947.

The population of Conway was 9791 in the 1960 census, and then problems in Pulaski County, and the efforts to create a number of industrial parks, caused the population to boom 58.4% to 15,510 in 1970. Besides the local industry, Conway serves as a regional shopping, educational, work, healthcare, sports, and cultural hub. The market area of Conway has grown greatly, including across the Arkansas River thanks to the 1969 opening of the Toad Suck Lock and Dam, which included a bridge across the river. In 1982, Toad Suck Daze was created, and now as many as 150,000 people attend the annual event. The population in the 2020 census was 64,134, making Conway the seventh-largest city in Arkansas.

Because of the universities, a number of well-known people have lived here, including Scottie Pippen (NBA basketball forward), Kris Allen (winner of *American Idol* Season 8), and Gil Gerard (actor known for the TV series *Buck Rogers*). Conway is also known for the large number of hotels and restaurants along Interstate 40, and the many rural recreational opportunities in almost every direction.

Conway is nationally famous for its annual Toad Suck Daze festival, named for the nearby lock and dam on the Arkansas River. The name dates back to steamboat days when in dry weather boats would be stuck here. It was said that the crews and passengers would drink and drink, and swell up like a toad.

373.3 CONWAY – The actual milepost used for Conway has changed several times over the years. In the June 15, 2021, employee timetable, Conway was shown to be at Milepost 373.3.

This area was once known as North Street by the railroad. North of here, the railroad had a number of tracks that served warehouses, wholesale dealerships, and other companies. Most of these tracks were to the east of the mainline and many of the old buildings still stand along Front Street.

373.7 SOUTH END OF 1904 CADRON RIDGE DIVERSION –

This five-mile route diversion was known as Detour No. 3 by Missouri Pacific. Starting at the former location of the Independence Street grade crossing, the St. Louis, Iron Mountain & Southern built a new route under Cadron Ridge as opposed to the older route that went over the east-west ridge. This required five miles of new track, but reduced the distance by almost one mile.

When the railroad was originally built, the grade headed north from Conway and through Cadron Ridge at Cadron Gap. Located along the west border of Hendrix College, this route is now used by Washington Avenue to Cadron Gap, and then U.S. Highway 64 westward. The route was described as being a hard climb out of Conway, a sudden peak of elevation in Cadron Gap, a sharp turn to the west, a steep drop down to Cadron Creek, and then the crossing of a long timber bridge. The grade over the ridge was 2.0% and required the doubling of the hill, the use of helper locomotives, or both.

At Conway, Washington Avenue uses the original grade of the Little Rock & Fort Smith as it heads northwards from downtown. This route was abandoned by the railroad in January 1904 when a new route opened through the tunnel underneath Cadron Ridge.

Using the current route of Washington Avenue, the railroad climbed to Summit Switch, a siding at the top of Cadron Gap. Located 2.6 miles north of the Conway station, by 1889 the siding was known as Alpine. From Cadron Gap, located near Exit 124 of Interstate 40, the old grade sharply turned west and closely followed today's U.S. Highway 64. The old grade crossed over the north end of the new tunnel about 1¼ miles west of Cadron Gap and rejoined the original grade near the Cadron Creek bridge.

The delays on the line as business increased forced the St. Louis, Iron Mountain & Southern to look for a new route over or through Cadron Ridge. In the March 7, 1902, issue of *The Railroad Gazette*, a news announcement stated that "surveys are reported in Arkansas for a new line between Conway and Cadron, seven miles distant, including a tunnel at the Cadron Gap. The object of the work is to shorten the existing line." Later in 1902, a new route was announced which would leave the current grade near Independence Street and curve to the northwest. At an elevation of 364 feet, the new line would pass through a tunnel about 160 feet below the top of Cadron Ridge. This new route would drop the grade to about 0.5% and allow trains to cross the ridge much quicker and haul more traffic. On January 10, 1904, all rail traffic was officially routed onto the new line and through the tunnel.

Cadron Gap is still a heavily used route through Cadron Ridge, being 150 feet lower than the top of the ridge. The gap was an early route used by settlers and explorers, and Interstate 40, U.S. Highway 64, and Arkansas Highway 25 still pass through the narrow opening in the ridge.

Rebuilding the Railroad with Convict Labor

Convict labor was still available to firms in Arkansas during the first few years of the twentieth century. Contractors reported that it was difficult to find sufficient labor to rebuild the Little Rock & Fort Smith, and convict labor was often the answer. Dalhoff Construction Company, one of the primary contractors on the project, and smaller subcontractors like Dickinson (working near Marche), were just some of the firms that worked on the project using convict labor. Newspapers reported heavily on the use of Arkansas penitentiary labor, noting that they had been convicted of crimes ranging from larceny to murder,

Housing the convicts was an early concern. A few contractors used traditional stockades, but most used railroad cars. For example, during June 1902, ten palace stock cars were converted to prison cars by the Iron Mountain at their Baring Cross shops. The cars were described as having heavy lumber in the ceilings, securely locked side doors, heavy screening to prevent any unauthorized items from being passed to the prisoners, heavy canvas that could be lowered to shield the prisoners during a rainstorm, and bunks installed lengthwise down the cars. Several prisoners did escape from the cars, but more often the escape attempt was discovered by guards and shots would end the plans of the convicts.

This photo shows the Dalhart Construction Company working on the west portal of the new tunnel near Conway during April 1903. Note the large number of convict laborers, apparently typical for much of the work that rebuilt the Little Rock & Fort Smith during the early 1900s. Photo courtesy of the Faulkner County Museum, Conway, Arkansas.

There were a large number of convict work camps, in addition to the many contractor labor camps. An article in the *Arkansas Gazette* (April 30, 1903) listed some of these convict camps, including Camp No. 52 near Conway (107 convicts), Camp No. 56 near Denning (96 convicts), Camp No. 57 near Pottsville (102 convicts), and Camp No. 58 near Coal Hill (49 convicts). Marche and Hartman were also listed as having convict labor camps, but no numbers were mentioned.

The use of the convict labor on the rebuilding of the Little Rock & Fort Smith did result in two State of Arkansas investigations. The first came about from the death of several workers, including some convicts, due to extreme heat during August 1902. There were also questions about the food being provided to the convicts. Arkansas State Physician, Dr. E. C. Witt, was reported as "making the rounds of the convict camps" and generally found that the convicts were doing well, and were "reasonably well-fed." These inspections were followed up during April 1903 by an Arkansas General Assembly joint legislative committee review. Reports were produced about each work camp, with most noting few issues, although a few of the camp wardens were noted as not being as good as others.

A second issue came about because the state discovered that the leasing of the convicts was providing far more financial benefit to the contractors than the state penitentiary system. An August 1902 report stated that the contractor of the convicts was making $1.50 per day, per prisoner, while paying the state 50 cents per day, per prisoner. Additionally, the state was bearing all the cost for guards, prisoner clothing and food. Several firms which had leased prison labor were subleasing the convicts to the Little Rock & Fort Smith for construction work, pocketing the difference.

The Arkansas penitentiary was not the only source of convict labor. Some labor also came from various county jails. Convicts from Pulaski County were under contract to Nicky Peay, who had leased them to the Gracie farm in Jefferson County. Several prisoners sued due to the work conditions and location of the farm. As a result, at least 50 convicts were leased to the Dalhoff

Construction Company for railroad work near Argenta, with an agreement to keep them in Pulaski County.

Despite these and other issues, convict labor was used across the railroad during the 1902-1904 rebuilding. Eventually, Arkansas created its own prison farm system, and ended leasing convict labor in 1913.

374.1 INTERNATIONAL SHOE COMPANY – Where the Conway Public Schools Administrative Annex now stands was the factory of the International Shoe Company, once served by a 556-foot-long private track. After World War II, the Conway Chamber of Commerce began efforts to attract businesses, especially manufacturing, to Conway. One of these was the International Shoe Company, at the time the world's largest shoe manufacturer. To help attract the shoe manufacturer, the Conway Corporation purchased $110,000 of bonds and agreed to provide about $5000 annually in electrical power over a 10-year period. The Conway Realty Company was organized to borrow the funds and erect a building on a five and one-half acre site on Hairston Street. Construction began in late 1945 and the factory opened on May 10, 1947.

The company initially employed about 400 workers to produce 7000 pairs of shoes a day. These shoes were for toddlers, children, misses and ladies. Most of these shoes were boxed and shipped to a St. Louis warehouse for national distribution. The plant was sold to R. G. Barry (shoes) during the late 1970s, and then San Antonio Shoe in 1983. The plant closed in 2009 and the building was purchased by Conway Public Schools later that year.

375.8 SOUTH PORTAL CONWAY TUNNEL – This new route left the old line at the old cotton oil mill, extended through the tunnel and joined the old route near the iron bridge across Cadron Creek, the total length being about six miles. Two miles of new track was required to reach the Cadron Ridge tunnel. Approaching the south portal of the Conway Tunnel, sometimes called the West Conway Tunnel, the railroad until recently passed through several miles of open pasture land. However, this area now consists of blocks and blocks of new housing. Because of this, the railroad passes under Salem Road at Milepost 375.5.

The tunnel is 1100 feet long, although a few sources state that it is 3960 feet long. The peak of the grade, located at an elevation of 364 feet, is at the south portal. Construction of the new route and tunnel between Conway and Cadron was big news and it was reported on in a number of newspapers and magazines. In February 1902, surveyors were finalizing the route. Various news stories stated that construction started in March 1902 and that several construction camps had been located along the new line. It was also stated that it would take seven months to construct, the tunnel would be 1300 feet long, and that the new route would save two miles of track over the thirteen miles between Conway and Plumerville.

On the last day of 1990, train GQNEMR pops out of the south portal of the Conway Tunnel, being pulled by Union Pacific 3430 (SD40-2).

Arkansas prison system convicts were used for some of the construction, and a stockade was constructed on the south side of Cadron Ridge to house them. Crews worked from both ends of the tunnel, with blasting with dynamite beginning in September 1902. The original pilot holes met on April 4, 1903, and the 21-foot-high and 16-foot-wide tunnel was lined with 3 inches of concrete and completed on January 10, 1904, when all traffic began to use the new line. The new line cut the grades from 1.75 percent to 0.6 percent. Because of this, train tonnage was increased by a reported average of 550 tons per train.

This 1990 view of the south portal of the Conway Tunnel shows how straight the tunnel is. Until recently, this area was rural, but it now is being encroached upon by housing. Because of this, the area is heavily marked as no trespassing by the railroad.

While the work was completed in 1904, some of the equipment used sat around for another seven years. A story in *The Log Cabin Democrat* (September 7, 1911) reported on the discovery of the equipment by a representative of the Dalhoff Estate.

> *A representative of the estate of Henry Dalhoff, deceased, was here yesterday and was surprised to find machinery said to be worth $4,000 or $5,000 which had been standing for the past seven years at the railway tunnel, just west of Conway. Mr. Dalhoff was the contractor who excavated the tunnel for the railway company, and a large air compression outfit used to operate the drills had never been removed from the job. The representative of the estate said he knew there was some property here belonging to the estate, but had no idea that such valuable machinery had been left here for so many years. He made arrangements to have it dismantled and removed to Little Rock.*

The tunnel has also been reported to be the lowest of the seven rail tunnels in Arkansas at 360 feet. After more than 80 years, Union Pacific had the tunnel's concrete lining replaced with steel support beams with a new concrete lining. This work was performed in 1987 by National Products, Inc., of Boise, Idaho.

376.1 NORTH PORTAL CONWAY TUNNEL – The north portal is located almost directly under U.S. Highway 64, which uses the original grade of the railroad. Reportedly, there was once a cemetery near here that was used for workers who died building the tunnel and new route around Cadron Ridge.

Leaving the tunnel, the railroad curves sharply to the west using a four degree curve. In about three miles, the new grade rejoined the original grade from the early 1870s.

On August 24, 1991, UP 2422 exits the north portal of the Conway Tunnel, pulling train 2NLKC. This train is basically what the LR&FS was built to serve, freight traffic between Kansas City and Central Arkansas.

377.8 SOLID WASTE ROAD – This area is full of various facilities of the City of Conway. To the north is the Department of Sanitation, with a landfill further north. The Conway Animal Shelter and the Conway Recycling Center are also located here. A bit further west is the large Roger Q. Mills, Jr. Water Treatment Plant.

378.1 SOUTH SWITCH GLEASON SIDING – Located to railroad-west, but actually to the south, was once the south end of the Gleason Siding. This end of the siding was shortened by 1644 feet in 1948, and later removed.

Cadron

Before the new route was built, there was a station known as Cadron in this general area, shown in the *Official Guide* by 1875. When the railroad arrived here, it built a few facilities. For example, two section houses (10' x 14' and 18' x 36') were built at Cadron in 1876.

Cadron, or often called Cadron Settlement, was located near the confluence of Cadron Creek and the Arkansas River. It was the first permanent white settlement in central Arkansas. During the 1810s, John McElmurry arrived in the area. He farmed and operated a small trading post. In 1818, McElmurry and three other investors laid out a town, using the name Cadron. Reportedly the town was big, including fourteen blocks, each with six half-acre lots, all located around a central square. Part of the plan for Cadron was to be the new capital of Arkansas. An interesting issue is that the land didn't even become officially the property of McElmurry until 1830, three years after he had died.

Early reports about Cadron questioned its location, stating that it was surrounded by swampy and infertile hills and forest. However, there was a ferry across both the Arkansas River and Cadron Creek, connecting to a number of area roads and trails. McElmurry built a protective blockhouse that was used as a residence, tavern, and trading post. In 1820, weekly mail service began and Cadron was being considered by the state legislature for both the territorial capital and the seat of Pulaski County. On June 28th, Cadron officially became the county seat of Pulaski County. Later, the state legislature approved $1400 to build the Pulaski County jail and courthouse at Cadron, but the spending was halted when the county seat was moved to Little Rock during October 1821. About the same time, the state capital was moved to Little Rock, and the political plans for Cadron almost ended. However, it was named the temporary county seat for the new Conway County in 1825. It kept some of these duties until 1831 when the county seat moved to Lewisburg. Within a few years, the community of Cadron basically disappeared.

A few other peaks of population did take place during the 1800s. The first was when the Cadron area was used as a temporary encampment in 1834 by a large group of Cherokee being removed to Oklahoma. The river level was low, so they camped here near some of the town's remains. Unfortunately, a cholera epidemic swept through the weakened Indians, and many died.

A survey from 1991 identified 44 Indian graves, 36 unidentifiable graves, and many unmarked graves.

The nearby ferry, roads, and several stage routes led to further efforts to create a town here, including one named Cadron Burg. Cadron was used as a Confederate base during the first year of the Civil War as there were several grist mills and sawmills nearby. Union forces also used the site off and on during the latter part of the war, and accepted the surrender of a number of Confederate troops here.

The area near the Arkansas River has been turned into the Cadron Settlement Park, a bicentennial project of the Faulkner County Historical Society, the Conway Chamber of Commerce, and the U.S. Army Corps of Engineers. A blockhouse was built based upon early sketches, and several trails allow visitors to wander the nearby woods. The park is leased from the Corps of Engineers by the City of Conway and was added to the National Register of Historic Places on May 17, 1974.

The Cadron Settlement dates back to about 1810. The most prominent structure was a two-story blockhouse used as a trading post, tavern, home, and a fort. This replica was built in 1998.

A Novel Turkey Story

The February 5, 1871, issue of the *New York Dispatch* had an interesting report about a "novel incident" on the Little Rock & Fort Smith Railroad at Cadron.

> *A flock of wild turkeys, more than five hundred in number, congregated on the track near Cadron Station. The down train rounded the curve, and the engineer soon discovered that the turkeys intended to hold possession of the tracks. Having one minute to spare, he stopped his train to allow them to depart, but they were not disposed to give away. The turkeys surrounded the train, walked up and down the track on either side of the cars, evidently delighted with the novelty of their situation. No hunting party aboard, and no fire arms of any description, the turkeys were safe, but one or two short, quick whistles from the locomotive upset their calculations, and they lost no time in gaining the bushes, where they soon hid from view, and the train moved on.*

The U.S. Highway 64 bridge at Gleason carries this marker that shows it was built across the "Mopac Railroad" in 1996, long after the line became Union Pacific.

378.5 U.S. HIGHWAY 64 – The railroad passes under U.S. Highway 64 near the Roger Q. Mills, Jr. Water Treatment Plant, historically called the Gleason Water Plant. This highway is 2326 miles long and connects Nags Head, North Carolina, with the Four Corners area of northeast Arizona. U.S. Highway 64 closely follows the railroad from here to Van Buren.

From near Cadron Gap to just east of here, U.S. Highway 64 is located on the original grade of the Little Rock & Fort Smith Railway. Where the highway curves to the west to cross the tracks, the original grade continued straight, essentially where Plant Road is now located.

On the last day of 1990, Union Pacific 3430 leads a northbound freight under U.S. Highway 64 and by the Roger Q. Mills Water Treatment Plant at Gleason.

378.7 NORTH END OF 1904 CADRON RIDGE DIVERSION – When the new line around Cadron Ridge was announced, known as Detour No. 3 by Missouri Pacific, it was stated that the ends of the line would be about seven miles apart. This was the distance via the original line, the new route was about five miles long thanks to the tunnel that cut through Cadron Ridge. The location of the north end of the detour was only 200 feet from the north switch of the Gleason siding, which was only 1800 feet long during the late 1940s.

With the completion of the rebuilding of the Little Rock & Fort Smith line, the Arkansas Board of Railroad Assessment raised the assessment value of the line in 1906 on the motion of Governor Jefferson "Jeff" Davis. Davis, a lawyer from Russellville, was known for blaming city-dwellers, blacks, and Yankees for problems on the farm, and his efforts to shut down large businesses. The raised assessment value created $1104.45 in new tax revenue for Faulkner County (19.90 miles of the main line and 5.25 miles of side-tracks), and $27.15 for the City of Conway (1.81 miles of the main line and 1.94 miles of side-tracks).

The former LR&FS passes just north of the Roger Q. Mills, Jr. Water Treatment Plant at Gleason.

378.8 GLEASON – Gleason was a small community located next to Cadron Creek. Several reports state that it was actually located at the intersection of U.S. Highway 64 and Arkansas Highway 319. This is just about the location of the Gleason Water Plant, now known as the Roger Q. Mills Water Treatment Plant. During the first decade of the twentieth century, a six-mile pipeline was built from Cadron Creek at Gleason to Conway as part of an improved water system.

Gleason was never large, but it was once the home of the Freeman Lumber Company. A post office was here from 1900 until 1915. For the railroad, Gleason was the home of Section

House 5, housing for the local track maintenance gang. A platform for passengers and less-than-carload freight was located on the east side of the tracks where a station sign stood at the siding's north switch. In 1918, the railroad installed a 12' x 18' shelter at the platform.

There was an 81-car siding, mail crane, and water tower in 1907, and a 62-car-long siding, plus a water tank and a company telephone in 1944. The old short siding wasn't needed after the installation of ABS signals, so it was shortened in 1948, and then later removed completely. Despite the siding being gone, the water tower and telephone remained for a few more years. Gleason isn't even shown in most current Union Pacific records.

The Gleason Water Station

In 1902, the railroad started drilling a well to obtain water for a water station at Conway. The well reached 389 feet and was capable of producing 108,000 gallons a day, less than the estimated need of 125,000 gallons. Despite this, the well began to be used with the result that many nearby wells went dry. In May 1903, a larger pump was installed in an effort to draw more water.

In May 1904, the well was abandoned and the 16-foot-diameter water tank was moved to the Cadron Creek bridge at Gleason. A pump house was also built in 1904 to fill the water tower from the stream.

During the Spring of 1915, the water stations at Gleason and Palarm were closed due to flooding on the Arkansas River. The main issue with the flooding was the large amount of mud that was in the water that backed up into the local streams, making the water unusable by the railroad's steam locomotives. Because of this, water was obtained from the city water system at Conway. At the time, it was reported that Conway Station Agent J. W. James had been instructed to obtain estimates from the municipal plant for a permanent water supply. The plan would be to close both the Palarm and Gleason pumping stations and water towers. No further action was taken at the time.

In 1920, a 9' x 21' carbody was installed as part of the water tower facilities at Gleason. In 1924, the original wooden water tower was replaced by a new 50,000-gallon steel tank. In 1930, the pump and coal bin were retired and the railroad began to use Conway city water to fill the tank.

378.9 CADRON CREEK BRIDGE – Immediately west of the U.S. Highway 64 bridge is the Union Pacific bridge across Cadron Creek, shown in some early documents to be Cadron River. The stream was likely named for Charles Cadron, an early Canadian trader who explored the area. Cadron Creek has its headwaters near Heber Springs, Arkansas. From there, the creek flows westerly across the northwestern corner of Faulkner County and enters the Arkansas River not far west of here. The stream is about 60 miles long. It is considered to be the largest free-flowing stream in central Arkansas and is a major canoeing, floating and fishing stream. Especially on the northern end of Cadron Creek, the stream flows next to towering bluffs which feature a number of caves and waterfalls.

On September 8, 2025, UP 1446 pulls a short train westward across Cadron Creek.

This was Missouri Pacific Bridge No. 102. It was a 199-foot-long through pin connected truss span (TPCT) set on sandstone abutments. In 1924, the bridge was replaced with a series of five deck plate girder spans, all set on concrete piers. The center span is 100 feet long, while there are a 49' 3" and a 30-foot span off each end. This makes the bridge over Cadron Creek 258 feet long.

The piers near each bank of Cadron Creek consist of cut-stone blocks with a concrete cap. These piers date from when the bridge consisted of a 199-foot-long through pin connected truss span. In 1925, this long span was replaced by a series of shorter deck plate girder spans.

County Line

Cadron Creek serves as the county line between Faulkner and Conway counties in this area. To the east is **Faulkner County**, created on April 12, 1873, as one of the last counties in the state. It was created by Republicans during the reconstruction area and was designed to break up the traditional power of the plantation owners. The county was named for Captain Sandford C. "Sandy" Faulkner (1803-1874), described as being a planter, raconteur (a person who tells anecdotes in a skillful and amusing way), and fiddle player. He has been given credit for writing the song *Arkansas Traveler*, the official historic song of the State of Arkansas since 1987. Faulkner was a unique choice as he actually served as an artillery officer assigned to the Trans-Mississippi Department of the Confederate States Army, managing supply depots at Little Rock and then Marshall, Texas.

Faulkner County was made up of small, rural farms and few towns of any size. Cotton, fruit and vegetables were the primary products grown. Construction of the LR&FS added some new residents, but the population was still only 12,786 in 1880. Conway, the county seat, grew due to its retail businesses, plus the three colleges that eventually located there. However, it wasn't until the 1960s that the population began to grow. The census in 1970 recorded 31,572 residents, and 46,192 in 1980. Much of this boom came about because of Interstate 40, which connected Faulkner County with the Little Rock area, where turmoil in the various school districts in Pulaski County led to movement to the surrounding counties. In the 2020 census, there were 123,498 citizens, making it the sixth-most-populous county in Arkansas.

Conway County, which is to the west, was the 11th county created in Arkansas when it was approved on October 20, 1825, taking land from part of Pulaski County. The county was named for Henry Wharton Conway, a member of the Conway-Johnson political family. Henry Wharton Conway was a territorial delegate to the U.S. Congress (1823-1827) at the time the county was created. He died in 1827 as a result of wounds from a duel with Robert Crittenden, a former friend and political ally.

When Conway County was created it comprised 2500 square miles and included most of the present Conway, Faulkner, Van Buren, White, Cleburne, and Perry counties and part of Yell County. Cadron was temporarily the county seat before it moved to Lewisburg in 1831, and then to Morrilton in 1883. Conway County is located along both sides of the Arkansas River, generally in a fertile, low-lying valley between the Ozark and Ouachita mountains. Farming has long been the dominant business within the county. Because of this, the population peaked in 1910 with 22,729 residents. As farming became more mechanized, many farm workers left the county and the population dropped to 15,430 in 1960. It has climbed back up to 20,715 in the 2020 census. Reports state that the railroad has 24 miles of track in the county.

379.0 GLEASON SPUR – In 1925, this station was listed as handling inbound and outbound freight. Gleason Spur was the track used to serve the local business after the Freeman Lumber Company closed. There were actually as many as three tracks here at one time. In 1929, several tracks were added to the original spur track, which was also extended. They were all removed in 1937.

While the spur tracks at Gleason Spur were removed in 1937, the location is still marked by northbound signal 3790.

Freeman Lumber Company at Gleason

The Freeman Lumber Company opened their mill at Gleason in December 1904. There was a great deal of news about the lumber company in 1908 as it was announced that the plant was going to add a shingle mill and a planing mill. The October 1, 1908, issue of *The Lumber Trade Journal* probably had the most detailed information about the plans.

> *A heading factory and two shingle mills are to be built and operated by the Freeman Lumber Company near Gleason, Ark. This announcement was made this week by H. H. Beekman of Gleason, secretary and general manager of the company, while he was in Little Rock attending to matters in connection with the opening of the new mills. He stated that the three plants are to employ about 400 men altogether and that they will be operated by the company in addition to the sawmill now operated at Gleason. The company is now building a new railroad, seven and one-half miles in length, known as the Gleason & Western, which will connect the plants with the Iron Mountain railroad, a trunk line. The new plants will start up as soon as this line is completed.*
>
> *The company has 3,700 acres of timberland where the plants are located and another tract of 5,200 acres elsewhere. Timber is secured from as far as Dardanelle, Ark. The logs are floated down the Arkansas river from there to the mouth of Cadron creek, where they are pulled up stream by a tug boat.*

A later article in the December 1, 1908, issue provided more information.

> *H. H. Beekman, secretary and treasurer of the Freeman Lumber Company at Gleason, Ark., states that the company will greatly increase its plant in the near future. Before the first of the year a shingle mill of large*

capacity and a big planing mill will be installed. This mill is now cutting exclusively cypress timber and shipping several cars a day. The timber is obtained from the big brake purchased several years ago known as the M. L. House brake, and is sufficient to supply the mill for a generation. A seven mile logging railroad is used to bring the logs to the mill. The third locomotive for the road has just been purchased.

During 1909, there were a series of issues for the Freeman Lumber Company. In May, flooding impacted the region and the sawmill was closed. A big reason for the closure was that the serving rail line was under water. According to Conway's *The Log Cabin Democrat* newspaper, there was a large force of men "engaged in raising the dump of the railroad on which the timber is brought to the plant. The dump is being raised an average of about six feet and will be completely above high water so that floods will not have the effect of causing the mills to be idle. There are now about three feet of water in the cypress bottoms, and until the dump was raised the water covered the track. The work will be completed in about a week and the mills will again begin to run on full time."

There was also a power struggle for control of the Freeman Lumber Company. On September 16th, S. D. Freeman filed for a receivership for the Freeman Lumber Company of Gleason, claiming mismanagement on the part of the present management of the company. S. D. Freeman also claimed that this management had ousted him from the company and misappropriated a large block of the capital stock which he owned. It was reported that H. H. Beekman of Kansas City, was the present head of the company, and that George Beekman of Louisiana and Harry Beekman of Gleason were also involved. The Beekmans were well represented in the fight, using Congressman Charles C. Reid and Judge W. L. Moose as their representatives in the case. The result seemed to be a change in management, but the sawmill kept operating.

Not all of the timber was obtained locally by the Freeman Lumber Company. For years, timber was rafted down the Arkansas River from as far away as Dardanelle. Later, cut timber from the area was brought in by train. Almost all of the finished timber was shipped out by rail.

On March 17, 1910, Freeman Lumber filed a complaint with the Interstate Commerce Commission (ICC) about the rates to move cypress lumber from Gleason. Apparently, the St. Louis, Iron Mountain & Southern had raised the rates soon after the mill opened for destinations in Missouri, Kansas, Illinois, Nebraska and Iowa. Since Freeman Lumber was based in Kansas City, this made it costly to move the lumber to market. One issue uncovered in the hearing was that "on that portion of the line of the St. Louis, Iron Mountain & Southern, running from Argenta, Ark., to Coffeyville, Kan., it is the only point on that division of said defendants line that produces cypress lumber in commercial quantities." The ICC did find the rates to be unreasonable and lowered them to what was considered reasonable rates.

The Freeman Lumber Company operated in several places in Arkansas and surrounding states. By 1910, its president was L. A. Hodge, the owner of a series of department stores in New York. The actual operations seemed to have been handled by vice-president T. H. Beekman, who operated a number of firms like the Boston & Kansas City Cattle Loan Company and the Beekman Lumber Company, another lumber firm that cut timber in Arkansas. G. H. Lowry, company secretary, also owned the Lowry Lumber Company, and by 1920 was president of the Turner, Dennis & Lowry Lumber Company. Finally, F. J. Mc-Clure, earlier the owner of the McClure Lumber Company at West Monroe, Louisiana, was the superintendent. The firm was basically a joint effort of a number of lumbermen and businessmen.

Things changed on March 15, 1911, when the saw and shingle mill plant at Gleason burned, causing a loss of $50,000. *The Iron Age* of March 30, 1911, stated that the Freeman plant "was one of the largest in central Arkansas and probably will be rebuilt, as the company holds timber rights on a large tract of land." More information could be found in the July 15, 1914, issue of *The Lumber Trade Journal*. "The Freeman Lumber Company's plant at Gleason, Conway county, has been placed in the hands of Sheriff Jim Gordon, who will act as receiver to dissolve the partnership and wind up the affairs of the company." Little was reported about the mill at Gleason after that.

379.8 CADRON CREEK CHIP MILL – To the west is the Cadron Creek Chip Mill, sometimes known as the Cadron Creek Woodyard, operated by Evergreen Packaging. This facility produces wood fiber using "100% U.S.-sourced wood that can be traced to the district of origin." Evergreen Packaging is part of Pactiv Evergreen, "the largest manufacturer and distributor of food service, food merchandising products and fresh beverage cartons in North America." The railroad does not serve this operation.

The firm can trace its history back to 1880 when John Cherry began his business, and 1908 when the Champion Fibre Company began mill operations in Canton, North Carolina. Pactiv began in 1959 when Central Fibre, American Boxboard, and Ohio Boxboard merged to form Packaging Corporation of America, a firm that manufactured paper for cardboard boxes. The name Pactiv dates to 1999. Evergreen Packaging dates to 2007 when International Paper Beverage Packaging Division, Blue Ridge Paper Products, and Cherry-Burrell merged to form a new company. This gave Evergreen the ownership of the former International Paper mill at Pine Bluff, Arkansas, where much of this wood fiber goes. Pactiv and Evergreen Packaging were part of Reynolds Group Holdings Limited until 2020, when they were sold under the combined name of Pactiv Evergreen. This organization was sold during October 2024 to Suzano SA of Brazil.

Just north of the Cadron Creek Chip Mill, and to the east of the tracks, is the site of an old quarry. Also to the east is the grade of Old Highway 64, one of the original vehicle roads through this area. It was later replaced by a modernized U.S. Highway 64, and then Interstate 40. Note that both the highways and the railroad loop to the northwest and then turn west to avoid a large swampy area that was once a series of old Arkansas River channels.

The Cadron Creek Chip Mill is located south of the tracks about a mile northwest of Gleason.

380.8 CONTROL POINT V380 – This is the South Switch Menifee, a 7576 foot-long siding on the east side of the mainline.

381.2 SECTION POST – This was at one time another dividing line between track gangs that maintained and repaired the railroad tracks.

381.3 MENIFEE (MF) – Menifee is one of a series of small communities along the Arkansas River that once had great dreams. This community began when Dr. Nimrod P. Menifee (spelled "Menefee" in some records and even Manifee for a time by the railroad) bought property west of Cadron Creek near the Cadron Settlement. Unlike Cadron, Menifee was located on higher ground and was a successful plantation for Dr. Menifee.

Dr. Nimrod Menifee was known as "the great dueling surgeon of early Arkansas" and was involved in a series of duels and fights over his lifetime. He probably came to Arkansas to avoid retaliation for winning a duel in Kentucky. He invested heavily in the region, and his wealth was mostly based on this land speculation. He provided the land for the creation of Lewisburg (the second county seat of Conway County), Point Remove, Oppelo, and Menifee. He also started several businesses to help in the development of these communities, including the Menifee Ferry on the Arkansas River. Menifee was also elected to a seat in the Arkansas House of Representatives in 1831 as the representative from Conway County, and served at the Constitutional Convention of 1836.

Despite his efforts to develop real estate and to serve in various Arkansas government offices, Menifee still was involved in some of the most bitter disputes and duels caused by the early political tensions in the Arkansas Territory. Many of these fights came about as different families and political groups tried to gain the most power in the territory and state. One of the most infamous was a fight with publisher William Woodruff. In this fight, Menifee used his cane to stop Woodruff from using his pistol. He even served as surgeon and second in a duel between two justices of the Arkansas Superior Court, Andrew Scott and Joseph Selden.

Menifee's luck ran out on January 29, 1842, when he had a knife-pistol duel with a neighbor named Phillips. In the fight, Phillips was shot, but he killed Menifee with his knife. As reported in the *Boston Medical and Surgical Journal* (March 2, 1842), "Dr. Nimrod Menifee of Lewisburg Co., Arkansas, was horribly and fatally mutilated in a savage combat with a neighbor – being stabbed and cut in no less than thirty-one places." Menifee was buried in the Old Lewisburg Cemetery, while Philips hung on for a year before he died. The properties of Menifee were so complicated that settling his estate went to the Arkansas Supreme Court.

The community of Menifee remained small until the Little Rock & Fort Smith built through the area. The Menifee family provided the right-of-way for the railroad in return for having a station stop at Menifee. With plenty of cotton farming in the area, Menifee grew with a significant migration of black families from states east of the Mississippi River. The Menifee post office opened in 1881. By 1890, the black population in Conway County was 39.4 percent of the total population, and Menifee was considered to be a model of black communities. It had Dr. G. W. McNeice, the first "colored" physician licensed in Conway County, a well-respected school, and a number of wealthy blacks who owned their own businesses.

A decade of floods and then droughts, plus the Great Depression, did heavy damage to area farming, and the population took a big drop as jobs went away. The population slowly recovered over the next several decades, but a large part of Menifee was destroyed by a May 6, 1960, tornado. Much of this rebuilding took place to the north along the new U.S. Highway 64 instead of next to the tracks.

Needing investment money for the community caused Menifee to incorporate in 1965. This led to street improvements, a city water system, a parks and recreation program, police protection, and a local district court. The 1970 census reported that the population of Menifee was 251. The Pinecrest Lumber Company opened in 1972 as a part of the Arkansas Kraft Company. Located on the west side of Menifee, the sawmill is now the Pinecrest Lumber Division of Green Bay Packaging. In 1979, a Federal District Court order consolidated the Menifee, Plumerville, and Morrilton school districts into the South Conway County School District. Despite this, the old Menifee High School Gymnasium (built in 1938) remains, located on the northwestern corner of North Park and East Mustang streets, and was listed on the National Register of Historic Places on June 6, 2002.

The population of Menifee peaked in 1980 with 368 residents, but it has dropped to 274 in the 2020 census. Of this, more than 75% were reported to be "Black or African American (non-Hispanic)." Menifee is still somewhat known in Arkansas for being the home of Thomas Alonzo Johnson, a graduate of Eastside High School at Menifee. Johnson was the first African American basketball player for the Arkansas Razorbacks.

On August 31, 2022, Menifee made national news when it was banned from writing speeding tickets for one year. Arkansas state law limits revenue from traffic citations to no more than 30% of a city's revenue, and it was almost half for Menifee. As stated by the district prosecuting attorney, "Clearly, they were writing substantially more tickets than other communities that were similarly sized." The defense of the community was that a change in leadership had made Menifee aggressive in dealing with unpaid bills and fines and that some of the revenue was from old tickets.

The Railroad at Menifee

The railroad arrived at Menifee during the early 1870s and used a right-of-way provided by the Menifee family. The community, with a listed elevation of 288 feet, was located west of Cadron Creek at the east end of five miles of almost flat grades through the Arkansas River Valley. The early business district was alongside the tracks, with Railroad Avenue (the old highway) in the same location. There was one problem as this area had some history of flooding during high water on the nearby Arkansas River.

In 1907, the railroad listed an 80-car siding at Menifee, plus a mail crane for the local post office. The year 1910 was a busy one for the railroad and Menifee as a series of hearings were held about building a depot to replace the boxcar that had served that purpose for years. After discussion between the citizens of Menifee and the railroad, a petition was sent to the Railroad Commission of Arkansas demanding that the St. Louis, Iron Mountain & Southern build a new depot at Menifee. The petition stated that the current boxcar was inadequate as patrons had to seek shelter elsewhere during rain or cold.

An interesting detail about the petition made the news, and almost ended the hearings. The petition had been signed by a number of women, who at the time did not have the right to vote or sign legal petitions. In fact, newspaper reports stated that women were not citizens under Arkansas law. However, enough men signed the petition that the Railroad Commission took action on the matter.

While the petition was submitted in early June 1910, it wasn't until the August meeting of the Railroad Commission of Arkansas that a hearing was held. At the meeting on August 3rd, the railroad was ordered to build a depot at Menifee. The 15' x 41' wood-frame building opened during October and cost a reported $824.

In 1925, the station and platform were on the west side of the tracks. It housed a ticket agency and a freight agency for carload and less volumes. The depot didn't last long as the train order signal was retired in December 1929, and the depot and its coal bin were removed in 1932. This left two storehouses and a 6' x 7' toilet on the east side of the tracks, plus a railroad telephone and a mail crane at Menifee. For the trains, there was a 91-car siding. In 1969, the siding was shown to be 4378 feet long, capable of holding 84 freight cars. The siding was extended to 7536 feet by the 1980s. Today, little of Menifee exists alongside the tracks, and the railroad has a siding in this area. Menifee is also known as where the railroad changes from generally heading north or northwest, to generally more of a westerly direction.

The Pinecrest Lumber Division of Green Bay Packaging is located west of Menifee near Milepost 383. There is a steady stream of inbound loads of timber and outbound loads of lumber. However, all is handled by truck as the plant is not served by the railroad.

382.4 CONTROL POINT V382 – This is the north switch of the siding at Menifee. Just a short distance west of CP V382, and to the north of the tracks, is the Pinecrest Lumber Division, part of Green Bay Packaging. The Pinecrest Lumber Division was founded in 1973 and the existing mill was constructed in 1974. The plant was expanded in 2019 with the addition of a new dry kiln to the existing two kilns. This project allowed a second shift in the sawmill and planer mill to be added to the plant.

To the south is a series of small ponds, known as Tank Lake, that can be much larger during wet periods.

382.6 TRACK REALIGNMENT – In 1930, almost 1100 feet of track and a bridge were removed and a new and straighter grade was built here. The old grade can still be found in the woods to the north of the tracks.

385.7 SITE OF 1945 COLLISION – On July 1, 1945, at 12:22pm, passenger train Nos. 116 and 117 collided here, resulting in the death of 1 train-service employee and the injury of 132 passengers and 21 employees ("1 railway-mail clerk, 12 dining-car employees, 1 train porter, 3 employees not on duty and 4 train-service employees on duty"). The Interstate Commerce Commission (ICC) reported that the cause was "failure to obey a meet order," but it was actually much more complicated than that.

Both trains were running behind schedule and the dispatcher was trying to arrange a meet location. According to train order No. 234, Plumerville was established as the meeting point. Train No. 116 was to receive the information at Conway, while No. 117 was to receive it at Russellville. However, before the orders could be delivered, the dispatcher issued a new train order No. 241, which changed the meeting point between these trains to Menifee. Before this train order was issued to the two train crews, train order No. 242, which annulled train order No. 241, was issued, and the meet was back at Plumerville. At Conway, train No. 116 received the proper train order to meet at Plumerville, but train No. 117 was to receive the updated train orders at Morrilton. Somehow, the train crew received a copy of train order No. 241 as well as the correct train order No. 234.

The ICC reported in detail what happened next. Basically, the locomotive engineer of No. 117 saw the Menifee meet while the conductor and flagman saw the Plumerville meet. As reported, "the flagman said that when their train was about 2 miles north of Plumerville he sounded the meeting-point signal on the communicating system. He did not hear the engine-whistle signal sounded in response to his signal, but he felt the brakes being applied and thought the engineer was preparing to stop the train in the vicinity of the north siding-switch." However, the train didn't stop, and the flagman used the communicating system to send a stop signal while the conductor opened the emergency valve at the south switch. Train No. 117 stopped about 1.5 miles south of the north siding-switch at Plumerville. The train's porter, who was riding on the locomotive, dropped off to flag while No. 117 began to back northward towards Plumerville at a speed of 15 miles per hour. Unfortunately, train No. 116 came around a curve, passed the porter, and hit train No. 117 at a speed of 45 miles per hour.

According to the report, the "engine of No. 116 was derailed and stopped on its right side, east of the main track and parallel to it, 220 feet north of the point of collision, and was badly damaged. The front truck of the first car was derailed. The engine of No. 117 was derailed and stopped upright and in line with the track, 320 feet north of the point of collision, and was badly damaged. The front truck of the first car was derailed, and the front end of the car was crushed inward about 6 feet."

The ICC report provided a great amount of detail about how the railroad was being operated. It stated that trains are operated by time-table and train orders and that "during the 30-day period preceding the day of the accident, the average daily movement in the vicinity of the point of accident was 20.2 trains." It also stated that the track was level and lined with vegetation.

The report also included information about the two trains, each of which was being pulled by Pacific-type locomotives (4-6-2) that had been built by Alco in 1924. "No. 116, a north-bound first-class passenger train, consisted of engine 6619, one baggage car, one baggage-mail car, three coaches, one dining-observation car and two coaches, in the order named. All cars were of steel construction. No. 117, a south-bound first-class passenger train, consisted of engine 6603, one baggage-mail car, one baggage car, two coaches, one tourist-sleeping car, one Pullman sleeping car and one dining-observation car, in the order named. All cars were of steel construction."

Later that year, Automatic Block Signaling (ABS) was installed over the Van Buren Subdivision, signals that would have made this type of accident less likely.

The train station at Plumerville was once located just to the west of the Van Buren Street Grade Crossing.

386.8 PLUMERVILLE (MR) – The train station at Plumerville was located just west of the grade crossing with Van Buren Street, with a benchmark indicating an elevation of 298 feet. Plumerville began as Plummer's Station, a stage station on the Memphis to Fort Smith line of the Butterfield Overland Mail stage route. The name of the community changed often, and the post office used at least four different names: Plummer's Station (1873-1875), Plummer (1875-1881), Plumer (1881-1881), and Plumerville (1881-Date). There was also a Plummerville (1882-1895) nearby. The railroad also changed the name several times: Plummers by 1871, Plummerville by 1875, and then Plumerville.

Plumerville is another river valley town that moved from the river to the stage road and then to the railroad. The name dates to 1833 when Samuel Plummer purchased 160 acres on what was claimed to be the "first high ground" north of the Arkansas River. A stage road and then a telegraph line were built across his property, and the railroad followed the same basic route during the early 1870s. A right-of-way was acquired from Plummer and Plummer's Station was established. The train station attracted businesses, especially those that supported local farming. The town was incorporated in 1880 with a population of 135.

One of the most significant events in Plumerville was the assassination of John Middleton Clayton on January 29, 1889. John Clayton was the younger brother of Powell Clayton, a Governor of Arkansas. He was elected to the Arkansas House of Representatives in 1871, and then to the Arkansas Senate in 1873 where he served as Speaker of the Senate pro tempore for part of his term. In 1888, John Clayton ran for the office of Arkansas' second congressional district in the United States House of Representatives as a Republican. The election was described as the most fraudulent in Arkansas' history, with at least one Conway County polling place being robbed by four armed and masked white men. They took what was described as being a ballot box full of votes for Clayton from a predominantly black voting precinct. Clayton lost by only a few votes out of about 34,000, and he started an investigation of the fraud by coming to Plumerville. During the evening of Tuesday, January 29, 1889, he was shot and killed through the window of the boarding house where he was staying. The assassin was never found, but a review of the election resulted in Democrat Clifton R. Breckinridge being removed from the office, which he won two years later. The event led to Plumerville being used as an example of corruption and violence in politics, and even was the subject of a speech by Frederick Douglass later that year.

Throughout the late 1800s, Plumerville remained a center for area farming, and it was described as being the best "mercantile town on the road from Little Rock to Coffeyville" in 1901 by the *Arkansas Gazette*. The local economy was so good that the Bank of Plumerville was a repeated target of robbers. The town was also known as having its own water system, and a natural gas system which was used with the city street lighting. The town's population peaked in 1920 with 702 residents. However, the farm disasters (flooding and drought) of the late 1920s, and then the Great Depression, hurt the area's economy. Another factor that impacted Plumerville was the construction of the new U.S. Highway 64, located north of town.

The population dropped to 541 in the 1940 census report, but during the 1930s, Plumerville had one of only four high schools in Conway County. The local school lasted until the 1979 merger of many area schools into the South Conway School District. The old downtown area of Plumerville burned in a 1987 fire, but most of the community still survives between the railroad tracks and Interstate 40 to the north. A few local retail stores and the Hixson Lumber Company still operate at Plumerville. Much of the town is basically a residential area for families who work in the region. The population again peaked at 854 residents in 2000, and has slowly dropped to 734 in the 2020 census.

One claim to fame of Plumerville is that it was the birth place of John Howard Yancey on April 27, 1918. Yancey was a highly decorated Marine Corps combat veteran of World War II and the Korean War who received two Navy Crosses, a Silver Star, a Bronze Star and three Purple Hearts. During the Guadalcanal Campaign, Yancey's leadership earned him a promotion to lieutenant and the Navy Cross. In Korea, he fought in the Battle of Chosin Reservoir and was awarded his second Navy Cross, a Silver Star, and a Purple Heart. While he was nominated for the Medal of Honor, no other officer survived the battle so no official report was ever submitted. Yancey was promoted to captain and was assigned as the commanding officer of the Marine Reserve unit in Little Rock. He attempted to serve in the Vietnam War, but his injuries, including losing all of his teeth, prevented it. His rejection led to the quote that he is known best for: "Hell, I wasn't planning on biting the sonsofbitches to death."

The Railroad at Plumerville

Like the town itself, the railroad used several different names for the station stop during the 1870s and 1880s. Much of the right-of-way for the railroad was acquired from Samuel Plummer and his family, and the station became somewhat important on the line. When the railroad was being rebuilt between Conway and Cadron, Plumerville was often cited in the reports. This trend continued when the Little Rock & Fort Smith Railway reported that the laying of new steel rails had reached Plumerville on August 26, 1903. The report also noted that "The work is being done principally by convicts." General improvements along the line in 1904 also cited Plumerville. In that year, a rock crusher was operating at Plumerville to produce ballast for the track.

Plumerville had a depot from almost the start of the railroad. On May 13, 1905, the railroad depot "was destroyed by fire, entailing a loss estimated at $2,500." An investigation determined that the fire was likely arson, done to cover-up the robbery of the depot's mail pouch. A boxcar was quickly located at Plumerville to serve as the temporary depot and telegraph office, with no room for baggage or passengers. This led to public meetings to demand a new station, which was built by July 1906, and described as possibly the largest depot between Little Rock and Fort Smith. In 1907, the depot housed a daytime telegraph office. Nearby was a 100-car siding, a mail crane, three old car-bodies, a store house, several tool houses, and an oil house, most located between Van Buren and Overcup streets. There was also a cotton platform to the west that served the Consumers Cotton Oil Company. It was removed in October 1943. Stock pens were installed north of the depot in 1923, but removed in November 1944.

Nothing remains of the Plumerville station, but signal 3868 marks its location.

Like many towns along the route of the Little Rock & Fort Smith, Plumerville has a street named Railroad, noting the importance of the rail line.

During March 1916, a fire burned part of downtown Plumerville. Damaged were two hotels, the plant of the *Plumerville Pilot*, the Iron Mountain depot, and two other buildings. The wooden depot was replaced by a 24' x 93' brick depot in 1917. It was soon being promoted as one of the finest stations in Arkansas. The agent at Plumerville handled the local business with 3 cotton dealers and 2 cotton gins. There was also 1 stock pen with a capacity of 2 stock cars. In 1916, the U.S. House of Representatives (64th Congress, 1st Session) conducted a hearing about the Arkansas River. The Board of Governors of the Arkansas River Improvement Association estimated that Plumerville received 2500 tons of freight a year (25 carloads of meal and hulls and 100 miscellaneous carloads) and shipped out 4000 tons (4000 bales of cotton, 50 carloads of cotton seed, 50 carloads of logs and staves, and 50 carloads of rock), all by rail.

The year 1925 was about the peak of the business at the Plumerville depot, located to the east of the tracks. The depot housed a ticket agency that also served as a coupon ticket station. It was also listed as a freight agency for less-than-carload freight all the way up to carload volumes.

In 1944, the station had a telegraph or telephone office but not a train order office. Outside there was a mail crane for putting mail onto passing trains. There was also a 77-car siding (2867 feet in length with the north switch 1924 feet north of the station) that was retired as part of the ABS signal installation the next year. As stated by the railroad, at certain locations, "the old short sidings were no longer needed." At a few locations, "it was desirable to leave short tracks for industrial purposes." Plumerville was one of these locations. It should be noted that the siding was on the west side of the mainline, and it was actually the original mainline. When a siding was installed at Plumerville, the mainline was moved slightly northward, creating the siding. By the late 1960s, Plumerville wasn't even listed in the employee timetables. However, Railroad Avenue can still be found on the north side of the tracks as the railroad passes through town.

Heading north, trains start an almost 3 mile climb at Plumerville, with grades as steep as 0.72%. The grade starts at an elevation of 289 feet and reaches the top at 363 feet.

387.9 SOUTH END OF DETOUR NO. 5 – This is another realignment of the railroad that reduced grades and curvature. Between here and Milepost 389.7, the original grade was to the south (railroad-west), curving back and forth along the low ridge.

389.7 NORTH END OF DETOUR NO. 5 – This is where the improvements on the track south of Morrilton ended.

391.2 ARKANSAS HIGHWAY 9 – The railroad passes under Arkansas Highway 9, which connects Arkansas Highway 5 at Crows (north of Malvern) with Morrilton and on north to Mammoth Spring. There is also a segment from Malvern southward to Eagle Mills. The bridge is part of a 1972 bypass built around Morrilton. Arkansas Highway 9 is one of the original state highways, created in 1926. Arkansas Highway 113 also uses this bridge as it heads south across the Arkansas River to Arkansas Highway 10. This road has traditionally marked the east end of Morrilton.

This area is the crest of a grade from both directions. The track peaks at an elevation of 382 feet, with grades of 0.5% in each direction. This grade is created by Burrow Mountain, located north of the tracks and peaking at an elevation of 613 feet. As stated in several Morrilton reports, Burrow Mountain creates a unique community landmark, located on the northeast side of town. This mountain forced most of the town's development to be to the south and west, "sandwiched in between the base around Burrow Mountain and the railroad."

During November 2019, UP 8264 headed north and past the south switch at Morrilton. This location has become a popular railroad viewing locations thanks to the opening of the Point Remove Brewing Company.

391.3 SOUTH SWITCH MORRILTON – To the east of the mainline are the remains of the old Morrilton Siding, now known as the Morrilton Business Track. The south switch is located just west of Ward Drive. The siding was often shown as being at Milepost 391.91. In 1907, it was shown to be an 80-car siding, a 53-car siding in 1944, and was expanded to a 90-car siding by 1951. In 1969, it was listed as being 4734 feet long, and later 4664 feet. Because the tracks are used only for switching, there are warnings that trains should stop before passing over street crossings "due to rusty rail conditions."

391.8 DETOUR NO. 5½ – This is another place where the railroad was straightened and the grades reduced. Here, the tracks were moved to the south, providing more room for U.S. Highway 64.

392.3 NORTH SWITCH MORRILTON – The north switch of the Morrilton Business Track is located immediately east of St. Joseph Street. To the west are the last of what were once a series of industry tracks that were located at Morrilton. The Morrilton Business Track is also known as the Old Siding by railroad workers.

Morrilton was once a very busy station along the LR&FS. Today, little remains except for a few tracks, the brick depot, and this sign.

392.5 MORRILTON (K) – Morrilton was not the first community in the area. By the time the railroad arrived in late 1870, this area was known as Lewisburg. When the railroad was built it was several miles north of Lewisburg, a port town founded in 1825 on the Arkansas River. During much of the 1800s, Lewisburg was an important port town, so being on the route northward into the farmlands and hills made the depot area important. Lewisburg started about 1820 when Major William Lewis, his son, Stephen D. Lewis, and Dr. Nimrod P. Menifee, established a port settlement where Point Remove Creek flowed into the Arkansas River. A trading post known as Lewisburgh was opened by Stephen D. Lewis in 1825. The combination of a river port and a trading post made Lewisburgh one of the most important locations in Western Arkansas.

In 1831, property was acquired from Menifee to be the location of a courthouse and jail for Conway County. Conway County was created as Arkansas' 11th county on October 20, 1825. When the county was created, the town of Cadron became the temporary county seat. In 1829, the county seat moved to the home of Stephen Harris (Harrisburg) until a more permanent location could be chosen. Menifee and Stephen D. Lewis built a log cabin courthouse and the seat moved to Lewisburgh in 1831. The following year, a post office opened and kept using the name Lewisburgh, even when the community shortened its name to Lewisburg.

By the early 1850s, Lewisburg was a thriving river town, but its location at the south end of the county created problems for many residents. Because of this, the county seat moved again in 1850 when Springfield obtained the title. In 1871, the Little Rock & Fort Smith Railroad was building west toward Fort Smith. This construction could place Lewisburg on both the Arkansas River and a railroad, and after donating $5000 for a new courthouse and $10,000 for a stone jail, Lewisburg was again the county seat starting in 1873.

Unfortunately for Lewisburg, the railroad was built about a mile to the north. Why was Lewisburg bypassed? Reportedly, the route used was shorter, although it required a grade over a low ridge where Morrilton now sits. However, the biggest reason was that the town of Lewisburg was certain that the railroad had to build through their community and they refused to provide any financial or land assistance. With this, the route went north of Lewisburg and a new town was platted on the property of Edwin James Morrill, George H. Morrill, and James Miles Moose.

When the new railroad station town of Lewisburg was created, Division Street was located on the property line between the lands of Morrill and Moose. One block to the east on his property was Moose Street, and to the west on the other owner's property was Morrill Street. Reportedly a flip of a coin made the town Morrilton instead of Mooseville. However, Moose Street was located just east of the railroad's station. Morrilton quickly grew with 770 residents in 1880 and 1644 in 1890. Meanwhile,

215

Lewisburg saw its population drop from a reported 2000 in 1860 to 356 in 1880. The Lewisburgh post office closed in 1882, and the county seat moved to Morrilton in 1883. Within a few years, Lewisburg was little more than a ferry landing with just a few residents.

The 1870s saw a number of German-speaking immigrants move to the area thanks to the sale of land grant lands by the Little Rock & Fort Smith Railroad, and other lands by the U.S. government. These new immigrants with their Roman Catholic and Lutheran religions immediately faced challenges from the Protestants who had lived in the area for half-a-century. This encouraged the new arrivals to create their own towns and communities, but none really competed with Morrilton for the business trade. In 1879, the Morrillton post office opened and the town incorporated on November 24, 1879. The name of the city was simplified in 1927 when the spelling was changed to Morrilton.

The first public school for white students opened in 1881, with a school for black students opening in 1895. Many of the schools in Conway County consolidated during the late 1970s to form the new South Conway County district, which now operates its high school as Morrilton High School.

By 1891, the businesses of Morrilton dominated the region. There were more than two dozen general stores, nine grocers, four drug stores, two hardware stores, a bakery, two barbers, a harness and saddlery, a jeweler, a gunsmith and machinist, a meat market, a marble yard, and a dentist. The town also featured a steam mill and cotton gin, a fur and hides dealer, three shoemakers, three blacksmiths and wagon makers, a tinwork and roofer, a horse and mules dealer, a custom tailor, a lumber yard, three furniture makers and undertakers, and a books and stationery dealer. There were two livery stables, eight building contractors, two brick masons, three dressmakers and millinery shops, 14 physicians, seven law offices, nine notaries, two newspapers, and nine hotels. As stated by the *Biographical and Historical Memoirs of Western Arkansas* (Goodspeed Publishers, 1891), Morrilton was a successful community.

> *Morrilton has ample reason to be proud of her
> business men. The enterprise of the Morrilton citizens
> has become proverbial over the State. No finer body of
> wide-awake, enterprising, thorough going men can be
> found in the South. It takes men to make cities, and
> right here permit us to remark that Morrilton has that
> kind of men.*

The city grew to 2424 residents by the 1910 census, and the lots around the railroad station were full of retail businesses. The Peer's Hotel was located across the street from the new brick depot. There were general stores, drug stores, barbers, a farm implement business, restaurants, groceries, hardware stores and an undertaker and furniture business.

The population had climbed over 3000 when the 1921 *Arkansas Marketing and Industrial Guide* was published. It listed a number of businesses at Morrilton, including the Morrilton Bottling Works, Morrilton Compress Company, Morrilton Cotton Oil Company, Morrilton Milling Company, Morrilton Ice & Fuel Company, Groblebe Lumber Company, and Arkansas Light & Power Company. A Missouri Pacific map of Morrilton shows companies like Earl Brothers, Federal Compress & Warehousing, Pierce Young Lumber Company, Lions Oil Company, Topeka Flour Company, Petit Jean Feed Company, Stalling Brothers, Otto Leinhart, and Morrilton Lumber Company. Over the next several decades, the population continued to grow as Morrilton supported the local farming, manufacturing, and retail businesses, plus the county government. During the Great Depression, Petit Jean State Park was created nearby using Civilian Conservation Corps (CCC) labor. The park has had enormous benefits for Morrilton since it was Arkansas' first state park and is currently the most visited state park in Arkansas. Interestingly, some of the land used by the park was earlier owned by the Little Rock & Fort Smith Railway.

Many of the retail businesses moved away from U.S. Highway 64 through downtown (Broadway Street) and north to the exits off of Interstate 40 when that route was built. However, downtown is still busy with most storefronts occupied and doing business. The population peaked at 7355 residents in 1980, settled to 6551 in 1990, and has grown back to 6992 in the 2020 census. John R. Stallings (1935–2008), who was born here, is often cited as a success story from Morrilton. Stallings was a mathematician known for his seminal contributions to geometric group theory and 3-manifold topology.

The Railroad at Morrilton

Ever since the Little Rock & Fort Smith was built, downtown Morrilton has been centered around the railroad. Lewisburg, which preceeded Morrilton, was an early goal of the construction. The *American Railroad Journal* (May 14, 1870) reported that the LR&FS was expected to have another 10 miles completed by the middle of May 1870, and to be completed to Lewisburg by July 4, 1870. A month later, the magazine reported that the railroad had completed grading to Lewisburg, with only the bridge over the Cadron remaining to be finished before track laying would begin. Scheduled train service to Lewisburg (Morrilton) began on November 21, 1870, and the first staffed railway station was reportedly opened in 1873. Town history states that the first station agent, J. W. Boot, was the one who flipped a coin to determine if the town would be named after Moose or Morrill. Various reports from the time stated that trains were regularly operating to Lewisburg, and that fifty more miles westward were graded with ties in place. To get to Fort Smith, passengers would connect with a stage coach until the line was built further westward.

In 1886, the town was known as Morrillton and the Little Rock & Fort Smith passed through the new town using the right-of-way of Railroad Avenue. The facilities of the railroad were between Moose and Division streets, with the depot to the south (railroad-west) and the freight house and cotton platforms to the north. The railroad also had a siding through town, located to the north of the mainline.

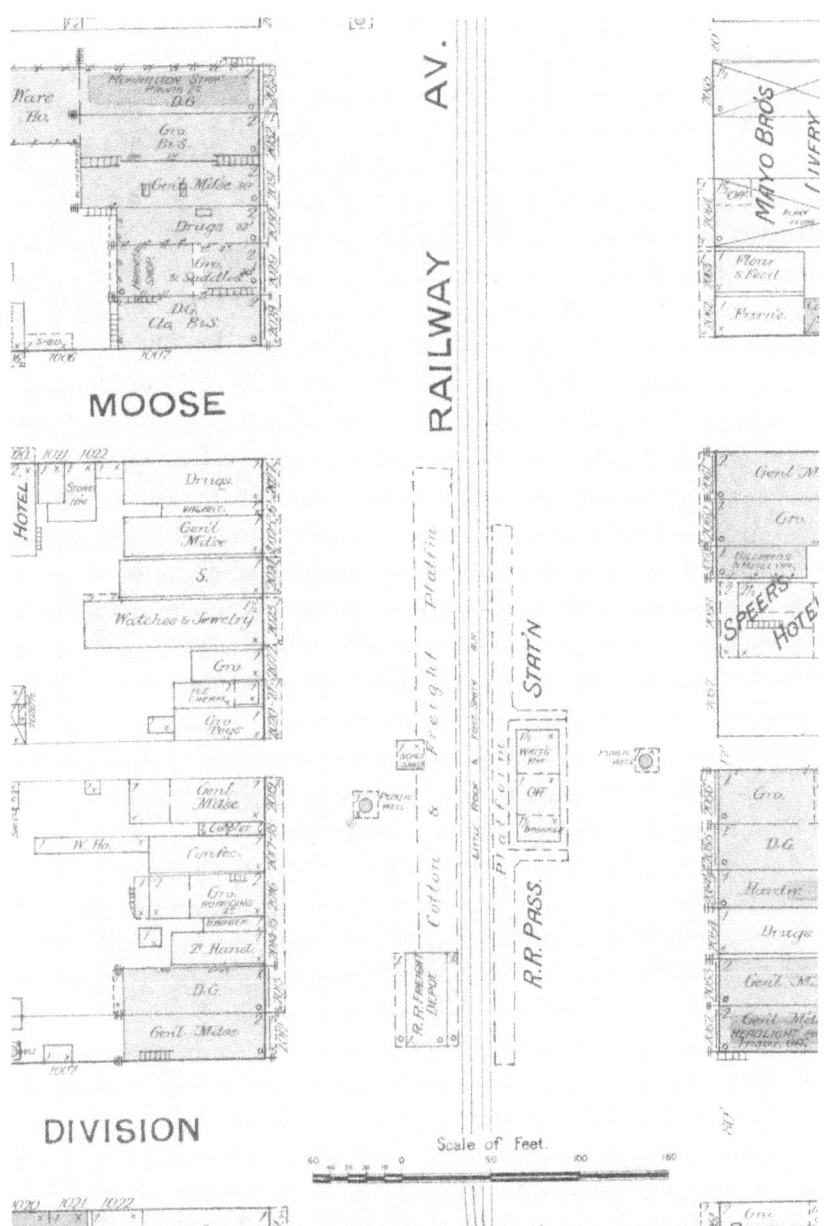

The Little Rock & Fort Smith passed through the new town of Morrillton using the right-of-way of Railroad Avenue. The facilities of the railroad were between Moose and Division streets, with the depot to the south and the freight house and cotton platforms to the north of the east-west running tracks. The railroad also had a siding through town, located to the north of the mainline. *Sanborn Fire Insurance Map from Morrilton, Conway County, Arkansas.* Sanborn Map Company, July 1886. Map. Retrieved from the Library of Congress, https://www.loc.gov/item/sanborn00310_001/.

To clean up the downtown area, within a few years the cotton platforms were moved to both ends of town. A small rail yard developed several blocks east of the depot by 1890. About the same time, the J. L. Lucas cotton gin and feed mill had located several blocks to the west of the depot. As traffic through the train station picked up, the Peer's Hotel located across the street. By 1896, the St. Louis Cotton Compress (capacity of 600 bales per day) was located east of Howard Street and south of the tracks. To the west, the J. L. Lucas operation had become the J. B. Wooten's cotton seed oil mill and gin. Within a few years, it had changed again to become the Moose Ginning Company.

After 1900, the railroad's right-of-way had been broken down into North Railroad Avenue and South Railroad Avenue. A challenge for the railroad was a grade that approached Morrilton from each direction. Over the years, the railroad has had several projects to raise the approaches and lower the main hill. In 1902, the railroad had a steam shovel working in the area, according to the *Arkansas Gazette* (July 4, 1902).

> *Morrilton – A steam shovel was brought up from Little Rock Sunday and put to work Monday cutting down the hill back of M. D. Shelby's residence. There is also one at work near Germantown. These steam monsters load a car full of dirt every four minutes, and are easily worked, as everything is done by steam. It is a great curiosity and a large number of our citizens have been out to see it work.*

Today, Morrilton is at the top of a 0.5% grade at an elevation of 379 feet. To make more room for the streets, the freight depot moved eastward several blocks in 1903-04, and was located at St. Joseph Street. Another ownership change had the St. Louis Cotton Compress become the Morrilton Cotton Oil Company, which had its own cotton gin. At the west end of town, the Moose Ginning Company had closed and been replaced by small warehouses, sheds, and oil tanks. A new Morrilton Cotton Oil Company facility was built further west of town within a few years. On the east side of downtown, the Morrilton Cotton

Warehouse Company was operating east of where the Morrilton Cotton Oil Company had been located, which simply had their cotton gin there. A fruit warehouse was also built across the street from the freight station.

A seasonal business at Morrilton was traveling shows. On October 23, 1910, the Miller Brothers' Carnival Company loaded and left Morrilton after a series of shows, and headed through Little Rock on its way to Camden, Arkansas.

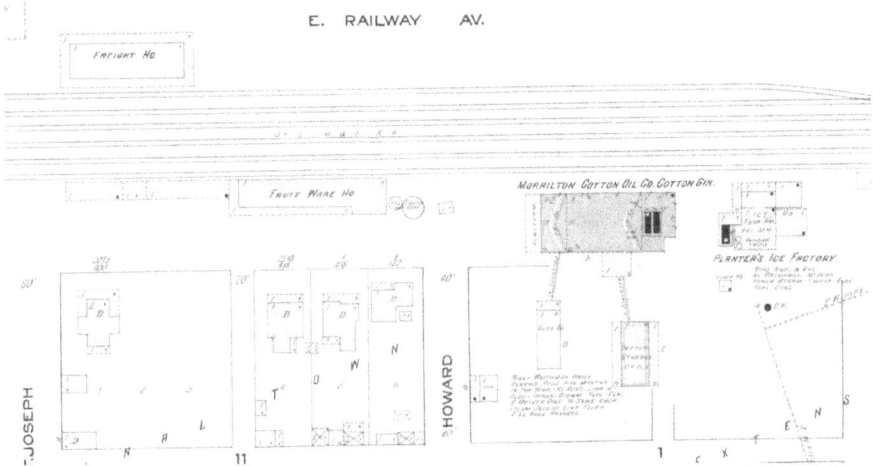

By 1913, much of the freight activity at Morrilton was located east of downtown around the freight house. On the south side of the tracks was a large fruit warehouse, the cotton gin of the Morrilton Cotton Oil Company, and the Planter's Ice Factory. Further east was the Morrilton Cotton Warehouse Company. *Sanborn Fire Insurance Map from Morrilton, Conway County, Arkansas.* Sanborn Map Company, October 1913. Map. Retrieved from the Library of Congress, https://www.loc.gov/item/sanborn00310_006/.

In 1915, the U.S. House of Representatives (64th Congress, 1st Session) held a series of hearings about making improvements on the Arkansas River to compete against the parallel railroad. As a part of the hearing, the Arkansas River Improvement Association of Morrilton provided data about the freight moving in and out of the town. It stated that 28,400 tons of freight per year were shipped out of Morrilton, while 51,220 tons per year were shipped to Morrilton. Among the leading outbound shipments were cotton (40,000 bales), meal and hulls (300 carloads), cotton seed (100 carloads), cattle (100 carloads), logs (100 carloads), fruit (100 cars), and railroad ties and rock (50 carloads each). Other products such as cottonseed oil, hogs, hay, strawberry plants, staves, and fertilizer shipped out in smaller volumes. Missouri Pacific also had 4 stock pens, with water, with the ability to hold 12 stock cars of livestock.

More than 44 different product categories were shown to be shipped to Morrilton. Some of the largest volumes included cotton into the compress (20,000 bales), cotton seed (200 carloads by rail and 30 by boat), dry goods and groceries (400 carloads) and miscellaneous groceries (375 carloads), coal (200 carloads), flour and feed (150 carloads each), fertilizer (100 carloads), meal and meat (50 carloads each), brick and sand (50 carloads), and logs (50 carloads). Many of the rest of the products moved in small volumes, but were essential for the community. These included various seeds and livestock feed, soap and lard, fruit jars, oils and gasoline, fruits like oranges and bananas, automobiles and farm implements, and construction materials.

A few changes took place during the late 1910s. The Peer's Hotel had become the Speer Hotel. The fruit warehouse had become a warehouse for soft drinks, feed and cotton seed. The Morrilton Compress Company had built a compress and warehouse east of where the Morrilton Cotton Warehouse Company was located.

Like many places along the line, tracks were added until about the 1920s, and then many were slowly retired. Union Pacific still showed a small yard east of the Morrilton depot soon after its merger with Missouri Pacific. Today, only one short house track remains. The siding was cut back east of downtown to avoid blocking grade crossings. And finally, services at the depot were reduced, and then they disappeared.

Trains heading north to Fort Smith head west from Morrilton and then curve to the northwest. It is also downhill as the track heads to the west, with the next grade near Atkins at Milepost 405.

Immediately to the east of the Morrilton depot is Moose Street, named for town co-founder James Miles Moose.

Across the tracks to the north of the Morrilton depot is the Morrill Building, built by the Morrill family in the town named for them.

Several towns along the LR&FS have cabooses on display. Located at the Morrilton depot is former Union Pacific caboose 25443. This caboose was one of 100 built in 1959 by Union Pacific in their own Omaha Shops, designated Class CA-7. They were the first new Union Pacific cabooses to receive five-digit numbers. This caboose was built in February 1959, retired on May 11, 1989, and then donated to the City of Morrilton.

Jay Gould's "Visit" to Morrilton

During April of 1890, Jay Gould was touring the southern lines of his railroad properties. Among these were the Little Rock & Fort Smith and the Kansas & Arkansas Valley. These rail companies connected the mainline at Little Rock with the agricultural lines in Kansas, and Jay Gould wanted to see the progress being made on this new route.

The private train of Jay Gould arrived at Little Rock about noon on Tuesday, April 22nd. The train left after being serviced and headed for Kansas. According to Little Rock newspaper reports: "At Morrilton, fifty miles from here, his special train ran through an open switch, and a considerable wreck resulted, but no one was hurt – at least it is so reported. The wreck caused considerable delay to traffic, as the passenger train due at five o'clock will not arrive until midnight." Other reports stated that the derailment of their engine and baggage car at Morrilton delayed the party several hours.

The Morrilton Train Depot

Lewisburg, later Morrillton, then Morrilton, had a train depot and freight office from about when the Little Rock & Fort Smith reached this location. Originally, both were located between Division and Moose streets, with the board and batten freight house to the north of the tracks and the wooden depot to the south. Before 1908, the freight house was moved several blocks to the east. The depot was a busy building as the railroad had a day and night telegraph office here. As business increased, the depot began to be called "entirely inadequate for present needs." In 1915, construction began on a new brick station at Morrilton.

This photo from the collection of the Conway County History Museum shows the early wooden Morrilton depot, busy for a big event. Photo courtesy of the Conway County History Museum, Morrilton, Arkansas.

The St. Louis, Iron Mountain & Southern announced in 1915 that it was going to spend about $15,000 to build a modern brick depot at Morrilton. Researchers will find numerous dates from 1907 through 1916 credited to the construction, but industry trade magazines clearly show that construction began in August 1915. The new depot was called a typical Missouri Pacific station with common elements used in stations across Arkansas. It was built as a single-story dark red brick building with a tile roof and Mediterranean styling. The details included a hipped roof with wide overhanging eaves and exposed rafters supported by decorative brackets. The building is 149 feet long and features five main sections. As described by the National Register, the main building has "a white waiting room (25' x 31') with restrooms for men and women in the east section (20' x 20'); a ticket office (31' x 16' 1") with a bay section (5' x 16' 1") extending northward toward the railroad tracks; a black waiting room (25' x 26'); an open breezeway paved with red brick (17' 7" x 20'); and a freight station (45' 5" x 20') on the west end of the building."

The brick station at Morrilton faces Railroad Avenue to the south. The building currently houses the Conway County History Museum.

In 1925, Missouri Pacific reported that Morrilton's depot served as a ticket agency as well as a coupon ticket station. The depot handled passengers at the east end of the station and baggage and express at the west end. At the nearby freight house there was a freight agency that handled volumes of carloads and less.

For years, Morrilton was shown to have a continuous train order office. The National Railroad Adjustment Board investigated the freight house staffing situation at Morrilton during the 1950s. The report provided the following staffing levels between 1928 and 1951.

November 1928 – cashier, warehouse clerk, cotton clerk, helper, porter
August 1937 – cashier, clerk, porter
December 1941 – cashier, warehouse foreman, porter
December 1943 – cashier, warehouse foreman, porter, ticket clerk
May 1946 – cashier, warehouse foreman, porter, ticket clerk
September 1947 – cashier, 2 check clerks, bill clerk, trucker
September 1949 – cashier, check clerk, bill clerk, trucker
February 1951 – cashier, bill clerk, trucker

On June 27, 1952, Missouri Pacific reduced the staffing level by abolishing the bill clerk position, a common change at several other stations as traffic volumes decreased. The report stated that at the passenger station there was an agent (actually a Star Agency who does not telegraph) with no assigned hours, and two telegraphers (6:30am-2:30pm and 2:30pm-10:30pm). These positions were "located at the passenger station across the railroad tracks and about two blocks distance down the tracks from the local freight station." At the time, the freight house cashier and trucker worked weekdays (8am-Noon, 1pm-5pm) while the bill clerk had a different weekday schedule (9:30am-1:30pm, 2:30pm-6:30pm).

The staffing continued to decrease as passenger traffic and less-than-carload freight declined. The last passenger train operated on March 28, 1960, and only a few freight and train order employees remained. The freight house soon came down and Missouri Pacific abandoned the passenger depot. Efforts started in the 1960s to acquire and preserve the depot. As an additional effort to save the station, it was listed on the National Register of

Historic Places on September 13, 1977. On the same day the depot was sold to a scrapper. With a move to save the building, the railroad delayed the destruction of the building for two weeks. During November, Missouri Pacific announced a plan to donate the Morrilton depot to either the city or a local civic group. The depot was acquired by the Conway County Historical Preservation Association which remodeled the building, turning it into a local history and genealogical museum. It reopened to the public in 1980. Trains still pass by the station on the north side and Railroad Avenue is still located to the south.

One of the railroad history surprises at Morrilton is this building, built around an old wooden refrigerator car and located two blocks west of the depot.

Petit Jean State Park

Petit Jean State Park, located to the south of Morrilton and across the Arkansas River on 3471 acres atop Petit Jean Mountain, was the first state park in Arkansas. In an interesting twist of fate, the Little Rock & Fort Smith (Missouri Pacific) and the Choctaw, Oklahoma & Gulf (Rock Island) railroads both played a role in the creation of the park. From the north, much of the Petit Jean Mountain was given to the Little Rock & Fort Smith as land grants during the railroad's construction. From the south, the Choctaw, Oklahoma & Gulf allowed the operations of the Fort Smith Lumber Company in the area.

The south side of Petit Jean Mountain was logged using a 30-inch narrow gauge logging railroad. Some reports state that this was the narrowest logging railroad in Arkansas, and it had a mainline about 6.5 miles long. The timber was hauled to the Fowler Mill of the Fort Smith Lumber Company, located on the Rock Island.

In 1907, a tour of the mill and the timber being cut led to a discussion about the difficulty in cutting much of the timber in the Seven Hollows area of the mountain, and the idea of donating it as a park. A leader of this suggestion was Dr. T. W. Hardison, the Fort Smith Lumber physician at the sawmill and nearby logging camps. Officials of the company approved of the idea and set the land aside and protected it from logging. Dr. Hardison was later the official who worked with the state in creating the state park, the first in Arkansas.

While the Fowler Mill closed in 1909, some timbering continued in the area, and it wasn't until 1921 that the timber company was ready to hand over the property. At first, the plan was for the creation of a national park, and a bill to create Petit Jean National Park was introduced in the U.S. House of Representatives. A meeting between Dr. Hardison and Stephen Mather, director of the National Park Service, resulted in a decision that the property was too small to justify the cost of development and administration. Instead, it was recommended that it be turned into an Arkansas state park.

During the time the State of Arkansas considered the gift, and the Fort Smith Lumber Company altered its agreement from giving the land to the federal government and instead to the state government, a group of eight Arkansas residents donated eighty acres that included the Cedar Falls area. This eighty acres was the first state park land ever acquired by Arkansas, and it led to the creation of Petit Jean State Park in 1923. Not long after, Fort Smith Lumber donated the Seven Hollows area. During 1926, Missouri Pacific signed a deed to 120 acres of land the firm still owned on the mountain, with plans to donate it to the park. However, the formal filing of the deed didn't take place until April 12, 1929, when a formal transfer ceremony took place. The Missouri Pacific's gift included one of the most popular parts of the park – Cedar Falls and Cedar Creek Canyon.

This photo is from the May 1929 issue of the *Missouri Pacific Lines Magazine*. It shows T. J. Cole, Missouri Pacific General Attorney (right), handing the title to 120 acres of former land grant property to Hal L. Norwood, Arkansas Attorney GeneraL. The property became part of Petit Jean State Park, Arkansas' first state park. From left, are also Charles H. Brough, former Arkansas governor, and John R. Hampton, Committee Chairman of the Arkansas Y.M.C.A.

A series of other acquisitions, plus the work of the Civilian Conservation Corps (CCC), helped create one of the highest rated state parks in the country. Today, Seven Hollows is a popular hiking area, and a visit will easily demonstrate why it would have been hard to log this country. A walk down the trail to Cedar Falls explains why the Missouri Pacific gift was so valuable to the park's development and continued popularity.

There is one other connection between Missouri Pacific and Petit Jean State Park. Based upon a story by Richard Davies, former director of Arkansas State Parks (1976-1990), a Missouri Pacific manual about building bridges was used in designing the Davies Bridge across Cedar Creek. The bridge was built by the CCC under the direction of his father Ladd Davies, who used his father's (Samuel Davies) Missouri Pacific manual from his work with the railroad. The bridge was listed on the National Register of Historic Places in 1990.

392.9 SOUTH CHEROKEE STREET – Heading west from Morrilton, the railroad's grade is higher than the surrounding terrain, built this way to reduce the grades that trains had to face. Because of this, there are railroad bridges over South Cherokee Street, using a 30-foot steel beam span with a 22-foot concrete pile trestle off each end, and South Cedar Street, using a 27-foot steel beam span with a 22-foot concrete pile trestle off each end. Cherokee Street is the route to Point Remove Park and Cherokee Park. This area on the Arkansas River was an early landmark for explorers on the river, and also the Cherokees in Arkansas.

If you look carefully under the South Cherokee Street overpass, you will find this 1946 date cast into the concrete headwall.

Point Remove played an important role in the development of Lewisburg and much of Conway County. However, the name is greatly misunderstood. Point Remove dates back to the French exploration of the area and was used for the location where Point Remove Creek flows into the Arkansas River. This created a whirlpool or eddy, a remous in French. In an 1813 document, William Lovely used the term "point remove byo," or Point Remove Bayou, for the creek. Thomas Nuttall, a naturalist who explored much of the region and wrote the book *Journal of Travels into the Arkansas Territory during the year 1819*, called the area Point Remu. During 1819-1820, Major Stephen Long led an expedition that passed along the Arkansas River. His report called the location Point Remove, or Eddy Point Creek.

Point Remove took on major significance when it became the southern point of the Treaty of the Cherokee Agency boundary line. This treaty established a line from "Budwells Old Place" at the mouth of Point Remove Creek, to the White River at Shields Ferry near Batesville, Arkansas. Lands to the west were traded to the Cherokees in return for lands east of the Mississippi River, and it temporarily became the western border of the Arkansas Territory. The agreement of 1828 that moved the border further west called Point Remove "Pointe au Remou." This use of the term led to some to believe that is was named for the removal of the Cherokees from what became Arkansas to Indian Territory in today's Oklahoma. For those who are interested, the Old Cherokee Boundary Line, also sometimes known as the Old Indian Treaty Boundary, still shows on many maps and is often used on land descriptions and surveys in Arkansas.

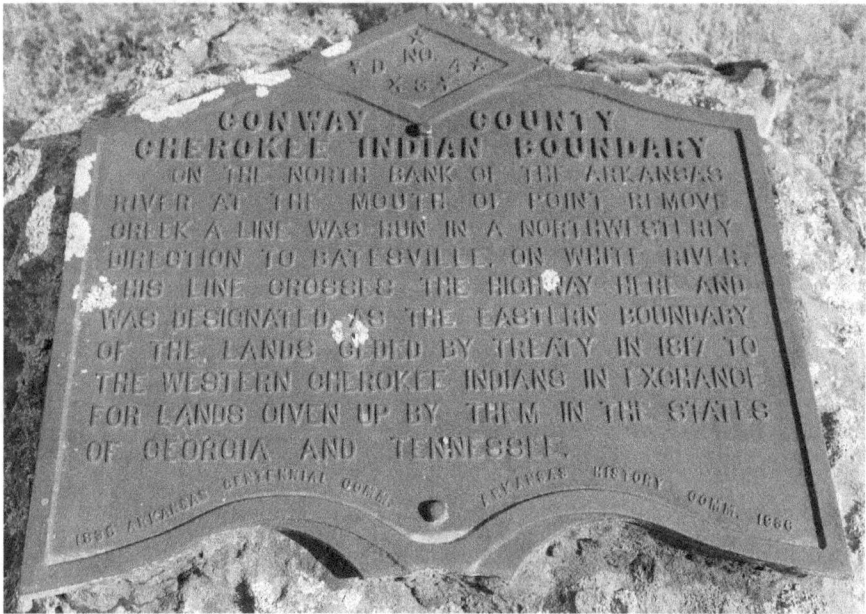

This marker in Morrilton tells the history of the Cherokee boundary line and Point Remove Creek.

During the early 1820s, Lewisburg developed east of Point Remove, but a post office also opened nearby in 1824 using the name Point Remove. The Point Remove post office opened and closed several times in slightly different locations, slowly moving northward up Point Remove Creek. By 1870, the Point Remove post office was located in the home of Dr. Francis Marion Crowell, Sr. At the time, Crowell's house was located on the Fryer farm, near Friar's Ford (now Fryer's Ford) on the East Fork of the Point Remove Creek. Reports state that Dr. Crowell moved closer to what became Solgohachia (several miles north of Morrilton) in 1873, still operating the Point Remove post office.

393.7 HORNS SPUR – This location was listed in the March 1, 1925, *Missouri Pacific Railroad Company Official List of Officers, Agents, Stations and Mileage.* It was noted that Horns Spur was used for prepaid freight, carloads and less. Maps from the railroad show a track looping to the south into Continental Oil Company. The track was built in 1920, could hold 19 freight cars, and was rebuilt in late 1926. The track was shown again in 1958, still with a capacity of 19 freight cars.

395.1 BRIDGE NO. 129 – This small bridge has a history that shows the work performed on the railroad over the years. It was initially a timber pile trestle, but was replaced by a 21-foot-long deck plate girder span. In 1940, it was replaced with a concrete deck slab.

395.5 BRIDGE NO. 130 – This bridge also shows some of the traditional bridge work performed along the railroad. In 1924, the existing deck plate girder (DPG) span was replaced with a heavier 45-foot DPG. In 1936, the timber approaches on each end were replaced with 20-foot beam spans.

396.0 WARD'S SWITCH – In 1879, a Rand, McNally and Company map showed the station of Point Remove immediately east of the Point Remove bridge. By 1889, the company's maps showed the station as Zeb. Railroad documents show that there is a short stretch of right-of-way that is 200 feet wide, instead of the normal 100 feet wide, on either side of the Point Remove Creek bridge. This is generally an indication that a siding or station was located in this area.

During the 1880s, Ward's Switch, or simply Wards, was listed as a small railroad station on the Little Rock & Fort Smith Railway in Conway County. It was stated that the mail came from Morrilton. Another name for this location was Ward's Junction. At the end of 1880, it was reported that there was a 1.0 mile branch from this location. In 1896, it was reported that 1.25 miles of track were abandoned between Wards and Zeb.

The stations of Zeb and Wards were named for Zebulon Ward, during the late 1800s known as one of the most influential citizens of Arkansas. Zeb Ward was born in Kentucky on January 14, 1822. He worked in the steamboat business, and later manufacturing after he leased the Kentucky Penitentiary in 1855. He worked the inmates on local farms and in manufacturing bagging. He then moved to Nashville and leased the Tennessee state penitentiary. Ward moved to Arkansas during the 1870s and started leasing the labor of convicts at the Arkansas penitentiary in May 1873. During this time he acquired and operated several plantations near Little Rock and Morrilton, often using prison labor. After the lease of the penitentiary ended, Ward engaged in a variety of business enterprises in Little Rock.

Among the activities of Zeb Ward was helping to create the Little Rock waterworks system, being one of the founders of the Mountain Valley Spring Water Company, and being the founding president of the Arkansas Agricultural Association. He was also the contractor for building the Little Rock, Mississippi River & Texas from Little Rock to Pine Bluff; president of the Mississippi & Little Rock Railway; a founding owner of the Little Rock Oil Mills and Cotton Compress Company; and a director of the Gazette Publishing Company in Little Rock.

The son of Mr. Ward, also known as Zeb Ward, was also a noted Arkansas businessman. The May 1911 issue of *Stone* magazine, reported that he had received a contract for 40,000 cubic yards of riprap stone to be used in revetment work on the Mississippi River in the vicinity of Memphis, Tennessee. "The stone will be taken from quarries in western Arkansas on the

Little Rock & Fort Smith road, and it will require 1,500 cars to transport it to West Memphis, where it is to be delivered."

396.1 POINT REMOVE CREEK BRIDGE – The railroad crosses the stream using 200 feet of deck plate girder spans. Known as Bridge No. 131, this bridge was rebuilt in 1923. The original bridge consisted of one panel of pile trestle, one panel of frame trestle, a 145-foot through pin connected truss span, and one panel of frame trestle. It was replaced with an 80-foot deck plate girder, plus two 60-foot deck plate girder spans.

During the first part of the 1900s, the railroad had a water station at Point Remove Creek. The tower and pump house were removed in 1929. Where the water tower once stood on the north side of the bridge was also a sign marking the boundary between track section gangs.

East Fork Point Remove Creek forms on the southwest side of Hunter Mountain near Formosa in southern Van Buren County. It flows generally to the southwest and merges with the West Fork northeast of Blackwell. These two streams separate the north end of Conway County from the south end. The combined waters then flow southward, passing west of Morrilton before flowing into the Arkansas River at Point Remove. The *Biographical and Historical Memoirs of Western Arkansas* (Goodspeed Publishers, 1891) described the stream by stating it "flows, in general, in a southern direction, but with a very winding course, and empties into the Arkansas 1½ miles above the City of Morrilton. Although there is much land under cultivation along the valley of this beautiful stream, there are thousands of acres yet a waiting occupation." Some sources state that locals called the stream a shortened Pointymove.

West of the Point Remove Creek Bridge, the railroad passes through a series of large fields, often planted with soybeans, cotton and even corn. The railroad also comes alongside U.S. Highway 64, which it follows closely all the way to Atkins, almost ten miles from here.

397.7 KENWOOD – Kenwood, originally known as Germantown, was once located at the grade crossing with Lemley Road, County Road 225. Germantown received a post office in 1874, soon after the railroad was built through the area. It was like many Arkansas Valley communities with farming, timber and light manufacturing dominating the economy. H. W. Burns owned and operated a shingle mill near Germantown, and the Arkansas Brick & Manufacturing Company was using convict labor at Germantown in 1902. Because of these industries, Germantown was listed as a principal town of Conway County during the early 1900s.

For a number of years, this was the home of the LR&FS Section House No. 7, which was removed in September 1928. The Germantown post office closed in 1904. There was still an 80-car siding shown at Germantown in 1907, but it was removed in 1938. The town changed its name to Kenwood during October 1918, likely due to anti-German feelings during World War I. By 1925, there was simply a platform and 8' x 14' shelter (built in 1916), plus a 9' x 15' carbody on the west side of the mainline. It was shown that freight handled at Kenwood, all moving in carload volumes, must be prepaid. Except for the mainline, the tracks are gone here and Kenwood is now an unincorporated town in southwestern Conway County.

Control Point V399 is at the Arkansas Highway 113 grade crossing, and the signs for both can be found on the signal box.

399.3 CONTROL POINT V399 – This is the south switch for the Blackville siding, which is located on the west side of the main-line just north of the Arkansas Highway 113 grade crossing. The siding was 63 cars long in 1944 and then extended to 90 cars by 1951. It was shown to be 4628 feet long in the late 1960s.

The 1982 issue of *Jane's World Railways* reported that the railroad had plans for a siding extension, and Blackville siding was listed as being 7754 feet by the early 1980s. Later, Union Pacific timetables showed it to be 7840 feet long until CTC signaling was installed. In 2021, the siding was shown to be 7780 feet long.

Just north of the control point is a switch off the siding into a small elevator complex. Recently, the complex has been unused.

The Arkansas River Valley is full of poultry, hog and cattle farms, and a series of feed mills can be found along the Van Buren Subdivision. This small one at Blackville has seen better days.

400.1 BLACKVILLE – Blackville, located at the grade crossing with Conway County Road 97, also known as Blackwell or Blackville Road, is a location that has had multiple names. Early maps show it to be Buckville, but the Little Rock & Fort Smith called it Blackville Station, or Blackville. The town was designed with streets 50 feet wide, alleys 20 feet wide, and lots that measured

50' x 150'. A post office opened in 1878 using the name Black-ville. Located at an elevation of 329 feet, the station was located on high ground above the Arkansas River bottomland, a prime agricultural area. The community grew large enough to support about two full blocks of stores, a doctor, a cotton gin, and a saw-mill. For years, the railroad bought crossties here.

While the railroad continued to use the name Blackville for the station, the town began to be called Blackwell. The original post office closed about 1889 and then reopened as Blackwell in 1897. Blackwell was often considered to be two separate com-munities – one black and one white. Each had their own schools (to the eighth grade), churches, and stores with the white facili-ties south of the tracks and the black facilities to the north. Both schools were merged into a new Morrilton Consolidated School District No. 32 in 1931.

On February 20, 1907, the Arkansas House of Representa-tives passed "An act to compel the erection and the maintenance of a suitable depot building and facilities at Blackville station, in Conway county, Arkansas." The railroad built a small wooden depot that featured a small freight and express room, and two small waiting rooms. There was also a mail crane and an 80-car siding. In 1925, Missouri Pacific stated that there was an agent at Blackville that worked a ticket agency and a freight agency for carload volumes and less. However, the train order signal had been removed in August 1922. The railroad also reported that the depot and platform were on the east side of the mainline. As the railroad closed facilities during the Great Depression, the depot was removed in August 1932.

By 1944, all that the railroad showed to be at Blackville was the siding, a company telephone, and a mail crane so passen-ger trains could pick up local mail without stopping. The Black-well post office closed in 1997 as the community shrank. Today, Blackwell is a scattering of homes along U.S. Highway 64. Near-by is the Ed Gordon-Point Remove Wildlife Management Area, about 9000 acres that include a waterfowl and wetland study area.

On August 16, 2023, a tired-looking UP 6538 pulls an Entergy coal train southbound through the siding at Blackville. This siding, with only one significant grade crossing, seems to be a popular location to meet trains.

Blackwell and the Titan II Missiles

The United States Air Force approved the Titan II program in October of 1959. These missiles would carry the largest nuclear warheads ever deployed on an ICBM (intercontinental ballistic missile) by the United States, and they featured a range of 5500 miles. Construction began in December of 1960, and the first unit went active on March 31, 1963. The missiles were located around three Air Force Bases, including the Little Rock Air Force Base (308th Strategic Missile Wing). Eighteen Titan II Missile units were located in central Arkansas, including one at Blackwell. During the 1980s, the Titan II system here was deactivated and torn out in August 1986, despite efforts to make it a tourist attraction.

400.9 CONTROL POINT V401 – This is the north switch of Blackville Siding.

401.0 COUNTY LINE – Not far north of the county line, the railroad turns directly westward and then passes through Atkins.

During late 2019, UP 8264 was photographed heading north from Conway County and into Pope County.

To the south is Conway County, while to the north is Pope County. **Conway County**, which is to the compass-east, was the 11th county created in Arkansas when it was approved on October 20, 1825, taking land from part of Pulaski County. The county was named for Henry Wharton Conway, a member of the Conway-Johnson political family. Henry Wharton Conway was a territorial delegate to the U.S. Congress (1823-1827) at the time the county was created. He died in 1827 as a result of wounds from a duel with Robert Crittenden, a former friend and political ally.

When Conway County was created it comprised 2,500 square miles and included most of the present Conway, Faulkner, Van Buren, White, Cleburne, and Perry counties and part of Yell County. Cadron was temporarily the county seat before moving to Lewisburg in 1831, and then to Morrilton in 1883. Conway County is located along both sides of the Arkansas River, generally in a fertile, low-lying valley between the Ozark and Ouachita mountains. Farming has long been the dominant business within the county. Because of this, the population peaked in 1910 with 22,729 residents. As farming became more mechanized, many farm workers left the county and the population dropped to 15,430 in 1960. It has climbed back up to 20,715 in the 2020 census.

Pope County was created from parts of Crawford County on November 2, 1829, the first Arkansas county to be formed from the old Cherokee reservation. It was named for John Pope, the third governor of the Arkansas Territory. Like all of the counties in the Arkansas River Valley, it started very rural with explorers and farmers being the first residents. The county had a population of 1483 in the 1830 census. Much of the county consists of flat and rolling land, and cotton and other farm crops were the primary economic activity for many decades. Pope County was famous for its Pope County Militia War after the Civil War, an effort by local Democrats to end Governor Powell Clayton's reconstruction efforts. Farming continued to dominate and the county's population peaked at 27,153 in the 1920 census. It began to grow again in the 1960s, mainly due to activity at the county seat of Russellville, the home of Arkansas Tech University. The population was 63,381 people in the 2020 census.

Coal was big business in Pope County during the first several decades of the twentieth century. The 1924 *Annual Report of the State Inspector of Coal Mines – State of Arkansas*, listed 12 coal mines that were served by Missouri Pacific in Pope County. All were shown to be small shaft mines employing only a few workers. They were also all shown to be about 4 miles northwest of Russellville. These included the following coal companies and their mine's name.

Allen-Mars Coal Co.	Allen-Mars
Austin-Maggard Coal Co.	Austin-Maggard
Douglas & Son Coal Co.	Douglas
Emerson-Wade Coal Co.	Mine #1
Harrison-Reynolds Coal Co.	Mine #1
Lewis Coal Co.	Mine #1
Noland Coal Co.	Noland
Harris-Price Coal Co.	Mine #1
Ouita Co-operative	Mine #1
Ouita Coal Co.	Lewis
Russel Coal Co.	Russel
Spainhire-Mars Coal Co.	Spainhire

402.8 FERGUSON SPUR – This long-retired station was located at the private grade crossing south of Bachelors Road. In 1925, the track was shown to only handle prepaid freight, both inbound and outbound. Located to the west, some tracks were abandoned in 1926 while the rest were removed in 1931.

When the railroad was built, this area was Perry Station, the end of the railroad for a short time after the railroad ran out of funds. During the summer of 1872, stages would meet trains at Perry on Mondays, Wednesdays and Fridays, and take passengers on to Fort Smith. Because of the location being the end of track, a small community grew up at the point, and the Perry Station post office was open 1872-1873. By mid-February 1873, railroad construction was again underway and rails had been laid "four miles above Perry" and past Atkins, and it was "expected that in two weeks trains will run to Russellville."

Perry Station made more news about the same time when Pope County Sheriff Elisha W. Dodson was shot in the back from ambush as he boarded a train bound for Little Rock. Dodson was one of several sheriffs who were killed during the late 1860s and early 1870s during the reconstruction era. Known as the Pope County Militia War, the shooting was part of a struggle between various political factions in the area, basically a continuation of the Civil War.

What was once known as Banquet Foods, located at Milepost 404.4, is now the facility of Livestock Nutrition Center.

404.4 BANQUET FOODS – To the south of the tracks (railroad-west) is a small feed mill facility, once operated by Banquet Foods, ConAgra Foods, Pilgrims Pride, and today by Livestock Nutrition Center (LNC). LNC operates almost twenty facilities in five states (Arkansas, Kansas, Oklahoma, Missouri and Texas) and specializes in premixed and specialized feed for livestock producers.

405.8 ATKINS (A) – Atkins was named for Elisha Atkins, a Massachusetts financier who became involved with the Little Rock & Fort Smith and helped to finance the completion of the railroad. He later became president of the railroad. Atkins first made his fortune importing molasses and sugar from Cuba, helping to make Cienfuegos, Cuba, one of the largest sugar ports on the island. Through a number of businesses, Atkins became one of the best known and successful businessmen in Boston. He used his funds to invest heavily in companies like Union Pacific and the Little Rock & Fort Smith.

The railroad had run out of funds when construction reached Perry Station, a few miles to the south. Elisha Atkins arranged for the funding to complete the railroad to Fort Smith, and the first town platted was named for him. A plat for the City of Atkins was created on December 29, 1873, about the time the Atkins post office opened. Atkins was officially incorporated on November 3, 1876.

Even before the town's official founding, several houses and businesses had been erected where it was believed the railroad would be built. Benjamin Towler Embry had built a house by 1872 and Ephraim Alexander Darr had opened a general store by the following year. Darr's store became the Atkins post office and even served as an informal bank. In 1895, Darr and several partners made it official when they opened the Bank of Atkins. Atkins soon became a one of the main trade centers for Pope County, attracting more residents. In the 1880 census, Atkins was shown to have a population of 519.

A number of the first settlers and businesses moved to Atkins from the nearby river town of Galley Rock (Galla Rock), once located seven miles southwest of Atkins. The first significant buildings at Atkins were located on the south side of the tracks, but a fire in 1889 led to new construction on the north side of the tracks along Rail Road Avenue (now East Main Street), where most of the town still exists. This area is now the Atkins Commercial Historic District, listed on the National Register of Historic Places on September 18, 2009.

Little of the old downtown Atkins still stands. This block of buildings, located just north of the depot, is about all that remains.

One of the attractions at Atkins is Lake Atkins, regionally famous for fishing (largemouth bass, bluegill, redear sunfish, crappie and channel catfish). Located south of town, Lake Atkins was built in 1956 as the first Arkansas lake partially financed under the Dingell-Johnson Act with funds from federal excise taxes on fishing equipment.

Area farming provided a great deal of business for the railroad during the late 1880s and early 1890s. In particular, corn, wheat, and cotton were the source of large volumes of rail traffic. To make more land available for farming, several drainage districts were created during the 1910s, and a number of local streams and bogs were channelized and drained. Because of all of the local farming, the population of Atkins peaked in 1920 at 1529 residents. In 1921, Atkins featured the feed company of Alewine Brothers, and the two lumber mills of Bell Lumber Company and Jess Anthony. There were also a number of salt manufacturers and fruit and vegetable dealers. However, the floods of 1927 destroyed crops in the fields and deposited as much as four feet of sand in the Arkansas River bottoms. Cotton prices dropped, a series of droughts followed, and many farmers lost their property just as the Great Depression started its decade-long grip on the country.

The Works Progress Administration (WPA) was responsible for five construction projects at Atkins. These included city projects like a new city jail, the waterworks pump house, and a gymnasium and agriculture building for the school. In 1945, an event occurred that has led to today's Picklefest. In that year, the Goldsmith Pickle Company built a pickle plant at Atkins. The town's population reached a low of 1291 residents in 1950. Over the next several decades, the poultry industry also grew in the area, including at least one poultry-processing plant and a number of broiler houses. Since 1992, Atkins has been the home of Picklefest, sponsored by the local pickle industry, as well as numerous companies around town. In the 2020 census, Atkins had a reported population of 2859. Twin River Foods has a facility on the southeast side of Atkins. The firm specializes in ready-to-cook chicken, and is based in Fayetteville, Arkansas. The Atkins schools are still located here, as well as numerous retail and service businesses.

The Railroad at Atkins

Atkins is located at an elevation of 352 feet and is at the bottom of a several mile 0.53% grade to the north. In May 1881, the Little Rock & Fort Smith moved their dinner stop for passenger trains from Russellville to Atkins. The passenger station was important to the railroad, and a number of services were provided here until late in the twentieth century. There were also a number of tracks, with 1028 feet of business track built in 1900, the same year that the passing track was extended 913 feet.

The tracks through Atkins run almost exactly east-west. Initially, the railroad had a passenger and freight depot on the north side of the tracks between Dover (today's Avenue One) and Gallarock (also Galla Street and today Avenue Two) streets. A 24' x 146' cotton platform and scale were located to the east, with several cotton sheds to the east of the cotton platform. By 1904, several industries were located east of town and south of the mainline on a long spur track. The spur track left the mainline at Galla Street and headed east to serve the American Cotton Company (cotton gin) and the Atkins Roller Mill. Further east was the planing mill of R. F. Yow. In 1907, the volume of business required a day telegraph office. A mail crane stood near the depot, and there was an 80-car siding. By 1908, the Morrilton Cotton Oil Company was located where the planing mill had been located. Downtown, the railroad had a 2-pen stockyard with a capacity of 4 stock cars.

In 1925, Missouri Pacific showed that the depot was busy with a ticket agency handling a coupon ticket station on the east end of the building. The west end of the station was the freight and baggage room. There was an official freight agency for carload and less shipments. There were also railroad stock pens (33' x 96'), several tool houses, an oil house with oil tank, and two toilets. The railroad freight house (20' x 53') was located south of the tracks and west of Everette Street (today's Avenue Three). The railroad section house (Gang 52, renumbered to Gang 13 during 1927) was removed in 1932 as the railroad cut back the number of employees and buildings during the Great Depression.

By the 1940s, the siding was shown to be 54 cars long. There was also a mail crane and the train order office had limited hours. All of this was gone by the 1960s, but several industry tracks remained. All of these are now gone, but they were once centered around the grade crossing of Arkansas Highway 105. The road also uses the name Avenue Two SE and Galla Street, named for the old Galla Rock community. The Atkins depot still stands just west of this grade crossing.

In 2023, this sign still stood across the tracks from the railroad depot at Atkins, Arkansas.

The Missouri Pacific Depot at Atkins

There have been at least three railroad stations at Atkins. The first was a small wooden building that was in a "dilapidated condition" by 1909. Local residents submitted a petition to the Railroad Commission of Arkansas during October, demanding a new depot. On November 5, 1909, the Commission met at Atkins to review the condition of the station. In 1910, a new wooden depot was built at a cost of $2100. A board and batten freight house also once stood here. The depot from 1910 didn't remain satisfactory for long and it was replaced in 1923 by a long rectangular single-story masonry building (24' x 114'), finished in brick and stucco and covered by a hip roof. The new platform was built of brick. The older depot was converted into a 6-room section house.

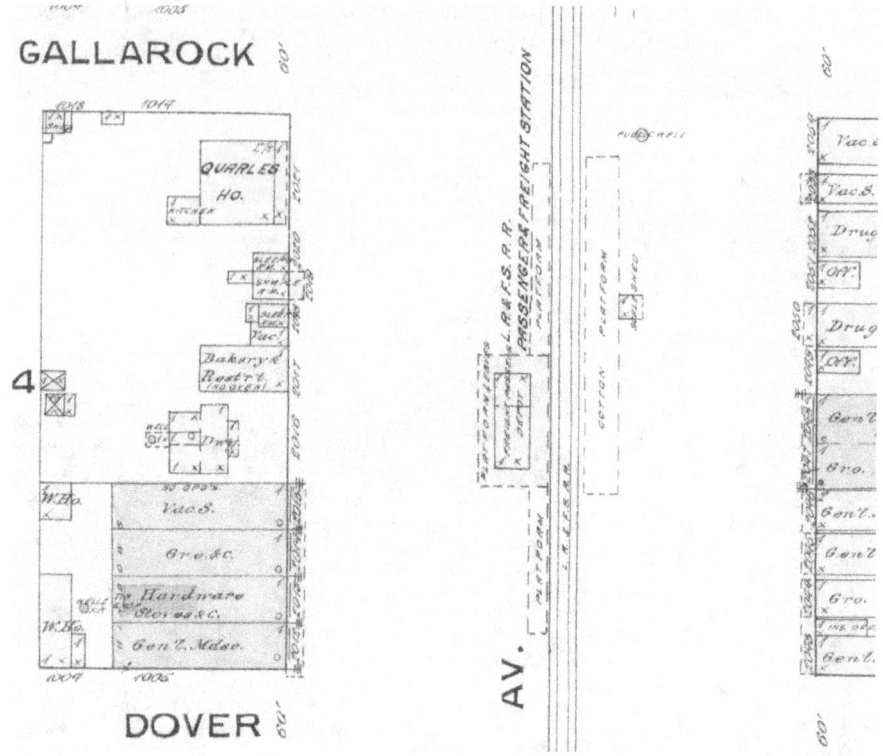

As shown on this Sanborn map, in 1886, the railroad had a passenger and freight depot on the north side of the tracks at Atkins, located between Dover and Gallarock streets. A cotton platform and scale were located to the south. This was also the center of the business district of Atkins. *Sanborn Fire Insurance Map from Atkins, Pope County, Arkansas*. Sanborn Map Company, July 1886. Map. Retrieved from the Library of Congress, https://www.loc.gov/item/sanborn00195_001/.

The brick and stucco station still stands at Atkins, and was listed on the National Register of Historic Places in 1992. Built in what is considered a Mediterranean style, the passenger waiting rooms are on the west end of the building with a covered portico outside. To the east is a small baggage and express section. The projecting telegrapher's bay is noted for its high roof, which like the rest of the building was once covered by ceramic tile.

Atkins was an important train order station on the line, and there was an agent-telegrapher assigned to the station in the first agreement with The Order of Railroad Telegraphers, negotiated in 1892. Atkins was the second highest paid position ($54.00 per month) on the line following Ozark ($55.00 per month). At the time, the various positions were rated and assigned a pay scale based upon the activity at the station. Until the 1920s, Atkins, Ozark and Spadra were the three highest paid positions, often swapping back and forth to be the highest paid position. For example, in 1904, Atkins was the highest paid agent-telegrapher, with Spadra having that title in 1906. In 1907, it was back to Atkins.

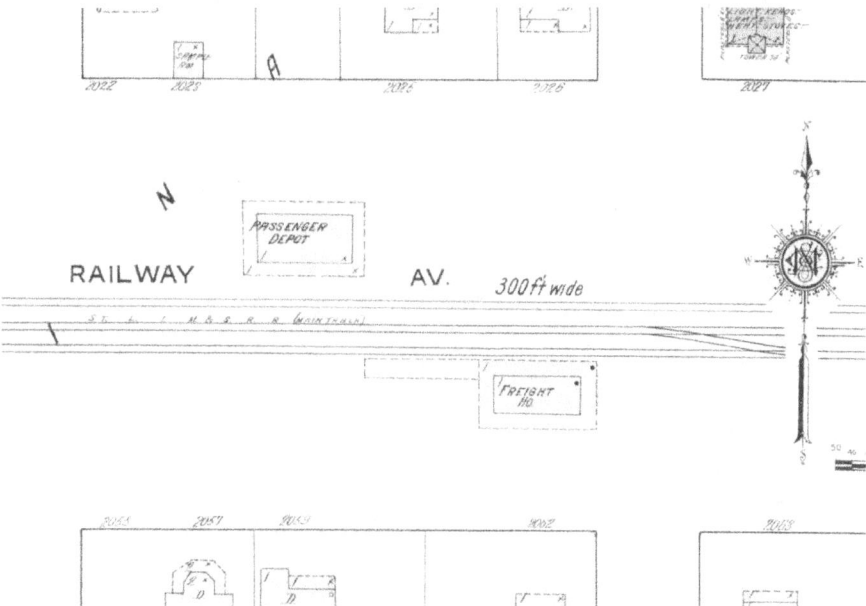

By 1913, the railroad's Atkins depot was located between Galla and Everett streets, a block to the east of its old location. Across the tracks to the south was a separate freight house. Additional tracks had also been built through Atkins, using the 300-foot-wide right-of-way of Railway Avenue. *Sanborn Fire Insurance Map from Atkins, Pope County, Arkansas.* Sanborn Map Company, October 1913. Map. Retrieved from the Library of Congress, https://www.loc.gov/item/sanborn00195_006/.

The Atkins railroad station, built of brick and stucco, still stands alongside the Van Buren Subdivision.

During World War I, the railroads were nationalized and operated by the United States Railroad Administration. In 1919, a new labor agreement was created that changed the agent jobs to hourly positions. At the time, Atkins still had an agent-telegrapher, while Ozark and Spadra had no telegrapher duties assigned to them. In the 1923 agreement, all three positions were classified by agreement as hourly-paid agent-telegraphers, and Atkins was the lowest paid of the three positions. In 1930, the agent-telegrapher worked the first shift and there were telegrapher positions on the second and third trick. By 1942, the two telegrapher positions were gone at Atkins due to fewer duties at the station.

On April 17, 1961, the railroad determined that train order service was no longer required at Atkins. On May 15, 1961, the agent position was reclassified from agent-telegrapher to agent-restricted operator. As defined by the railroad and union agreement, an agent could operate a station but with few train order and communication responsibilities. "At small non-telegraph or non-telephone agencies it will be permissible at the option of the carrier to require the agent to handle Western Union service, railroad communication service confined exclusively to the transmission of car orders and securing reports on the probable arrival for bulletin board information." The change was protested by the Transportation-Communication Employees Union (formerly The Order of Railroad Telegraphers), but the National Railroad Adjustment Board ruled that the change was legal under the contract. Within a few years, even that position was eliminated.

409.8 CONTROL POINT V410 – This is the south switch of Worthen siding, a 7897-foot siding on the west side of the mainline.

410.1 WORTHEN SOUTH SWITCH – In November 1928, the original Worthen siding was extended south to here, located near the grade crossing with Worthen Road. In April 1931, a 300-foot track was built across the mainline at Milepost 410.4. This track was only temporary and was removed in October 1931.

During December 1990, Worthern was the scene of a coal train derailment. This is what it looked like on Christmas Day of that year.

410.7 WORTHEN – For the railroad, Worthen is a siding, The location of the station sign was for years just east of Edwards Road at an elevation of 394 feet, almost a mile west of Worthen Road. Worthen was shown as holding 80 cars in 1907. It was 91 cars long in 1944 when there was also a company telephone here. The siding was extended to 141 car-lengths by 1951. During the 1960s, it was shown to be a 122-car siding due to longer freight cars, but a defined length of 6388 feet. Later sources showed it to be 7945 feet long. The siding was shortened slightly when CTC signaling and new turnouts were installed during the late 2010s.

For the general public, Worthen is an unincorporated community in Galla Township of Pope County. Most maps show that it is located north of the tracks along U.S. Highway 64. A few houses and at least one manufacturing company are located here.

Source of the Name Worthen

So where did the name Worthen come from? Records are not clear on this, but many of the stations along the LR&FS were named for investors. One of these investors was William Booker Worthen of Little Rock. W. B. Worthen, as he was generally known, started in the banking business in 1874. On January 1, 1877, he helped form Parker & Worthen, "Bankers, Brokers and Real Estate Agents." He bought Parker's share in 1888 and created W. B. Worthen & Company.

Apparently among the holdings of the company were Little Rock & Fort Smith Railway bonds. Starting in 1885, Worthen began a series of lawsuits against the railroad to enforce the payment by the road of over-due coupons on the railroad aid bonds issued under an Arkansas Act of 1868. As reported, the value of the bonds was about $1,250,000 and nearly all were held in New York City. Conflicting court rulings on the liability of the railroad were made even more complicated by several laws that were passed in Arkansas that reversed the earlier acts, actually making payment illegal.

Despite the work involved in these legal cases throughout the latter part of the 1880s, W. B. Worthen stayed involved with railroads. Among those that he served as a director or officer included the Little Rock & St. Louis Railroad; Arkansas Northern Railroad; Little Rock & Pacific Railway; Dardanelle & Mount Nebo Railway, and the Little Rock Railway & Electric Company. The W. B. Worthen Company also provided financing to the Dalhoff Construction Company. During March 1909, Worthen took possession of four locomotives, 24 dump cars, one steam shovel and one spreader owned by the Dalhoff Construction Company to pay off debts owed to the Worthen Company.

By 1902, the W. B. Worthen Company was one of sixteen banks in Little Rock. In 1906, Worthen wrote a history of Arkansas banking at the request of the Arkansas Bankers Association. He passed away in 1911, but his firm was one of the few that survived the Great Depression, becoming the largest bank holding company in the state. It is now part of Bank of America.

411.5 CONTROL POINT V412 – This Control Point is the north switch of the 7897-foot Worthen siding, which is located railroad-west (compass-south) of the mainline. Older timetables showed this to be North Worthen Siding.

This is the sign for Control Point V412 at the north switch of the Worthen siding.

411.6 ARKANSAS HIGHWAY 247 – The railroad passes under a new overpass that is part of a four-lane divided highway that bypasses Pottsville. It connects Interstate 40 with Arkansas Highway 7 near the Arkansas River and south of Russellville.

411.9 GALLA CREEK BRIDGE – The railroad uses an 83-foot deck plate girder span to cross Galla Creek. The stream forms in the Carrion Crow Mountain region located several miles to the north of here. It flows south and is dammed to form a drinking water reservoir known as Galla Creek Lake, often called Pottsville Reservoir or Pottsville City Lake. Downstream alongside the Arkansas River is the Galla Creek State Wildlife Management Area. Galla Creek attracted settlers, including various Indian tribes, several early European settlements, and a stagecoach stop.

This plaque on the Arkansas Highway 247 overpass shows that the bridge was built across the Union Pacific tracks in 2009.

412.1 POTTSVILLE – This area has had many names, including Galla Creek, Galla, Potts Station, Pottsville Junction, and Pottsville. If you include nearby communities which moved about, there were at least six post offices: Galley Rock (1837-1839), Galla Rock (1842-1890), Gally Creek (1844-1866), Gally Rock (1858-1871), Potts Station (1874-1897) and Pottsville (1897-Date). This caused confusion during the 1800s and early 1900s as the town that developed alongside the railroad was called Pottsville, while the railroad station used the name Galla. An 1890 map of Galla Township showed this as Galla Creek or Potts.

The town of Pottsville traces its history back to Kirkbride Potts, a New Yorker who moved to Missouri in 1820, and then to Arkansas in 1824. Potts moved to Choctaw lands near Mount Magazine, located south of the Arkansas River in what became Logan County. The area acquired the name Logan's Bottom after William Logan and Robert A. Logan, brothers who arrived with Kirkbride Potts. In 1828, the Cherokee were removed from their reservation land on the north side of the Arkansas River. Some reports from the time state that Potts was a government agent for the Choctaw and Cherokee removals, and his knowledge allowed him to buy land along Galla Creek alongside the

Arkansas River, helping to create the port town of Galla Rock. During the 1840s, he bought 160 acres on the south side of Crow Mountain where the military road crossed Galla Creek. He eventually used various land patents to acquire a total of 650 acres.

Potts' home became a stage stop when the Butterfield Overland Mail Company acquired a contract to carry mail between Memphis, Tennessee, and San Francisco, California. Potts had by this time built a large two and one-half story home with many fireplaces and a large detached kitchen. It became a rest stop and was called Potts Station, Potts Inn, or Potts Tavern. The large structure housed the post office, an inn, a dining room, and served as the local social center. During construction of the railroad, surveyors and engineers building the Little Rock & Fort Smith lodged and ate here.

Potts Inn has been described as "one of the best preserved stagecoach stations on the Butterfield Overland mail route between Memphis and Fort Smith." It occupies a large block in the town in Pottsville, and was lived in by members of the Potts family until being sold to Pope County in the early 1970s. It is now managed by the Pope County Historical Foundation.

A small town grew up around the stop, which expanded in 1851 when the Associate Reformed Presbyterians (ARP) from the Carolinas sent a group to settle the area. The group soon became the center of an ARP movement in the region, and became leaders in farming, business, education and politics.

Mail was handled by James Potts, the son of Kirkbride Potts. James was appointed postmaster by the president of the United States, and in 1879 asked that the post office be named Pottsville in honor of his father. On May 7, 1897, Pottsville was incorporated and had a population of 192 in the 1900 census. For the next several decades, the town had less than 300 residents supporting five brick stores and a bank, all located near the historic Potts Inn. The town moved northward when U.S. Highway 64 was built, and then most of the businesses moved to nearby Russellville as farming diminished and roads improved.

The Potts Inn, a former Butterfield Overland stage stop, was used by the Little Rock & Fort Smith to house their surveyors and engineers during the railroad's construction. The large house is now listed on the National Register of Historic Places and is part of the Potts Inn Museum complex.

In the March 1, 1925, *Missouri Pacific Railroad Company Official List of Officers, Agents, Stations and Mileage*, the station of Pottsville had replaced Galla Station, a move that officially took place on August 6, 1924. It was shown that the Pottsville station was on the west side of the tracks. It housed a railroad agent, ticket agency, and freight agency for carload volumes and less.

Starting in the late 1960s, the population of Pottsville began to grow as it became a suburb of Russellville. The population reached 564 in 1980, 1271 in 2000, and 3140 in the 2020 census. During the late 1990s, new schools were built at Pottsville, and they are nationally rated in their use and education of technology. The Potts Inn Museum (placed on the National Register of Historic Places on June 22, 1970) is a centerpiece of the community, which hosts an annual homecoming event known as Butterfield Days. With Arkansas Highway 247 serving as a bypass of Russellville for trucks connecting to industries south of the Arkansas River, Pottsville has grown to include numerous houses and subdivisions, retail stores, and several manufacturing companies.

Galla Station

Galla Station, located at Milepost 411.9 in the community of Pottsville, has never been a large or important station along the railroad, although it did include two large railroad water tanks in 1887, and a mail crane by 1907. On February 23, 1905, the Arkansas State Legislature passed "An Act to require the St. Louis, Iron Mountain and Southern Railway Company to keep and maintain a depot agent at Pottsville, a station on its line known as Galla, in Pope County, Arkansas." The law contained details about the community and the railroad at Pottsville.

The incorporated town of Pottsville, in Pope County, Arkansas, is located on the Little Rock and Fort Smith Division of the St. Louis, Iron Mountain and Southern Railway Company; and is a station on said line known as Galla, in Pope County, Arkansas, and is located about six miles west of the town of Atkins, and about six miles east from the town of Russellville, and does an annual business of about $60,000 a year.

Said town has a population of about 225 inhabitants of prosperous and industrious people, with five general merchandise stores, which buy and ship about 1,500 bales of cotton each year, and one drug store, one wholesale mattress factory, one wholesale broom factory, one cotton gin, two grist mills, one blacksmith shop and wagon factory, three church houses for whites, and a high school with 125 pupils, and is surrounded by fertile and productive lands, and by a densely populated community.

There is already a good and convenient depot and side track at said station.

In the reconstruction of said road a few years ago, in consideration of certain changes in the streets and public roads, in and near said town, and the elevation

> *of the track and other physical changes incurring inconveniences forborne by the citizens of said town and community, the division superintendent of said road agreed and promised to keep and maintain a depot agent at said town and community.*

Orders from the Arkansas Railroad Commission didn't end with the station and agency. In early March 1910, the Commission ordered the railroad to install a road crossing for easier access to the Galla Station at Pottsville. At the time, the railroad had a small board and batten depot with a V-shaped bay window. In October, the St. Louis, Iron Mountain & Southern moved the depot from the east side to the west side of the track. This was necessary so that a hill behind the depot could be cut down to make way for a new switch and track to a cotton gin.

Railroad reports stated that the agent handled the business of two grain dealers, a feed mill, lumber mill, and cotton gin. During August 1922, the train order signal was removed, and the station was no longer listed by 1925. A mail crane stood near the depot until the late 1940s. During February 1947, an 8' x 12' freight house was built to store local freight movements, and an 8' x 8' shed was added to the east end of the freight shed in 1951, replacing the depot. There was also a 16' x 79' cotton platform. No side tracks exist at Pottsville today. At Milepost 412.4, the railroad uses a concrete structure, built in 1921, to bridge over River Road, what was once the old highway around the east side of Russellville.

412.4 SOUTH END OF DETOUR NO. 6 – The original mainline was moved to the north and then swung around the low ridge, basically where U.S. Highway 64 is now located. The new route was built straighter with fewer grades thanks to a series of fills and cuts.

413.5 TYSON FOODS FEED MILL – Known as the Russellville Feed Mill, this complex is large, but started as a smaller feed mill in September 1985. Over the years, it has become a consolidated facility replacing several other Tyson feed mills. The site now includes truck and equipment maintenance facilities, equipment storage areas, a Tyson distribution center, and an Americold Logistics freezer warehouse.

Tyson has a number of facilities around Russellville, including this large feed mill. Surrounding the towering structure are other Tyson operations including a truck and equipment maintenance facility, which explains all of the trucks and trailers that encircle the complex.

Tyson Foods is big, producing 20% of the chicken, beef, and pork in the United States, and it is the largest U.S. food company. Tyson Foods started in 1931 when John W. Tyson moved to Springdale, Arkansas, and to feed his family, began buying chickens locally and selling them across the Midwest. The business grew rapidly during World War II as poultry was one of the few foods not rationed, and Tyson moved into chicken production. The company was incorporated in 1947 as Tyson Feed and Hatchery, Inc. During the late 1950s, the company built its first processing plant, meaning that it raised, processed and sold poultry, one of the first firms to control the entire process.

In 1963, Tyson's Foods went public, allowing it to continue to expand. The name became Tyson Foods in 1972, and other product lines were added throughout the 1980s. By 1990, Tyson

Foods was the world's largest fully-integrated producer, processor, and marketer of poultry-based food products, and was quickly expanding its international market. Thanks to further expansion and several acquisitions, Tyson became the world's largest processor and marketer of chicken, beef, and pork by 2001. Since then, the company has continued to expand and the product names on the side of their trailers will surprise almost anyone.

The railroad has several tracks to the north of the mainline that are used to switch grain and freezer railcars in and out of the facility. The west end of the complex is where Tyler Road (Pope County Road 38) bridges over the railroad at Milepost 414.1. These tracks are within the Russellville yard limits.

The Tyler Road Overpass can be a great place to watch trains as they climb the grades on the east side of Russellville. Here, Union Pacific 5588 is pulling a long freight southward towards Little Rock.

414.1 TYLER ROAD OVERPASS – This road crosses the Union Pacific mainline, which is passing through a deep, wet cut at the top of a series of hills. The cut is at an elevation of 432 feet, with grades of 0.7% to the south and north. The bridge over the tracks was once owned by the railroad. At one time, it was a seven-panel frame trestle. In 1937, Missouri Pacific replaced the older timber bridge with a 4-panel timber frame trestle on concrete pedestals. It was built with a concrete floor, giving it a much more substantial look.

Heading west into Russellville, there are a number of tracks that are used to serve manufacturing and warehousing firms located in the East End Industrial Park. These include JW Aluminum (Milepost 414.5), Bemis/Amcor and International Paper (Milepost 415.1), and Americold (Milepost 415.2). West of Arkansas Highway 331 (Milepost 415.8) is a short runaround track that is used for switching.

415.8 NORTH END OF DETOUR NO. 6 – The north end of the 3.4-mile-long Detour No. 6 is located a short distance east of the El Mira Avenue grade crossing. Where the railroad curves to the southeast, the original grade once curved off to the northeast.

To the north of the Russellville Wye was once a series of railroad facilities, including a coal chute and a water tower. These footings still remain at the location. The carloads of treated railroad ties were loaded on the Dardanelle & Russellville Railroad by Stella-Jones at their wood treatment plant.

This marker, which notes that the bridge crossed the Missouri Pacific Railroad and North Detroit Street, can be found on the Main Street Overpass in Russellville.

On October 14, 1990, Union Pacific 5020 was found heading north at Russellville, pulling a company business train. It was photographed as it passed under the Main Street – U.S. Highway 64 Overpass.

417.6 D&R CONNECTION – To the south and between Knoxville Avenue (Milepost 416.9) and Detroit Street (Milepost 417.4) is a wye that connects Union Pacific with the Dardanelle & Russellville Railroad (D&R). The D&R is a five-mile railroad that serves several customers between Russellville and the Arkansas River. While the railroad currently handles pulp board, plastics, and forest products, it once was also a mover of significant volumes of coal and cotton. The Dardanelle & Russellville Railway began operations in August 1883, and was reorganized as Railroad in 1900. During the railroad's coal era, it was owned by the McAlester Fuel Company, and is currently owned by Arkansas Shortline Railroads, Inc. For those wanting the entire story, check out the book *The Dardanelle & Russellville Railroad* by Hull and Pollard.

To the north of the wye is the actual D&R Connection, located under the U.S. Highway 64 overpass. The connection is the north switch of a short siding to the west (compass-south) that connects directly with the wye at an elevation of 354 feet.

At the north end of the wye and to railroad-east is the Tyson Foods Russellville Distribution Center. This complex features a large cold-storage facility with a rail loading dock.

In this photo from 2025, Dardanelle & Russellville 16 is switching freight cars near the interchange track with Union Pacific. The D&R dates back to 1883, not long after the Little Rock & Fort Smith was built.

417.7 RUSSELLVILLE (RS) – Russellville was a clear landmark during the construction of the Little Rock & Fort Smith. Construction work towards the Pope County city was reported on frequently, especially as the track got close.

Track-laying on the Little Rock and Fort Smith rail-road goes rapidly on. The iron is already down four miles above Perry, and, in pleasant weather, about one mile per day is laid. It is expected that in two weeks trains will run to Russellville.
Daily Arkansas Gazette, February 12, 1873

The construction train on the Fort Smith railroad will be within two miles of Russellville to-day.
Daily Arkansas Gazette, February 27, 1873

The Fort Smith railroad will be completed to Russellville to-day.
Daily Arkansas Gazette, March 4, 1873

The Russellville area was once a popular hunting region, being located between the mountains to the north and the Arkansas River to the south. The area featured plenty of water and grassy prairie for first the Osage, and later the Cherokees. The Osage relinquished their ownership of their hunting grounds in what was to become Arkansas by treaty in 1808. In 1817, much of northwest Arkansas became a reservation for the Cherokee, of which about 4000 relocated into Arkansas. Many of the Cherokee established farms and orchards in the area. In 1820, Cherokee leader Tahlonteskee assisted in creating a Protestant mission – the Dwight Mission – near today's Russellville. The mission grew into a small town with a post office, library, sawmill, gristmill, blacksmith shop, gardens, and residences.

The region had many names including Cactus Flats, Chactas Prairie, or The Prairie. In 1828, the Cherokees, who for a decade had a reservation in northwestern Arkansas, were moved further west into Indian Territory and white settlers began to move here. Dwight Mission moved with the Cherokee, but a new community began to grow in its place. The first house at what became Russellville was built in 1834 by P. C. Holledger, and a general store was built nearby the following year. About the same time, Dr. Thomas Russell acquired the log cabin of Holledger, and there was soon a small community.

Russellville was often the destination of Union Pacific excursions out of Little Rock. On October 25, 1996, UP 949 pulled such a train. While the passengers had time to wander town, a southbound freight behind UP 2265 passed the excursion train at Russellville.

The home of Dr. Russell was located along the Little Rock-Fort Smith road (today's Main Street), an old north-south buffalo trail that led to a ford on the Arkansas River (today's Arkansas Avenue), and several trails into the mountains to the north. As the town grew, two important figures seemed to have dominated the new community. The first was Doctor Thomas Russell, who many give the title of "Founder of Russellville." His home was used for area meetings and he seemed to be the lead of the community's social events. The second leader of the town was Jacob Shinn, who had bought the first general store from his uncles, James and Silas Shinn. Jacob was the business leader of the community since almost everyone had to buy goods from him. Jacob Shinn built a new masonry structure in 1875, and the building still stands as a part of the city's historical district.

As the town was being organized, there was competition between the names Shinnville and Russellville. Reportedly a vote was taken and the name Russellville was chosen, resulting in a post office using that name opening in 1852. Despite some promise, Russellville remained a small farming community until the Little Rock & Fort Smith was surveyed through town, causing Russellville to be incorporated as a town on June 7, 1870. The population that year was recorded as being 240 residents. With the arrival of the railroad in 1873, new residents arrived and the freight docks along the tracks brought in farm products from across the county. By 1876, there were fifteen stores, two cotton gins, and six doctors at Russellville, and the population was 514 in the 1880 census.

As the town grew, schools were required. The first school opened in 1820 at the Dwight Mission, and a series of private and subscription schools replaced the earlier school as the Cherokees were moved westward. In 1870, the Russellville Public School District was formed, but it only had classes through elementary school. This was increased until there were ten grades in 1890, and then a full high school by 1893. With Russellville growing to be the largest city in Pope County, there were efforts to move the county seat from Dover, where it had been located since 1842. An election on March 19, 1887, developed into a contest primarily between Atkins and Russellville, with Russellville narrowly winning the title. The change led to more growth of the city, and the population reached 1832 in the 1900 census.

Farming was the early business that supported Russellville, but the railroad allowed timber and coal to become important. The early 1900s saw cotton and coal dominate the local market, and the wealth they brought to Russellville allowed the city to rebuild using brick after a 1906 fire that burned most of the central business district. In 1909, the Arkansas Polytechnic College opened, which is today Arkansas Tech University.

In 1921, Russellville was shown to have a long list of industries, businesses, and manufacturers. These included J. G. Butler & Sons (steam laundry and bottling works); the coal mines of Claude Humphrey, Ouita Coal, Southern Anthracite Coal, and H. K. Vines; the cooperage works of John Kopp; the Russellville Roller Mills; Russellville Iron Works; the Arkansas-Oklahoma Ice Company; the lumber mills of J. J. Shoptaw and William Westphal; and the soap works of M. B. Cassell. The population at that time was 4505 and it has continued to grow until the 2020 census, when it reached 28,940.

Manufacturing is still found throughout the city, with firms making everything from railroad crossties to frozen dinners, from graphite electrodes to aluminum foil, and from parking meters to aircraft and automotive parts. Almost fifty manufacturing plants employ more than 8000 people. Tourism is also big business, especially with Lake Dardanelle State Park at the edge of town. Also nearby is Arkansas Nuclear One, the state's only nuclear power plant.

The area around the Russellville Depot is known as the Depot District, and is noted by banners like this one. Numerous events are held in this area, supporting the downtown area of Russellville..

Russellville residents are quick to point out some of the famous people from the community. These include 1982 Miss America Elizabeth Gracen; the actress Natalie Canerday (*Sling Blade, October Sky, Walk the Line*); composer Scott Bradley (*Tom and Jerry* cartoons); and noted knifemaker James Buel Lile (Rambo Knife).

A significant part of the Depot District is the Mr. Conductor sculpture, located near the entrance to the Russellville train station.

The Railroad at Russellville

Just as Russellville was an early destination for the railroad, it was also an important station and yard for many decades. One of the reasons was that it was located near the center of the railroad between Little Rock and Fort Smith. Local freight and passenger trains ran in each direction for many years, and all trains stopped at the station and freight yard. This led to a railroad dining facility being opened at Russellville.

Apparently, the operator of the "Railroad Eating House" at Russellville changed regularly, and *The Russellville Democrat* newspaper reported on the changes. For example, the May 31, 1877, issue reported that "The Russellville Railroad Eating House is again in the hands of Capt. T. A. Barrelle, and under his management the traveling public may rest assured that they will be favored with a table supplied with the best the market affords." By September, the newspaper reported that J. W. Cummings was running the railroad dining hall, and that he was building a new frame residence next door. In March 1878, Yerzley & Davis became the new proprietors of the Russellville Railroad Eating House. However, in May 1881, the dinner stop for Little Rock & Fort Smith passenger trains was moved from Russellville to Atkins. Despite this, Russellville remained a freight division point with a train dispatcher's office.

Cotton was an early business at Russellville. *The Russellville Democrat* newspaper reported on March 21, 1878, that there "had been 6,643 bales of cotton shipped from this station up to the 13th just." On November 13, 1879, the newspaper stated that the "L. R. & Ft. Smith Railroad took 21,000 bales of cotton into Little Rock last month. Russellville station sent in 3890 bales of that amount – more, by nearly 1000 bales than any other station on the road. By September 1887, the railroad had enlarged the cotton platform to handle the growing volumes being shipped.

During the fall of 1879, fruit was also shipped from Russellville. *The Russellville Democrat* of November 13, 1879, reported on this "new source of revenue for Pope County." Several local farmers had shipped 1021 bushels of green peaches to St. Louis, and the peach business began to grow in the region.

Russellville wasn't the only growing source of business along the railroad. The Russellville newspaper reported on November 30, 1882, that "Freight and passenger traffic over the railroad each way is just now immense, necessitating the running of ten trains daily....The railroad company, in order to expedite the increasing business at this place, has placed a night telegraph operator on duty. This will prove a great convenience."

As traffic increased and coal began to move in volume over the line, a list of improvements were made at Russellville. New section houses, several yard and industry tracks, and a "prairie turntable" were installed in 1894. In 1902 alone, a wye was built and the freight and passenger depots were moved east to between Jefferson and River streets, with the passenger station located on the south side of the mainline. Along with the station move, new platforms were built and an additional track was built on the south side of the station. This track was used by Dardanelle & Russellville trains which also served the station. In 1903, the yard at Russellville was rearranged and three miles of track were added. By 1907, the railroad had a 138-car siding at Russellville, as well as a wye, track scale, water tower, and coaling tower. At the depot was a train register and a day and night telegraph office.

As the fruit business grew in the area, the railroad built a re-icing station at Russellville. The 1908 annual report of the Missouri Pacific Railway Company included information on the reason for, and the construction of, an icing platform at Russellville.

> *Fruit shipments growing heavier each year in the Van Buren District, facilities were found inadequate for proper handling of fruit movement; an icing platform 10 x 142 feet has been constructed at Russelville, Ark., ice to be elevated by standing car on 4 per cent. incline to coal chute.*

In late 1911, the citizens of Clarksville petitioned the Railroad Commission of Arkansas to force the St. Louis, Iron Mountain & Southern to move its freight division point from Russellville to Clarksville. A law passed in 1907 required that the railroad maintain a point halfway between Little Rock and Fort Smith as a terminal point for local passenger trains. When passed, the law intended to ensure that daytime local passenger trains operated over the entire line. A local passenger train could operate from Little Rock and Fort Smith and turn at Russellville, making the round-trip in one day. The Railroad Commission refused to get involved by saying that the Arkansas General Assembly had ordered the railroad to establish a single terminal point, but that it was up to the railroad to determine the location. It also stated that the current operating plan met the requirements, so they had no authority to change it.

The local coal business, especially the mines on the Dardanelle & Russellville, forced Missouri Pacific to make further changes in the yard tracks in town. In 1930, local freight trains and their crews were still based at Russellville, and operated to North Little Rock and Van Buren. These crews overnighted at these locations, and there were numerous reports about small schedule changes made to ensure their timely return to Russellville. Changes kept happening at Russellville as technology and shippers changed. A water column was added in late 1927 (more in 1943), a tool house and the section house were removed in 1937, the coal chute and its track were removed in 1938, and the stock pens were removed in 1954.

For years there were also other jobs at Russellville. One of the forgotten jobs was crossing watchman. Just south of the passenger station at the Commerce Avenue grade crossing (north side of tracks and to the east of the street) was a watchman tower. The watchman in the tower worked gates at both Commerce and Arkansas Avenues until about 1950. Today, only a bit of the foundation remains from this structure. Additionally, there were track maintenance forces, a switch oiler who oiled and inspected the many switches on a daily basis, and often several local switching crews.

In 1944, Missouri Pacific had a 118-car siding at Russellville, plus a track scale (40 feet long, 100,000-pound capacity), water, coal, turntable, and wye. The station operated with a continuous train order office. These facilities were still here during the early 1950s, but the station's train order office had limited hours. In 1969, the station's office was still busy, with it serving as a train order office and a radio base station. Because several train crews were based here, the depot housed a general order book and a standard clock. There was still a wye, a track scale, and a 6143-foot siding (east side of mainline), all protected by yard limits. These were all still there in the early 1980s.

Today, north of El Paso Street (Milepost 417.9) is a small yard that serves as a base for local freight trains. This yard, and the second track at Russellville, end north of the new Phoenix Avenue overpass (Milepost 418.5). Across the tracks from the depot is the local landmark of Stoby's Restaurant. This restaurant has for decades used several passenger cars as part of the restaurant. One of these was former Rock Island Railroad commuter car #2572. A second car that was built into the main building is former Illinois Central coach 3661. The third car was former Rock Island parlor car 3505. This car was built in 1930 by Pullman Car & Manufacturing Company, one of six such cars bought by the railroad. In 1951, the car was converted to instruction car #1815, a mobile classroom for railroad training and rules examinations. It was rebuilt in 1966 at the company's Silvis shops into a Maintenance of Way food service car, and it was also used in wreck train service. The cars were bought by Russellville businessman John Harris after the Rock Island closed and he moved them to Russellville where they have been used by various businesses. After several years of not being used, the Rock Island cars were moved to the Dardanelle & Russellville Railroad during early October 2024.

Just south of the passenger station at the Commerce Avenue grade crossing was a watchman tower, which controlled vehicle traffic when trains were approaching. The concrete foundation of the tower can still be found in the brush on the east side of the tracks.

The Missouri Pacific Depot

Visitors to Russellville today will find a large brick station northwest of North Commerce Avenue, two blocks from Arkansas Avenue, more properly known as Arkansas Highway 7.

The railroad arrived at Russellville in early 1873, and the first depot was apparently a local business, with several freight cars and small buildings also serving various roles. The first independent depot was built in 1880. It was a frame structure and was called "the largest on the Little Rock and Fort Smith road outside of Little Rock." The depot was actually a union depot as it was also used by the Dardanelle & Russellville Railroad (D&R). On May 2, 1904, the D&R signed a 15-year agreement for the joint use of the Iron Mountain depot and yard. The payment for these rights was only $420 a year.

During late September 1910, the St. Louis, Iron Mountain & Southern and city officials announced that a new brick passenger and freight depot would be built at Russellville, costing about $6000. Later, it was announced that to make room for the new station, the old depot was to be moved about a block away and become a freight depot. However, arguments about exactly where to locate the new depot delayed the work for years.

In January of 1915, the Russellville Depot Act was passed by the Arkansas Legislature. It required that a new brick or stone depot be built at Russellville by October 1, 1915. It was also included that the depot was to cost not less than $25,000 and that it not be located at the current location so that River Street could be reopened and extended to the new Agricultural School.

The location of the new depot was still hotly debated. One possible site was east of a local residence and the other was in the wye opposite of the railroad's coal chute. Basically, almost every location through town was supported and opposed. The leaders of the city wanted the new depot to be built in the same spot as the original depot. The Iron Mountain company was willing to work with the city, but they legally could not build the depot in the same spot. This resulted in an impasse that lasted a year.

The lack of action led to a hearing by the Railroad Commission of Arkansas. In April 1916, the Railroad Commission ordered the construction of a new depot on the existing depot site. The railroad proposed a station similar to the one it had recently built at Conway, but larger. It would feature dark red brick and stucco construction with a breezeway separating the passenger and express sections of the building. The building would be topped by a red tile roof. A covered portico was included on each end of the building.

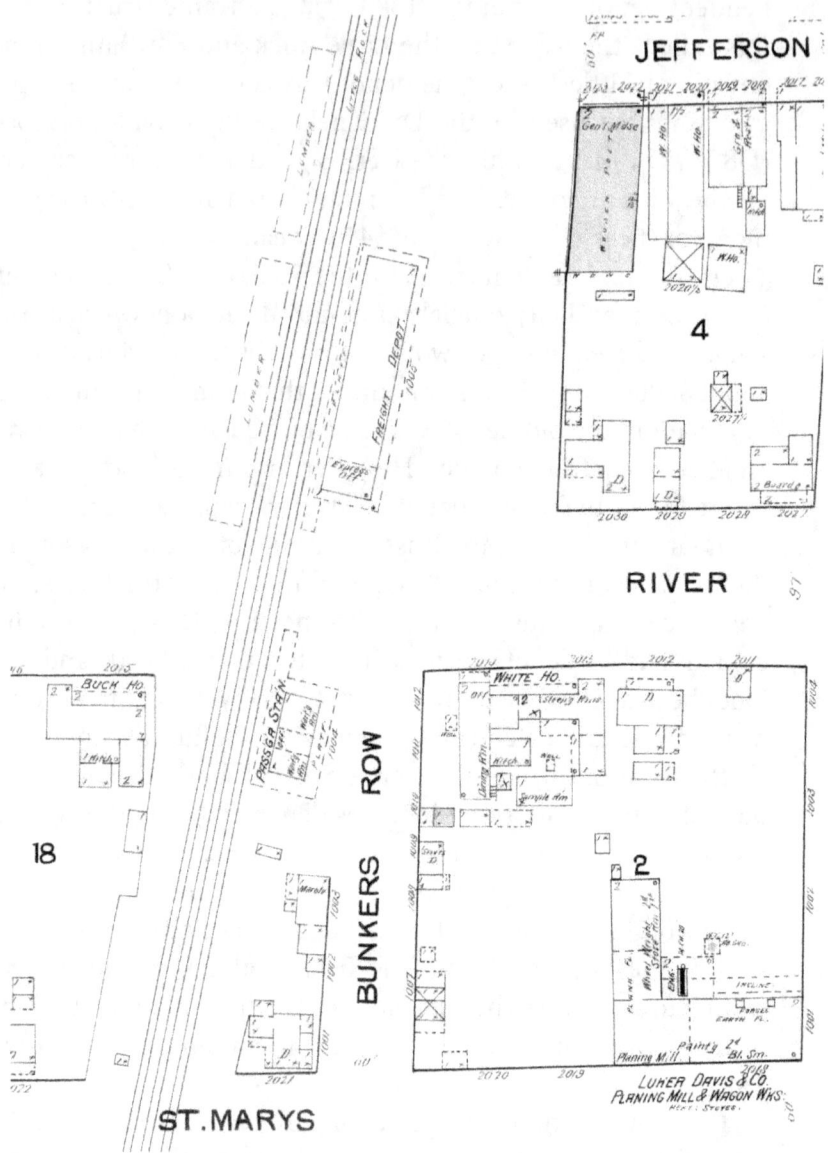

In 1892, Sanborn showed that the freight depot and passenger station at Russellville were centered around River Street, both located on the south side of the tracks. *Sanborn Fire Insurance Map from Russellville, Pope County, Arkansas.* Sanborn Map Company, July 1892. Map. Retrieved from the Library of Congress, https://www.loc.gov/item/sanborn00339_002/.

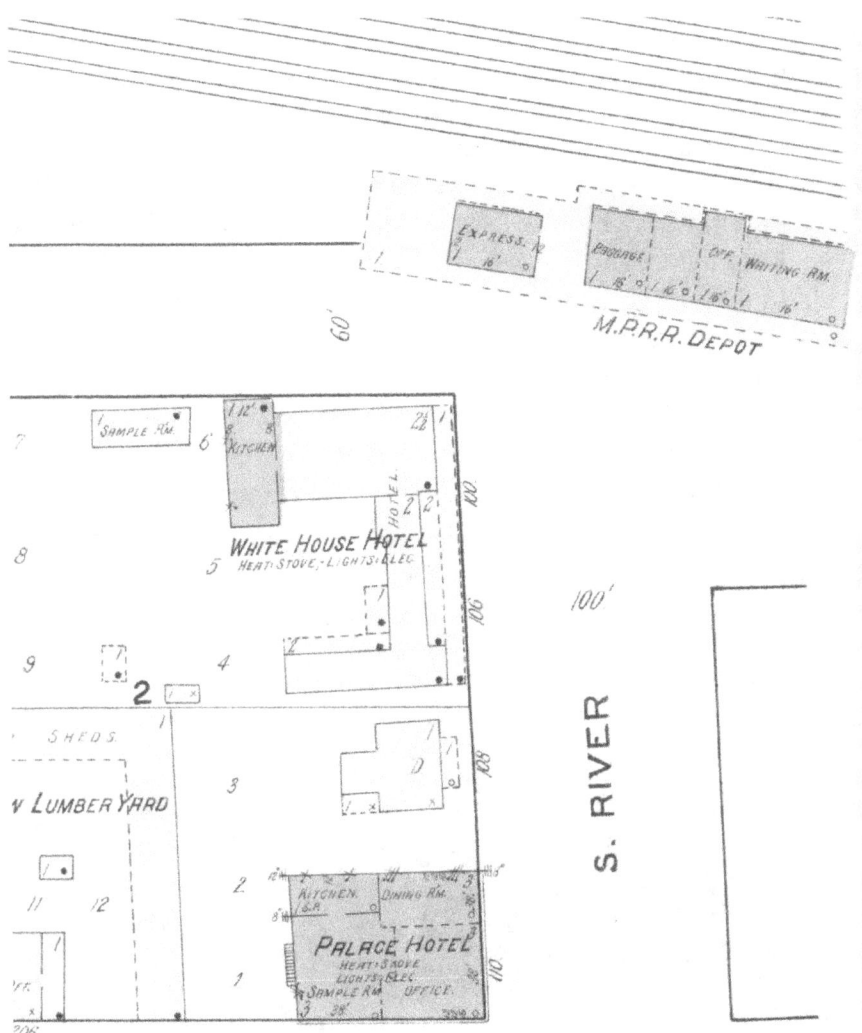

The new Russellville passenger station opened in early 1917, as shown by this Sanborn map from 1919. *Sanborn Fire Insurance Map from Russellville, Pope County, Arkansas.* Sanborn Map Company, February 1919. Map. Retrieved from the Library of Congress, https://www.loc.gov/item/sanborn00339_007/.

Construction began in May, with part of the old depot moved to be used as a temporary depot, with the rest of the building razed. The old 32' x 145' freight house was also moved from the southeast corner of River (Denver) Street to the southeast corner of Jefferson (Commercial) Street. Even during construction, several legal challenges continued about the depot's location.

However, the orders of the Railroad Commission of Arkansas held and the new 22' x 216' St. Louis, Iron Mountain & Southern Railway station opened in February 1917.

During the fall and winter of 1888-1889, a government survey party determined elevations along the railroad from Van Buren, through Ozark, Hartman, Montana, and Clarksville to Russellville. The line was rerun during the winter of 1932-1933. In the survey from the 1930s, it was reported that the elevation for the "top of rail opposite the Missouri Pacific Railroad station" was 351.8 feet.

In 1925, Russellville was a very busy place. There were separate freight and passenger stations on the west side of the main-line. The passenger depot housed a ticket agency and a coupon ticket station. There was also a freight agency in the wooden freight depot that handled carload freight and smaller shipments.

In 1984, the Russellville depot was still used by the railroad and was showing a bit of age, as demonstrated by this trackside view.

The station continued to house local offices, telegraphers, agents, and even dispatchers and many other employees. However, these numbers decreased until it housed only local agents and telegraphers to handle train orders, passenger needs, and freight shippers. Even into the 1950s, Russellville was a continuously operated station for train orders and was supported by telegraphers. The last passenger train to leave the depot was southbound No. 125, which departed at 9:01pm on March 28,

1960. As stated by the National Railroad Adjustment Board, the "work at the station diminished to the point where there was no need for two clerical positions which were abolished at the freight office and the remaining work was assigned to the telegraphers who were assigned to work at the passenger station."

In 1984, railroad vehicles were often parked around the Russellville depot, which housed the office of the local Roadmaster, track inspector, and section crews.

In 1999, the City of Russellville acquired the depot and restored it as part of a downtown revitalization project. The building currently houses the offices of Main Street Russellville and also contains a local museum.

Union Pacific used the station into the early 1990s as a base for railroad freight and maintenance activities, and the depot was listed on the National Register of Historic Places in 1992. In 1999, the City of Russellville acquired the depot and restored it as part of a downtown revitalization project. Groups like Main Street Russellville and its Friends of the Depot committee were involved with the effort, and the building currently houses the offices of Main Street Russellville and also contains a local museum. The open areas outside are often used for public events and is the home of Mr. Conductor, posed with "pocket watch in hand, calling any last passengers to hop aboard."

Depot Rooms and Original and Current Names

Following the plan view above, the various areas and their original and current uses are as follows:

- West Porch – shelter and receiving freight. This will continue to be called the West Porch and will be for special outdoor events, bands, etc.
- Railway Express – for rail freight, with large sliding freight doors and a counter for paperwork. This area now contains public restrooms and a general use office.
- Breezeway
- Baggage Room – passenger baggage and a counter for paperwork. This area will be the Model Train Room and Depot Store. It can also serve as a small meeting space.
- Colored Waiting Room – this area will currently serve as the Main Street Russellville office.
- Station Agent Office/Ticket Office – this area is now the Main Entrance for the building and contains interpretive materials.
- White Waiting Room and White Ladies Waiting Room – this area is the Community Meeting Room with adjacent break area, restroom and custodial closet.
- East Porch – used as shelter for passengers, this provides another public event space.

Main Street Russellville has a large amount of information posted about the depot's history. For example, this sign explains the various parts of the depot and their current use.

The baggage room of the Russellville depot currently houses a number of displays about the area's railroad history.

418.8 CONTROL POINT V418 – This control point protects the north end of the many tracks at Russellville.

420.2 DETOUR NO. 6½ – Between Mileposts 420.2 and 421.0, the original mainline looped a short distance to the north.

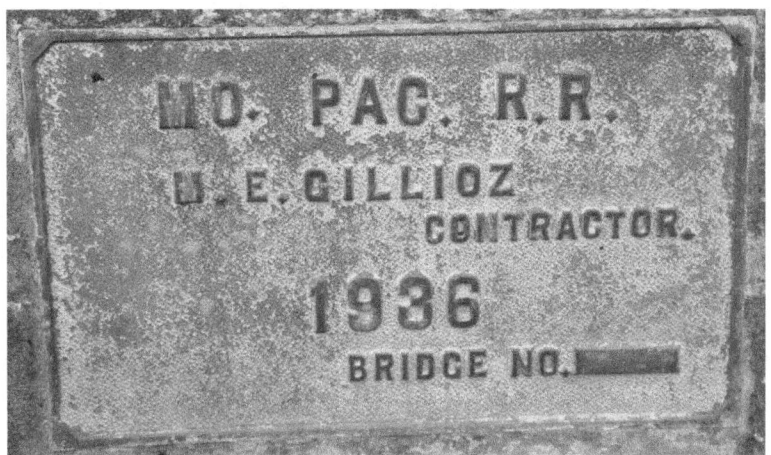

On the west side of Russellville, Main Street (U.S. Highway 64) again bridges over the Van Buren Subdivision, this time at Milepost 420.4. This bridge was built in 1936, as shown by this contractor plate.

420.4 OUITA – This former coal mining community was located where the railroad currently passes under U.S. Highway 64, known locally as West Main Street. This area now features Washburn Park, the Bona Dea Trails and Sanctuary complex, the Illinois Bayou part of Lake Dardanelle, Lake Dardanelle State Park – Ouita Area, and several residential areas. During the late 1870s, the Ouita Coal Company was mining coal in this area, the first in Russellville and the surrounding region.

Coal production had been active for years for local use, but it increased greatly in 1873 when the Little Rock & Fort Smith Railroad arrived. The Ouita post office was open 1876-1877, quickly replaced by nearby Russellville. In 1887, the Ouita Coal Company produced 3500 tons of coal from the Ouita mines, "used entirely for domestic purposes in Little Rock and surrounding towns." A geology report stated that the coal lands in the Ouita basin covered an area of approximately two square miles. The coal was described as being of excellent quality. This was the description of the Ouita Coal Mine of the Ouita Coal Company, which also had mines at Coal Hill. "The principal opening is a slope about 500 feet long, which enters the coal near the outcrop, and this is provided with a steam hoisting plant." This mining activity ended by the 1930s and all of the tracks were removed.

A community using the name Ouitaville eventually formed here, and it had a post office 1899-1901. The town never incorporated until an effort was made to do so as the Town of Ouita during the late 1960s. A series of court cases determined that the incorporation was done to prevent the territory from being annexed by the City of Russellville. With the construction of Lake Dardanelle, most of the lands of the Ouita Coal Company were flooded. The Bona Dea Trails and Sanctuary complex was built on the south bank of the Illinois Bayou section of Lake Dardanelle, while the Ouita Coal Company Trails were built on the north bank.

This sign points the way to the Ouita Coal Company Mountain Bike Trails near the Illinois Bayou.

There were once several spur tracks here that served different mines. In the 1880s, two miles of spur tracks were shown to exist. In 1925, the 0.28-mile-long Ouita Branch left the mainline from Ouita Branch Junction, located 0.50 miles west of Ouita. The track was shown to have both inbound and outbound freight movements, all prepaid.

420.9 OUITA BRANCH JUNCTION – A track once curved to the north to serve the Ouita Coal Mine operation. The tracks at the end of the line were taken up in March 1917, and the rest of the line was removed in August 1939. Near where the switch was located was once a section post used to define the limits of track gangs assigned to the line.

Over the years of the mining activity, tracks were built, moved, and retired numerous times. Some were built by the railroad, while others were built by the Ouita Coal Company to move its "Ouita Anthracite Coal" to market or between facilities. For example, during late 1925, there were numerous newspaper reports that the Ouita Coal & Railroad Company (sometimes listed as the Ouita Railroad and Coal Company) was planning to build a new railroad into the Ouita Coal Basin. As stated in *The Calico Rock Progress* (October 16, 1925), "all preliminary arrangements have been perfected by A. M. Malone and his associates and articles of incorporation will be applied for in a few days by the Ouita Coal and Railroad Company, which will build a railroad line into the old Ouita coal basin and carry on extensive mining operations in that section, which was the scene of the first mining activities in the Russellville field." The *Malvern Times=Journal* (November 12, 1925) later reported that a carload of steel rails had arrived for the spur to be built into the Ouita coal basin.

421.8 ILLINOIS BAYOU BRIDGE – At about Milepost 421, the railroad heads to sea and starts to cross the Illinois Bayou section of Lake Dardanelle. This almost mile-long causeway was built when the lake was formed. Lake Dardanelle, also known as the Dardanelle Reservoir, was created when the Army Corps of Engineers worked to make the Arkansas River navigable from the Mississippi River as far west as the Tulsa Port of Catoosa. This project became known as the McClellan-Kerr Arkansas River Navigation System and opened on June 5, 1971.

Raising the level of the Arkansas River forced Missouri Pacific to raise its track through seven different sections between Russellville and Spadra Junction. The track work was expected to cost $5,428,000 and was paid for by the Corps of Engineers. The work included new steel bridges over Illinois Bayou, Mill Creek and Little Spadra Creek, and was scheduled to be completed by September 30, 1964. The new bridge over the Illinois Bayou, replacing the old Bridge No. 197, included seven deck plate girder spans, measuring 501 feet long. The earlier bridge included two 74-foot deck plate girder spans with four 17-foot concrete slab approaches.

During April 2023, UP 7295 went to sea across Lake Dardanelle and the Illinois Bayou Bridge. The train was heading south to North Little Rock with a trainload of oil cars.

Despite the work to raise the Van Buren Subdivision, the line could still be closed by high water. Probably the worst flooding event was in 2019 when an Arkansas River levee near Russellville broke on May 31st, leading to major flooding in the area. It took almost two weeks before the Van Buren Subdivision was reopened.

The Illinois Bayou

In 1873, the Illinois Bayou, often shown on maps as Illinois Creek, was a barrier for the railroad to build westward from Russellville, and the construction was reported on in the March 14, 1873, issue of the *Daily Arkansas Gazette*. "Mr. E. P. Curry, of Memphis, the contractor in charge of the track laying on the Little Rock and Fort Smith railroad is pushing things. Rails are now laid as far up as Illinois Bayou, three miles above Russellville. The road will be finished to Clarksville, forty miles above Russellville, by the 15th of April next."

The Russellville Democrat newspaper reported often on the local railroad activities. It noted that the original Illinois Bayou bridge was temporary, and the railroad soon planned on installing a new structure. During late March of 1878, the newspaper reported that a "new railroad bridge over the Illinois Bayou" would soon be installed. At the time, the LR&FS built a number of 109-foot-long wooden Howe truss spans. Many were sheathed to reduce weathering of the wood, and in late December 1879, *The Russellville Democrat* reported that the "railroad bridge at Illinois Bayou has been covered over and sided up."

The Arkansas Nuclear One power plant is clearly visible from the Illinois Bayou Bridge. On this June 2025 morning, a southbound American Electric Power Company (AEPX) coal train passes the plant producing an interesting mix of coal and nuclear power generation.

Like many streams that flow into the Arkansas River, the Illinois Bayou was named bayou by early explores who seldom followed the creeks into the mountains where they were actually mountain streams. Instead, the bayou name came from the sluggish waters in the valley lands alongside the Arkansas River. However, some researchers believe that the French word may have originated from the Choctaw word "bayuk", which means "small stream." This use of the term would be appropriate for many of the streams that the Little Rock & Fort Smith bridged as it built across western Arkansas.

The Illinois Bayou is created from three streams – North Fork of Illinois Bayou, East Fork of Illinois Bayou, and Middle Fork of Illinois Bayou. Illinois Bayou is located in Pope County and starts at the confluence of the East Fork and Middle Fork. It then flows about 30 miles southwest into the Arkansas River, now Lake Dardanelle. The East Fork is 15 miles long and includes the East Fork Wilderness. It flows to the southwest and helps to form the Illinois Bayou. The Middle Fork is almost 25 miles long and flows southward through the Ozark National Forest. The North Fork forms near the community of Ben Hur in Pope County. It flows about 25 miles southward to the Illinois Bayou near Scottsville. All of its route is within the Ozark National Forest.

When the region was being explored for coal, the Illinois Bayou Basin was an early target since the coal was rather close to the surface. However, it seemed to just start and stop, and was mainly found in several concentrated areas. A geological report stated that the Illinois Bayou "flows across the basin and has no doubt eroded a great deal of the shallow coal, so that much of the area included in the basin is not coal land."

Timothy Dwight Mission

In 1820, the Dwight Presbyterian Mission opened on the west side of Illinois Bayou to serve the Arkansas Cherokees. The efforts of the mission actually date back to 1818 when Western Cherokee Principal Chief Tahlonteskee visited the Brainerd Mission in Georgia. He felt that it would be useful for the tribe's children to be formally trained in Anglo-American ways. As a number of Cherokee moved west to Arkansas, it was felt that this would be a good time to expand the efforts. The decision wasn't always popular, and a series of tribal leaders debated the decision but allowed some education to take place here. The Dwight Mission was sponsored by the American Board of Commissioners of Foreign Missions (ABCFM), a Presbyterian organization. It was one of the first Protestant missions established west of the Mississippi River, and the first formal Protestant effort directed at the education and conversion of Native Americans in Arkansas.

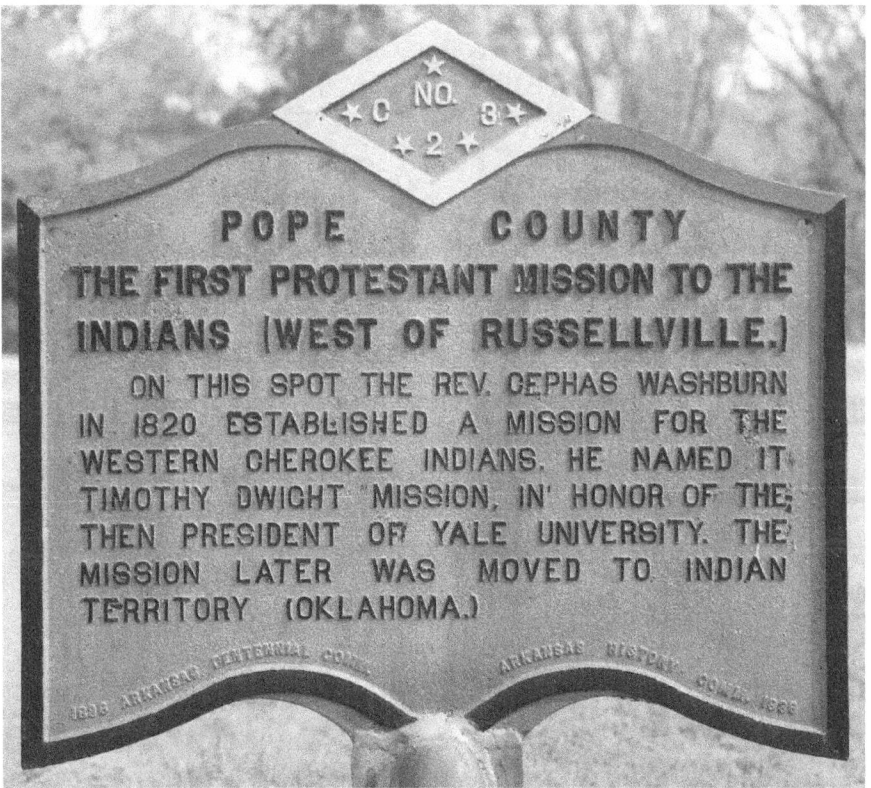

This marker is located at the north end of the Illinois Bayou causeway. It tells the story of the Timothy Dwight Mission, an early religious mission that served the Cherokee Indians during their brief time in northwestern Arkansas.

The mission was established here during August 1820. Its location was chosen by New Englanders Cephas Washburn and Alfred Finney, plus War Chief Takatoka, who opposed the efforts. Takatoka had his headquarters at nearby Spadra Creek (now Clarksville), and felt that he could watch the mission carefully from his home. The mission was named after Timothy Dwight, who had been president of Yale University and was the first corporate member of the ABCFM.

Most of the staff came from New England, and they had arrived by December 1821. The school opened on January 1, 1822, and as many as 100 students attended class each year. The mission expanded and eventually included fifteen residences and twenty-one other buildings. There were also a sawmill and gristmill, along with several houses and outbuildings, located a mile to the west on Mill Creek. In 1828, the Cherokee were required to move further west to Indian Territory, and the Dwight Mission closed at the end of summer 1829. It then moved west to near what became Marble City, Oklahoma.

422.8 MILL CREEK – In 1852, the Arkansas State Legislature passed a bill that allowed a Mr. Hanger and Mr. Howell to build a toll bridge across Mill Creek near here. During the early years of the railroad, a small community developed between Illinois Bayou and Mill Creek, using the name Mill Creek Station. The community was scattered along the railroad and the Little Rock to Fort Smith military road a short distance to the north. A Mill Creek post office only existed 1892-1894. Today, Mill Creek is an unincorporated community in Clark Township of Pope County. A number of country homes can be found in the area on the lake and surrounding hillsides.

The railroad built a small board and batten depot at Mill Creek. In 1907, there was also a mail crane and an 80-car siding. The depot was closed and removed in February 1920, but a platform remained on the east side of the mainline. A freight room and passenger shelter replaced the depot, and a railroad telephone was also available at Mill Creek. With no agency here, all freight was required to be prepaid. The freight house and shelter were removed in May 1932. When ABS signaling was installed on the railroad in 1944, some sidings were lengthened while others were retired. The 84-car siding at Mill Creek was retired and removed, leaving no side tracks here. The telephone was also removed since trains no longer stopped at Mill Creek.

422.9 MILL CREEK BRIDGE – This is one of several bridges that were installed as part of the line's rebuilding due to the Arkansas River navigation project of the early 1960s. The old bridge, known as Bridge No. 203, consisted of a 76-foot deck plate girder with several panels of timber pile trestles off each end. In 1925, the bridge was rebuilt with a 75-foot deck plate girder and two concrete trestle approaches. The newer bridge was replaced with this higher 3-span, 240-foot deck plate girder bridge.

Mill Creek forms several miles to the north. It has several small branches on the north side of Ouita Ridge. It then consolidates and flows through a narrow gap through the ridge, just a short distance north of here. Heading westward, over the next 1.5 miles, the track climbs 37 feet to pass over a low ridge between London Mountain (to the north) and Round Mountain.

Three deck plate girder spans replaced the older bridge over Mill Creek about 1965. The higher and longer bridge was necessary due to the creation of Lake Dardanelle as part of the McClellan-Kerr Arkansas River Navigation System project. Most of these new bridges are identified by the concrete piers like this one.

423.4 CARGILL – While the short spur track to the north has historically been known as Cargill, the small feed mill is now operated by JBS Live Pork. JBS Live Pork serves Arkansas, Texas, Missouri and Iowa, and this is their London facility, which specializes in feed corn. The company is a small part of JBS Foods, the leading beef producer in the world and the majority shareholder of Pilgrim's, the leading poultry producer in the world.

This small JBS Foods feedmill is served by Union Pacific at Milepost 423.4. It has historically been known as Cargill.

423.7 SOUTH END OF DETOUR NO. 8 – This is another detour from the early 1900s when the Iron Mountain rebuilt parts of the railroad to reduce grades and the number of curves. The original line looped to the north while the newer line was straighter and had fewer grades due to several cuts and fills.

The industrial line that heads south to serve Arkansas Nuclear One breaks off of the Van Buren Subdivision next to U.S. Highway 64. The track hasn't been used in years and trees have grown up next to it, making travel almost impossible today. The turnout on the mainline remains, and now includes a jump frog. A jump frog is a type of flange-bearing frog where the mainline railhead through the frog is solid, and trains taking the turnout side climb over the frog on the wheel flanges of each car and locomotive.

424.5 AP&L SPUR – To the south (railroad-west) is a several-mile-long track into Arkansas Nuclear One, the state's only nuclear power plant. Unit 1 of the facility began commercial operations on December 19, 1974, with Unit 2 starting commercial operations on March 26, 1980. The plant provides more than half of the electrical power required by Entergy's 700,000 customers in Arkansas. Unit 1 uses Lake Dardanelle for cooling water while Unit 2 uses the 447-foot-tall cooling tower that marks the plant's location. While the plant is owned by Entergy, the name Arkansas Power & Light (AP&L) has been used since before the plant's construction began as that was the name of the local power company. AP&L was founded in 1913 by Harvey Crowley Couch, and the company eventually became the primary electrical utility company for much of Arkansas. It became part of Middle South Utilities in 1949, and then Entergy Corporation in 1989. Trains seldom move on the line and parts of it are heavily overgrown.

The milepost used for this location has historically been 424.5, but by 2021 it was shown to be Milepost 424.7. Just west of the switch at an elevation of 387 feet is the top of a 0.41% grade that started at Ouita, and a 0.48% grade that started to the west at Scotia.

425.1 NORTH END OF DETOUR NO. 8 – The north end of this detour is almost impossible to find, but some of the old grade is to the north in the woods.

425.5 LONDON – London was another small farming community that grew with the construction of the railroad. It was dominated by nearby Russellville and Clarksville, so it never grew large, but the basics of the community still exist. The community developed on the high ground north of the Arkansas River and centered itself on the Little Rock & Fort Smith Railway. While there were scattered settlers already, Isaac Haddox and his family, plus a large number of slaves, moved here from Tennessee about 1860. The family moved elsewhere by the end of the Civil War, but the area took on the name Haddoxburg. The only clear reminder of their presence is a slave cemetery with sixteen graves, now clearly marked as Slave Cemetery.

The possibility of being on the new railroad brought a number of new settlers, and a Methodist church was founded in 1870. The railroad passed a short distance north of the Haddoxburg community, and a post office opened in 1877. John McClure was the first postmaster and he named the post office London, for no known reason. The community and the railroad also adopted the name, especially after the town was incorporated on March 2, 1882, with a population of about 100. The population was 282 in the 1900 census, and London featured several stores, two schools, a bank, a doctor's office, a grist mill, and three blacksmith shops. There was a community building used by various churches and groups, a Masonic temple was active, and there was a railroad depot.

Unlike towns to the east and west, London was not a coal town. A mineral survey stated that "in the vicinity of London, there is an area of land containing something over one and one-half townships which is underlain by Spadra shale and Hartshorne sandstone." Prospect wells near London revealed no coal, although there was coal just south of the Arkansas River. The changing channels of the local streams were blamed for this as coal would be washed away and then sands would be deposited in its place as the streams moved.

By 1920, the population had reached 386 residents and three cotton gins had been built to handle the area's annual cotton crop. With the reduced need for farm labor due to the addition of farm machinery, and the depressed prices for cotton, the population of London dropped to 355 in 1930. It jumped back up to 418 in 1940, and then dropped until hitting a low of 282 in 1960. It has generally grown since then with 936 residents reported in the 2020 census. London also still has its own elementary school, several retail stores, and it has essentially become a bedroom community for nearby Russellville.

The tracks are located on an east-west alignment through here. When the railroad was first built, a siding was included at London. In 1900, the passing track was extended 605 feet. A small wooden depot stood here until 1938, located on the south side of the tracks and west of Price Street. The depot housed an agent who operated both a ticket and freight agency. A three-room section house stood at London for years, located east of Price Street. The railroad also had a cotton platform (removed 1939), store house, and a tool house. The siding was gone by the 1930s, but a spur track for local customers remained for many years, and a mail crane stood here until the end of railroad mail service. The London spur track disappeared in 1981. However, Railroad Street still exists on the south side of the tracks.

Like many towns along the route, London has its own Railroad Street, located immediately south of the tracks.

Heading towards Fort Smith, the railroad turns to the southwest to reach the Arkansas River. It then runs along the shoreline and follows the river to the northwest to near Knoxville. There, the railroad continues almost northward, avoiding several large river bends. This was another part of the track that the railroad had to raise in the early 1960s due to the Arkansas River navigation project.

Union Pacific 7369 pulls a freight southbound into London, Arkansas, on July 31, 2025. This curve has the train changing from heading northeast to heading southeast.

426.0 MIXER– A station was listed in this area in public timetables during the 1890s and the first few years of the twentieth century. Mixer and Georgetown were apparently the same community, or at least the station of Mixer was replaced by the station of Georgetown.

During the fall and winter of 1888-89, a survey team conducted field work along the railroad between Van Buren and Russellville. The line was rerun during the winter of 1932-33. The elevation of the top of rail opposite Missouri Pacific Railroad Milepost 426 was 356.6 feet. This was part of a gentle three-mile-long downhill grade for westbound trains.

426.5 SOUTH END OF DETOUR NO. 9 – This is another of the many track realignments made by the St. Louis, Iron Mountain & Southern about 1904. The old line curved back and forth along the low ridge and around the many wetlands to the north, sometimes near U.S. Highway 64. This line change impacted 3½ miles of the original Little Rock & Fort Smith, a significant investment for the Iron Mountain.

426.6 CONTROL POINT V427 – This location has historically been known as South Switch Scotia or South Scotia. The 8160-foot siding is located on the west side of the mainline, directly beside the Arkansas River. Over the years, the siding has been listed as being between 8200 and 8300 feet long. Even earlier, the south switch was at Milepost 427.6.

426.9 GEORGETOWN – As stated in many local histories, Georgetown (also known as Mixer) is an unincorporated community in Clark Township of Pope County. The community is actually located to the north along the route of U.S. Highway 64. This was where a local road reached the tracks making it the closest rail point to Georgetown. The name was actually found in timetables from the 1870s, years before the name Mixer was used for the area.

427.5 SCOTIA – The elevation at Scotia is 345 feet, and the railroad has an almost steady grade as it heads north alongside the Arkansas River. In 1907, the railroad had an 80-car siding here. In 1944, the Scotia siding could hold 67 freight cars, and was extended to 90 cars as part of the ABS signaling project of the mid-1940s. There was also a company telephone for train crews to talk with the dispatcher. By the 1920s, there was no depot or railroad agency at Scotia, just a simple station sign, and all freight movements were prepaid.

The original LR&FS grade curved around the hillsides to the north of the current Van Buren Subdivision. Some of this old grade was substantial and can be seen passing across ranch lands near U.S. Highway 64.

Scotia predated the railroad, with the land being acquired by Judge Andrew Horatio Scott in 1828 from former Cherokee lands that had just been opened for settlement. He chose land along the military road and near the Arkansas River. Scotia was described as being about two and a half miles below the mouth of Big Piney Creek on the north bank of the Arkansas River. The property was soon used as the county seat of Pope County, which was created on November 2, 1829. The site was always to be temporary, but the Scotia post office opened in 1830 to support the new center of government. The same year, the county seat moved to Norristown, and then on to Dover. The post office at Scotia lasted until 1855.

Judge Andrew Horatio Scott was an important early political leader in Arkansas, and the earlier Missouri Territory. Scott was the first Clerk of the House of Representatives for the Territory of Missouri, and later the sheriff of Jefferson County, Missouri. President James Monroe appointed Andrew H. Scott as a Superior Court Judge for the newly created Territory of Arkansas on March 3, 1819. He was the first governmental official to report for duty at the village of Arkansas Post, the capital of the Arkansas Territory. He arrived on July 4, 1819, and being the first Superior Court Judge to arrive, led the effort to create a set of laws for the new territory. He later served as Circuit Court Judge for the First District and was the first County Judge of Pope County. Scott County, Arkansas, was named for him when it was created in 1833.

428.3 COUNTY LINE – The county line between Pope and Johnson counties is a short distance east of the north switch of the siding at Scotia. The Arkansas River is on the west side of the tracks while a small pond is to the east. **Pope County** was created from part of Crawford County on November 2, 1829, the first Arkansas county to be formed from the old Cherokee reservation. It was named for John Pope, the third governor of the Arkansas Territory. Like all of the counties in the Arkansas River Valley, it started very rural with explorers and farmers being the first residents. The county had a population of 1483 in the 1830 census. Much of the county consists of flat and rolling land, and cotton and other farm crops were the primary economic activity for many decades. Pope County was famous for its Pope County Militia War after the Civil War, an effort by local Democrats to end Governor Powell Clayton's reconstruction efforts. Farming continued to dominate and the county's population peaked at 27,153 in the 1920 census. It began to grow again in the 1960s, mainly due to activity at the county seat of Russellville, the home of Arkansas Tech University. The population was 63,381 people in the 2020 census.

To the west (railroad-north) is **Johnson County**, site of most of the coal mining in Arkansas. The county was created from parts of Pope County on November 16, 1833. Like most of the counties along the railroad, the southern half is in the Arkansas River Valley while the northern part is in the Ozark Mountains. This county was once located in the Cherokee lands, and one of three factories (trading posts) was located at Spadra Bayou, near today's county seat of Clarksville. In 1840, the county's population was 3433. Some coal was shipped on the Arkansas River, but with the construction of the railroad, large volumes began to be mined. Almost 20 different mines operated in the county at the peak of coal mining. Timber, cotton, fruit (apples, pears, and peaches), poultry, and natural gas all are major sources of business in the county. In particular, the Missouri Pacific Railroad heavily promoted the Johnson County peaches across the country.

The population temporarily peaked in 1920 with the county having 21,062 residents. With the end of manual labor in farming, and coal and timber production, the population dropped to 12,421 in the 1960 census. Since then, retail and light manufacturing have moved to the county, and even a Walmart Distribution Center has brought fame after it earned the "Grocery Distribution Center of the Year" award for four straight years. Since 1938, Johnson County has hosted an annual Peach Festival, and outdoor activities have brought many visitors to the county. Even the notorious bandit Bill Doolin, the founder of the Wild Bunch, is an attraction as he was born in Johnson County in 1858. The population in the 2020 census was 25,749.

428.3 CONTROL POINT V428 – Once known as North Scotia, this is the north end of the Scotia Siding.

430.0 NORTH END OF DETOUR NO. 9 – The end of Detour No. 9 was just south of the former station of Piney. Little of the original line can be found except for a few locations where it is used as field roads.

430.1 PINEY – Piney Creek was an early area of German settlement along the Arkansas River, with Hugh Gilbert operating a grist mill on the stream by 1833, and Abraham Clark operating a saw mill by 1840. A post office opened at Piney in 1844, and then repeatedly closed and opened until 1934, when it closed for good during the Great Depression. To support the post office, the railroad had a mail crane at Piney. The community, which was on the south or east bank of Piney Creek, was a trading post and market for people who lived upstream on the east side of the creek. A stone quarry was also worked nearby.

This was where ferry boats and bridges crossed the creek to reach the towns towards Fort Smith. On April 18, 1920, a tornado destroyed the county bridge across Piney Creek. This was the second time that the bridge had been destroyed by a tornado (a tornado in late 1908 killed a number of people and did large amounts of damage at Piney), and a ferry took over the task each time, adding some local business to the community.

The railroad had a few industry tracks at Piney, shown as Piney Bridge in early timetables, during the first few decades of the twentieth century. At least one of these tracks came about due to a November 23, 1911, petition by citizens of Piney who wanted the St. Louis, Iron Mountain & Southern to build a spur track to handle the stone and lumber that were shipped from Piney. There was also a small wooden station that was built in October 1912, but was closed by the mid-1920s and removed in August 1936. In 1925, Missouri Pacific reported that there was a platform to the west at Piney, with all freight (carloads and less) required to be prepaid. The government survey during the winter of 1932-1933 reported that the elevation for the "top of rail opposite the Missouri Pacific Railroad station" at Piney was 347.4 feet.

Piney was at one time the home of a track section gang. The gang was supported by a store house, tool house, and a section house. The section house was removed with the depot in 1936. The other structures were eventually removed and nothing remains at the site today.

430.2 BIG PINEY CREEK BRIDGE – The railroad crosses Big Piney Creek, shown as Big Pine Creek on some early maps, using a 5-span deck plate girder bridge that is 463 feet long. The bridge, once known as Bridge No. 221, is just a few feet from the Arkansas River and just downstream of the U.S. Highway 64 and Interstate 40 bridges. The two spans on the west end of the bridge have a higher clearance over Piney Creek, important due to the boat traffic from the Arkansas Game and Fish Commission boat ramp to the north.

This sign is located several hundred feet north of the railroad alongside U.S. Highway 64.

UP 7369 heads east across the Big Piney Creek Bridge pulling a freight train. This photo is taken from the nearby U.S. Highway 64 bridge. A joke among local rail enthusiasts is that a boat may be the best chase vehicle along this section of track.

This bridge and the track around it have been replaced several times over the years. In 1925, the existing 199-foot-long through pin connected truss span was replaced by a new bridge consisting of a series of deck plate girder spans. The work included moving almost a mile of track northwards away from the Arkansas River. The new line was straighter, cutting 220 feet from the mainline.

Big Piney Creek is about 70 miles long and starts between Limestone and Fallsville, both in Arkansas. Most of the stream is in the Ozark National Forest as it flows south to Lake Dardanelle on the Arkansas River. Also called a river, Big Piney Creek is popular for canoeing and sportfishing. It has been designated as a National Wild & Scenic River and a number of campgrounds can be found along its length.

431.1 SECTION POST – This was another dividing line between the territories assigned to track gangs. In this area, the railroad runs along backwaters of the Arkansas River. This was some of the railroad grade that was raised as part of the construction of Lake Dardanelle.

431.5 ZIEGLER SPUR – A spur track once headed to the east. It was retired in April 1931.

During the early 1930s, the Ziegler Construction Company of Nashville, Tennessee, had a number of contracts to build roads for the State of Arkansas. In Johnson County, Ziegler Construction had a $175,840.96 contract to do grading, build drainage structures, and install concrete paving on 7.442 miles of roadway. This spur track was used to deliver construction materials for the project.

433.6 KNOXVILLE (KO) – Knoxville, located at an elevation of 390 feet (the top of rail opposite the Missouri Pacific Knoxville station was 392.1 feet according to a 1932-1933 survey), is in the middle of a 0.45% grade against northbound trains. Knoxville was an early station, initially called Mayville. In 1900, the passing track was extended 1548 feet and a new 731-foot business track was built. A small board and batten depot stood at Knoxville, with the first one reportedly opened by 1881. The station was justified during the early 1900s when the railroad served a timber company's sawmill (lumber and railroad crossties), two fruit growers, and several cotton gins. In 1907, the railroad had a day and night telegraph office, a mail crane, and an 80-car siding at Knoxville. In 1925, the station and platform were to the east, located south of Plum Street, and there was still a ticket and freight agency here.

The agency seemed to come and go and the staffed station was replaced by a station sign by 1927. The station was soon staffed again, but after the agency was closed again, the depot and train order signal were retired in August 1937. About the same time, the section house (March 1938) and the cotton platform (March 1939) were also removed. In 1944, there was a 91-car siding on the west side of the mainline at Knoxville, plus a company telephone, tool house, and a mail crane (installed July 1921). The siding and other structures were later removed, but there is still a short double-ended business track north of Plum Street. Alongside this house track is a very unique platform, built from several flatbed truck trailers.

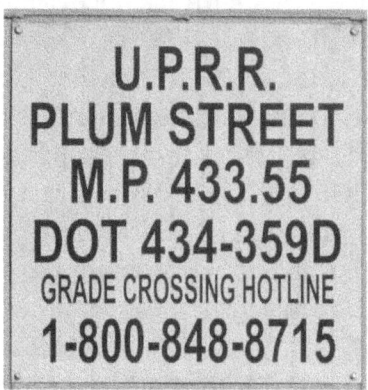

Plum Street was the center of the railroad facilities at Knoxville, Arkansas, for many years. The station and platform were located south of Plum Street while a siding once passed through town.

The Community of Knoxville

During the mid-1800s, what became Knoxville was essentially a one-man town. Thomas May was an early settler in the area and by 1850 owned almost 800 acres of bottomland in Johnson County, creating a small community that he called Mayville. Besides the land, May also owned 14 slaves, a sawmill, a lumberyard, a general store, a hardware store, and an ice house. His farm produced cotton, corn, wheat, oats, potatoes, and hay. By late 1872, the railroad work reached Mayville, and a temporary depot was built on the property of Thomas May, shown as a flag stop for many years. A post office opened at Mayville in 1873, but it used the name Black Fox. At the time, W. D. Epperson operated the post office, plus a small store and the railroad depot.

A few years later, M. H. Hobbs purchased eighty acres of land from May. Hobbs had first come to Arkansas in 1868 and then returned home to Virginia, returning to Arkansas in 1877. He brought a large amount of stock to Mayville and opened a store. He worked to establish a more formalized town and helped to name it Knoxville, or Knoxville Station. The post office also changed its name that year, using Knoxville instead of Mayville since there was already a town with that name in Arkansas. In 1887, Hobbs sold his store to P. J. Carr, who operated a 250-acre farm. Carr became his father-in-law the next year.

This unique platform at Knoxville seems to have been built from several flatbed truck trailers.

New residents, businesses, and churches arrived as the town developed. One of the larger buildings was the Methodist church, built in 1883. Later, the church built a new building and sold their old church building to the school board. A new drug store opened in 1909, a new five-room school was built in 1913, and a small business district developed. However, much of the town burned in a fire in late 1923. The fruit business – apples, peaches, and pears – developed during the first few decades of the twentieth century. Cotton also remained important, especially on land that had recently been logged. The local farm incomes allowed for three stores at Knoxville. Unlike many towns in the area, Knoxville was never a coal mining community. A mineral survey reported that between Knoxville and Russellville to the east, the Hartshorne sandstone comes to the surface but without coal. To the west were the Spadra and Ouita coalfields.

The successful local economy changed as the Great Depression of the 1930s took effect. Many local residents moved away, stores and schools closed, and many farms were foreclosed upon. As the Arkansas River navigation project was underway, Knoxville incorporated on January 5, 1962, to take advantage of possible financial assistance. The population was 202 in the 1970 census, and it grew to 731 by the 2020 census. The creation of Lake Dardanelle introduced tourism to the community, now one of the largest businesses in town. Other businesses include manufacturing, stone, concrete, steel, natural gas establishments, trucking companies, restaurants, and a few retail stores.

This very leaning sign warns employees that the south turnout at Knoxville uses a jump frog. These frogs are for slow speed train movements when heading in or out of the house track, and are difficult for hirail equipment to use.

Besides the house track and platform, Union Pacific also has a train defect detector (hot box and dragging equipment) at Knoxville, Arkansas.

The Collision of October 23, 1928

Knoxville was the scene of another train collision that was investigated by the Interstate Commerce Commission (ICC). In this case, it was a collision between a passenger train (gas-electric motorcar) and a freight train. The two trains involved included southbound passenger train No. 143 and northbound freight train No. 168. The passenger train consisted of steel gas-electric motor #654, built in 1926 by St. Louis-EMC. The northbound freight train was pulled by steam locomotive #1708 (2-10-2 built for the St. Louis, Iron Mountain & Southern by Alco-Brooks in 1916) and consisted of 58 cars and a caboose.

Each train had received a train order to meet at Knoxville, with No. 168 to hold the main track. No. 143 had received their order at Knoxville Junction while No. 168 received theirs at Russellville. However, the crew of No. 168 got distracted and passed Knoxville without stopping and collided with train No. 143 shortly afterwards. The ICC report included information about rail operations around Knoxville.

The passing track at Knoxville is 5,010 feet in length and parallels the main track on the west. A State highway is also located west of the right-of-way and parallels the main track for a considerable distance.

The accident occurred 2,521 feet north of the north passing-track switch at Knoxville; approaching this point from the south, beginning at the south passing-track switch, the track is tangent for a distance of 6,588.3 feet, followed by a 0 degree 57' curve to the left 2,516.7 feet in length, the accident occurring on this curve at a point 942.7 feet from its southern end. Approaching from the north there is a 4 degree 02' curve to the left 1,675.7 feet in length, then tangent for a distance of 106 feet, followed by the curve on which the accident occurred. The grade is generally ascending for northbound trains, being 0.42 per cent at the point of accident. The accident occurred in a cut, the maximum depth of which is 15 feet, and there is some shubbery on the inside of the curve; approaching the point of accident, the range of vision is restricted to approximately 875 feet from the engineman's side of a southbound train and to about 200 feet from the engineman's side of a northbound train.

434.9 SOUTH SWITCH CLARKSVILLE JUNCTION – Located just north of the grade crossing with Old U.S. Highway 64 is a switch for a track to the east. The short siding to the east is part of the old junction between the two lines to the north. The original route went via Clarksville, while the new route went directly west to Spadra, saving 4.68 miles.

Details about the Clarksville Subdivision, the original mainline between BB Junction and AA Junction, are found in the route guide for the Clarksville Branch starting on Page 463.

This AAR-DOT Crossing Sign marks the Old Highway 64 grade crossing at the South Switch Clarksville Junction.

435.6 CLARKSVILLE JUNCTION – Located just north of the Pittsburgh Road grade crossing is the north switch to the siding at Clarksville Junction, now known simply as Clarksville. The switch off of the siding that led to the Clarksville Subdivision was also here, shown as being at Milepost 435.66. For years, this switch was known as BB Junction, located at Milepost 435.85, and also Knoxville Junction, located at Milepost 435.95.

In 1907, the St. Louis, Iron Mountain & Southern showed that there was a train register booth at Knoxville Junction. Knoxville Junction was originally the site of a section house, which was destroyed in March 1923. In late 1926, a number of facilities were built at Knoxville Junction. This included a telegraph cabin (10' x 12') and train order signal, a coal box, a toilet, and a section post sign. To protect the junction, there were warning and stop signs, all with lamps. By the 1940s, the location was shown as being BB Junction and only a company telephone was available for use by train crews.

In 1958, the employee timetable of Missouri Pacific had a number of instructions about BB Junction. It stated that the spring switch at BB Junction was normally lined for the Van Buren Subdivision, and that it was a train register station only for trains moving via the Clarksville Subdivision which were instructed by train order to register at that point.

Heading towards Fort Smith, the railroad curves to the west to the Arkansas River, and then stays on the riverbank to Spadra.

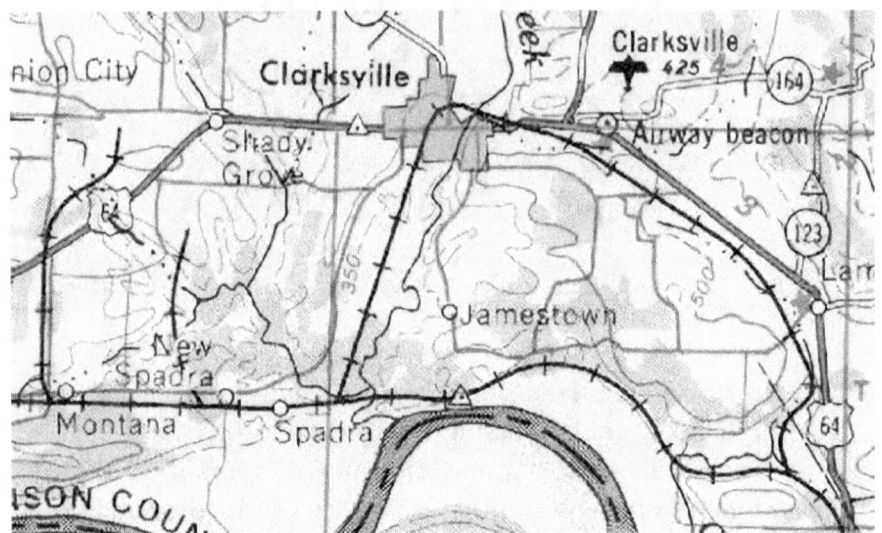

In 1904, a new rail route opened between Knoxville and Spadra, bypassing the route through Clarksville. This topographic map from 1956 shows both routes. Also note the coal mine spurs located just west of Spadra. *Russellville (AR) Quadrangle, 1956.* U.S. Department of the Interior, U.S. Geological Survey.

The mainline and Clarksville side track create an interesting picture on this early October morning in 2022.

This sign marks the switch at North Clarksville, also once known as Clarksville Junction and BB Junction.

This signal directs traffic off of the Clarksville Junction siding.

437.5 SOUTH END OF DETOUR NO. 10 – Detour No. 10 was completed in 1937. This detour is somewhat unique in that the new route is 2766 feet longer than the original route, which went straight for about four miles. While straight, the old line dropped down into the river valley through Cuba Bottom, creating several significant grades. The new line curved to the northeast to go around them.

This detour was built for a very different reason than many of the other detours – it was forced upon the railroad by the Arkansas River. During Spring 1935, there were multiple storms that dropped five or more inches of rain along the Arkansas River in Oklahoma and Arkansas. Between June 12th and 21st, a week of storms dropped almost nine inches of rain upstream, and more than six inches of rain in this immediate area. With the river already high, flooding occurred all along the river and washed out the former LR&FS in this area. Missouri Pacific detoured all trains through Clarksville on the original LR&FS route.

During March 1936, officials of Missouri Pacific announced plans that were reported in *Railway Age* and local newspapers. The news announcement stated that the railroad "plans to undertake the construction of 3.71 miles of track between Spadra Junction, Ark., and Knoxville Junction, to replace a line that was washed out by the Arkansas river in June, 1935. By moving the line back a maximum of 4,000 ft. from the river to the face of the river bluffs, it is felt that it will be safe from further flood damage. This project will cost approximately $260,000, will require about six months to complete and will provide employment for about 150 men."

Eventually, 3.7 miles of new track and grade were built, with a total of six miles of new track installed. All of the tracks were moved and/or raised to be above flood level. The first freight train operated over the line at noon on December 16, 1936. Work continued on the line into 1937, with passenger trains continuing to go through Clarksville during that time. Since then, the creation of Lake Dardanelle has brought the Arkansas River back alongside the Van Buren Subdivision

437.6 CAZORT SPUR – In the March 1, 1925, *Missouri Pacific Railroad Company Official List of Officers, Agents, Stations and Mileage*, Cazort Spur was shown to handle prepaid freight in carload volumes and less. This track curved to the northeast and was abandoned by 1937 when a new alignment for the mainline was built.

The Cazort family moved to the area when Sidney Cazort acquired the Adams plantation in 1850. Cazort cleared land in the area and helped to develop the community of Cabin Creek, later Lamar, on the original rail line via Clarksville. The Little Rock & Fort Smith arrived at Cabin Creek in 1873 and located a depot and water tower there. William Alexander Cazort, the son of Sidney Cazort, was made the first station agent for the railroad, and then the first postmaster when a post office opened in 1874. When the new rail line bypassed Clarksville, a spur track was installed here to handle the local business that was once handled at Lamar.

437.8 CABIN CREEK BRIDGE – This bridge is located where the railroad rejoins the Arkansas River. This bridge was specifically mentioned in an October 2, 1963, newspaper article. It stated that the bridge was to be raised about eight feet and extended as part of the Arkansas River navigation project. The bridge consists of 40 feet of reinforced concrete trestles, a 24-foot beam span, a 75-foot through plate girder span, a 48-foot beam span, and 36 feet of reinforced concrete trestles. The concrete spans on each end were added when the bridge was raised. The through plate girder span has long been noted as limiting the side clearance on the main line over the bridge.

This is one of the old Cabin Creek bridge abutments, now standing in the waters of Lake Dardanelle. It is visible from the Cabin Creek Slough Access boat ramp just east of the Van Buren Subdivision.

The remains of the pre-1935 Cabin Creek Bridge can be seen under the new bridge, raised in 1964 to stay above the new Lake Dardanelle.

This sign marks the Cabin Creek Slough Access, located at the former Missouri Pacific Cabin Creek Bridge.

South of the current bridge are the concrete remains of the earlier bridge on the original route. The abutments are now surrounded by the waters of Lake Dardanelle.

Cabin Creek forms in the low hills northwest of the town of Lamar, once also known as Cabin Creek. The stream received its name in the mid-1830s when Samuel Adams, acting governor of Arkansas in 1844, built a number of cabins along the stream to house his slaves. The waterway was soon called Stream of Cabins, and then Cabin Creek.

440.7 COAL MINE LEAD – A ½-mile-long spur track curved off to the southeast until it was removed in late 1943.

441.2 NORTH END OF DETOUR NO. 10 – This is the north end of the 1937 detour. Much of the original mainline is long gone, washed away by the Arkansas River as it has moved to the north. The construction of Lake Dardanelle has also flooded much of the route.

441.4 COAL LOADER TRACK – This is another track that was built for the local coal industry, including several strip mines that are now lakes. Several short tracks were built in July 1944 to the east of the mainline. They were removed in August 1948. By this time, many of the new coal loaders were served by trucks hauling coal from area mines.

441.5 SPADRA PARK – Jamestown Road crosses the tracks and heads to the Arkansas River and Spadra Park. This is a Corps of Engineers park that includes camping, restrooms and showers, boat ramps, and a picnic shelter. The boat ramp area at the west end of the park provides views of the Spadra Creek Bridge. Warning – fees do apply.

From here to near Hartman, the tracks are heading east-west, and those directions will be used.

Spadra Trading Factory

During the late 1810s, a trading post opened near here to trade products for furs with the Western Cherokee settlements in the area. A marker noting the presence of the Indian Trading Post was erected at Spadra Park in 1983.

The Spadra Trading Factory was initially operated by Isaac Rawlings, and then Barak Owens. In 1820, President James Monroe appointed Matthew Lyon as U.S. Factor to the Cherokee Nation in the Arkansas Territory. Matthew Lyon had an interesting history, serving in Congress 1797 to 1801 (representing Vermont) and 1803 to 1811 (representing Kentucky). Lyon is somewhat famous as being the only person to be elected to Congress while in jail. During a series of political battles in 1798, the Federalist party pushed through the Alien and Sedition Acts, which prohibited "malicious" writing about the president, the houses of Congress, or the American government as a whole. On October 10, 1798, Lyon was found guilty of violating the law for criticizing President John Adams. He became a regional hero and won re-election. After his death, the law was found to be illegal and his family was eventually reimbursed for all expenses related to the trial, plus interest. After Lyon arrived in Spadra, he again ran for Congress, but lost. He died on August 1, 1822, and was interred in Spadra Bluff Cemetery, but later re-interred in Eddyville, Kentucky.

The trading factory officially closed in 1822, but remained open as a private trading post. Area reports state that people traveled from more than 100 miles to buy and trade goods at the Spadra trading post. In 1828, the Cherokees were moved west to Indian Territory in today's Oklahoma, and white settlers moved into the area. The trading post and river port along Spadra Creek attracted enough residents that it became the first county seat when Johnson County was created on November 16, 1833. However, the government seat moved to Clarksville very shortly afterwards.

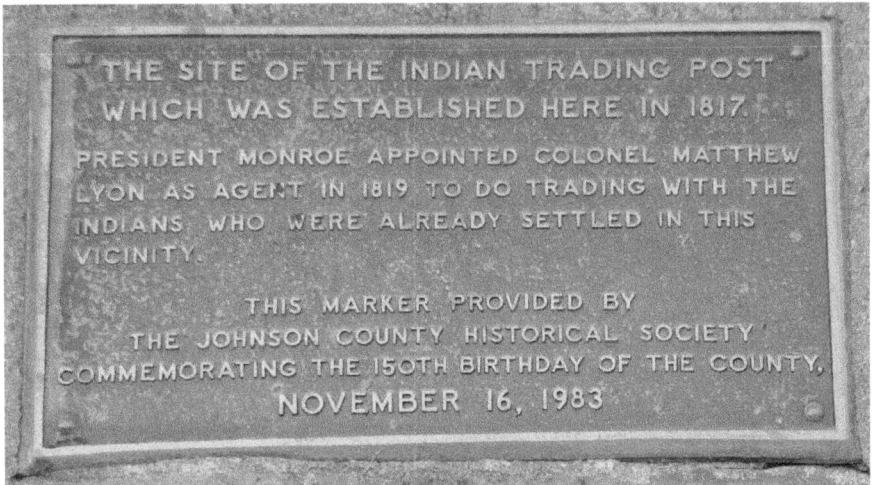

This marker at the Spadra Park notes the one-time presence of the Spadra Trading Factory.

Spadra was also along one of many routes used by what became known as the Trail of Tears. This sign at Spadra Park notes the route.

442.2 SPADRA CREEK BRIDGE – This bridge is more than 1000 feet long and includes from the east, 486 feet of concrete pile trestle spans, 5 deck plate girder spans that measure a total of 400 feet, and 162 feet of concrete pile trestle spans. Spadra Creek marked the east end of coal mining country. Coal was initially discovered near the east side of Spadra Creek in 1840. East of the bridge and to the north are several large ponds, old coal mining pits from the days when the area was strip mined.

When this bridge was rebuilt in the early 1960s, the alignment was also changed slightly to keep the railroad above the higher water levels on the Arkansas River. At the grade crossing with Jamestown Road (Milepost 441.5), the railroad now curves to the south to reach the new bridge over Spadra Creek. The railroad once headed almost straight west to cross Spadra Creek. Part of this grade is now used by Marina Road. There was once a short track to the north at Milepost 441.8, but it was removed in 1939.

Spadra Park is a good location to photograph train action on the Spadra Creek Bridge. On May 22, 2023, UP 7248 pulls a train southbound across the 1050-foot-long bridge.

The railroad once crossed Spadra Creek at Milepost 441.9 where the Spadra Waterfront Marina now sits. The bridge consisted of two 75-foot deck plate girder spans. The west abutment of the retired bridge can still be seen from the marina's docks, while the east abutment is part of the marina. From there, the old grade made a gentle S-curve to the southwest and then back to the west, squeezing its way between Spadra Creek and Little Spadra Creek. Part of this grade is now a series of islands. The two grades rejoin a short distance west of the current Spadra Creek bridge.

Spadra Creek starts as a small stream on the east side of Mac Wood Mountain west of Ozone, Arkansas. It drains parts of the Boston Mountains in northern Johnson County. It flows through downtown Clarksville and then widens as backwaters from the Arkansas River.

This is the western abutment of the pre-1960s bridge over Spadra Creek. The view is from the Spadra Waterfront Marina.

442.4 CONTROL POINT V443 – This is the south switch of Spadra Siding, located to the east of the mainline. The siding was recently extended from 7447 feet long to 7824 feet long.

442.6 AA JUNCTION – This was the junction between the original line through Clarksville, and the new line that opened in 1904. Early documents showed this location to be Spadra Junction, and the name Clarksville Line Junction was also sometimes used. A railroad telephone was located here for years so that train crews could get permission to enter the new mainline, or to enter the line through Clarksville. This area is now deep in the woods alongside the current Union Pacific Railroad, and only an old fill to the north where the bridge across Little Spadra Creek once was helps to mark the location. The available water resulted in the erection of a water tower at Spadra Junction.

The name AA Junction comes from a general practice that Missouri Pacific used to name locations that didn't already have a name. The railroad tended to simply use two letters of the alphabet, often the same letters as shown with AA Junction and BB Junction. Details about the Clarksville Subdivision, the original mainline between BB Junction and AA Junction, can be found in the route guide for the Clarksville Branch starting on Page 463.

At one time, the railroad had a number of facilities here. This included a section house and cistern, two tool houses and a toilet, and a section bunk house made from a 9' x 30' boxcar. A station sign and a section post were both located here. There was also an "engineman's bath house" (4' x 6') and a "pumpers dwelling" built from two 9' x 34' carbodies. The water tower and related facilities were retired in November 1943.

The 1958 employee timetable had a number of instructions for AA Junction, simply called Spadra at the time. It stated that the spring switch at Spadra was normally lined for the main track. Northward trains moving from the Clarksville Subdivision must, unless otherwise specified, move through Junction Cut-off into Spadra siding and through the siding, entering the Van Buren Subdivision main track at the north switch of the siding. It also stated that Spadra was a train register station only for trains moving via the Clarksville Subdivision, and that the train order delivery device at Spadra was on the west side of the main track at the depot.

443.0 SPADRA (RA) – Where the railroad had a station named Spadra was actually New Spadra. The original Spadra was a river port on the Arkansas River and was located on the east side of Spadra Creek near the current Spadra Waterfront Marina. The area developed as a trading area and the U.S. government had an authorized Indian trading factory (trading post) located at Spadra. New Spadra, actually called Spadra, developed with coal mining, and then the construction of the railroad.

The land around Spadra was initially promoted for farming. In 1840, a land advertisement stated that Spadra was "situated in the centre of the rich and fertile county of Johnson, on the north bank of the Arkansas River, about four hundred and fifty miles from the Mississippi, one hundred and thirty-five miles above Little Rock, and one hundred miles below the Indian line, by the course of the river." One of the early settlers was E. B. Alston who owned about 1400 acres in the area. Most of his land was on the west side of Spadra Creek and he built the first bridge across the stream to connect his land with the early town of Spadra. Alston is credited with the start of the move to the west side of the creek when he built a cotton gin and store on his property, about where today's Spadra sits. The existence of coal on the west side of Spadra Creek also attracted attention, and some coal was used locally or shipped on the Arkansas River to the Little Rock market. The Civil War slowed area development, and probably forced many settlers to move away due to numerous cases of guerrilla warfare.

Despite the coal production, the hope of Spadra regaining its importance went away when the Little Rock & Fort Smith Railroad built through the county seat of Clarksville and then along the west side of Spadra Creek, bypassing the old river port. By the arrival of the railroad, a series of small coal mines were operating both east and west of Spadra Creek. A large area of anthracite coal, known as the Spadra field, as well as a layer of bituminous coal, could be found throughout the area. The product of the mines was described as being excellent domestic coal. There was also a layer of what was called Spadra shale here.

The new Spadra soon became a known coal mining center, and some of the early commercial mines were operated by the Johnson County Coal Company, Spadra Anthracite Coal Company, and Stiewel Coal Company. The growth in population and business led to the creation of the Spadra post office in 1871, which finally closed for good in 1954. The production of coal also had some negative issues, including labor unrest, strikes, and personal feuds. During the first half of the 1880s, the U.S. Commissioner of Labor reported that Spadra was the home of two of the three major strikes in Arkansas. The coal miners were strong members of various fraternal organizations, and groups like Knights of Labor, Knights of Pythias, Farmers' Alliance, and several lodges of the United Mine Workers of America were located at Spadra.

In 1921, five mines were listed in the *Arkansas Marketing and Industrial Guide*. These included the Consolidated Coal Company, Lucas Mardis Coal Company, McWilliams Ward & Company, Smokeless Anthracite Coal Company, and the Spadra Creek Coal Company. The railroad directly served many of these mines as spur tracks seemed to curve everywhere around Spadra. The town also had its own school, replaced with a new school building in 1929. However, as mining activity dropped, the school was consolidated into the Clarksville school system during the late 1940s. Today, Spadra is a scattering of houses and at least one church. But there are also several major industries. One of these is the large Tyson Spadra Feed Mill, located across Crawford Street from the Spadra Cemetery.

Coal is still moved through Spadra by the railroad. On April 7, 2023, UP 2635 pulled an Entergy coal train southward through the siding at Spadra. Car ETRX 750415 stopped above rail markings that alert employees as to which track is the main track and which is the siding.

At the grade crossing near Milepost 443 is a large radio tower. South of the tracks are several foundations, a truck scale, and a number of old buildings from the era of coal mining. Views of the rail yard and large feed mill are also available from this location.

To the west at the intersection of Crawford Street and Arkansas Highway 109 (Milepost 444.8) is a truck stop (closed in 2025) and the huge Walmart Clarksville Distribution Center. Highway 109 connects Clarksville with Arkansas Highway 217 near Booneville. A short distance to the south on Highway 109 is the Morrison Bluff Bridge, also known as the Ada Mills Bridge, a 1.6-mile-long bridge over the Arkansas River. It is reportedly the longest bridge in Arkansas, and the longest bridge across the Arkansas River anywhere in the United States.

The Railroad at Spadra

Somewhat unique for the towns along the Little Rock & Fort Smith, there was already an established freight business at Spadra. Coal was big business, and the railroad allowed it to grow and to reach new markets. It was big news when the Little Rock & Fort Smith reached Spadra, and it was a point of pride when chief engineer George W. Hughes made the announcement in early March 1875. A number of local tracks were built to serve the area coal mines. For example, in 1900, two tracks were built to serve the Anthracite Coal Company. One was a simple 600-foot spur track while the other was 346 feet that was built as the Slack Track to handle the coal fines from the sorting process. For many years, coal was loaded at Spadra, and the Hardin Coal Company had several air tunnels and a mine slope actually pass under the mainline at Milepost 442.9.

With the railroad's arrival, a depot and coal house were built at Spadra, and in 1892, The Order of Railroad Telegraphers showed that there was an agent-telegrapher at Spadra, with telegraphers who assisted the agent in his work. The 1903 *Missouri Pacific Annual Report* showed an expense to build a new combination depot at Spadra. The construction was due to the new route that bypassed Clarksville. By 1907, Spadra was a large facility located at Milepost 445.34. Yard limits between Mileposts 443.6 and 450.1 protected the switching of the many coal mines. The depot was equipped with a day and night telegraph office and a train register used to keep track of the various trains working the coal lines and the route through Clarksville. A mail crane was used to hand mail up to passing trains. To pass trains, there was an 80-car siding.

In 1910, passenger train service at Spadra became an issue. During February, the town of Spadra petitioned the Arkansas Railroad Commission to require the St. Louis, Iron Mountain & Southern to have a passenger train stop at the town at night. At the time, only the daytime locals served the station and residents wanted other alternatives for taking a train to and from Spadra. The petition was at first denied on April 6, 1910. However, the decision was challenged and in mid-May the railroad agreed to stop train Nos. 105 and 106 at Spadra. At this time, the passenger trains and several local freight trains operated on the original line through Clarksville, but through freight trains used the new line that had been built several years earlier. This stopped in June 1935 when the Arkansas River flooded and washed out much of the track on the new line between Knoxville Junction and Spadra Junction. Plans were announced to repair the damage in March 1936. The track was finally reopened at noon on December 16, 1936. To make the repairs, some of the track was moved away from the bank of the Arkansas River and raised above flood levels. Missouri Pacific reported that it spent $265,000 to rebuild the line.

In 1923, the station featured an agent-telegrapher plus two telegrapher helpers. Spadra was shown to have a ticket and freight agency in 1925, located in the station on the west side of the tracks. In 1930, the agent-telegrapher worked the first trick with telegraphers handling the work on the second and third tricks. By 1942, the telegrapher work at Spadra had diminished to the point where the reduction in duties and responsibilities resulted in the elimination of the second and third shift telegrapher positions. A 1933 survey determined that the elevation of top of rail opposite the Missouri Pacific Railroad Spadra station was 372.1 feet. The elevation shown by Union Pacific for the location today is 369 feet.

A new, larger depot (24' x 61') was built at Spadra in 1915. In 1919, a two-story section house was built to house track maintenance employees. For the trains, there were sidings, a 100,000-gallon water tower fed by Spadra Creek, and a 40-foot track scale with a capacity of 100,000 pounds. In 1944, there was a 62-car siding at Spadra, increased to 90 cars by the time the ABS signals were installed. The depot had a train order office on a limited schedule. There was also a mail crane to serve the local post office. A wye track was also shown at Spadra. In 1943, the 24' x 100' depot lost 40 feet of its east end. During the early 1960s, the track southward as far as Russellville was raised, with some new bridges installed, as part of the Arkansas River navigation project. By 1969, the siding had been extended to hold 144 freight cars (7517 feet) and the depot was closed. Today, the siding and a short house track at Spadra remain. A yard with five tracks is located on the east side of the mainline and siding. The yard is used to serve the Tyson Spadra Feed Mill located at Milepost 443.2. The south switch of the yard is at Milepost 443 while the north switch is at Control Point V445.

The Spadra location has changed quite a bit over the past several decades, including the installation of CTC along the line and the construction of the Tyson feed mill. This is UP 3732 hauling an empty coal train northward on July 8, 1989, without the feed mill yard tracks.

UP 2635 pulls an Entergy coal train southward through the siding at Spadra and by the large Tyson feed mill.

The official location of Spadra is marked by this milepost sign.

UP 6324 heads north at Spadra, passing an ETRX coal train at Milepost 443.

Because of the various changes on the railroad, several different sets of mileposts have been used between Little Rock and Van Buren. This has been a challenge around Spadra as several line changes were made just to the south and north. In 1983, Union Pacific showed that there was a milepost equation of 443.00 = 442.53. This means that for trains heading towards Van Buren and Fort Smith, there was a Milepost 443.0 that then reverted back to Milepost 442.5. Because this created two mileposts with the same number (443), the railroad made some minor adjustments and current employee timetables state that there is not a milepost equation here.

443.4 SCALE HOUSE – This area had several yard tracks and other facilities designed to serve the many coal mines in the area. In 1940, a more modern track scale was installed in a two-track yard, replacing an older one with insufficient capacity. There was also a garage and tool house made from a 9' x 30' carbody, as well as a carbody bunkhouse, all located on the north side of the tracks.

The Tyson feedmill at Spadra uses a Trackmobile to handle switching. On this June day, the Trackmobile is shoving a cut of empty grain cars northward from the mill so that they can be picked up by a Union Pacific train.

443.9 SUNLIGHT MINE LEAD – In September 1927, a coal line was built northward from here to serve the Sunlight Mine of the Spadra Coal Company. The track was described as being 10,395 feet long, and it curved to the north and crossed several streams, requiring timber trestles to be built. A small yard was located at the coal tipple at the end of the line. The mine was later shown to be owned by the Smokeless Coal Company. Missouri Pacific reported that the line was abandoned during October 1943.

444.1 CONTROL POINT V445 – This switch has historically been known as North Spadra.

To the south was a wye that served the tipple of the Clarksville Coal Company. Further south was a several-block community that was shown to be New Spadra on maps from around 1960. Because of all of the switches and coal cars, oil was often needed by track crews and car inspectors. An oil house, using a 9' x 34' carbody, was located here to store the various oils required.

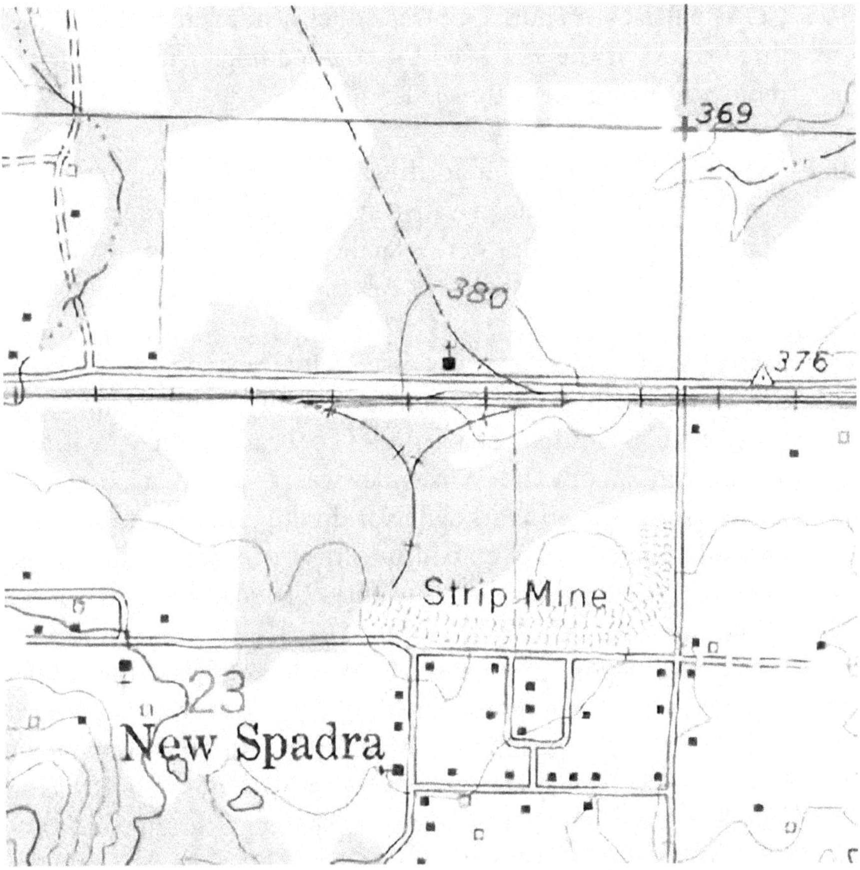

This 1961 topographical map shows the 2-mile-long Sunlight Mine Lead to the north, and the wye and spur track southward to the Clarksville Coal Company near New Spadra. These grades can still be seen where they pass through open pasture and recently established woods. *Hartman (AR) Quadrangle, 1961.* U.S. Department of the Interior, U.S. Geological Survey.

This sign on the signal box at Control Point V445 is easily visible from Johnson County Road 2351.

444.6 COAL SPUR – A short spur track once headed north here, with three tracks at the end used for coal loading. The tracks were removed during the early 1930s.

445.0 COAL TIPPLE – To the north was a railroad siding, and then five private tracks. The private tracks passed under a large coal tipple. Nothing remains of this facility as the site is now covered by the county road just west of Arkansas Highway 109.

445.1 MONTANA – Montana was essentially the center of the Spadra coal fields. A history of Johnson County, published in 1921, stated that "Spadra is but a series of coal camps almost without break from Spadra Creek six miles west to Montana, a station created some fifteen years ago. Nor do the camps end there, for beyond Montana they extend into the corporate limits of the town of Hartman, and north to the Wire road along the foothills of the Ozarks."

Coal mining in the area was reported as early as 1818. Montana was one of a number of coal mining towns that supported a series of coal mines. A post office called Montana was established in 1881 and was reportedly named after the Montana Territory. Two of the largest coal companies operating at Montana were the Western Anthracite Coal Mine Company and the Arkansas Anthracite Coal Mine Company. The Smokeless Anthracite Coal Mining Company also operated a shaft opening on the railroad here during the 1920s. During the 1910s and 1920s, the Sunshine Mine of the Spadra Coal Company had a shaft mine near Montana on the Iron Mountain/Missouri Pacific. The Kneed More Mine of the Lucas Mardis Coal Company, and the Pig Mine of the Spadra Creek Coal Company, also had shaft mines on the Missouri Pacific at Montana.

Johnson County was an important producer of coal, but after World War II, mining decreased quickly. "The recorded production of coal mined in the Arkansas Valley coal field for the calendar year ending December 31, 1954, was 477,268 short tons, the lowest recorded production since 1890." In that year, almost half of the total coal production took place in Johnson County. With the decrease in coal mining, and the local population, the post office closed in 1954, and the Montana mail crane was removed. Today, Montana is simply an unincorporated community in Johnson County.

On the mainline of Missouri Pacific at Montana were a number of facilities. The right-of-way for one-half mile, between Mileposts 444.9 and 445.4, was 200 feet wide instead of the typical 100 feet. There was a small (14' x 36') wooden depot set up on short stilts. This depot was built because of an act passed by the Arkansas General Assembly on May 17, 1907. The act required the St. Louis, Iron Mountain & Southern to build within 90 days a passenger and freight depot at Montana. The act also required that the depot would be open every day, sell tickets, receive freight, and issue bills of lading. All local freight trains and at least two passenger trains would stop at the depot daily to handle the local business. A mail crane also stood here.

An agent was assigned to the Montana depot in 1925, which was located on the east side of the tracks. The agent, identified as Miss E. Wallis, worked a ticket and freight agency (carloads and less). It was noted in railroad documents that the Montana Railway connection was 0.13 miles to the north (compass-west). In 1933, the depot still stood and the elevation of the top of rail opposite the Missouri Pacific Railroad station at Montana was 394.2 feet. In 1941, railroad documents showed that there was a mail crane and a telephone booth, as well as several tracks that curved off to the south. Nothing is here today except for the mainline of Union Pacific.

445.1 MILEPOST CHANGE – The mileposts along the Little Rock & Fort Smith changed a number of times as the railroad became part of the St. Louis, Iron Mountain & Southern, and then a number of track realignments took place.

The station of Montana can confuse many people as it actually had two different official milepost locations. As shown in *Missouri Pacific Railroad Company Southern Kansas and Central Divisions Time-Table No. 17* (Effective 12:01 a.m., Sunday, September 21, 1941), these were officially Mileposts 445.12 and 445.65. The timetable explained the situation with the following statement. "Two mile post locations at Montana, Ark., are one and the same point, 445.65 being new mileage account change in line south of Montana made November 1936, and 445.12 being old mileage."

According to the Missouri Pacific "Right of Way and Track Map" dated January 31, 1941, there was only a single Milepost 444 and Milepost 446, located 13,230 feet, or 2.5 miles apart. However, there were two locations identified as Milepost 445. The southernmost Milepost 445 was 5258 feet north of Milepost 444, while the northernmost Milepost 445 was 7812 feet north of Milepost 444. At the northernmost Milepost 445 was a concrete milepost, apparently making this the official Milepost 445 since Missouri Pacific had installed concrete markers at the mileposts that were multiples of 5.

The miles through this area tended to be more than 5280 feet long. For example, the distance between the northernmost Milepost 445 and Milepost 446 was shown to be 5418 feet, while it was 5360 feet between Mileposts 446 and 447. Union Pacific now makes an adjustment in the mileage at Milepost 446.

445.2 MONTANA RAILROAD JUNCTION – According to an Interstate Commerce Commission (ICC) valuation report from 1933, the Montana Railroad was incorporated April 5, 1915, under the general laws of Arkansas. With a capital stock of $7000, some reports state that the railroad was owned and built by a series of coal companies to serve at least six coal mines near Clarksville, with the Johnson & King coal mine specifically mentioned. The ICC reported that the Montana Railroad was "an industrial road controlled by the Clarksville Coal Company, one of the principal industries served." The railroad was a single-track, standard-gage, steam railroad that connected the "Missouri Pacific Railroad Company at Montana, to end of track at North Spadra, a distance of 2.647 miles." The railroad also had 0.035 miles of yard tracks and sidings.

The 1933 report by the ICC was correct for the time, but the Montana Railroad had originally been built as a narrow gauge operation to serve the coal mines of the Johnson & King Coal Company. On August 16, 1918, the charter was amended and the railroad changed from narrow to standard gauge. The railroad at first was simply a plant railroad serving just the Johnson & King Coal Company, but it changed to being a common carrier in May 1921 when the railroad actually acquired its property to perform freight service. The Clarksville Coal Company acquired the Johnson & King Coal Company and the railroad, which served several mines including those owned by the Clarksville Coal Company.

The ICC described the grading of the railroad as "very light averaging about 2,000 cubic yards per mile and is all common material. There are no important bridges on the line. Drainage is crossed by means of timber trestles and culverts. Ties in main track are all untreated oak. The main track is laid with new 60-pound rail, and is ballasted with burnt shale." The railroad only owned 1 freight car and 1 piece of miscellaneous rail equipment. The locomotives were rented from the Missouri Pacific Railroad Company as needed. Near Clarksville at North Spadra, the Montana Railroad had a small station on the property of the Clarksville Coal Company, and shared space in a building that was used jointly with the coal company.

A later ICC report stated that the line was operated with Missouri Pacific crews and equipment. Several old steam locomotives were still on the property and used to work the various coal mines. One of these was an old Class B37-2 Shay locomotive (Shop Number 1759, built in October 1906 for the Bering Manufacturing Company at Bering, Arkansas) that was scrapped during the late 1930s. As the coal mines closed, the railroad began to abandon various spur tracks. On October 26, 1934, the Montana Railroad applied to the ICC for permission to abandon its entire railroad from North Spadra to Montana. On February 9, 1935, the ICC approved the abandonment, but Missouri Pacific purchased some of the track and used it as a spur until abandoned during December 1944. The old grade is now simply a grassy path across several fields on the west side of the Walmart Distribution Center, with parts used as farm roads.

445.8 HOYT – Between Spadra and Hartman, there were a series of coal mines, coal camps, and coal spurs that opened and closed as the local coal field was worked. Many of the locations were named after the coal company, owner, or local manager. Hoyt was actually an early name on the railroad that was listed as a passenger station in some timetables. In 1907, there was an 80-car siding at Hoyt, located on the north side of the mainline. Until 1987, the railroad listed a business track at Hoyt, generally shown to have a capacity of 10 cars.

The location of Hoyt was moved around as needed by the railroad. Milepost 445.8 was generally the cited location, which is now the grade crossing with Johnson County Road 2301. However, by the 1960s, the spur track was actually at Milepost 446.2, where Johnson County Road 2271 is now located. Maps from the same period also show Hoyt here. There were strip mines to the north, and a mine dump and Goose Camp to the south. Goose Camp was a coal mining community in those days, and the area still uses the name. Further south were once a series of fruit orchards, but today the hill is a stone quarry.

446.0 MILEPOST EQUATION – Current Union Pacific timetables show a milepost equation here instead of at Montana. It shows that 446.00 = 446.43.

446.4 P. A. CONNECTION – This station was listed in 1925 as a 0.46-mile spur track to the P. A. Coal Mine, located south (railroad-west) of the mainline. The coal traffic from the mine, and any inbound freight, was shown to be prepaid. The track was removed in November 1941.

446.9 KEMP-JOHNSON COAL COMPANY – About a mile west of Hoyt was another coal spur that was listed in railroad timetables into the 1970s. It headed to the northeast from the mainline and ended at a coal dump along today's Johnson County Road 2250. There was a telephone booth at the mainline switch to allow train crews to communicate with the railroad's dispatcher.

Missouri Pacific records show that the main spur track, plus a three-track yard, were installed in 1914. In 1922, the Kemp-Harding Coal Company had a shaft mine served by the railroad in this area, using a 9-car loading track. Over the years, many of the coal companies merged and changed names, causing quite a bit of confusion in trying to track the histories of the region. The tracks were also shown to be the McWilliams Spur for a few years.

In 1958, the railroad had instructions that engines must not be operated under coal tipples at Milepost 447 Pole 2, and 446 Pole 28, both at Spadra.

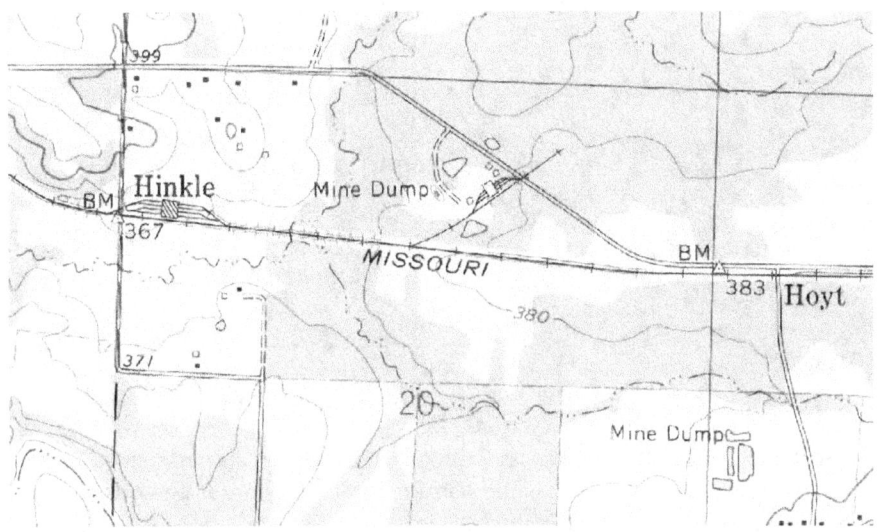

Hinkle (Peabody) and the spur track to the Kemp-Johnson Coal Company are shown on this 1961 topographical map. *Hartman (AR) Quadrangle, 1961.* U.S. Department of the Interior, U.S. Geological Survey.

447.5 PEABODY – This was another coal mining area, shown as Hinkle during the 1950s. There was a 4-track coal loader on the north side of the mainline, located just east of County Road 2241. Reports from the 1940s showed that there were four tracks to the north of the mainline that served the Arkansas Stripping Company coal tipple. The tracks measured 1687 feet, 931 feet, 612 feet, and 608 feet long, and reportedly had a capacity of 40 coal cars.

A 1959 report from the Arkansas State Mine Inspection Department stated that the average thickness of coal in the area was about three feet, and that the Peabody Coal Company had leased several hundred acres of coal lands here. The tracks are now gone, but the tipple still stands.

On September 1, 1992, the Arkansas Railroad Club sponsored a passenger train trip behind UP 3985 (4-6-6-4) across the Van Buren Subdivision. A photo runby was conducted at the coal tipple at Peabody.

While the tracks are gone and coal is no longer loaded at Peabody, the coal tipple still stands beside the Van Buren Subdivision at Milepost 447.3.

447.9 MCWILLIAMS – This was another early railroad name (McWilliam's Spur) that moved about and was used as needed by the railroad. In 1922, the Igo mine, a shaft coal mine of the Clark-McWilliams Coal Company, was located here and was served by the railroad.

In the March 1, 1925, *Missouri Pacific Railroad Company Official List of Officers, Agents, Stations and Mileage,* the station of McWilliams was shown to be at Milepost 446.9. All freight, carload volumes or less, using the track had to be prepaid.

There were also other coal mines near here. The Tight Wad Mine of the Collier Dunlap Coal Company was located on the Missouri Pacific Railroad about one and one-half miles east of Hartman, and the Blue Bird Mine of Johnson Coal Company was a bit further to the west. In 1941, this was shown to be the Collier-Dunlap Coal terminal, consisting of four tracks.

Between Johnson County Road 2250 and the railroad tracks are the remains of an old coal complex at McWilliams. This tower is one of the larger structures that still stand.

448.7 COAL SPUR – A spur headed southeast to a three-track terminal, once used to load area coal. The railroad had instructions that engines must not be operated under the coal tipple at Milepost 448 Pole 27 at Hartman.

448.8 HORSEHEAD CREEK BRIDGE – In 1875, the LR&FS used a 109-foot covered Howe truss and a 40-foot truss beam span, along with 29 bents of a wooden pile trestle and 3 bents of a wooden frame trestle, to cross Horsehead Creek. This was one of many wooden bridges that were replaced with a steel through pin connected truss span (111 feet long). Because of the through truss design, there were tell-tales on each end to warn brakemen of the overhead obstruction. In 1923, the steel through truss span was replaced with a 115-foot through plate girder span, creating limited side clearances for trains. In 1935, the timber pile trestles on each end were replaced with concrete slabs. On the south approach is 123 feet of concrete spans (7 slabs), while the north approach has 316 feet of concrete spans (18 slabs).

Horsehead Creek was another stream that attracted early settlers as it formed in the mountains to the north and flowed across the fertile Arkansas River Valley to reach the Arkansas River. The stream forms on Batson Mountain near Interstate 40, and flows southward collecting a number of small streams. The name Horsehead Creek apparently comes from a horse's head that was stuck on a pole along the stream. There is no explanation of who did it or why, but the horse's head was described as being "of dimensions larger than an ordinary animal of that type."

449.3 HARTMAN (N) – Hartman was the west end of the Spadra coal fields, although more coal was mined to the west around Alix, Denning, and Coal Hill. Oren Davis Hogins purchased land here in 1837, and soon there was an unorganized community for the local farmers who grew cotton and various fruits and vegetables. Livestock was also an important business.

After the Civil War, the community took a few years to recover from the guerrilla warfare, but the construction of the Little

Rock & Fort Smith helped to redevelop the community. Before the railroad arrived, the community had been named Coalburgh by Mary Hogins, a prominent landowner. The railroad station briefly used the name, but was using the name Horsehead Creek during the early 1880s. A post office opened in 1879 using the name Coalburgh, but changed to Hartman later that year. A local legend is that a "railroad conductor remembered only as T. Hartman promised to have a depot and sidetrack built at the settlement if the residents would name the city for him." In reality, T. Hartman was Theodore H. Hartman, the General Superintendent of the Little Rock & Fort Smith Railway during the late 1870s and 1880s.

Within a few years, Hartman was being described as "one of the most prosperous towns in the state," citing the agriculture, fruit, berry, livestock and coal mining productions. Many of the local residents were recent immigrants who had arrived from Germany, and they were heavily invested in farming on the nearby hillsides, or in local businesses in town. By the 1910s, Hartman produced 3000 to 4000 bales of cotton annually through three different cotton gins. The railroad also hauled more than 200 carloads of Elberta peaches, several carloads of berries and other fruits, 200 carloads of cotton seed, 100 carloads of coal, and 25 carloads of logs annually from Hartman. Building stone was also being produced locally, explaining the many stone buildings in the area. The waste stone was often sold to the United States government which used it to rip-rap the banks of the Arkansas River. The businesses allowed Hartman to feature its own bank (moved from Spadra), several large mercantile establishments, two drug stores, a millinery store, a jewelry business, and even local telephone service. The Daley Mine of the Boston Spadra Coal Company was located nearby.

Hartman was incorporated on October 13, 1911. A one-room schoolhouse opened about the time the railroad arrived, and then it was replaced by a two-story schoolhouse with three classrooms. With the local mining, a brick schoolhouse with six classrooms opened in 1926. At the time Hartman also featured a bank, several stores, two livery stables, two hotels, a restaurant, two blacksmith shops, a tinshop, telephone facilities, three doctors, and churches of almost all denominations. Much of downtown burned in November 1926 and then was flooded in the Flood of 1927. With these events, the population of Hartman was 542 in 1930.

The Great Depression ended much of the coal mining and the value of cotton and many of the local farm products dropped to almost nothing. Following World War II, the town was mostly abandoned and down to only a few stores, a Masonic lodge, a post office, and a barbershop. The population in 1950 was 418, and there were only 299 residents in the 1960 census. Hartman was bypassed by Interstate 40, and most businesses moved northward to be near the highway.

By 1970, Hartman began to recover, and the Westside School District has an elementary school here. The population has stabilized at about 500 and the community basically serves as a quiet residential area outside of the urban area of Clarksville. Agriculture has also returned, especially hay production and vineyards for the local wine industry.

The Railroad at Hartman

Legend states that the name Hartman came about in return for the town getting a depot. The 1890 annual report of the St. Louis, Iron Mountain & Southern reported that a new depot had been constructed that year at Hartman. Earlier that year the Iron Mountain had leased the Little Rock & Fort Smith and started to include the improvements on the line in their reporting. The depot was located at the Main Street grade crossing. In 1900, the railroad built a 541-foot passing track at Hartman. In 1904, the St. Louis, Iron Mountain & Southern operated a rock crusher at Hartman as part of a series of track improvements along the route.

By 1907, there was an 80-car siding at Hartman. The local post office used a railroad mail crane, and there was a daytime telegraph office and a train register at the depot. There was also a water station for the steam locomotives. During the 1920s, Hartman had a 75-car siding and the depot (located on the east side of the tracks) featured a train order office on a limited schedule, a ticket and freight agency, and a mail crane for the local post office.

Hartman also featured two tool houses, stock pens (35' x 80') constructed in 1939, and a 16' x 48' store house. The replacement frame depot, built in 1913, was shown to measure 20' x 76' and had train order signals that were removed in July 1939, and then reinstalled in March 1942 as business picked back up.

A survey in 1933 stated that the elevation of the top of rail opposite the Missouri Pacific Railroad Hartman station was 369.6 feet. Today, nothing remains except for the mainline of Union Pacific.

This old signal base can be found along Burlison Street in Hartman. It dates from the junction that was once here.

449.4 HARTMAN JUNCTION – Hartman Junction was located immediately west of the depot at Hartman, which explained why there was an agent here for many years. The original route built by the Little Rock & Fort Smith passed through Coal Hill and Altus, passing over several ridges that required stiff grades on the railroad, a line that was generally called a hilly route. With the track changes, the new line was eventually called Detour No. 11.

During 1902-1904, the management of the Little Rock & Fort Smith implemented plans to make improvements on the entire line between North Little Rock and Fort Smith. These improvements included reducing grades, decreasing curves, cutting the distance over the line, and reducing the travel time required for trains to cover the route (a planned 12 miles and 40 minutes of running time). As the improvements began, the St. Louis, Iron Mountain & Southern took over the railroad and pushed more improvements. These included installing 85-pound rail and replacing older bridges with new steel bridges. As many as 1000 workers were hired to do the work, and the railroad and its contractors operated thirty work trains and eight steam shovels.

There were a large number of reports that the "contractors on the reconstruction work on the Iron Mountain's Fort Smith line are experiencing great difficulty in securing labor, in spite of the good wages which are being paid." Many local workers apparently would go home once they were paid, while others left when they saw the work involved. Some foreign labor was brought in for the work, such as "nearly two carloads of Greek railroad laborers" that was reported on in late 1903. However, most labor reports were about convict labor.

At the time, prisons could rent out convicts, and the railroad's contractors used hundreds of them. The prison system would cover the cost of guards and prisoner clothing and food. It would then be paid a set amount per worked day. One issue during the work was that the Arkansas penitentiary board realized that the state was being paid 50 cents per day while the contractor was paid $1.50 per day for each worker. Another issue that came up was that some convicts died from the heat, resulting in field visits by several doctors and the Arkansas General Assembly's joint legislative committee. While there were numerous reports of escape attempts, there were also reports that the men were better fed and preferred the work to what they had been doing on several farms. The convicts were kept in a series of camps along the railroad work. Most used what were called prison cars, actually converted stock cars, that were preferred over the more traditional stockade. Camps in this area included Hartman, Coal Hill and Denning.

On Saturday, January 9, 1904, the last steam shovel finished its work and it was reported that this left the railroad between Van Burn and Little Rock clear of construction equipment for the first time in two years. A month later only a few small projects were still to be completed. It was stated that the railroad spent $2,500,000 to build the tunnel at Conway, lay 85-pound rail, rebuild all the bridges, and lower the grades to an average of six-tenths from the previous two percent. Because of this, trains could handle 45 to 50 cars instead of the previous 20 to 25.

When completed, the new line between Hartman Junction and Ozark Junction became the mainline. The original route via Coal Hill and Altus became the Altus District. Because of the lack of large populations, several of the premier passenger trains were moved to the new mainline. However, the older route still handled local service and some passenger trains until it was abandoned in 1936. Details about the Altus District can be found in the route guide for the Altus Branch starting on Page 493.

451.5 HARTMAN LAKE – This was not a station on the railroad, but this Arkansas River oxbow lake forced the new line to curve around a large wetland area. To the north is a low ridge that was once the bank of the Arkansas River.

This signal is located at the grade crossing with Johnson County Road 2051 at Milepost 453.8. This very rural location receives electrical power from several sources, including wind and solar.

454.3 HOING SPUR – To the north were two tracks that were leased by Joseph George (J. G.) Hoing until the tracks were removed in 1934. Joe Hoing was the manager of the Joe Hoing Coal Co., which operated several coal mines in the area. Hoing was born in Illinois in 1876 and moved to Coal Hill by 1906. He died in 1957 and was buried in the Coal Hill Cemetery.

Today, the remains of several coal strip mines and coal dumps can still be found on the north side of the tracks where trains heading towards Van Buren curve from heading west-south-west to the northwest.

454.6 SPUR TRACK – There were several tracks to the north that were used to serve a coal mine. A seldom-used private road crosses the tracks here.

455.1 COUNTY LINE – Located a short distance east of Kenny Hole Road is the county line between Johnson County and Franklin County. The area was once active with several strip mines. During the 1920s, there were at least five coal mines east of Alix in this area. The Wallace McKinney Mine of the Blue Hill Coal Company was identified as being three miles east of Alix. Both the Fafter Coal Company and the Douglas Coal Company had shaft mines two miles east of Alix. The Alix Coal Company had their Superior Mine one and one-half miles east of Alix. Finally, the Sambo Mine of the Semi-Anthracite Coal Mining Company was located one mile east of Alix. All were served by the St. Louis, Iron Mountain & Southern, later Missouri Pacific.

Johnson County, located to the east, was the site of most of the coal mining in Arkansas. The county was created from parts of Pope County on November 16, 1833. Like most of the counties along the railroad, the southern half is in the Arkansas River Valley while the northern part is in the Ozark Mountains. This county was once located in the Cherokee lands, and one of three factories (trading posts) was located at Spadra Bayou, near today's county seat of Clarksville. In 1840, the county's population was 3433. Some coal was shipped on the Arkansas River, but with the construction of the railroad, large volumes began to be mined. Almost 20 different mines operated in the county at the peak of coal mining. Timber, cotton, fruit (apples, pears, and peaches), poultry, and natural gas all are major sources of business in the county. In particular, the Missouri Pacific Railroad heavily promoted the Johnson County peaches across the country.

The population temporarily peaked in 1920 with the county having 21,062 residents. With the end of manual labor in farming, coal and timber production, the population dropped to 12,421 in the 1960 census. Since then, retail and light manufacturing have moved to the county. Since 1938, Johnson County has hosted an annual Peach Festival, and outdoor activities have brought many visitors to the county. Even the notorious bandit Bill Doolin, the founder of the Wild Bunch, is an attraction as he was born in Johnson County in 1858. The population in the 2020 census was 25,749.

In the June 30, 1924, *Annual Report of the State Inspector of Coal Mines – State of Arkansas*, a total of 27 coal mines were listed as being on the railroad in Johnson County. These included the following coal companies, their mine, and location.

Albro Martin Coal Co.   Strip
    3 miles north of Spadra
Arkansas Coal & Land Co.   Mine #2
    1½ miles southwest of Montana
Blue Hills Coal Co.   Blue Hill
    2 miles east of Alix
Blue Valley Coal Co.   Blue Valley
    At Coal Hill
Cater-Simmons Coal Co.   Love
    3 miles north of Spadra
C. C. & E. Coal Co.   Strip
    2½ miles north of Spadra
Clark-McWilliams Coal Co.   Igo
    West of Spadra
Clarksville Anthracite   Brook-Bryant
    2½ miles north of Spadra
Collier-Dunlap Coal Co.   Collier-Dunlap
    1 mile east of Hartman

Denning Branch Coal Co.　　　Galic
　　¼ mile south of Coal Hill
Diamond Anthracite Coal Co.　　James
　　3 miles north of Spadra
Douglas & Son Coal Co.　　　Mine #1
　　¼ mile south of Coal Hill
Douglas Coal Co.　　　Douglas
　　2½ miles east of Alix
Ellington Coal Co.　　　Sterling
　　2½ miles south of Clarksville
Fernwood Coal Co.　　　Mine #1
　　2½ miles south of Clarksville
Fort Smith Spadra Coal Co.　　Blue Bird
　　¾ miles east of Hartman
Franklin Coal Co.　　　Strip
　　1½ miles southwest of Coal Hill
Hartman Anthracite Coal Co.　　Mine #1
　　At Hartman
Johnson-King Coal Co.　　　King
　　3½ miles north of Spadra
Kemp-Harding Coal Co.　　　Kemp-Harding
　　½ mile northeast of Montana
King-Nichols-Lasser Coal Co.　　Joe King
　　3 miles south of Clarksville
Koontz-Thompson Coal Co.　　Needmore
　　½ mile northeast of Montana
Smokeless Anthracite　　　Duck Nest
　　1 mile south of Montana
Spadra Anthracite Coal Co.　　Daily
　　¼ mile west of Montana
Spadra Coal Co.　　　Sunshine
　　At Montana
Werner-Dunlap Coal Co.　　　Strip
　　3 miles north of Spadra
Western Coal Mining Co.　　　Rafter
　　2½ miles southwest of Coal Hill

To the west is **Franklin County**, created on December 19, 1837, from part of Crawford County. Franklin County covers mostly very rural and rugged country on both sides of the Arkansas River, each with its own county seat – Ozark north of the river and Charleston to the south. When created, the county was named for Benjamin Franklin, and the population was shown to be 2665 in 1840. Forestry, mining (coal, clay, iron, shale and other minerals) and farming have traditionally been the largest economic activities, especially after Swiss-German immigrants moved to the area, settling in the mountains that reminded them of home. Wine grapes soon became a major crop grown and were shipped out on the railroad for decades. The first oil strike in Arkansas happened in Franklin County and natural gas is still produced. Poultry has become a major activity, and the wine industry and its annual Winefest makes the county a major tourist attraction. One interesting feature about the county is that because of the wine, the north part of the county is "wet" and alcohol is sold almost everywhere. Meanwhile, south of the Arkansas River the county is "dry" with no alcohol sales. The current population is 17,097 and the county is still very rural.

Coal was big business in Franklin County during the first several decades of the twentieth century. The peak production was 423,452 tons in 1907, with the peak in revenue being in 1920 when 278,450 tons was sold for $1,261,000. The 1924 *Annual Report of the State Inspector of Coal Mines – State of Arkansas*, listed 22 coal mines in Franklin County that were served by the former Little Rock & Fort Smith route. These included the following coal companies, their mine, and location.

Allison Coal Co.	Mine #1
5 miles northeast of Ozark	
Allison Coal Co.	Mine #2
5 miles northeast of Ozark	
Alix Coal Co.	Superior
1½ miles east of Alix	
Big Six Coal Co.	Dodson
1 mile northeast of Alix	
Black Diamond Coal Co.	Black Diamond

343

2 miles west of Alix

Burley Coal Co.	Burley

6 miles northeast of Ozark

Chase Coal Co.	Mine #1

¾ mile east of Alix

Denning Coal Co.	Denning

1¼ miles west of Denning

Douglas Coal Co.	Douglas

2 miles east of Alix

Godsey Coal Co.	Godsey

1½ miles west of Denning

Hoing Coal Co.	Mine #1

1½ miles southwest of Coal Hill

Kline Coal Co.	Denton-Kline

2 miles west of Altus

Lewis Coal Co.	Packett

1¾ miles east of Alix

Liberty Coal Co.	Evans

1½ miles west of Denning

Melton Coal Co.	Dodson #1

1 mile southwest of Alix

Ozark Coal Co.	Red Devil

1¾ miles west of Denning

Paige-Strickland Coal Co.	Mine #1

1¾ miles west of Denning

Pyron-Levy Coal Co.	Mine #1

2 miles west of Altus

Semi-Anthracite Coal Co.	Sambo

¾ mile northeast of Alix

Western Coal Mining	Mine #2

At Denning

Western Coal Mining	Mine #6

1¼ miles west of Denning

White Eagle Coal Co.	Strip

1 mile east of Alix

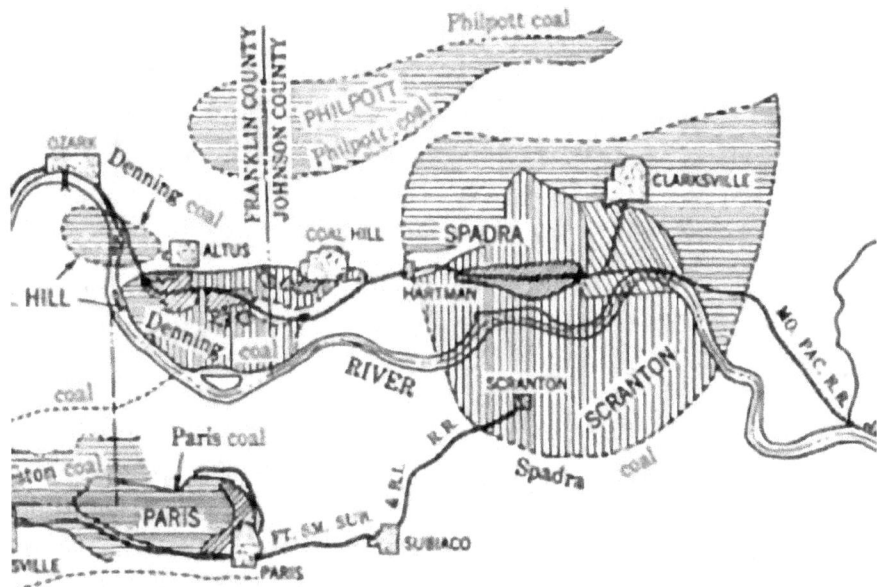

shows the coal fields between Spadra and Ozark, and comes from *Bureau of Mines Information Circular 7562 – Report of the Health and Safety Division for Fiscal Year 1949.*

455.2 SPUR TRACKS – At one time there were a large number of spur tracks into coal mines in Johnson and Franklin counties. Here, a spur track headed to the northeast to connect to a small yard at a coal loading facility. There were then two spur tracks that headed northwest to serve other facilities. One of these was the slope mine of the Joe Hoing Coal Company.

In the *Missouri Pacific Special Instructions No. 1 for the Central Division*, effective July 1, 1958, a 20-car capacity track was shown to be at Milepost 455.16 and used by the Philpot Mine.

455.6 CONTROL POINT V456 – This is the South Alix siding switch. Located on the east side of the mainline, the siding is shown to be 7606 feet long.

CP V456 ALIX

This sign marks the south switch of Alix Siding, today known as Control Point V456. The switch is a short distance from Kenny Hole Road, once an access road to several coal mines.

455.6 SANDBOE MINE #1 – A 2000-foot-long spur track once headed off to the south to serve this mine, owned by the Semi-Anthracite Mining Company. The track was also used by the White Eagle Coal Company. This coal mine worked a 42-inch layer of the Lower Hartshorne Seam using a 36-inch gauge mine railroad pulled by mules. The company was owned by the Parmelee family of Coal Hill. H. C. Parmelee handled almost all of the offices of the coal company, and was also shown to be the superintendent of the Blue Valley Coal Company and the Blue Hills Coal Company, both of Coal Hill.

456.2 SOUTH ALIX WYE SWITCH – This was the switch for the south lead of Denning Yard, later Alix Yard. The lead connected all five yard tracks to the mainline, and then curved to the northeast and connected with the Coal Hill Branch, forming the south leg of the Alix Wye. Immediately north of Yard Track No. 5 was the location of the original Detour No. 11 mainline. The Alix Yard complex, and a new mainline, were all built to the south. Because of the number of trains entering and departing the yard, a telephone booth was installed at the switch.

456.5 ALIX – Alix was the name chosen by the residents of this community, and it was adopted by the post office when it opened in 1906. However, the railroad used the name Denning Yard until May 28, 1925, when it finally made the change to Alix.

Just a block north (railroad-east) of the railroad at Alix is Alix Lane.

Denning Yard came about when the Little Rock & Fort Smith built a branch line from Coal Hill to several coal mines in this area in 1885. Construction on a seven-track yard at what became Denning Yard started in 1893, and by 1904 there were almost five miles of track. By this time, local coal mines shipped more than 100 cars per day. When the railroad built a new and more level mainline in 1903, Denning Yard was on the route and became the junction with the Coal Hill Branch. Some timetables listed the Coal Hill Branch Connection at Milepost 456.9. The yard stretched between Alix Pond on the north end (now gone) and Mikes Creek at Milepost 456.1. Because of the nearby coal mines and the junction with the Coal Hill Branch, during fiscal year 1904, a new seven-track yard and a combination depot/yard office/train order office were built here. The Denning Yard train order office was important and operated continuously since it was the only train order office on the new mainline between Ozark Junction and Hartman Junction.

In 1907, the employee timetable of the St. Louis, Iron Mountain & Southern showed that Denning Yard featured a 180-car siding, mail crane, water, coal, a wye, and four miles of yard limits. The depot featured a day and night telegraph office, a train register, and a train order signal, In 1922, the state of Arkansas listed three coal mines around Denning Yard that were served by the railroad. These were the W. A. Hill Coal Company's Hill Mine (two and one-half miles east of Denning Yard); George E. Dodson Coal Company's Mine No 2 (one mile east of Denning Yard); and George E. Dodson Coal Company's Mine No.

1 (one mile south of Denning Yard). The larger region, known as the Denning-Alix Coal District, or even the Denning-Coal Hill District, produced most of the Franklin County coal before 1943.

The local residents didn't like the name Denning Yard. There was a community named Denning less than two miles to the west, and they wanted their own name. One of the early settlers who had sold land to the railroad was Constant Alix, so the residents chose the name Alix. The railroad ignored the name, but the post office chose it when the post office opened in 1906, probably because there was already a Denning post office a few miles to the west. On May 28, 1925, the wooden depot, located on the west side of the tracks, was renamed Alix. At the time, the depot of Denning Yard (telegraph symbol DG) had a ticket agency as well as a freight agency for carload volumes and less.

In 1923, Denning Yard (Alix) was a busy place with a large number of train and crew services. Besides the yard, there was a 180-car siding and a wye. Coal and water was available for the steam locomotives, and there was a track scale to weigh the many carloads of coal moved from the local mines. A cotton platform was located immediately west of the depot, which was removed in 1951. The depot featured continuous train order service to handle the trains that operated day and night. The Great Depression of the 1930s greatly reduced the traffic on the line and Missouri Pacific closed a number of agencies along the Little Rock & Fort Smith. At Denning Yard (Alix), the train order office was reduced to a day office by the late 1930s. It was finally closed in 1952.

Alix was also the center for area track maintenance. A section gang was located here from when the new mainline was built. To house the track workers, a one-story section house was built in 1907. The house (24' x 34') featured four rooms and a porch.

In 1944, the siding was shown to be 81 cars long, and then 125 cars by 1951. There was still water available, and a wye track. The train order office was only open during limited hours. In 1969, the siding was 6014 feet long and capable of holding 115 freight cars. Today, the siding is about 7600 feet and the railroad faces grades of as much as 1.13% heading towards Fort Smith.

The yard is all gone, but a few tracks remain to serve the Butterball Alix Feed Mill that is located west of the main grade crossing at Alix. Butterball is one of the largest producers of turkey products in the United States and has several processing plants in western Arkansas. This feed mill serves a number of turkey producers in the area.

On May 3, 2023, UP 8006 pulls an oil train southward past the Butterball Alix Feed Mill.

Where coal trains once switched, the big business is now the Butterball Alix Feed Mill.

The Butterball Alix Feed Mill uses its own car mover to switch the plant, as shown here on a sunny spring day in 2023.

The Butterball Alix Feed Mill switches its own cars on its own tracks, so a derail and a track maintenance limits sign mark the track ownership limits.

Alix is now a small collection of houses, churches and a post office scattered over several blocks. It never had its own census until 2020 when a population of 100 was recorded.

The Train Collision of August 23, 1934

On August 23, 1934, a Missouri Pacific train was switching at Denning Yard, by then known as Alix. During the first move, the train actually had a side collision with another part of its own train, resulting in the death of one employee. The investigation and report by the Interstate Commerce Commission provided a great deal of information about the railroad at the time.

At Alix there is a yard consisting of 10 tracks paralleling the main track on the east, the tracks being known from west to east as the passing track and then numbered from 1 to 9, respectively. The north switch of the yard is located 2,047 feet north of the station, and the accident occurred at the fouling point of this switch, approximately 123 feet south of the switch point. Approaching the point of accident from the south, there is tangent track for a distance of 1,433 feet, followed by a 3 degrees 03' curve to the right 956 feet in length, the accident occurring on this curve at a point approximately 55 feet from its southern end. The grade for north-bound trains is 0.146 percent ascending at the point of accident.

North-bound freight Train Second No. 160 consisted of 42 cars and a caboose, hauled by engine 1544... This train arrived at Alix at 7:55 a.m., and after taking water the train proceeded to the north end of the yard where a cut was made behind the fourth car, preparatory to picking up cars in the yard, leaving 38 cars and the caboose standing on the main track with the head car approximately 123 feet south of the switch. The engine and four cars then pulled ahead and started to back in on the lead track. The four cars being handled by the engine passed the first car of the portion of the train left standing on the main track, but the left rear corner of the tender struck the right front corner of that car while moving at a low rate of speed.

456.7 ALIX OVERPASS – With the busy Alix Yard, a highway bridge was built over all of the tracks. The main span consisted of a 134-foot-long steel Pratt truss set on timber bents. The north approach was 118 feet long and consisted of an eight-panel frame trestle and 30 feet of rubble. The south approach had the same 30 feet of rubble approach, plus 211 feet of frame trestle consisting of 13 panels. The bridge is gone, as is the rail yard, but Arkansas Highway 186, shown as Coal Road in documents of the Federal Railroad Administration, still crosses the tracks here.

West of the overpass were once a a number of railroad facilities, all located on the north side of the yard. These included a section house, tool house and scrap bin for the track gang. There was also an oil house, coal bin, bath house and a pump house

(18' x 20') on a reservoir to the north. The road to the Butterball Alix Feed Mill is located where these structures once stood.

457.0 ALIX TRACK SCALE – This was the north end of the Alix Yard. The north yard lead had a switch with the mainline while a single lead continued through the 50-foot, 100-ton track scale before connecting to the mainline at Milepost 457.3.

457.2 CONTROL POINT V457 – This is the switch at North Alix.

This sign marks the Cherry Street grade crossing at Denning, Arkansas.

458.2 DENNING – The former station at Denning was located at to-day's Cherry Street grade crossing. The town traces its start to about 1890 when coal was discovered a few miles south of Altus. Benjamin Denning of the Western Coal Mining Company began buying up leases for coal mining, with much of the land dating back to an 1839 land patent for Samuel Davis. Ground was broken for the first mine shaft in December 1893, and soon there were at least a half-dozen mines in operation. A town was developed to house the workers, and an early report stated that it included 77 houses, a general store, post office (opened 1894), schoolhouse, a bank, a blacksmith shop, dance halls, saloons, gambling establishments, four churches, and a railroad depot. Western Coal Mining reportedly owned the general store and operated it as a company store for its employees. The mining company also built a stone vault to hold the gold and currency that it used to pay employees, and a stone prison for those who needed it.

Needing a name for the community, the residents chose Denning for the person they credited for starting the coal mining. The town was incorporated on December 2, 1903, and some sources state that there were 4000 residents, making it the largest city in Franklin County. However, the first census in 1910 counted only 757, the highest ever recorded here. Western Coal Mining kept opening mines as it acquired more coal rights, and eventually it owned six mines at Denning, employing more than 1000 miners.

Denning, Arkansas, still exists today, as shown by the Denning Town Hall sign, although the town simply consists of a scattering of houses north of the tracks.

A mining union moved to Denning in 1899 and the workers immediately went on strike demanding higher wages, shorter hours, and better working conditions. In 1903, the strike was finally settled and the union became recognized by the mining companies in the area. Mining at Denning seemed to have peaked in 1915 when Western Coal Mining Company Mine No. 1 closed. In 1922, the census reported a population of 608 at Denning. Despite the reduction in mining, the report *Minerals in Arkansas*, published in 1922 by the Commissioner of Mines, Manufactures and Agriculture for the State of Arkansas, listed seven mines around Denning. These were the Mine No. 2 of the Western Coal Mining Company (one half mile west of Denning), Mine No. 6 of the Western Coal Mining Company (one and one-half miles west of Denning), the Pendergrass Mine of the Denning Coal Company (two miles west of Denning), Liberty Coal Company (two and one-half miles west of Denning),

Mine No. 10 of the Harbottle & Bailey Coal Company (two and one-half miles west of Denning), the Black Diamond Coal Company (two and one-half miles west of Denning), and the Altus Domestic Coal Company (two and three-quarter miles west of Denning). All of these mines were served by the Missouri Pacific Railroad.

Many of these mines were actually former Western Coal Mining Company properties. Following World War I, Western began selling its mines as their production began to drop. In 1922, Denning suffered more injury as part of the town burned, and few of the businesses or homes were rebuilt. The Great Depression caused most of the mines to close, but World War II kept several open for a few more years. Mine No. 6 finally closed in 1943 and No. 2 closed in 1947, making it the last shaft mine at Denning. The population in 1950 was only 268 and the town was down to a general store and the post office.

By this time, Denning was being called a ghost town and only a few of the old coal tipples still stood, and a few sinkholes marked where the underground mines had once been worked. The post office closed in 1965, and in 2004, the Altus-Denning School District closed and students started attending the Ozark School District. Denning does still exist and is a scattering of houses over more than a dozen blocks north of the tracks. The population in the 2020 census was only 200.

The Little Rock & Fort Smith reached the Denning area when it built a branch line from Coal Hill to reach the developing coal mines in the area in 1885. It was extended to Denning when the mines here were opened. The railroad reported building four tracks in 1900. These tracks were Siding No. 1, the 1981-foot Denning Lump Track; Siding No. 2, the 1614-foot Egg Track at Mine No. 3; Siding No. 3, the 600-foot Rock Track at Mine No. 3; and Siding No. 4, the 1409-foot Slack Track at Mine No. 3.

The railroad also built a wooden depot here, and as the coal mines expanded, a ticket and freight agency were installed in the Denning depot. Located on the west side of the tracks, the service was very limited after the mines began to close. A mail crane was located at Denning, but it was removed by 1960. Like many stations between Fort Smith and Little Rock, the depot at Denning was closed during the Great Depression. It was removed in December 1933, and all local freight billing took place at Denning Yard (Alix). The local cotton platform had been torn down the year before. Today, the Union Pacific mainline is located south of town, but a number of old grades can still be found nearby.

Coal Tipple

A short distance west of the depot was once a private coal line that served a coal tipple on the north side of the mainline. Three tracks served the tipple and then 2122 feet of track continued to curve to the northwest to provide room for switching the facility. This was just one of a number of coal spurs that once kept the railroad busy.

A number of old railroad grades remain around Denning, including this one used as a farm road west of Cherry Street.

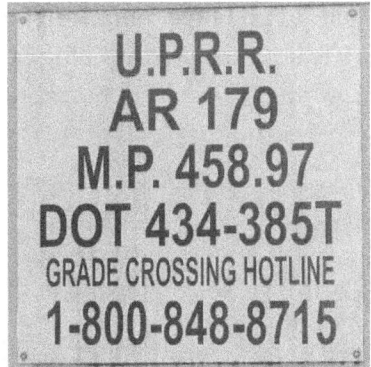

A grade crossing with Arkansas Highway 179 is located just railroad-south of the switch at Carbon.

There are a number of signs at the Carbon switch, including station and jump frog signs.

459.2 CARBON – Carbon is located near the top of a several mile grade from the east that exceeds 1.0%. Heading west, the tracks drop at more than 0.5%. The elevation here is 431 feet. Not far west of Carbon, the railroad turns back to the north to reach Ozark, Arkansas.

Carbon is also the mainline switch for a several-mile-long spur track to the south that serves the Tokai Carbon USA plant. Tokai Carbon is one of the largest graphite electrode manufacturers in the world. The company was founded in 1918 and is a pioneer in the Japanese carbon products industry. This plant opened in 1981, and later became owned by SGL Carbon, which began operations in Arkansas in 1996. In 2013, SGL Carbon invested $26 million in the plant to upgrade it and to expand the products that it could produce. The electrodes made at the plant are used in electric arc furnaces used to recycle scrap steel. SGL Carbon was acquired by Tokai Carbon about 2019.

During the early 1990s, Great Lakes Carbon operated the plant on the spur track at Carbon. The company switched the plant using this small GE locomotive.

A short distance west of Carbon is the grade crossing with Pond Creek Road, where there was once a coal tipple. A short distance to the south is Coal Road, an indication of what was once mined in this area.

459.4 COAL TIPPLE – There used to be a coal tipple and loading track to the south, where Pond Creek Road now crosses the tracks. The original track had switches on both ends, but the south switch was removed in January 1941. In December of that year, the track was expanded.

459.7 PENDERGRASS SPUR – This track was listed throughout the 1920s and required that all carload movements (in and out) be prepaid. The track was for the Pendergrass Mine of the Denning Coal Company, located about two miles west of Denning. The track was removed in 1934.

The Pendergrass Mine was named for William Joshua Pendergrass, a co-owner of the firm. Will, or W. J., grew up poor in Tennessee and moved to the coal fields of Arkansas to work as a miner. While working in the mines, he was self-taught in mine engineering and law. In 1912, Pendergrass created the Denning Coal Company along with his brother Dave and two other miners. The firm eventually owned several mines in the region. In 1920, William Pendergrass acquired and operated The Western Grain Company, a wholesale grain business, in Fort Smith, Arkansas. He also acquired other coal companies in Oklahoma.

459.8 CREEK ROAD – The railroad turns to the north to follow the Arkansas River to Ozark. There was a coal spur just west of Creek Road that headed to the southwest. This track was abandoned January 1941.

The Douglas Coal Company, often known as Douglass Brothers, had a track to the northeast at Milepost 460.0. The mine, known as the Saffire Mine, employed 150 workers and produced about 20,000 tons of coal a year. The mine had a 36-inch gauge railroad, with trains pulled by mules and electric locomotives.

461.1 SPUR TRACK – A track once headed to the northeast from here. This was about the west end of the coal district around Denning and Coal Hill. This track was abandoned in October 1941.

461.3 POND CREEK BRIDGE – Pond Creek forms on the west side of Pond Creek Mountain, located north of Altus. The stream flows to the south and southwest before flowing into the Arkansas River a short distance to the southwest from here. The railroad uses a 60-foot through plate girder span to cross the stream. Because of this, the bridge was routinely listed as having limited side clearance affecting the main track.

461.5 SPUR TRACK – This was another track that once headed to the northeast. This track was also abandoned during October 1941.

The Thomas B. Fitzburgh Generation Station burns natural gas to produce electricity for the seventeen electric distribution cooperatives in Arkansas. Named for the first full-time employee of the Arkansas Electric Cooperative Corporation, the plant no longer has a business track.

462.9 CO-OP SPUR – This retired track once served the AECC Thomas B. Fitzhugh Generation Station to the west of the tracks. The plant started operations in 1963 and is owned by the Arkansas Electric Cooperative Corporation (AECC). In 1942, the electric cooperatives of Arkansas formed a statewide association, Arkansas Electric Cooperatives, Inc., (AECI), to produce and share electrical power between its members. The Arkansas Electric Cooperative Corporation was created in 1949. Today, AECI and AECC, and the seventeen electric distribution cooperatives, are known collectively as the Electric Cooperatives of Arkansas.

During the late 1950s and early 1960s, the AECC developed plans to produce its own electrical power. The first plant, a 59-megawatt natural gas-fired generation plant, opened here in 1963 and cost $7.5 million. Unit 2 opened in 2003 and the plant now produces 170.6 Megawatts using natural gas. In 2024, it was announced that two natural gas generating units that could also operate on fuel oil were to be added to the plant. At a cost of $93 million, this will bring the total capacity to 270 MW.

The name Thomas B. Fitzhugh Generating Station honors the first full-time employee of the AECC. Fitzhugh was the AECC's attorney who helped create the electric cooperative association and ensured that it had the right to build its own generating plants.

A barge tow is working its way through the Ozark – Jeta Taylor Lock and Dam, with several of the barges below the dam and the line boat still in the lock. The locks on the McClellan-Kerr Arkansas River Navigation System measure 110 by 600 feet and some larger barge tows require two lifts through the lock to get all of the barges and line boat through the dam.

463.5 LOCK AND DAM 12 – To the west, the Arkansas River flows through Lock and Dam 12, later known as the Ozark Lock and Dam, and today known as the Ozark – Jeta Taylor Lock and

Dam. The lock and dam was built as part of the McClellan-Kerr Arkansas River Navigation System to help ensure a 9-foot navigable channel for commercial barge traffic. When completed in 1969, it created Ozark Lake, a 10,900-acre reservoir that offers great fishing for catfish, bream, crappie and bass.

The Ozark – Jeta Taylor Lock and Dam can cause a bit of confusion. It is Lock and Dam 12, but there is no Lock and Dam 11 since Dardanelle Lock and Dam (Lock and Dam 10) was built larger than originally planned. Additionally, a dam was built near the mouth of the McClellan–Kerr Arkansas River Navigation System as Lock & Dam 99. A further bit of confusion is that some sources call the road to the dam on the north bank Lock 13 Road.

U.P.R.R.
LOCK 13 ROAD
M.P. 463.52
DOT# 434392D
GRADE CROSSING HOTLINE
1-800-848-8715

While the Ozark – Jeta Taylor Lock and Dam is Lock and Dam 12, this Union Pacific grade crossing sign calls the dam's access road Lock 13 Road.

Jeta Taylor was a founder and first President of the Ozark Development Association. He also served as President of the Ozark Dam Society, Chairman of the Arkansas River Basin Interstate Committee, as a representative of the Governor of Arkansas to that Committee for many years, and First Vice President of the Arkansas Basin Association. As stated on October 18, 1976, in the bill that proposed the name change of the lock and dam, "Jeta Taylor was a pioneer in the movement that led to navigation on the Arkansas River and worked for more than 30 years to see the Ozark Lock and Dam become a reality."

To the east is Reed Mountain, named for Randall Reed, a former slave who bought the land from the railroad. On top of the mountain is Reed Mountain Park, a former Corps of Engineers park that is now managed by the City of Ozark. The park includes an overlook, trails, playground, restrooms, and a pavilion.

463.9 OZARK JUNCTION – Ozark Junction had few facilities beyond the railroad telephone available for train crews and track maintenance employees. This was the north end of the Altus District, the original route built by the Little Rock & Fort Smith during the 1870s. It was replaced by the more level route during 1903-1904. The original route via Coal Hill and Altus became the Altus District or Altus Branch, and a train register in a register booth was installed here to track movements on and off the old mainline. This route handled local service and some passenger trains until it was abandoned in 1936. The old grade was later used for Lock and Dam Road and Shady Lane. Details about the Altus District can be found in the route guide for the Altus Branch starting on Page 493.

On July 15, 1936, a train hauling bridge girders derailed 2400 feet south of the sign board marking Ozark Junction. The northbound extra train consisted of 37 cars and a caboose, and was hauled by steam locomotive #7, a 2-8-2 built by Baldwin in 1905. Many of the cars in the train were flat cars, twin-loaded with bridge girders. Apparently a bridge part came loose and fell off one car, derailing several cars further back in the train. The Interstate Commerce Commission reported that the "track is laid with 90-pound rails, 39 feet in length, with 24 ties to the rail length, single-spiked, fully tie-plated, and ballasted with washed gravel to a depth of 8 inches below the ties. The track is well maintained."

464.4 GAR CREEK BRIDGE – The railroad has a 181-foot bridge, consisting of 4 spans of beam construction. Before the Arkansas River was dammed and numerous bridges on the railroad rebuilt, this bridge (Bridge No. 344) consisted of three deck plate girder spans. They measured 46 feet, 80 feet, and 55 feet.

The railroad calls this Gar Creek, but most maps show it to be Hicks Creek. In reality, it is both. Hicks Creek forms a few miles to the east and flows to here. It once flowed into Gar Creek, but when the river level was raised due to Lock and Dam 12, the Arkansas River backed up into this area. Gar Creek forms on the west side of Ozark and flows around the north side of town before turning south and flowing into the Arkansas River here.

Approaching Ozark, the railroad curves again so that the tracks run east-west between the Arkansas River and the downtown area of Ozark.

Turkey King of Ozark

To the north of the Gar Creek Bridge is the turkey processing plant of Butterball. While the facility isn't served by the railroad, the Missouri Pacific Railroad can claim credit for the production of commercial turkeys at Ozark.

In 1928, Harold Dodgen partnered with his father to form the Ozark Creamery. By the early 1940s, Harold Dodgen had begun processing small volumes of turkeys. After World War II, Missouri Pacific was looking to help develop industry along the line, and George Trollope, an agricultural representative of the railroad, thought that turkeys might be a product that could be produced in the area. In 1947, Trollope asked Dodgen to process 35 turkeys for the dining cars of the Missouri Pacific Railroad. They were popular on the passenger trains and led to orders from retail stores. A small plant was built on River Street and production reached 750 turkeys per day by 1955. To meet the increasing demand, a new production facility was built in 1957 on the east side of town. This plant could process 2500 turkeys per day, and Harold Dodgen became known as the Turkey King of Ozark, and the father of the Arkansas turkey industry.

Turkey production spread across the region with several dozen processing plants eventually being built. About 1970, Dodgen sold his plant to Cargill, which expanded the facility, basically building a new and larger production facility during the early 1990s. During March 2003, the plant was sold to ConAgra Foods, which sold it to Butterball in late 2006. The feed mill at nearby Alix supports the local production of turkeys which are processed here at Ozark.

The turkey industry at Ozark was reportedly started by Harold Dodgen before World War II. It was supported by Missouri Pacific, which bought many of the processed turkeys to serve on the railroad's dining cars. Today, after passing through the hands of several companies, the large processing plant is operated by Butterball.

464.6 PHILPOT LEAD – For years a long spur track, also known as the Philpot Mine Lead, headed north to serve what was called the Philpot Mine, or the Ozark-Philpot Coal Mine. The Philpot Valley Coal Field, often spelled Philpott, was located about six miles northeast of Ozark and produced many tons of coal. The track was built to handle coal trains, with cars weighing a maximum of 251,000 pounds in 1958.

This county road sign shows the spelling used for Philpot Road, which runs through much of Philpott Valley.

The coal was reportedly discovered by Lindon Simeon Philpot, who moved into the valley during the early 1880s and acquired 120 acres on the stage road in the east end of the valley which later took his name. Philpot accidently discovered the coal vein from an outcropping in the creek bed while digging a water hole to supply water for the steam cotton gin he had just built. With the discovery, Philpot operated a small coal mine, as did several other farmers to meet local demands. Lindon S. Philpot died on March 16, 1916, and was buried in Mount Olive Cemetery, Midland, Sebastian County, Arkansas. The marker over the grave spelled his name Philpott. By the 1920s, Philpott was the most common spelling and maps showed the region to be Philpott Valley.

The Philpot property was later leased to larger coal companies. Several mineral reports called the coal the best west of West Virginia, and unsurpassed in the world in quality. Mines here worked a bed of Charleston coal that was known as the Philpott Seam. The coal mines were considered to be in the Philpott District. Reports on the coal field stated that only a small part of the Philpott District was in Franklin County, with most of it being in Johnson County. It was actually just a few miles north of Coal Hill, separated by a high ridge.

The Philpot Valley Coal Company was listed as being active in the coal fields here in 1944. Things really boomed in 1948 when "Utah crews stripped a layer of very high-grade coking coal from the Ozark – Philpott Coal Mine." This coal, "18 or 20 carloads a day," was shipped west to Colorado Fuel & Iron for use in making steel, requiring several new tracks to be constructed in the Philpott Valley.

According to a March 9, 1957, hearing of the Special Subcommittee on Coal of the U.S. House of Representatives, there were other users of Western Arkansas coal in steel making. Kaiser Steel (Fontana, California) and United States Steel (Geneva, Utah) were using the coal, which had a low sulphur content and was excellent for coke production. Much of this coal was being sold by the Sinclair Coal Company, which advertised the coal as *Utah's Arkansas Smokeless Coal "From the Famous Philpot Seam"* starting in August 1949. The coal name was last advertised during the early 1970s.

By Summer 1961, the Utah Construction Company had closed the Ozark Philpott mine for lack of economic coal. At the time, the Arizona Public Service Company was building their Four Corners Powerplant and needed a machine to open the first coal pit. A Marion Model 5323, a 23-yard stripping shovel, was located at the Ozark Philpott mine. It was dismantled and shipped to the construction site, where it was reassembled and used to open the first coal pit. This equipment move essentially ended large-scale coal mining in the Philpott Valley.

This is the emblem often used for Utah's Arkansas Smokeless Coal.

Ozark & Philpott Valley Railroad Company

The Ozark & Philpott Valley Railroad Company was incorporated with capital of $100,000 in Arkansas on September 11, 1929, to build a seven-mile-long railroad from Ozark to a proposed coal mine in Philpott Valley. The line would head north along the East Fork of Gar Creek, and then east into the valley, following what was described as "an easy grade, without substantial cutting or filling." The Interstate Commerce Commission (ICC) reported that the line would cost $133,953.44, including 80-pound rail and equipment consisting of two secondhand locomotives, one secondhand combination coach, and one box car.

The application with the ICC stated that the rail line would pass through territory used for agriculture and the raising of livestock, and that the railroad would also haul forest products from the easterly part of the line. However, moving coal was the primary purpose of the railroad, and it was owned by the stockholders of the Philpott Valley Coal Company, with J. S. Turner serving as president of the railroad. Turner had previously worked as a clerk, operator, relief agent, accountant, and agent (at Ozark) for Missouri Pacific/St. Louis, Iron Mountain & Southern. He was also involved with the Arkansas Valley Bank in Ozark, was the president of the Ozark Board of Education, and served on the state highway commission. His farm was used several times for experimentation, including fruit trees. He also raised American Trotting horses.

Listed as vice-president of the Ozark & Philpott Valley was Charles G. Kershaw, who was also president of the Kershaw Mining Company and C. G. Kershaw Contracting Company, both of Birmingham, Alabama. At the time, Kershaw was operating several coal mines across Alabama, Tennessee and Kentucky, and had handled grading for railroads (including Florida East Coast and Louisville & Nashville) and highways. In the book *Men of the South: A Work for the Newspaper Reference Library* (1922), it was stated: "There is undoubtedly no better known figure in the railroad construction and general contracting field than Charles G. Kershaw." Reports stated that Kershaw had subscribed for $52,300 of the $100,000 of capital stock of the railroad.

In 1929, the coal company leased about 5,000 acres of coal-bearing lands in west Johnson County and east Franklin County, Ark. Drillings and test pits indicated above 14,000,000 tons of recoverable coal in this field. It is estimated that there are 6,000,000 tons additional not yet fully explored. A large portion of the coal will be reclaimed by strip mining, in which the overburden is removed by means of steam shovels. Where the coal is too far below the surface for removal by this method the company will resort to tunneling.

The applicant states that Philpott Valley coal is semianthracite, high in carbon and British thermal units, exceedingly low in sulphur, moisture, and ash, and especially adapted to domestic use. At the present time there are 11 mines in the Philpott Valley field, with a total maximum output of approximately 250 tons per day.

Despite the local enthusiasm for the Ozark & Philpott Valley Railroad, there were also numerous groups in opposition to the granting of the application for a charter and ICC approval. Among these were the Arkansas-Oklahoma Coal Institute and the Midwest Coal Traffic Bureau, both of which stated that there was too much coal produced in the region, that coal prices had declined, that oil and natural gas was replacing coal with many users, and that the existing mines were able to operate only about half the time due to low demand. A number of coal companies and miners also provided testimony about the lack of demand for the existing Arkansas coal. Railroad officials responded by pointing out that the Philpott Valley coal was different and that it would replace Pocahontas and New River coal from West Virginia due to its coking abilities. Kershaw noted that several firms had already spoken for the mine's output.

With the testimony, the ICC issued a certificate of public convenience and necessity on September 19, 1930, with the requirement that the work be started on or before January 1, 1931, and completed on or before December 31, 1931. Over the next year, this date was extended to December 31, 1933. Some reports state that construction of the railroad grade began in 1929, but that the economic depression prevented funding from being obtained to complete the line. On June 22, 1933, the Ozark & Philpott Valley Railroad applied to the Interstate Commerce Commission for a Reconstruction Finance Corporation loan for $75,000, but it was denied due to a lack of economic potential because of the depression's impact on the railroad's owners.

Our action in granting authority to construct this railroad, while evidencing our willingness at a time of industrial activity to waive the doubts inherent in a proposition to bring into production additional new coal areas in favor of the optimism of those who were at that time willing to back their judgment by their capital should not now be construed as a reason why we

should authorize the expenditure of Government funds
for the purpose at a time when the promoters are either
unwilling or unable to carry out their undertaking.

At the time that the application for a loan through the Reconstruction Finance Corporation was made, no part of the railway property was in operation. However, the line was eventually built, but the Ozark & Philpott Valley Railroad was never listed as a railroad by the Railroad Retirement Board. Instead, a rail line was built from Ozark to the coal fields of Johnson County during the late 1940s. Reports from The United Mine Workers stated that the Utah Construction Company built a railroad in 1949 "into the Philpott Field." The Department of the Interior, Bureau of Mines, published *Mineral Resources and Industries of Arkansas* in 1969. The report covered the Philpott Coal District in Johnson County and supported the 1949 date for the construction of the railroad.

Inaccessibility allowed only scant production prior
to 1950. Construction of a railroad spur in 1949 stim-
ulated mining so that about half of the coal produced
from strip mines in Arkansas from 1952 to 1961 was
mined in this district. Since 1961, economic conditions
have caused coal output to regress to the position com-
parable with the period prior to 1950.

The construction of the railroad did allow coal to move off of the line for the next decade. In 1958, Missouri Pacific restricted train speeds on the Philpot Lead to a maximum of 15mph and had special instructions for operating on the line due to the sharp grades that were involved. Note that the railroad still used the spelling of Philpot.

Crews handling loads from Philpot Mine to Ozark
must stop train at top of Hill about four miles north of
Ozark and set pressure retaining valves on all cars in
the train to high pressure of 20 pounds and leave them
in this position until stop is made at foot of hill for de-

rail, where all retainers must be turned back to exhaust position before proceeding with train.

The mine of the Utah Construction Company closed in 1961, and the railroad was abandoned soon after. Today, little remains of the route except for a few grades and bridge piers. The line headed north, just a short distance east of the Ozark depot. Bridge piers can still be seen across Gar Creek just north of East Side City Park. The rail line then followed the East Fork Gar Creek to near the intersection of Stagecoach Road and Horseshoe Loop. It then turned east on what would be the south side of Interstate 40, with a few parts still used as farm roads. It briefly becomes Champaign Drive, a private road, where it crosses Arkansas Highway 186 and continues east past an old strip mine before turning north alongside McKinney Creek to pass between ridges. Here, Interstate 40 passes over the old grade. The tracks passed through a series of rock cuts and then crossed Philpot Road and turned east and northeast into Johnson County, reaching the Utah Strip Mine just west of Hunt, Arkansas. Parts of this route are marked as "Old Railroad Grade" on topographical maps from the early 1960s, especially the Hunt Quadrangle of 1963.

These old bridge bents, which once supported a Philpot Lead bridge over Gar Creek, can still be seen from East Side City Park at Ozark. The rail line once crossed the very eastern part of the land that the park sits on.

Just south of the Altus exit on Interstate 40 (Exit 41) is a gated road that uses the grade of the Philpot Lead. To the west of here are several ponds that mark the site of a coal mine.

Little remains of the many coal mines that once operated in Philpott Valley. This building, located alongside Philpot Road, is one of the few that still stands.

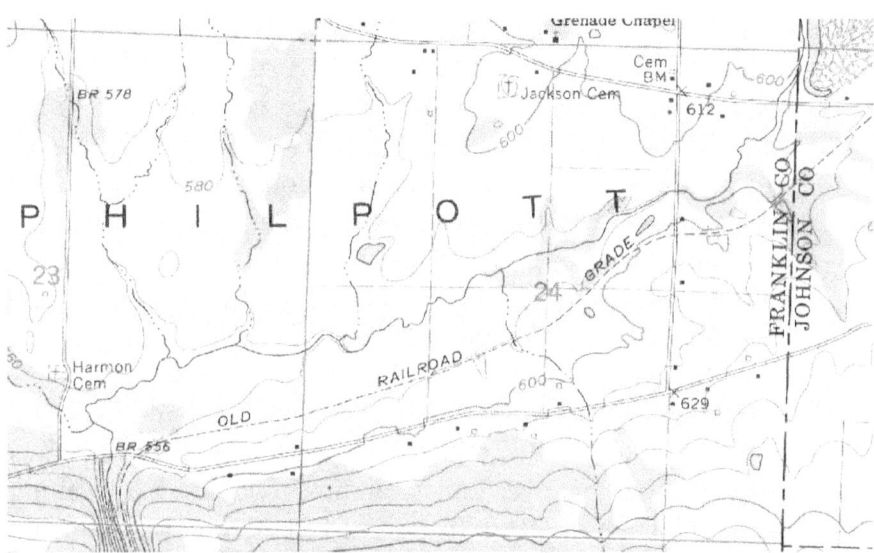

This topographic map from 1963 shows the grade of the Philpot Mine Lead as it passed through the Philpott Valley. At the bottom left, the grade followed part of McKinney Creek through a high ridge using a series of deep rock cuts. The former Utah Construction Company strip mine was located just east of the county line. *Hunt (AR) Quadrangle, 1963*. U.S. Department of the Interior, U.S. Geological Survey.

The last of the mines in Philpott Valley are now being reclaimed. Hunt operated as the mining headquarters for several of these coal mines, and this sign was standing in 2025 to note the reclamation of this strip mine site.

464.8 OZARK (Q) – Ozark is a well-known location along the Arkansas River, and the former Little Rock & Fort Smith Railway. This is the point where the Arkansas River is farthest north in the state. The name Ozark came from the French words "Aux Arc," which means "at the bend." French explorers, fur trappers, and traders traveled through the area and often stopped here as it was a noted landmark. The river bend was the closest navigable point to much of northwest Arkansas, and the location became the destination of a number of roads and trails, making it a noted trading point.

During the early 1830s, Ozark became a supply point and temporary stop on the Trail of Tears, especially when there was low water on the river and steamboats would stop awaiting rains. The town of Ozark had existed for several years when a post office opened on July 3, 1837. Later that year, Ozark was made the county seat of Franklin County and the first court house opened in 1840. The town was officially incorporated in 1850, the same year the census showed a population of 82. During the late 1850s, Ozark was publicized numerous times as an early goal for construction of the planned Little Rock & Fort Smith. Several contracts were signed to build a 32-mile section of track from Van Buren to Ozark. While a bit of earthwork did take place, no track was built at the time.

In 1860, Ozark celebrated the opening of a two-story brick school building. For the next five years, Ozark was impacted by the Civil War. At first, the town grew as farmers moved to town to be away from guerrilla warfare in the surrounding hills. In 1862, the town became an important Confederate base after the battles of Pea Ridge and Prairie Grove. In 1863, a force gathered here as part of a campaign towards Fayetteville, Arkansas. The campaign failed and Union forces captured Ozark, burning every business, church, government building, and all but three homes. The town ceased to exist and lost its incorporation.

A few years after the war ended, Ozark began to grow and was reincorporated in 1869. By this time, business along the river had returned and there was word that a railroad would be built through the community. Businesses opened and a number of new buildings were erected. By 1870 when Ozark had a population of 210, the town featured several banks and general stores, and a number of saloons. The town became known as a trading center for horses and cattle.

The railroad was being built towards Ozark, and an expected arrival date was May 1, 1875, although it was actually completed to here by the start of February 1876. A story is told that the railroad was originally going to bypass Ozark. However, the chief engineer fell in love with a young lady from Ozark and he was persuaded to change the route so that it passed through her town. With the railroad in town, the 1880 census reported 824 residents at Ozark.

The first freight moved from Ozark included general farm products, but in 1888, a vegetable canning factory opened at Ozark on the south side of Water Street (now River Street), between Second and Third streets, and shipped many carloads of freight each year. The Ozark Milling Company (grist and flour mill) was in operation on the north side of the tracks east of Third Street by 1897. There were plans to add a stave mill and barrel factory, but the facility was vacant by 1904. Other businesses such as lumbering, feed and grain production, and even coal mining developed in the area. In the 1920 census, the population was reported as being 1262 residents. At the time, Ozark was the home of P. F. Jones (wagon stock and oak lumber), the grist mill of F. N. Wilson, the lumber mill of B. F. Jones, the foundry and machine shop of E. R. Protheroe, and the monumental works of Johannes J. Jones & Son and the Wade Monumental Works. Four coal mines were also listed as being based at Ozark – Jones Mine, Moomaw Coal Company, Ozark Coal & Mining Company, and Smith Brothers Coal Company. Across Water Street from the depot (west to east) were rail shippers W. M. Cochrane & Sons, Ozark Packing Company, and the peanut shelling plant of Homer Hillard.

With the industry came modern utilities like electricity (1909), natural gas (1930), and city water and sewer (1930). In 1937, a little bank known as the Bank of Ozark was founded. Today, it is Bank OZK, which has a national presence but still many offices downtown. The Ozark Campus of Arkansas Tech University is located here, as are the schools of the Ozark School

District. The high school is the home of the Hillbillies. On the east side of town is the large Butterball turkey processing plant. Scattered throughout Ozark, with a 2020 population of 3542, are restaurants, retail stores, hotels, gas stations, and numerous other businesses.

Over the years, Ozark has been the home of a number of famous people. Elizabeth Gracen, the 1982 Miss Arkansas and Miss America lived here, and Harold Sells was born here. Few people know who Harold Sells was, but he was responsible for the creation of Foot Locker and was once the CEO of the F. W. Woolworth Company. On the music front, Ozark was where Leroy "Roy" Buchanan, a guitarist and pioneer of the Telecaster sound, was born.

This station sign for Ozark still stands alongside the Union Pacific mainline.

The Railroad at Ozark

Ozark, already a busy river port town shipping out products like coal, was another goal of the Little Rock & Fort Smith Railroad. The April 8, 1876, issue of *Railway World* reported that the track was laid and that trains were running to Ozark, 125 miles from the eastern terminus at Argenta. By 1882, the railroad was advertising that stages connected with the railroad at Ozark for Eureka Springs. With the railroad's arrival, Ozark immediately became a collection of railroad facilities. A 50,000-gallon wooden water tower stood here, watered by the Arkansas River. A wooden depot was built soon after the railroad arrived, and it was rebuilt as the freight house when the stone depot was built in 1910-1911. By 1907, there was a 100-car siding at Ozark, plus a mail crane and water tower. Stock pens operated for several decades, but were removed in 1925. Track Section No. 10 was based at Ozark, and a new four-room section house was built in 1910. The depot (18' x 94') was open 24 hours a day thanks to its day and night telegraph office.

Visitors to Ozark now find the cut-stone depot that was built in the winter of 1910-1911. Located at the intersection of River Street and First Street, it is often known as the Missouri Pacific Ozark Depot. The building now houses the Ozark Area Depot Museum and was listed on the National Register of Historic Places in 1992. The planning and construction of the depot took almost a year and a series of petitions and Railroad Commission of Arkansas hearings. After several years of requests to the St. Louis, Iron Mountain & Southern, the citizens of Ozark petitioned the Railroad Commission to require the railroad to make improvements to the local depot and other facilities. The petition resulted in a February 12, 1910, meeting at Ozark to review the town's request, which now included an entirely new depot since the existing depot was located too far from the town.

At the February hearing, the railroad stated the company realized the depot and its location was inadequate and that it proposed to move and remodel the old depot, locating it at the end of First Street. However, the Railroad Commission ordered that the railroad plan for and build an entirely new depot at the First Street location. By March, plans had been submitted for a new depot based upon the one built at Clarksville. A series of hearings continued through the summer on the plans and a schedule for the new building's construction. By September, the discussion was between a wooden and a stone depot. The local citizens wanted a native stone station while the railroad had proposed a timber frame depot. During mid-September, in spite of hearings still underway, the St. Louis, Iron Mountain & Southern announced that contractor Claud Talley had started work on the new Ozark depot and that completion was expected within six months.

The completed station has been described as "a single-story stone masonry passenger and freight depot" with a "composition-shingled hipped roof with Craftsman exposed rafters and large brackets underneath the projecting eaves." The building faces the Union Pacific mainline along the Arkansas River, with River Street immediately to the north. A survey benchmark is located 3 feet up in the face of the wall on the track side, between the windows of the agent's office. At the time in 1933, the elevation of the benchmark was shown to be 385.219 feet.

This photo from 1984 shows the track-side of the Ozark depot, a view that is currently hard to get due to fencing and vegetation.

In 1984, there was still a house track on the north side of the Ozark depot. This area is now used as parking for the Ozark Area Depot Museum.

The new depot, while in a better position for downtown, did block access to a small neighborhood south of the tracks and east of the train depot, as well as a horse barn, a lumber company, propane tanks, and the city's dump. A new grade crossing was built just east of the depot. These houses and buildings were removed when the Army Corps of Engineers built Lock and Dam #12 and flooded the area. Eventually the crossing was closed and removed, although this eliminated access for several landowners, despite almost all of their land now being underwater.

For years, Ozark was a staffed station with 24-hours train order service. Much of this was because of the coal business to the east, and the mainline and Altus District routes south of Ozark Junction. In 1892, the agent-telegrapher position was the highest paid in the area. At first they were paid a monthly wage, but this was changed to hourly during World War I when a new contract was signed with The Order of Railroad Telegraphers.

By the 1920s, Ozark had the continuous train order station, a 100-car siding, a water tower, and a mail crane. In 1923, Ozark had an agent-telegrapher on the day shift, with two telegrapher helpers handling the rest of the day, making Ozark a continuous train order station. In 1925, a Missouri Pacific report described the facilities at Ozark. There were both a freight and passenger station on the east side of the tracks, away from the Arkansas River and towards the town. The ticket agency was located in the passenger depot, while the freight agency (carloads and less) was located "0.1 mile to south of passenger agency."

In the labor agreement of 1930, there were three telegrapher positions to assist the agent (non-telegrapher) at Ozark, Within a few years the Ozark depot was back to an agent-telegrapher and two telegrapher helpers By 1942, the two telegrapher positions were gone, and Ozark was shown in timetables to have only limited train order service, which lasted until the end of passenger train service.

The siding was shown to only hold 78 freight cars by 1944, but the cars were longer by this time. The water tower was gone by the end of steam service, and the mail crane was removed with the end of passenger service in 1960. The siding was shown to be 3859 feet long by the 1960s, and is currently shown to be a business track in Union Pacific timetables. The south end is just north of the Gar Creek Bridge, while the north end is north of the Arkansas Highway 23 bridge.

There is still a long house track south of the depot and maintenance-of-way equipment is often found there. This track was once part of several tracks that served local industries. Along River Street were companies like Ozark Packing and the Homer Hillard peanut shelling plant. The open area between the Ozark post office and Gar Creek was the site of a large coal tipple and truck ramp. Missouri Pacific showed that the facility was used by the Franklin County Coal Company and the Pearless Coal Company. Across the tracks to the south was the tipple of the Ozark Smokeless Coal Company.

This view of the north side of the Ozark depot dates from 2022. The building has been cleaned up and is now the home of the Ozark Area Depot Museum.

Ozark and Railroad Disasters

Between the many tall bluffs and the nearby Arkansas River, if there was a train derailment on the Little Rock & Fort Smith, it was likely at Ozark. For example, during January 1889, a passenger train on the Little Rock & Fort Smith struck a landslide west of Ozark and was wrecked, injuring several people and killing the engineer. Two years later in March, an eastbound passenger train derailed near Ozark, injuring a number of passengers. It was reported that three coaches and the baggage car left the track and toppled over, with the derailment caused "by a spreading rail."

Much more was reported about the July 29, 1905, derailment at Ozark. This wreck involved the "Little Rock & Kansas City special on the Little Rock & Fort Smith branch of the St. Louis, Iron Mountain & Southern railway." About 50 crew and passengers were injured, including many members of the Little Rock baseball team and the "daughter of Superintendent Walsh of the Missouri Pacific railway." Reports stated that the wreck injured "forty-three passengers, five of whom will die" and that relief trains brought all the injured to Fort Smith.

This derailment was covered in great detail in newspapers across the region, including the *Topeka State Journal* (Topeka, Kansas) and *Omaha Daily Bee* (Omaha, Nebraska). The *Topeka State Journal* stated that the "train jumped the track at a switch while running full speed, and the engine and forward part of the train left the rails and went into the ditch." Meanwhile, the *Omaha Daily Bee* added that the "wreck was caused by spreading rails. All the coaches left the track and the second coach and the first Pullman were telescoped. The wreck occurred fifty feet from the bank of the Arkansas river, and had it not been for some cottonwood trees the derailed coaches would have rolled into the river."

It wasn't just derailments that made the news. During February and March of 1882, there were numerous news articles about the LR&FS being damaged by heavy rains. This seemed to be an almost yearly event. During February 1884, the *Las Vegas Daily Gazette* (Las Vegas, New Mexico) and other newspapers reported that the Arkansas River was flooding and that a Little Rock & Ft. Smith railroad bridge over a bayou near Ozark was washed away on February 12th. It was also reported that the railroad had suffered several landslides which hurled immense quantities of rock, earth and trees into the river, and that it would be several days before the trains resumed.

465.2 ARKANSAS HIGHWAY 23 – Above the railroad is another reason why Ozark is well-known. The bridge across the tracks and the Arkansas River is lit each evening and has been selected by the American Institute of Steel Construction as one of the most beautiful long spans in the country. It also provides great views of the railroad alongside the Arkansas River, but no sidewalks are actually provided on the bridge.

In June 1995, Union Pacific Challenger-class (4-6-6-4) 3985 headed southbound on the Van Buren Subdivision. These photos from the Arkansas Highway 23 Bridge shows it approaching Ozark, Arkansas.

In November 2019, an even larger steam locomotive headed north from Ozark on the former Little Rock & Fort Smith. This was Union Pacific Big Boy (4-8-8-4) 4014.

This photo in the collection of the Ozark Area Depot Museum shows one of the deep cuts north of Ozark, long an issue due to rock falls and limited side clearances. The gentlemen are standing next to the Section 40 limits sign.

Arkansas Highway 23 is also known as one of the most scenic highways in Arkansas, connecting Elm Park in western Arkansas with the Missouri border north of Eureka Springs. Its 130 miles pass through the heart of the Ouachita and Ozark mountains. North of Ozark, the highway is officially designated as the Pig Trail Scenic Byway due to its steep hills and hairpin turns.

Heading railroad-north, the railroad stays on the shore of the Arkansas River and actually turns to the southwest. In this area, contractors for the Little Rock & Fort Smith used 8239 kegs of black powder and spent $85,000 to make a 1200-foot-long cut through a bluff. For more than a decade, the railroad warned that the rock cut produced limited side clearances for the main track. Construction began in December 1875 and was finished in April 1876.

The Milepost 468 sign seems to be a popular target for local shooters.

468.6 ZENO – There was once a siding to the west (railroad-east), but it was retired and removed in December 1923. The location was still listed in the index of railroad stations in the March 1927 issue of the *Official Guide of the Railways*. The *Guide* stated "On the line indicated but not shown in time tables." At one time, there was a road bridge overhead to a stone quarry.

The name Zeno traces back to an ancient Greek philosopher from about 450 BC. He is best known for his paradoxes, but also for the dialectical method, where issues would be debated from two or more points of view, with Zeno often taking both sides of the argument.

United States Stone Company

For several years, there was a quarry at Zeno that provided stone for various government levee projects, mostly in southeast Arkansas along the Arkansas and Mississippi Rivers. During late 1913, the United States Stone Company was incorporated by Zeb Ward, J. J. Ball and W. D. Cammack, with a capital stock of $50,000. The firm moved into the area during December 1914 to obtain rock for their contracts. The August 3, 1915, issue of *The Ozark Spectator* newspaper reported on the naming of the site.

> *The rock quarry and railroad switch west of Ozark have been christened "Zeno" by employees of the railroad and the United States Stone Co. It looks as tho the name will stick and we hope to see the day when Zeno will outrival Poping, not that we have anything against Poping, but Zeno is nearer Ozark and will properly belong to Ozark.*

A few weeks later, the newspaper reported that employees of the United States Stone Company were arrested on a charge of Sabbath breaking. Apparently, the workers had performed blasting at the quarry, described as being "about five miles west of town where the government is securing several thousand car loads of rock for use on the Mississippi river," on Sunday, August 8th. The six workers pled guilty and were fined $1 each and costs, amounting in all to $90.40. Not long after, the quarry shut down when the stone contract was fulfilled. The quarry re-opened in late 1916, and *The Ozark Spectator* reported that the quarry shipped "several thousand carloads of rock annually to the Mississippi river for government use for levee and bridge purposes."

468.8 CONTROL POINT V469 – This is the south switch of Poping for a siding to the west of the mainline. The siding length has changed many times over the years, although some of these changes simply came about as the definition of a car length was changed. These car lengths included 100 (1907), 98 (1923), 81 (1944), and 131 (1951). The installation of ABS signaling on the line resulted in the lengthening of the Poping Siding. By the late 1960s, the siding was shown to be 118 cars long, or 6178 feet.

The 1982 issue of *Jane's World Railways* reported that the railroad was planning a siding extension at Poping. When the work was completed, the siding was shown to be 7488 feet long. After the installation of CTC signaling, the siding is shown to be 7590 feet long and is located alongside the Arkansas River.

This sign marks the country road that serves the gas wells in the Poping (Poppin) area. The tracks are very inaccessible throughout this area unless you are in a boat on the Arkansas River.

469.7 POPING – Poping is located in an isolated area alongside the Arkansas River at an elevation of 377 feet. When the railroad was being improved during 1903-1904, the St. Louis, Iron Mountain & Southern operated a gravel pit for ballast at Poping.

The 1904 annual report of the railroad stated that a "gravel pit was opened up at Poping, Ark., late in the season, but high water forced suspension after we had secured only sufficient gravel to complete the first raise of ballast on about 8 miles of the Little Rock & Fort Smith Railway."

A lawsuit from 1910 indicated that there was a station at Poping, but that it was not a regular passenger stop. Railroad documents showed that there was a depot (8' x 14'), coal bin and toilet located at Milepost 470.0. In 1933, the railroad was surveyed by a government team, and they reported that the elevation of top of rail opposite the Missouri Pacific Railroad station signboard for Poping was 384.8 feet.

Poping, reached by Poppin Bottoms Road, was never much of a community and never had a post office. Today, this area is gated due to the number of operating natural gas wells.

For years, the cuts that allowed trains to operate between the Arkansas River and the hills to the north were trouble spots for the railroad. Falling rocks, flooded ditches, and debris on the tracks were all reported. Many employee timetables included warnings about these potential dangers around Poping (Milepost 472.90 in 1907 during the Iron Mountain days) and White Oak (Milepost 477.87 during the same time period).

> *Passenger Trains will not exceed 20 miles per hour, and Freight Trains 10 miles per hour, passing Stone Bluffs between 2150 feet north of M.P. 471 and 2363 feet south of M.P. 473, and between 1956 feet north of M.P. 477 and 2193 feet south of M.P. 479; and while passing these points will look out for stone on track.*

There were also a number of warnings about the limited side clearances affecting the main track as it passed through several cuts and alongside a series of rock bluffs between Mileposts 471 and 472.

470.4 CONTROL POINT V470 – This is the North Switch Poping. The railroad continues to follow the Arkansas River and has turned back to the northwest as it heads towards Fort Smith.

The land to the north is known as the North Cecil Gas Field. The hills and woods are full of gas and oil wells.

474.5 WHITE OAK CREEK BRIDGE – Heading towards Fort Smith, the railroad curves away from the Arkansas River and starts to pass through miles of pasture lands. The railroad crosses White Oak Creek with a bridge consisting of three deck plate girder spans (184 feet total) and 33 feet of concrete pile trestle on the north end. This is another bridge that was improved with the construction of the Arkansas River navigation project. Before that, it was known as Bridge No. 360 and was located at Milepost 474 Pole 18.

This pier, located at the north end of the center deck plate girder span, shows some of the complexity caused when the bridge was raised.

The north end of the White Oak Creek Bridge was rebuilt as a concrete span in 1929, and then raised and rebuilt during the 1960s.

On May 3, 2023, Union Pacific 7899 pulls an AEPX (American Electric Power) coal train southward across the White Oak Creek Bridge. The locomotive is surrounded by a swarm of cliff swallows that nest under the railroad and nearby county road bridges.

While today this is a Union Pacific rail route, locomotives from other railroads are not uncommon. In this example, CSX 878 works as a DPU (Distributed Power Unit) on a southbound coal train.

Earlier, this bridge was rebuilt in late 1929. At the time the bridge consisted of three deck plate girder (DGP) spans, each 52 feet long, plus three timber pile trestle panels. The bridge was rebuilt with a 2-panel concrete slab, a 52-foot DPG, an 82-foot DPG, and another 52-foot DPG span. It is these spans that were raised and improved with the Arkansas River navigation project.

The use of steel bridges on the line accelerated during the 1890s as the St. Louis, Iron Mountain & Southern worked to improve the LR&FS. In 1896, the railroad reported in its annual report that it installed several 28-foot "Steel Eye Beam Girder" spans in this area.

Also known as Whiteoak Creek and Allmand Creek, the stream starts when the North Fork and South Fork merge near White Oak, Arkansas, about a dozen miles northeast of here. North Fork White Oak Creek forms in Wildcat Hollow, another dozen or so miles to the northeast. South Fork White Oak Creek forms northeast of Altus and flows westward. Just north of Ozark, it is dammed to create Ozark City Lake, a source of drinking water for the community.

During the Civil War, White Oak Creek was used as a defensive line by Confederates attempting to protect Van Buren and Fort Smith. With the stream flowing out of the rugged mountains to the north, it essentially blocked any movement from the east. As early as 1863, a series of battles were fought along the creek. On September 29, 1864, the Skirmish at White Oak Creek was fought as Union forces moved westward from Clarksville to take Van Buren.

475.0 WHITE OAK – This was a small community that existed along the railroad on the northwest side of White Oak Creek. It was never incorporated and never had a post office, although a mail crane (likely for the nearby Hight post office) and a 70-car siding were here during the first several decades of the twentieth century.

In 1925, the railroad reported that there was a platform on the east side of the mainline, and that prepaid carload freight moved in and out of White Oak. A cotton platform once stood at White Oak, but it was removed in June 1930. A 1933 survey report stated that the "top of rail opposite the Missouri Pacific Railroad station and milepost 475" was 395.6 feet. By 1934, the depot, section house, tool house, coal house, two toilets, and three bunk car bodies had all been removed. Today, only a private grade crossing and a small ranch complex marks the location of White Oak.

475.6 KD SIDING – In 1923, KD Siding (or K. D. Siding) was shown to hold 70 cars. By 1944, the siding had been extended to 90 cars long. A company telephone was also located at KD Siding.

This siding was immediately west of White Oak, and a grade crossing that provides access to a field on the south side of the railroad marks the location where the KD Siding station board once stood. In 1933, the elevation of the top of rail opposite the Missouri Pacific Railroad KD Siding station signboard was 407.3 feet. This was the top of a short grade from each direction. Throughout this area the railroad crosses a series of low ridges and the track keeps climbing to about 415 feet and then dropping back to about 390 feet.

KD Siding was located in what was called Pleasant Valley, with some maps showing it to be Hight. The community of

Hight is marked by the Hight Cemetery and its approximately 800 marked graves. One of the first buried here was William Green Hight, once a farmer in Bedford County, Tennessee, who moved to Arkansas with much of his family in 1867.

To the south is a small hill with a peak elevation of 686 feet. To the north is a series of low hills that are now covered with scattered houses, hay fields, pastureland, and poultry houses. About Milepost 478 was a small community known as Pleasant View. The Pleasant View Cemetery is located about a mile to the east.

476.2 SECTION POST – This was the location of another section post that marked the limits of the track section gangs in the area.

479.5 MULBERRY RIVER BRIDGE – Union Pacific now crosses this river using three deck plate girder spans totaling 316 feet, plus short concrete spans on each approach. Designated as a National Wild and Scenic River, the Mulberry River is one of Arkansas' wildest rivers and is used extensively for canoeing and kayaking, The river forms in southwestern Newton County and flows westwardly through Johnson and Franklin counties before turning southward to the Arkansas River, about three miles south of here. Most of this length is through the Ozark National Forest. In 1976, the United States Board on Geographic Names declared that the stream was the Mulberry River, settling disputes on whether it was a river or creek.

This bridge has been replaced a number of times since it was originally built by the LR&FS. For example, in 1890, the railroad reported that during early March, the Mulberry River Bridge washed out due to flooding. In 1916, this bridge was shown to include 3 concrete slabs, a 60-foot deck plate girder (DPG), four 56-foot DPGs, a 33-foot DPG, and then one concrete trestle panel. The bridge had been upgraded with concrete abutments and piers. To supply water for the steam locomotives, there had been a pump house and coal bin installed in 1928, but removed in late 1940. At the same time, the old water tank in Mulberry was replaced with a new one that measured 12' x 14'.

In 2011, a railroad contractor conducted a project to retrofit two existing piers on this bridge. The repairs came about due to a deteriorating pier cap and spread footing foundations that were being undercut by the river. The two piers were demolished while temporary falsework continued to support the bridge under traffic until new piers were installed, taking about two weeks.

This is the southern pier of the Mulberry River Bridge that was replaced in 2011. In the background is part of the old highway bridge, which has mostly been removed.

County Line

For much of its length, the Mulberry River is now the border between Franklin and Crawford counties. The county line was once further to the west, but it was moved here in 1895 when Crawford County agreed to build a bridge over the Mulberry River. On the east side of the Mulberry River is **Franklin County**, created on December 19, 1837, from part of Crawford County. Franklin County covers mostly very rural and rugged country on both sides of the Arkansas River, each with its own county seat – Ozark north of the river and Charleston to the south. When created, the county was named for Benjamin Franklin, and the population was shown to be 2665 in 1840. Forestry, mining (coal, clay, iron, shale and other minerals) and farming have traditionally been the largest economic activities, especially after Swiss-German immigrants moved to the area, settling in the mountains that reminded them of home. Wine grapes soon became a major crop grown and were shipped out on the railroad for decades. The first oil strike in Arkansas happened in Franklin County and natural gas is still produced. Poultry has become a major activity, and the wine industry and its annual Winefest makes the county a major tourist attraction. One interesting feature about the county is that because of the wine, the north part of the county is "wet" and alcohol is sold almost everywhere. Meanwhile, south of the Arkansas River the county is "dry" with no alcohol sales. The current population is 17,097 and the county is still very rural.

To the west of the river is **Crawford County**, created on October 18, 1820, from part of Pulaski County. When created, it acquired the nickname of "Empire County" since it covered western Arkansas and much of Indian Territory, later part of Oklahoma. Five Arkansas counties were carved out of Crawford County, plus several in Oklahoma. Because of its location on the western border of Arkansas, and between the Arkansas River and the mountains to the north, numerous roads and trails passed through the county, including the Butterfield Overland Mail stage route. The county became known nationwide when radio comedian, newspaper columnist, and movie star Bob Burns would joke about his family and friends back in Crawford County. The county was also the birth place of former slave Bass Reeves, who later became a noted lawman working out of Fort Smith and covering much of Indian Territory during the late 1800s. The population of the growing county was 60,133 in the 2020 census.

Crawford County was named for William H. Crawford of Georgia, a long-time politician. Crawford was elected to the U.S. Senate in 1807, and was president pro tempore of the Senate when Vice President George Clinton passed away in 1812, essentially making him vice president. During the War of 1812, President James Madison appointed Crawford as the minister to France. He then became Secretary of War, and then the 7th Secretary of the Treasury on October 22, 1816, and held the position until March 6, 1825.

479.7 MULBERRY (MY) – This area was hunted and fished by the Osage before it became part of the Cherokee lands during the early 1800s. In 1828, the Cherokee were moved further west to what became known as Indian Territory, and today Oklahoma. The clear-running Mulberry River attracted many settlers when the land was opened for settlement, and it became known for its farming and even recreational gatherings. The name Mulberry came from the large mulberry trees lining the local river's banks.

The first community in the area was Pleasant Hill. It formed around the school on the site of what was called the Presbyterian Campground, The campground was created to hold evangelistic religious gatherings each fall, and it actually predated the arrival of the Cherokee in the region in 1818, and the activity continued during the ten years that this was part of the reservation. After the Cherokee left, white settlers quickly grew the town. The community was soon large enough to have its own school, and a post office that opened and closed from 1828 until 1879. The settlement also featured a stage stop, several stores and druggists, and a few doctors.

To the south and towards the Arkansas River, another community began to develop, and a post office using the name Mulberry opened in 1830. Like just about every community in the region, Mulberry and Pleasant Hill were destroyed by roaming Confederate and Federal guerillas. Many residents fled to southern Arkansas or Texas to avoid the fighting, and many lost their livestock and homes. Settlers, some new and some old, started redeveloping the towns during the late 1860s. During the 1870s, there was almost a contest to see which town could become part of the route of the Little Rock & Fort Smith.

To make land available for the railroad, land was acquired south of Pleasant Hill along the road to the small port on the Arkansas River, now Main Street at Mulberry. Thomas A. Carter bought the land east of the road and Robert Henry Hicks purchased the property to the west. Carter is credited with building the first home near the tracks while Quesenbury and Company built the first business building. During early August 1876, the *Daily Arkansas Gazette* announced that "The Fort Smith Railroad Company has commenced work on a depot to be erected at Mulberry."

Mulberry was incorporated on November 8, 1880, and its population in the 1890 census was 321. At the time Mulberry supported local farming, and the town never grew very large or featured more than a few stores. It grew generally northward to join with the older Pleasant Hill, and the railroad essentially became the southern border of Mulberry. Most of the businesses in Mulberry were north of Second Street on Main Street, several blocks north of the railroad depot. The town's population peaked in 1920 at 1095 residents, and then dropped to 895 in the 1930 census. The population didn't exceed 1000 again until the 1970 census (1340 residents). The 1927 Flood, several droughts, and then the Great Depression forced many local farms to close and many residents to move away.

The 1960s saw Mulberry start to recover as Interstate 40 was built north of town where Pleasant Hill once was, and the work on the Arkansas River reduced the flooding in the farm fields to the south. Farming and livestock have again become important activities, and an industrial park was created west of town, but not on the railroad. One of the companies there, American Vegetable Soybean, produces a specialized soybean product known as edamame, and Mulberry has been called the "edamame capital of the United States." For those that want to know, edamame is a preparation of immature soybeans in the pod, found in cuisines with origins in East Asia.

Recreation has become big business in the Mulberry area with a number of parks (Bluff Hole Park is particularly well known) and canoeing and kayaking on the Mulberry River. The population has climbed to about 1600 and it supports a few retail stores, restaurants, gas stations and even the Mulberry-Pleasant View Bi-County School District and its Mulberry High School.

The Railroad at Mulberry

Today, the railroad passes by the south side of Mulberry with a short spur track into a local industry. However, during the first seventy years of the railroad, Mulberry was a busy railroad station. A small building served the railroad until a new wooden combination station was built in 1905. It featured a covered portico on the passenger end and was described as being larger than most on the line. In 1907, the station featured a day and night telegraph office. Nearby was a 62-car siding, mail crane, and a water station.

In 1909, the Arkansas Legislature passed a bill (Act No. 344) requiring the railroad to build a viaduct over the railroad at Mulberry. The viaduct was built at Church Street and was removed in 1937. An old warehouse still stands where the south approach to the viaduct once was. The fill for the north approach can still be easily found.

For some reason, the station was jacked up 2-3 feet and moved a short distance in 1915, and was located on the north side of the tracks and west of Main Street on Railroad Drive. The railroad received several complaints about the work and at least one lady fell off the temporary platform and hurt herself, and later sued the railroad over her injuries. The elevation at Mulberry is shown to be 392 feet, but a 1933 survey reported that the elevation of the top of rail opposite the Missouri Pacific station at Mulberry was 394.1 feet.

The first major rail shipper at Mulberry was the Mulberry Cotton Oil Company, located south of the tracks and west of Main Street. It became the Mulberry Plant of the Osage Cotton Oil Company during the late 1910s, and then the Mulberry Plant of the Cherokee Cotton Oil Company.

To handle some of the cotton shipments, the railroad built a 24' x 75' cotton platform. The cotton oil plant was retired and the machinery sold and shipped off by 1930. However, some of the buildings still stand and are used for other purposes. Other shippers included the James N. Farmer lumber mill; a cotton gin and several cotton dealers; a butter, egg and poultry dealer; and several livestock dealers who used the railroad's two stock pens with a 4-car capacity.

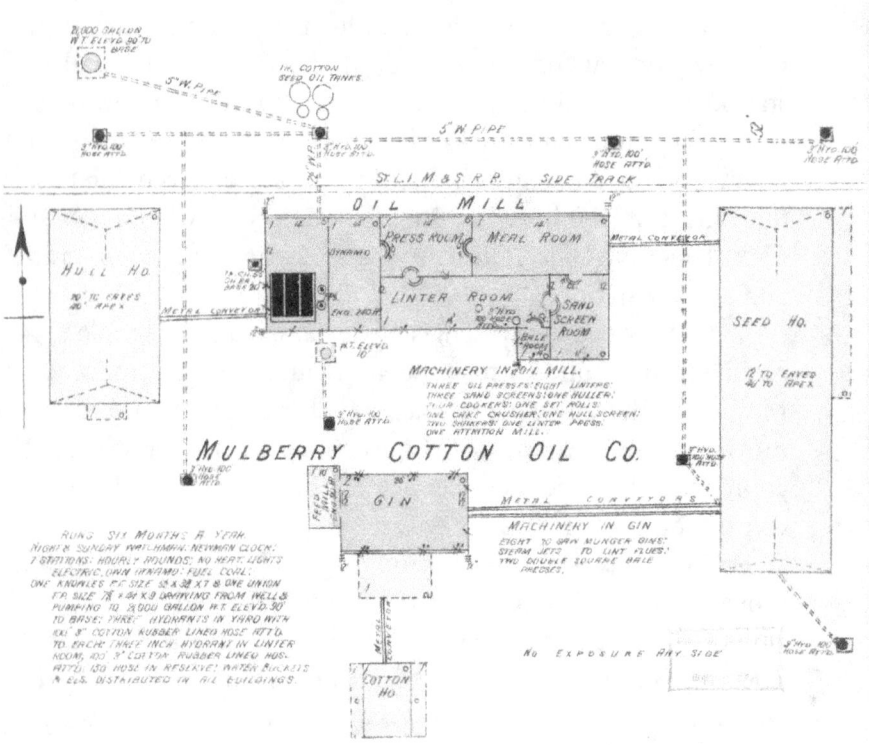

The Mulberry Cotton Oil Company was probably the largest rail shipper at Mulberry, Arkansas. This Sanborn map from 1908 shows the layout of the plant, located south of the mainline and west of Main Street where the spur track remains. *Sanborn Fire Insurance Map from Mulberry, Crawford County, Arkansas.* Sanborn Map Company, June 1908. Map. Retrieved from the Library of Congress, https://www.loc.gov/item/sanborn00311_001/.

For the railroad's operations, the station provided continuous train order service during the 1920s. There was a mail crane for the post office, a water tank supplied by city water, and a 62-car siding. About 100 yards east of the depot was a railroad section tool house used to store tools and track parts for local railroad repairs. In 1925, the Mulberry station was located on the railroad-east side of the tracks. It housed a ticket agency (coupon ticket station) and a freight agency for carload volumes and less. By 1944, the siding was shown as being only 45 cars long and 38 feet of the depot were removed. The mail crane still stood, but the train order office was closed and only a railroad telephone was available for the train crews.

Prior to installing the new ABS signaling during the mid-1940s, certain sidings had been lengthened to be long enough to hold trains of up to about 90 cars. At Mulberry, the siding was retired but a short track was left for industrial purposes. Employee timetables from 1951 show no siding, and only a telephone and mail crane. After 1960 when passenger service ended, only a business track remained.

The street signs for Railroad and Main mark the location where the Mulberry train depot once stood.

480.1 LITTLE MULBERRY RIVER – The Little Mulberry River, also known as Mulberry Creek, forms in the mountains east of Mountainburg, Arkansas, and flows to the south until near Dean Springs, where it turns to the southeast. It flows around the west side of Mulberry before flowing into the Mulberry River a short distance north of the Arkansas River.

The October 9, 1878, issue of the *Arkansas Democrat* reported that the Little Rock & Fort Smith's 90-foot Howe Truss bridge over the Little Mulberry River burned on the night of October 8, 1878. Today, the bridge consists of 85 feet of concrete pile trestle and two deck plate girder spans that measure a total of 142 feet. These spans were installed in 1924.

481.3 GIN TOWN ROAD – Some county road signs show this to be Gun Town Road. Gin Town was apparently an early settlement that is long gone. Note that the road on the south side of the tracks is Caboose Road.

Before 1895 when the county line was moved east to the Mulberry River, this was the location of the border between Franklin and Crawford counties. Some maps show this to be Old County Line Road.

Also known as Gun Town Road and Old County Line Road, Gin Town Road was the county line between Franklin and Crawford counties before 1895.

The Unsuccessful Train Holdup of Mulberry

The March 15, 1883, issue of *The Railway Age* reported on a train robbery on the Little Rock & Fort Smith that took place near here. The report follows.

> *On the Little Rock & Fort Smith road, March 7, two miles west of Mulberry station, Arkansas, the east bound passenger train was boarded by four men, who ordered the passengers to throw up their hands and began firing pistols. Conductor John Cala was killed and brakeman Milton Lester fatally injured. The robbers started for the engine, but the engineer started and the robbers became alarmed and jumped off without obtaining any booty. Superintendent Theo. Hartman has offered a reward of $5,000 for the capture of the rob-*

> *bers, and the authorities of Crawford county $1,000.*
> *One of the robbers has been captured. He was wound-*
> *ed in the face and arm. Being unable to keep up with*
> *his companions, he took refuge in a farm house where*
> *he was traced by the officers. A vigorous search is being*
> *made for the rest of the band and it is thought they*
> *cannot escape.*

More information on the robbery and the pursuit of the crim-
inals was reported nationwide, with the March 8, 1883, issue of
the *Indianapolis Journal* reporting many of the same facts.

> *At 8:30 to-night, the east-bound passenger train on*
> *the Little Rock & Fort Smith railroad was boarded by*
> *four men, two miles west of Mulberry Station, Craw-*
> *ford county, 140 miles from Little Rock. They ordered*
> *the passengers to throw up their hands, and began fir-*
> *ing pistols. Conductor John Cain was in the rear car,*
> *and was fatally shot. The robbers then rushed for the*
> *engine, but before reaching it Engineer Rogers pulled*
> *out. Brakeman Lester was also shot during the firing.*
> *The robbers jumped off after the train was in motion.*
> *The superintendent offers $5,000 reward for the cap-*
> *ture of the robbers.*

Conductor John Cain was buried in the Oakland Fraternal
Cemetery in Little Rock. A public fundraising effort raised the
money for the burial, headstone, and Cain's widow and children. Within a few weeks, the names of the robbers became
public and the rewards led to many efforts to catch them. The
three who fled were identified in *The New York Times* of March
18, 1883, as "the Johnson brothers and a noted desperado
named Herndon." Reports from the time stated that the four
men were encouraged by a series of books about Frank and Jesse James. James Johnson, known as Gov since he had the same
name as the governor of Tennessee, had moved from Tennessee
to Illinois. His brother Benjamin had made the same moves and
then moved on to Kansas, and then to Washington County in

Arkansas. James Johnson came to visit his brother Benjamin, where his 17-year-old nephew Jim became quite taken with Gov while a train robbery was being discussed. After a short period of time, James Johnson had persuaded his nephew Jim, James Herndon, and Monroe McDonald to participate in the holdup.

No real planning was made by the four robbers, and despite there being a large payroll package in the express car of the train, they got away with nothing. The two Johnsons and Herndon fled to Washington County. The first caught was Monroe McDonald, who had a reputation of being a bully, conducting dishonest transactions and making threats of retaliation against neighbors, and just being a disreputable person. McDonald was severely wounded during the robbery, reportedly by James Herndon, and didn't join the other three robbers as they fled. Instead, he pretended that he was an innocent victim but was immediately identified and arrested.

Within a few days, the rest were captured, especially due to a local insurance salesman who hired a pack of dogs and managed to trace the would-be robbers into the hills. It should be noted that the insurance salesman was later convicted and hanged for murder in Texas. James Herndon was described in newspapers as being in his 20s, single, and apparently aimless in life but with no history of misdeeds. James Johnson was described as the mastermind of the robbery, but rather clueless in planning the event. Finally, 17-year-old Jim Johnson was described as excitable and having only the most basic education.

The men were taken to Clarksville, tried, and sentenced to be hung. It was determined that the shooting of John Cain was unintentional, and no one was sure who had fired the shot. However, Jim Johnson admitted that he may have been the only person who fired his weapon. During the first days after the robbery, Ben Johnson's wife reportedly worked with neighbors to make sure that food was available in case the Johnsons and Herndon showed up. After the trial, Ben Johnson reportedly approached several people to help free his son Jim from custody. The efforts were unsuccessful and all four men were hung on Friday, July 22, 1883. A full report was printed in the *Arkansas Gazette* the next day.

483.9 SOUTH SWITCH DYER – For years, this was the south switch of the siding at Dyer, which was located on the railroad-east side of the mainline. The siding was removed by the 1960s. Directions through this area can be a bit of a challenge as trains heading towards Van Buren – north on the railroad – are actually heading to the southwest.

484.7 DYER – Dyer is another town along the Little Rock & Fort Smith Railway that was created after the railroad was built. The land where the town sits was owned by the railroad and sold to Stephen M. Dyer in 1870. The Dyer family had been living in the area since at least 1840 when Joel Dyer acquired a farm adjacent to the East-West Military Road which had opened by 1828. Joel started operating a small store and rest stop for wagons heading west on the road. It became a designated stage stop in 1858, which also handled the local mail. Joel's sons Stephen and George took over the work when their father died in 1864. The community grew enough that a small school opened in 1867.

W. U. Casey is credited with building the first house and store on the former railroad property, and members of the Dyer and Hays family also soon had houses here. A depot opened about the same time on the railroad, and the town's history states that the Dyers provided the materials for the depot, which was at first called Dyer Station. With the railroad completed, Stephen Dyer built the first cotton gin in the area by 1880. In 1884, the community was platted and lots laid out by George E. Dyer (often spelled Dyre) and John William Moss. The plat had the streets being 60 feet wide, alleys 20 feet wide, and all lots 50 feet wide. The new town was named for the landowner Stephen Dyer. As part of an effort to grow the community, some town lots were given away. The town soon had two stores, a sawmill, a blacksmith shop, and a cotton gin. A post office opened in 1885.

Dyer became the local market town for farms in the area which grew everything from corn and cotton to watermelons, peaches and apples. Alfalfa and hay were important as residents also raised cattle, hogs, and poultry. A school opened on land donated by Stephen Dyer, and the town was incorporated on July 22, 1889. Its population in the 1900 census was 343.

The Dyer Gin Company, owned by the Cherokee Cotton Oil Company, opened a new cotton gin in 1903. It burned in 1921 and was replaced by a modernized electric gin which later burned in 1939. Fires also burned much of the business district in 1909, and it was replaced by seven brick buildings within a year. Dyer hit a high in its population of 609 in 1920. Joel Dyer opened a gas station during the 1920s after U.S. Highway 64 was paved through town. Other businesses also opened to take advantage of the highway traffic, including an ice cream parlor and a beer joint. A furniture manufacturing and repair business, as well as a clothing store were located at Dyer until the Great Depression of the 1930s, when many of the businesses in town closed. The town also closed its high school and sent students to schools in nearby Alma. By 1950, the population of the town was down to 398. After that, Dyer began to slowly grow again.

Some of this growth was not entirely welcomed. In 1975, the Tony Alamo Christian Ministries established its headquarters in Dyer. The organization was sometimes called a cult, having started as a street ministry in Hollywood, California. The group built a compound at Dyer and started up a number of businesses, using labor supplied by its followers (many street people from urban areas) who lived in the organization's housing. Many of these businesses, as well as the church, were investigated for tax fraud and for violations of the Fair Labor Standards Act. Tony Alamo was convicted and served time in prison, moved, was convicted again, and the church's activities at Dyer are now all gone.

Dyer was reincorporated as a second-class city in 1981. Today, Dyer is a small community with several stores along U.S. Highway 64 north of the old downtown, which was located around the Washington and Main street grade crossings. Its population is about 800 and the town has its own fire station, drinking water plant, and sewage treatment system.

The Railroad at Dyer

To the north of the tracks between Washington and Main streets is Railroad Lane, located where the depot once stood.

The original depot burned in September 1888, reportedly set ablaze by disgruntled Republicans upset over a recent election. The replacement depot was a small wooden structure, built in 1890. In 1905, the Arkansas legislature passed an act that required the Iron Mountain to open the depot and to stop trains at Dyer. Apparently, this was done as it housed an agency until the late 1920s, but with the train order semaphore removed in November 1922. A mail crane had been installed by 1907, as had a 52-car siding.

On the north side of the tracks at Dyer is Railroad Lane. It seems that almost every town along the old LR&FS has a street named Railroad.

During the 1920s, Dyer was one of a number of stations that saw a sudden increase in strawberry shipments. Missouri Pacific was promoting strawberries to local farmers, especially with the railroad's ability to haul the strawberries to northern markets. In 1924, local farmers shipped 9 carloads of strawberries from Dyer, averaging 420 crates per car.

In the March 1, 1925, *Missouri Pacific Railroad Company Official List of Officers, Agents, Stations and Mileage*, Dyer was shown to have a ticket agency and a freight agency in the depot, located on the west side (compass-south) of the tracks at Washington Street. On October 31, 1929, the Arkansas Railroad Commission authorized the closing of the agency at Dyer, but required the railroad to employ a caretaker at the station. In 1933, a survey stated that the top of rail opposite the Missouri Pacific Railroad Dyer station was at an elevation of 425.4 feet. In the summer of 1936, the station was removed from Dyer. There was still a loading platform, tool house, and toilet. Several tracks once looped to the south between Main and Washington streets, but they were mostly gone by this time. By 1944, a mail crane was used to send out mail and a railroad telephone was here to be used by train crews and track workers. The siding was shown to be 80 cars long, and it had been extended to 90 cars long by 1951. The siding was gone by the 1960s, but a new one was installed west of town by the 1980s.

During May 2023, Union Pacific 7496 pulls a westbound train across Main Street at Dyer. Also at the grade crossing is a WPA 1940 marker, noting the construction of several nearby roads by the Works Progress Administration.

484.9 NORTH SWITCH DYER – The north switch of the mile-long Dyer siding was once located here.

485.1 CONTROL POINT V485 – This is now the south switch of the siding at Dyer. The siding is located on the east side of the mainline. This siding was built during the early 1980s due to an increase in train traffic on the line – mainly coal trains.

486.0 DYER – This is the new Milepost of Dyer as shown in railroad timetables. This marks the location of the new siding that replaced the former station and siding of Dyer to the south. It is shown to be at an elevation of 438 feet.

486.8 CONTROL POINT V487 – This is now the location of the north switch at Dyer.

Union Pacific 6162 pulls an eastbound oil train out of the siding at Dyer on September 22, 2022. The current Dyer Siding was built during the early 1980s as capacity on the Van Buren Subdivision was increased to handle a surge in coal traffic.

This plaque on the Arkansas Highway 162 overpass shows that it was built over the Union Pacific Railroad in 2015.

489.1 ARKANSAS HIGHWAY 162 – The railroad passes under a new highway bypass, built in 2015. This is actually the third route assigned the title of Arkansas Highway 162. The original route, designated in 1937, was near Luxora (northeast Arkansas), and was removed from the state highway system by 1939. The second Highway 162 lasted only a few years during the late 1940s at El Dorado (south Arkansas). This Arkansas Highway 162 connects Alma with Van Buren via Kibler, less than a dozen miles long. It was designated about 1952. The highway originally went through the old downtown of Alma, but this bypass opened in 2015 to relieve congestion around the Alma High School complex.

Like many bridges along the Little Rock & Fort Smith, the old pilings of the previous timber trestles can still be found under the more modern structure of the Little Frog Creek Bridge.

489.2 LITTLE FROG CREEK BRIDGE – While the railroad shows this to be Little Frog Creek, most call it Little Frog Bayou. The stream forms on the southwest side of Winn Mountain and flows generally to the south. It flows into Lake Alma, a local source of drinking water, and then south a few miles around the east side of Alma and into Frog Bayou.

During the 1940s, the bridge was 157 feet long and consisted of a 12-panel timber pile trestle. At the time it was known as Bridge No. 396. It was soon rebuilt with a 30-foot steel beam span, plus about fifty feet of timber pile trestles on each end. Today, it consists of five concrete ballast-deck spans. The remains of the older timber piles can still be found in the streambed.

489.5 ALMA (AX) – Welcome to the "Spinach Capital of the World."

The Alma area was once part of the early Cherokee territory of northwest Arkansas, and it opened to non-Cherokee settlement in 1828. One of the first buyers of land was Armstead "Ira" Smoot, who bought land from the government on August 3, 1836. The land was used for farming, but a small community began to develop nearby with a drugstore, cotton gin, and a few houses. The name Gum Town was used by some, noting the number of gum trees in the area.

Alma was the scene of an event that almost started a war between Arkansas and Utah. In 1857, Parley Parker Pratt, Sr., was killed by the estranged husband of his twelfth wife. Pratt was one of the first members of the Quorum of the Twelve Apostles of the Latter Day Saints faith. He had been part of the large movement of members to Utah, and then was assigned to a mission in the eastern United States. Here he ran into the husband of one of the wives (they had never divorced) he had taken, moving her and her children to Utah to be out of the reach of her husband, Hector McLean. A series of legal battles ensued, including charges involving the kidnapping of his children. The judge admitted that he sympathized with the wife due to Hector's reported drinking and wife-beating, and secretly released Pratt. However, Hector McLean found him and fatally shot and stabbed Pratt. The motive for the murder was understood by many in the Alma area, but in Utah it was considered to be martyrdom, being killed "by a small Arkansas band antagonistic toward his teachings." The killing was used by some as justification for the Mountain Meadows Massacre a few months later. The massacre involved a wagon train heading from Arkansas to California. It was attacked and all adults killed by a band of Mormon followers. The surviving children and family possessions were given to Mormon families. Pratt was reportedly buried near Alma, but when family tried to move his body back to Utah, his remains could not be found.

Early in 1871, a post office opened using the name Alma. There is no clear explanation for the name Alma, but several stories try to explain the reason. One states that the name came from the sweetheart of Sam Daugherty, a nearby postmaster. Another story states that residents got to drop names in a hat and then one was chosen.

Later in 1871, a log house was built as the first school, and a public hall was built in 1872 to be used as a meeting space, church, school, and Masonic hall. Businesses and small industries also opened. These included several general stores, groceries, dry goods stores, a saloon, a cotton gin, a sawmill, and a flouring mill. Several churches were also built. On January 7, 1874, Alma was incorporated, and reports from the time stated that the town's economy was based upon serving the local agricultural interests.

The Little Rock & Fort Smith Railway was building towards Fort Smith during the mid-1870s. To make sure that the railroad came through Alma, Mathias F. Locke, an early landowner, provided $1500 to the railroad company and worked to make sure the railroad had the required land and survey available. With the arrival of the railroad in 1876, businesses that served the travelers also developed. The King Hotel opened on the corner of Railroad Street and Fayetteville Avenue. A sawmill to cut local timber (black walnut, locust, cedar, and sweet gum) began to ship on the railroad. Cotton became big business at Alma during the 1870s and about 3000 bales of cotton were shipped from here each year, producing about $120,000 in income for local farmers and cotton dealers. With this success, Alma made an attempt to become the county seat of Crawford County in 1877, but lost the vote to Van Buren on July 10, 1877. The census of 1880 reported a population of 504.

During the late 1800s, Alma developed a number of businesses to serve the traveling public. In public timetables, it was stated that stages connected at Alma for Fayetteville. Downtown Alma took a hit when much of it burned in December 1884.

However, the town rebuilt and even grew as the Alma Canning and Evaporating Company was incorporated in August 1888. The company provided a new market for local fruit and vegetable farmers, and drew more business to Alma. Strawberries were also shipped to national markets on the railroad. By the early 1900s, new crops like spinach, mustard greens, various beans, potatoes, and tomatoes gained importance as the fruit business was hit by new competition from Texas and Florida. Coal and natural gas also provided some new economic activity in the area. In 1921, Alma had a number of industries, including a cannery (Garrett Canning Company), feed dealer (J. R. Roberts), and a coal mine (John Owens). There were at least four cotton gins operated by William Meyers, the New Town Gin Company, the O'Neal Gin Company, and the Planters Cotton & Gin Company.

Like most of the country, the Great Depression of the 1930s hurt the local economy, but Alma remained the second-largest town in Crawford County, and its population actually grew. On June 23, 1933, Alma made the national news as Alma city marshal Henry Dallas Humphrey was killed by Buck Barrow and W. D. Jones of the Barrow Gang. Humphrey was looking for members of the Barrow Gang who were fleeing south after robbing a grocery store in Fayetteville. At the time, the Barrow Gang was staying with Bonnie and Clyde and others at the Dennis Motel Tourist Camp on Midland Avenue in Fort Smith.

By 1940, the population of Alma had reached 774. Like many places across the country, World War II offered new adventures and opportunities for the residents of Alma. David Brinkley even discussed Alma in his book *Washington Goes to War*. "In the town of Alma, Arkansas (population 776), one-fourth of the girls in the 1944 high school graduating class signed up to leave for Washington, and several of their teachers cast aside their low-paying jobs and went with them, all of them climbing aboard a Pullman car for their first train ride, looking for more money and excitement than they had any reasonable expectation of finding in Alma."

In 1961, the Alma Canning Company was purchased by H. L. Hunt. Soon, the company canned over half the spinach consumed in the United States (about 60 million pounds annually) and Alma acquired the nickname of "Spinach Capital of the World." A statue of the cartoon charachter Popeye, a water tower painted like a can of spinach, and even the Spinach Festival helped to promote this important business. In 1974, Alma was essentially invaded by Tony Alamo and his followers, who bought up or started twenty-nine businesses in town. Since many of the workers were former street people who volunteered their time, many existing businesses folded. However, after Alamo was arrested on and found guilty of various tax-related charges, the businesses closed and the workers moved away.

Today, Alma has a population of about 6000 people, but it still serves a large rural area with thousands of more residents. The town has four public schools – Alma Primary School, Alma Intermediate School, Alma Middle School and Alma High School – with attendance of almost 4000. Being at the junction of Interstates 40 and 49, the town is full of restaurants, gas stations, hotels, and many other retail businesses. Heading through town, the railroad passes the former spinach canning plant, now closed and used for other purposes. Where the cotton platform once stood is a pavilion used by the local farmers market. The former downtown to the south has now been replaced by several large retail areas near the freeway exit.

The Railroad at Alma

The area around Alma was a busy one for the railroad. One of the major reasons were the steep grades to the west used to climb what was called Alma Hill. At one time the grades exceeded one percent and trains often failed to make the hill, which was more than three miles long. As part of a series of improvement projects in 1902-1904, the Little Rock & Fort Smith/St. Louis, Iron Mountain & Southern spent almost two years cutting down the hill. The work included lowering the hill by digging a better cut, filling several other cuts and raising fills, and widening the roadbed by four feet. One major issue was that the work included the area around Frog Bayou, described as soft ground that prevented some of the work from being accomplished. At least one steam shovel was used on the project and it wasn't until July 1904 that it was moved from Alma Hill to other work at Ozark. Even with the work, Alma Hill was still a noted grade on the railroad. In 1933, a survey of the route measured the elevation of the top of the rail. These were as follows.

Milepost 490	426.6 feet
Milepost 491	442.6 feet
Milepost 493	490.8 feet
Milepost 494	464.2 feet
Milepost 495	436.0 feet
Milepost 496	416.9 feet

At Alma, the railroad had a wooden depot. Apparently, the station was replaced several times. For example, in 1893, it was announced that a "depot is being built in Alma to fill the place of the one recently burned." Other reports state that a frame depot (20' x 52') was built about 1900. In 1907, the Iron Mountain reported that Alma was the home of a day telegraph office, a mail crane, and a 62-car siding. In 1913, maps show that the passenger depot was to the east of Fayetteville Avenue and south of the tracks. Across three tracks to the north was a freight house. A house track looped around the south side of the depot to serve a cotton platform on the west side of Fayetteville Avenue. Immediately south of all of this was Railroad Street. In 1933, a survey showed that the elevation of the "top of rail opposite the Missouri Pacific Railroad station" at Alma was 432.9 feet.

In 1923, the station had a train order office that was open 24 hours a day, plus a ticket and freight agency. In 1925, the depot was extended to 21' x 93'. Stock pens were installed at Alma in 1928 and removed in 1940. A cotton platform (16' x 197') was built in April 1918 and had a 24' x 75' extension added in 1947. However, the freight house (22' x 48') was removed in October 1932. There was also a mail crane and a siding that was 80 cars long. As freight cars got longer, the siding was shown to hold fewer cars – 60 in 1944. The siding was extended to hold 75 cars by 1951. By this time, the station had only limited hours when train orders could be obtained. The siding was shown to be 3810 feet long by the late 1960s, but was gone by the 1980s. A short spur track east of Fayetteville Avenue is now all that is left at Alma.

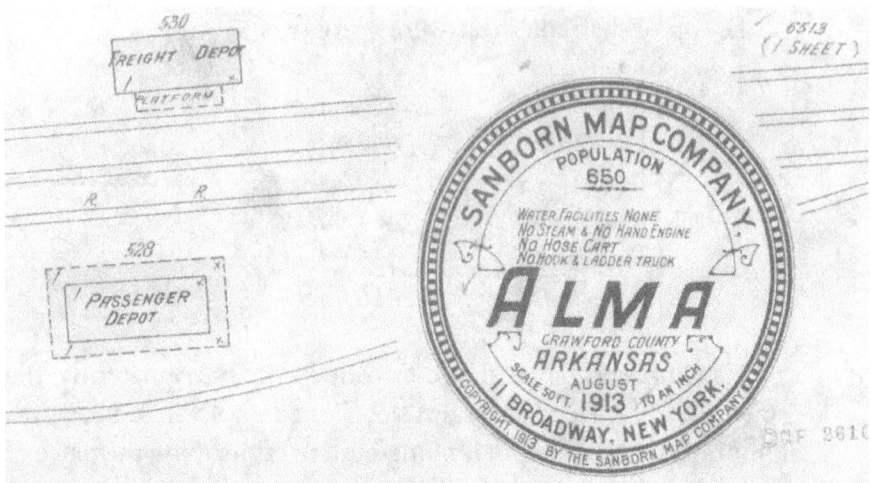

In 1913, the Alma passenger station was east of Fayetteville Avenue and on the south side of the main tracks and sidings. Across the tracks to the north was the railroad's freight house. *Sanborn Fire Insurance Map from Alma, Crawford County, Arkansas.* Sanborn Map Company, Aug, 1913. Map. Retrieved from the Library of Congress, https://www.loc.gov/item/sanborn00187_001/.

Missouri Pacific caboose 13523 is now located in downtown Alma at the intersection of Fayetteville Avenue and Railroad Street. The caboose was built in 1971 by the International Car Corporation and was one of the last Missouri Pacific extended vision cupola cabooses in service. It was retired in 2010 and then donated to Alma, Arkansas. For several years, it was used by the Alma Chamber of Commerce.

490.1 BRIDGE – This bridge consists of 144 feet of six reinforced concrete spans. This unnamed stream has been channelized and drains the west side of Alma. When the Arkansas River is high, water can back up Frog Bayou and into this canal. To the south are a series of large fields, often growing soybeans.

490.5 FROG BAYOU BRIDGE – In this area, Frog Bayou has changed from being a mountain stream to being a wide delta waterway. This is one of several areas where the stream takes on an almost swampy characteristic.

This bridge consists of about 50 feet of concrete pile trestle on each end with 150 feet of deck plate girder spans in the middle. It once was a much longer bridge but parts have been filled in over the years. An early bridge consisted of two 84-foot through plate girder spans installed in 1896. They were replaced with three 50-foot deck plate girder spans during June 1924. During the early 1930s this was listed as Bridge No. 400, and was described as being 20 poles west of Milepost 490.

The channel beneath the bridge is often dry except during the winter and spring, or after a recent rainfall, when Frog Bayou fills up with water from the surrounding mountains.

UP 5749 heads south across the Big Frog Bayou Bridge near Alma, Arkansas.

The south headwall of the Big Frog Bayou Bridge shows both the new concrete and older cut-stone construction.

The Big Frog Bayou Bridge at Milepost 490.6 has been rebuilt over the years, piece-by-piece. The north end of the structure still shows fresh markings from the work, like this piece with the bridge's location written on it.

490.6 BIG FROG BAYOU BRIDGE – To differentiate between the two bridges over Frog Bayou, the railroad added the word Big to the stream's name. This bridge has 24 feet of concrete trestle on the north end and then 225 feet of deck plate girder spans to the south. In June 1924, the railroad replaced two 84-foot through plate girder spans with three 75-foot deck plate girder spans. Heading west towards Van Buren, trains start to face grades up to 0.54% as they leave the bridge. The top of this grade is at Milepost 493.2.

Frog Bayou was a noted location used in the 1808 Osage Treaty. The treaty had the Osage move out of northwest Arkansas and cede approximately 48 million acres to the United States. Frog Bayou originates in the steep rocky highlands of the Boston Mountains. This area is in the Ozark National Forest in the very northern part of Crawford County, located west of the source of the Mulberry River, and south of the source of the White River. The primary headwaters of Frog Bayou are on the north slope of Shepherd Mountain. Frog Bayou flows generally southward, draining fairly rugged terrain before emptying into the Arkansas River. The main branch has been dammed, forming Lake Fort Smith. Just below the dam, the stream joins with the Howards Fork of Frog Bayou, sometimes called Clear Creek during the late 1800s, and then again starting in the mid-1900s.

In 1861, during one of the first attempts to build the railroad, the company had their headquarters in Van Buren. One of the first projects was building a bridge over Frog Bayou in preparation for laying of track. However, the bridge wasn't built and little grading was actually accomplished.

494.0 SHIBLEY – Shibley was once located between Hill Top Road and Shibley Road (County Road 2). This was a small station during the late 1800s and early 1900s. In 1860, Henry Shibley moved from Missouri and bought 120 acres about 4 miles east of Van Buren. His son, William Henry Harrison Shibley, became a leading businessman in the Van Buren area within a few years, where he co-owned Shibley, Wood & Company, a wholesale grocery company. The Shibley & Wood Grocery Company was sold to the Wood Brothers during the 1880s, and it became the Fort Smith Wholesale Grocery Company about 1905. In 1888, William Shibley became president of Van Buren Canning Company and was also invested in many Van Buren businesses. These included the Crawford County Bank (director and stockholder); Van Buren Building and Loan Association (treasurer); Van Buren Land and Improvement Company (treasurer); and the Van Buren Ice and Coal Company (stockholder).

The community that grew around the Shibley farm obtained a post office in 1895, but it closed in 1917. Shibley was the home of a 70-car siding and a mail crane in 1907. Railroad timetables still showed a mail crane at Shibley in 1923, despite the closing of the local post office six years earlier. In 1925, the railroad showed that there was a platform to the west with a 6' x 14' shelter (built 1912), and that a track handled carload freight. By the 1940s, natural gas was found in the area and the local wells were part of what became the Shibley Gas Field. Where the railroad stop was once located is now a scattering of houses and churches about a mile south of U.S. Highway 64.

In 1932-1933, a government survey team checked older benchmarks that had been installed along the railroad during the 1880s. The results were published in several reports, including *Leveling in Arkansas* by the Coast and Geodetic Survey of the U.S. Department of Commerce. The report called the area around Milepost 494 the Box Springs siding. It also stated that the elevation of the "top of rail opposite Missouri Pacific Railroad milepost 494" was 464.2 feet.

This Union Pacific sign marks the grade crossing with Shibley Road, at the former station of Shibley, Arkansas.

494.4 BX SIDING – This was a siding located a few miles east of Van Buren, called Box Springs Siding in some documents. In 1923, it was shown to be 70 cars long. In 1944, the siding was shown to be 56 cars long, with the south switch at Milepost 494.1 and the north switch at Milepost 494.7. There was also a railroad telephone at BX Siding. The siding was removed with the ABS signaling installation in 1945.

BX siding once had two berry facilities on its north side. One was removed in 1923 while a larger 10' x 71' berry shed remained until the tracks were abandoned in late 1947. Fruits and berries, especially strawberries, were big business for the railroad. The company not only hauled the fruit and berries to market, but it also moved crates, baskets and cans to the farms. The Arkansas Bureau of Mines, Manufactures and Agriculture had the following to say in 1901 about the fruits and berries in Crawford County.

> *Peaches of many varieties are grown here. Many crates are shipped to market and many bushels are put up at the canning factories each year. Plums, pears, cherries, etc., grow well here and are being grown more and more each year. Strawberries, raspberries and blackberries are also grown very extensively. There are some of the largest berry farms in the vicinity of Van*

> *Buren that are to be found anywhere in the State. It is estimated that there are more than 3,000 acres in strawberries alone within marketing distance of Van Buren. The berries mature early and grow very fine. They always command a high price on the market.*

Strawberries have been grown commercially in Arkansas since about 1890, and the Van Buren district in Crawford County probably led in production during the early years. Even during the 1920s, Van Buren was one of the four largest strawberry shipping points in Arkansas, with the primary shipping time running from late April through early June. Starting in 1926, Van Buren even held an annual strawberry festival to celebrate the business that the berry brought to town. What made the strawberry business possible was the railroads, which hauled the berries to markets across the Midwest. This business lasted until about World War II when California and Florida took over the market.

495.0 NORTH END VAN BUREN SUBDIVISION – In 2021, this was the dividing line between the Van Buren Subdivision of the North Little Rock Area, to the south, and the Wagoner Subdivision of the Kansas City Area, to the north. With this, the terminal at Van Buren has been assigned to the Kansas City Area management.

495.5 FLAT ROCK CREEK BRIDGE – Look for the 115-foot concrete pile trestle. It crosses Flat Rock Creek, a stream with some history of area flooding. It forms from several streams north of Van Buren and flows southward into Hollis Lake, an old oxbow lake created many years ago when the Arkansas River changed its channel. South of there, Flat Rock Creek has been turned into a drainage ditch to protect area fields. It eventually flows into the Arkansas River downstream of the James W. Trimble Lock & Dam 13.

495.7 INTERSTATE 540 – The railroad passes under Interstate 540, also designated as U.S. Highway 71, on the east side of Van Buren, Arkansas. Construction on this highway began about 1965 and it was completed between Interstate 40 and U.S. Highway 271 near the Oklahoma state line (about 14 miles) during the early 1970s. It was one of the original five Arkansas Interstates and connects Fort Smith and Van Buren with a bridge over the Arkansas River.

Early timetables showed that the south end of Van Buren Yard was somewhere in this area. The yard limits for the Van Buren area still start here.

496.2 ARKANSAS HIGHWAY 162 – The railroad passes under the highway, known locally as Kibler Road. The overhead bridge pretty much marks the entrance to the Van Buren yard and series of tracks for rail shippers. In fact, just compass-north of the bridge were once several large shippers on the railroad.

Arkansas Zinc & Smelting Corporation

The first railroad shipper was a large zinc plant, one of three in the Fort Smith-Van Buren area, and one of the fifty-one zinc smelters in the United States. Zinc and lead were found in a number of places in northern Arkansas along the upper White River, and in large volumes in southwest Missouri. Zinc (Zn) is "a malleable, corrosion-resistant metal." Zinc has a number of manufacturing uses, including "as an alloy to make brass, rolled into sheets for roof cladding, melted for 'hot dip' and other galvanizing, and pulverized for paints." It is also used for batteries. Most of the zinc ores found in Arkansas were forty-eight percent zinc or more, but the energy required led to the smelter burning natural gas from the Arkansas River Valley gas fields.

About 1915, the Arkansas Zinc & Smelting Corporation was formed to build a smelter at Van Buren. The railroad actually reported that the start was due to L. Vogelstein & Company, which had the first tracks built here. To make it easier for workers to reach the smelter, which was located several miles east of downtown Van Buren, the zinc company contracted with the Fort Smith Light & Traction Company to extend their Van Buren streetcar line to the smelter in 1917. The new streetcar line was described as being one mile long and reportedly cost $20,000. Arkansas Zinc was acquired by the American Metal Company in 1920, but the plant kept its name. The ownership of the smelter again changed in 1922 when the Falcon Zinc Company of William Lanyon acquired the property. At the time it was shown to be a 75-ton zinc smelting plant with 3 Ropp furnaces and 3200 retorts used to purify the zinc.

About 1927, the smelter shut down and sat unused, principally because it was worn and out-of-date. In April 1929, the smelter was acquired by the owners of the New Chicago Mining Company, which operated several mines at Joplin, Missouri. The smelter was set up as the Van Buren Zinc Company and improvements were made to reopen the smelter. By the end of World War II, this was the Arkansas Smelting Company, owned by the Eagle-Picher Mining & Smelting Company, at one time the nation's leading zinc manufacturer. Operations were suspended in January 1946 with the end of the World War II military demand, although the plant was still listed as a zinc facility into the early 1950s.

Farmland Feeds

Also just north of the Kibler Road overpass is a large concrete grain elevator. This elevator is generally known as the Farmland elevator due to the faded lettering on its sides. On January 1, 1959, the Consumers Cooperative Association began construction on a soybean crushing plant at Van Buren, with a feed mixing plant nearby. Opened on October 27, 1959, the plant could turn 8700 bushels of soybean a day into oil and meal. The facility later became part of Land O'Lakes Farmland Feeds. Farmland Feeds was an animal feed subsidiary of Land O'Lakes, an American member-owned agricultural cooperative based in Minnesota and founded on July 8, 1921.

In August 1983, Land O'Lakes sold off five soybean processing plants to the Boone Valley Cooperative Processing Association. The Van Buren plant was one of these, and it was closed on March 5, 1987. While Land O'Lakes sold off its soybean processing, it continued to focus on its dairy, butter and cheese products. It also continued with its farm supply businesses. In 2001, the company acquired animal feed producer Purina Mills, once part of Ralston Purina. In 2004, Land O'Lakes Farmland Feed was renamed Land O'Lakes Purina Feed. Today, this facility is abandoned and the property is up for sale.

The abandoned Farmland Feeds elevator and bean plant still stands alongside the railroad on the east side of Van Buren.

496.3 CONTROL POINT V496 – Located just east of 28th Street (Milepost 496.4) in Van Buren is this switch that provides a lead into the Van Buren Yard. On the north side of the mainline is a switch for the industrial lead into the former Farmland facility.

For years, Missouri Pacific showed that the south switch into the Van Buren Yard was at Milepost 496 Pole 12, or about this same location. In 2021, the railroad stated that it had a 10,165-foot siding from here to CP 498.

Hudson Excavation, a dirt contracting firm, is located next to the tracks at Control Point V496. The company has a display of old excavating equipment alongside the tracks.

497.2 VAN BUREN – This was the location cited in Missouri Pacific and Union Pacific employee timetables from the 1960s through the 1990s. Van Buren is essentially the north end (geographically west) of the Little Rock & Fort Smith, although it did cross the Arkansas River to Fort Smith at two different locations, using ferry boats. These two routes were replaced with trackage rights on the Frisco's bridge, and later a connection directly to Fort Smith at Greenwood Junction, Oklahoma. However, the track in Oklahoma was actually built and owned by the Kansas & Arkansas Valley Railway. A bit of the track was originally graded and built by the Little Rock & Fort Smith, but since it was on Cherokee lands and was not approved, the track was removed. The Kansas & Arkansas Valley later relaid the track as part of its route from Van Buren to Coffeyville, Kansas.

    The facilities at Van Buren changed frequently, and the mileposts used for the various locations at Van Buren also changed frequently. The locations used from the 1920s through the 1950s will be the primary mileposts cited for the Van Buren Yard and the Van Buren station. The following mileposts have been used for these facilities over the years.

497.2 – Van Buren (1969, 1983, 1986, 1994)
497.3 – Van Buren Yard (1923, 1944, 1951)
498.0 – Van Buren (1944, 1951)
498.4 – St.L.-S.F. Crossing / A&M Crossing (1944, 1951, 2003, 2011)
498.5 – Van Buren (2003)

497.3 VAN BUREN YARD – Probably the first report about the Van Buren locomotive shops was in the January 25, 1879, issue of the *Van Buren Press*. It stated that "The turn-table is completed and whirled the engine this morning." At the time, the railroad had a rail yard down the middle of Columbus Street, what would have been Second Street today. A small frame engine house stood at Van Buren, replaced in 1890 by a new frame round house, with a new water station. In 1892, the railroad installed new water tanks and stand pipes at Van Buren. A new sand house was installed in 1893. In 1894, new stock pens were erected here. As the railroad was improved, more and more facilities were built south of the roundhouse. In 1895, the railroad announced that it had built a coal hoist at Van Buren at an expenditure of $2,555.56. This was the first of many coal facilities built at Van Buren. At the time, the Little Rock & Fort Smith Railway had their roundhouse, machine shop, and turntable immediately south of Jefferson Street and between the mainline and the Arkansas River. This area is now used by the river levee and a parking lot for trucks serving the nearby Simmons food processing plant.

As downtown Van Buren grew, the railroad needed larger repair shops and a rail yard. At 7am on July 19, 1901, the St. Louis, Iron Mountain & Southern broke ground on a new yard complex in the "eastern suburbs" of Van Buren. It was announced that the new Van Buren yard would be capable of holding 4000 railroad freight cars. On September 28, 1901, the yard opened and was claimed to hold 900 freight cars, what was considered to be the largest single yard in the Southwest. An additional mile of track was added to the Van Buren yard in 1903, but by late 1905, reports stated that the yard was suffering badly from congestion. At the time two switch engines were being used to work the trains passing through the yard and stories from the time state that trains were arriving faster than they could depart. Reportedly, local businesses were complaining that it was taking two, three, and even ten days to have cars spotted.

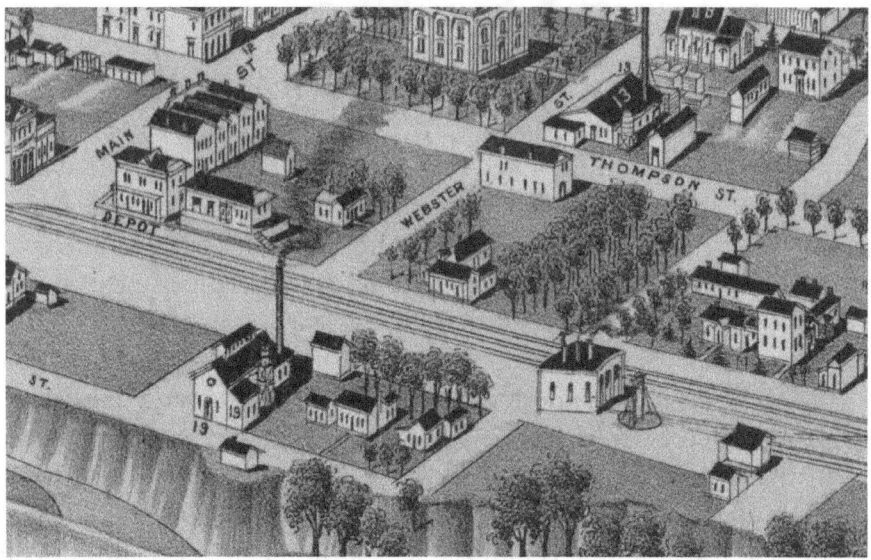

In 1888, Henry Wellge & Co. of Milwaukee published a "Perspective Map of Van Buren, Ark. County Seat of Crawford County." It showed several details about the LR&FS, including this scene showing the shops and turntable in the lower right, and the depot in the upper left. *Perspective map of Van Buren, Ark. county seat of Crawford County.* [Milwaukee, Henry Wellge & Co, 1888] Map. Retrieved from the Library of Congress, https://www.loc.gov/item/75693085/.

In 1902, the railroad announced plans to build a big roundhouse at the new yards in Van Buren. The 20-stall roundhouse was completed during 1904. Ten of the roundhouse stalls were 85 feet 5 inches deep while ten were 79 feet 5 inches. The new shops also included a 320-foot-long car repair shed, store room, and a power house. There was also a 150,000-gallon steel water tank that was supplied by the Van Buren city water system. The water tower fed two water columns that were used to water the railroad's steam locomotives. To provide coal, a new coaling tower was completed in January 1904. Newspaper reports stated that the new wooden coaling tower was capable of pulling 50-ton coal cars up a 400-foot incline with a steel cable. The coal was then dumped into a bin. The empty cars were then lowered back down the incline. The hoisting mechanism consisted of a 32-horsepower gasoline motor driving the hoisting drum. One man operated the tower, which held eight bins with a total capacity of 500 tons for fueling locomotives. The coaling tower burned in early 1910 and plans for a larger and more efficient coaling tower were announced. Meanwhile, the coal was loaded into the tenders of the steam locomotives using a steam shovel.

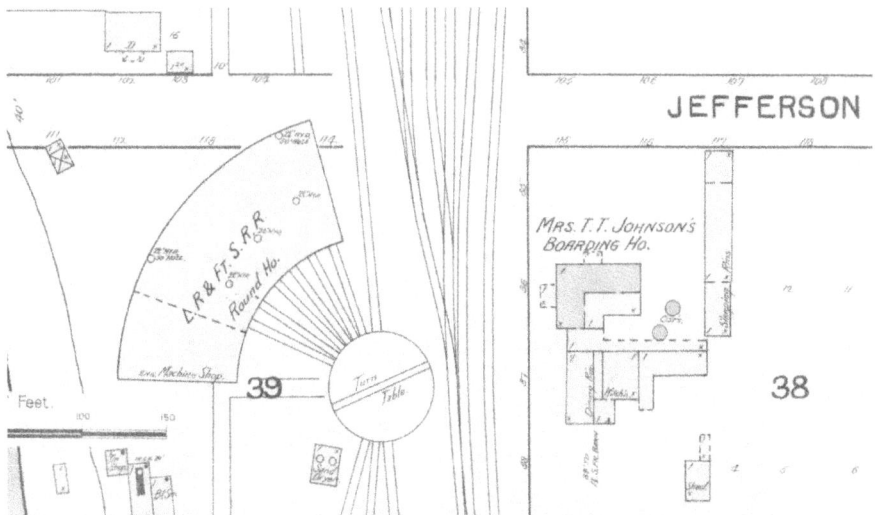

In 1892, the Little Rock & Fort Smith Railway had their Van Buren roundhouse, machine shop, and turntable immediately south of Jefferson Street and between the mainline and the Arkansas River. *Sanborn Fire Insurance Map from Van Buren, Crawford County, Arkansas.* Sanborn Map Company, August 1892. Map. Retrieved from the Library of Congress, https://www.loc.gov/item/sanborn00358_002/.

The future of the Van Buren locomotive and car shops became uncertain in 1908 when many of the shop workers went on strike. The railroad tried to operate with non-union workers, but with the community's support, the strikers were able to hang on and the new workers were made to feel very un-welcomed. As the strike went on, the St. Louis, Iron Mountain &

Southern made announcements about closing the shops and moving them to Fort Smith. During June 1908, there were several violent confrontations between the strikers and strike breakers, and in July, the railroad announced that the car repair shops would be moved across the Arkansas River to Fort Smith. The new location for the shops was reportedly next to the Fort Smith freight house. Additional strikes in 1910 also led to threats to move the shops to Fort Smith, but they remained here until the end of steam.

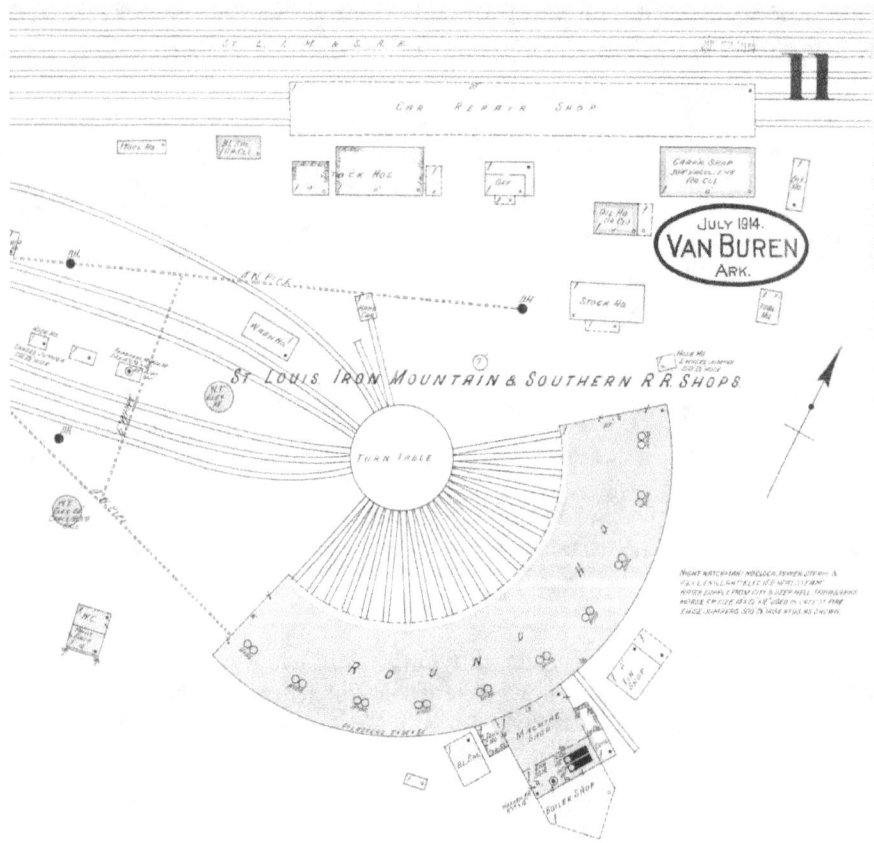

In 1904, the St. Louis, Iron Mountain & Southern built a new and enlarged shop complex further south in Van Buren. This included a larger roundhouse, and the foundations can still be found in the middle of the current wye. *Sanborn Fire Insurance Map from Van Buren, Crawford County, Arkansas.* Sanborn Map Company, July 1914. Map. Retrieved from the Library of Congress, https://www.loc.gov/item/sanborn00358_006/.

Signs like this are found at the various entrances to the current Union Pacific Van Buren rail yard.

During the 1920s, the Van Buren Yard had a continuous train order office to handle train crew changes. There was also a track scale (50 feet long with a capacity of 150,000 pounds), water station, coal station, and a turntable. The water station was greatly improved in 1922 by Joseph E. Nelson & Sons of Chicago, Illinois. The firm received a contract to erect a pumping station and water treating plant at Van Buren, as well as four other Missouri Pacific terminals.

These facilities stayed in place through the end of steam locomotives. The first diesel locomotives made their appearance on Missouri Pacific in 1937. By 1951, the Van Buren yard featured fuel oil and diesel fuel, and the railroad was fully converted to diesel locomotives in 1955. Today, the yard is basically used for switching and all of the shops are gone. There are 11 yard tracks, a base radio, and wye, all protected by yard limits. The railroad has an office on the north side of the yard that houses local management and is used for crew changes. Across the yard to the south is a wye, with the old roundhouse foundation in the center.

Over the years, several crossover tracks were installed at Van Buren Yard. Special instructions were printed in employee timetables about these tracks.

Crossover located at MP 497, Pole 17, leading from main track to track No. 1 (facing point for northward trains), is designated "CROSSOVER No. 1, VAN BUREN".

Crossover located at MP 497, Pole 22, leading from main track to track No. 1 (facing point for southward trains), is designated "CROSSOVER No. 2, VAN BUREN".

The 4th Street Overpass, located at Milepost 497.7, marks the north end of Van Buren Yard.

Camp Jesse Turner

During World War II, Van Buren and the Missouri Pacific shops and yard were the home of Camp Jesse Turner, a military railroad training facility. In 1941, Van Buren applied to host a railroad training facility. By 1942, a small camp was established on Pickett Hill, a small knoll on the east side of Van Buren, just north of the south end of the current Van Buren yard. Thirty-five acres were bought on July 15, 1942, for the camp. On July 18th, materials for the camp arrived and 34 buildings were quickly constructed. The camp officially opened on December 4, 1942.

The camp was at first known as Camp Walter Johnson, but was changed to Camp Jesse Turner during September 1943. The purpose of the camp was to train soldiers on how to repair and operate railroads, especially those in foreign countries. Most of the training for the four Railroad Operating Battalions (ROBs) – the 733rd, 734th, 748th, and 759th – happened in the local Missouri Pacific Railroad yards and roundhouse. Each battalion featured four companies with different expertise. Company "A" consisted of those troops and officers in charge of building and maintaining the railroad tracks and bridges. Company "B" consisted of the machinists and mechanical workers who maintained the equipment. Company "C" consisted of the train crews – engineers, firemen, conductors, and switchmen. The "H&S" Company included officers, clerks, medical personnel, and telegraph operators who were the headquarters and services soldiers. These units were sent to locations like North Africa, Sicily, Italy, France, and the China-Burma-India theater,

During the 1943 floods, the troops assisted with repairing roads, railroads, levees, and even houses. Some of the local residents who had to flee their homes wound up staying at Camp Jesse Turner. More troops arrived from other units to help reclaim farmland and crops. By late 1944, the four battalions had all received their training and left for their assignments, and Camp Jesse Turner was closed. In 1949, the land was used for the new Crawford County Hospital and a low-income housing project.

498.0 VAN BUREN (D) – The Van Buren depot was always located somewhere between the Frisco Crossing and Broad Street, later Broadway Street. Over the years, Van Buren has had a number of depots to serve the trains on the Little Rock & Fort Smith route. A depot opened when the railroad was completed to Van Buren on July 11, 1876, with the first train from Argenta arriving on July 24, 1876, carrying officials and dignitaries. It was soon reported that the Little Rock & Fort Smith Railway was rip rapping the river front in order to save the depot grounds. They were planning to line about fifteen hundred feet of the riverbank using rock "taken from the cuts in the Ozark mountains." At the time, it was announced that the distance from Van Buren to Little Rock, by railroad, was 159 miles, and it was 9 miles from Van Buren, by railroad, to the depot opposite Fort Smith.

Within a year, regular train service between Van Buren and Little Rock had been established. A Little Rock & Fort Smith Railway passenger timetable was published in the March 5, 1878, issue of *The Van Buren Press* which demonstrated this early service. "Trains leave Van Buren for Little Rock, daily, Sundays excepted, at 7:37a.m. Trains arrive at Van Buren, from Little Rock, at 6:12pm, daily, except Sundays. Trains run by St. Louis time, which is 20 minutes faster than Van Buren time."

The railroad started adding offices at Van Buren within a few years. In early July 1889, "The train dispatcher for the Little Rock & Fort Smith and the Kansas, Arkansas and Valley Roads [sic] has been removed from the [Little Rock] Union Depot and established at Van Buren, a more central location for those roads."

In 1891, a brick "Union" depot that served both the Little Rock & Fort Smith and Frisco railroads was built on South Second Street between Main and Webster. This station had both a passenger and a freight section and was located on the north side of eight LR&FS tracks. Within a few years, the Frisco built their own station at 813 Main Street. By the late 1890s, Missouri Pacific/Iron Mountain had an office with an oil and tool room located on the north side of Main Street, east of the tracks. There was a second railroad office further to the north by 1909. The older building was shown simply as offices by 1914, and was gone by the 1920s. The area is a gravel parking lot today.

At 213 Main Street is a nice one-story brick building, with its cast iron columns still visible. In 1897, this was shown to be a "Railroad Eating House," a common business where train crews were changed. For the Little Rock & Fort Smith, crews changed at Van Buren, so a restaurant catering to the crews was often found near the station or yards. In addition, many passenger trains did not have dining cars, so longer stops were scheduled for certain stations to allow passengers to grab a meal. These stops were generally for about twenty minutes, allowing the railroad to change crews and steam locomotives. In many cases, the "Railroad Eating House" was owned by the railroad or a contractor. The restaurant was gone by the 1910s, and the building was the Dobyn's Brothers Laundry. It was shown as a garage by 1922, and today is a store.

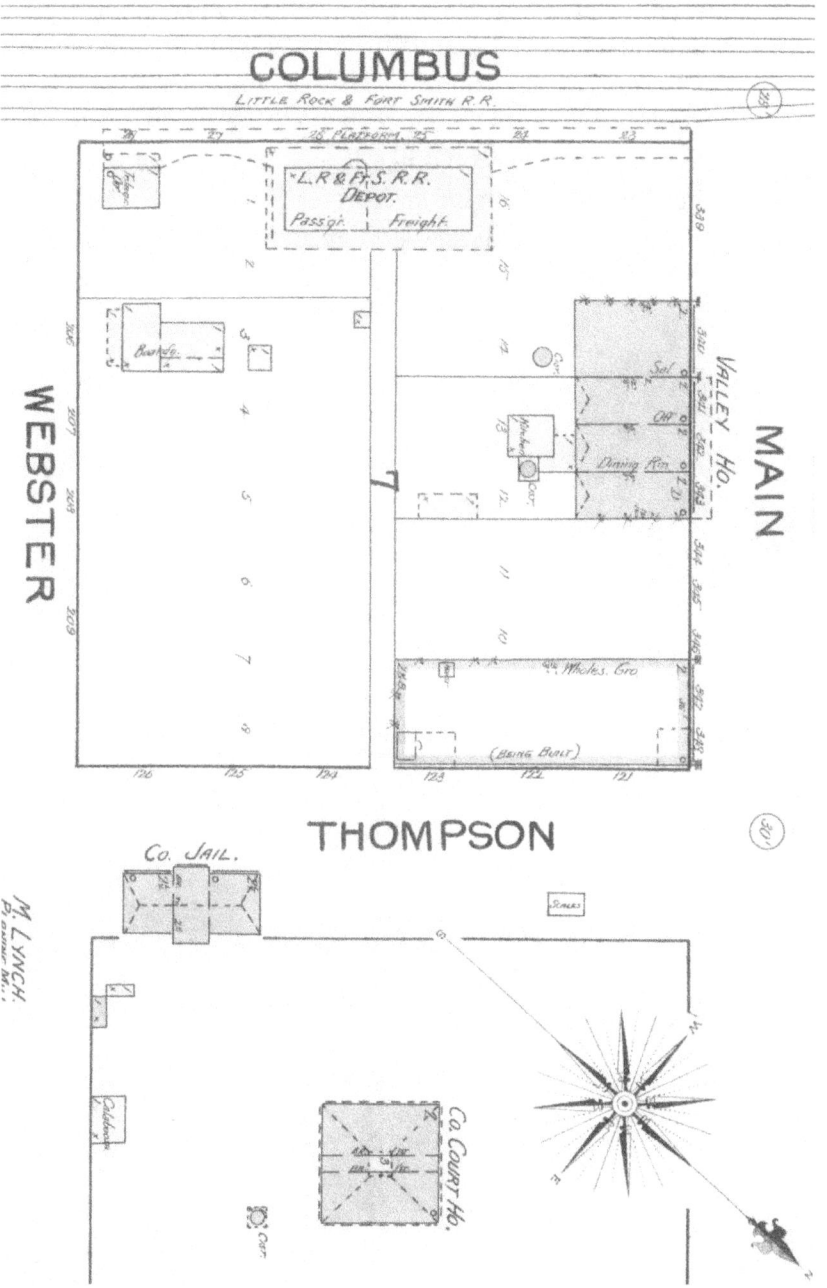

During the late 1800s, the Little Rock & Fort Smith Railway had their Van Buren depot a block southwest of the Crawford County courthouse. *Sanborn Fire Insurance Map from Van Buren, Crawford County, Arkansas.* Sanborn Map Company, August 1892. Map. Retrieved from the Library of Congress, https://www.loc.gov/item/sanborn00358_002/.

By 1904, the Missouri Pacific Hotel stood on the south side of Main Street, to the east of the tracks. This building featured a lunchroom, dining room, and hotel rooms. By 1914, the railroad hotel was stores and storage. To the south of the depot there was also a telegraph office. The St. Louis, Iron Mountain & Southern listed a large number of facilities that were located at Van Buren in 1907. There was a day and night telegraph office, a standard clock in the dispatcher office, and a train register.

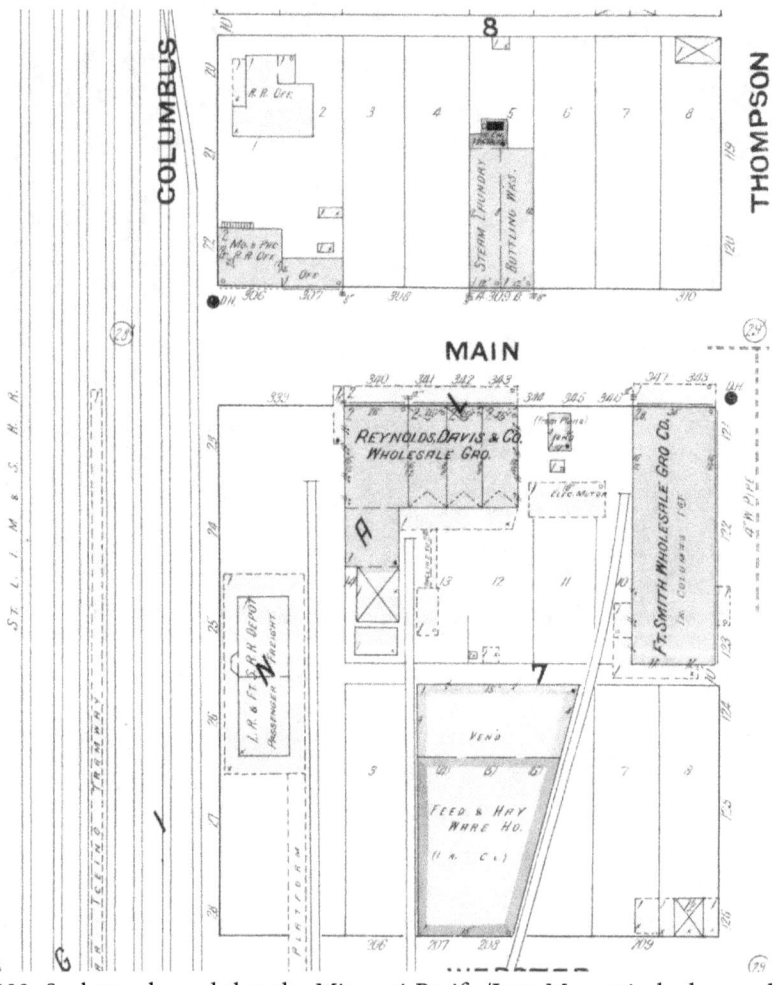

In 1909, Sanborn showed that the Missouri Pacific/Iron Mountain had several office buildings to the north of Main Street and east of the mainline. *Sanborn Fire Insurance Map from Van Buren, Crawford County, Arkansas.* Sanborn Map Company, March 1909. Map. Retrieved from the Library of Congress, https://www.loc.gov/item/sanborn00358_005/.

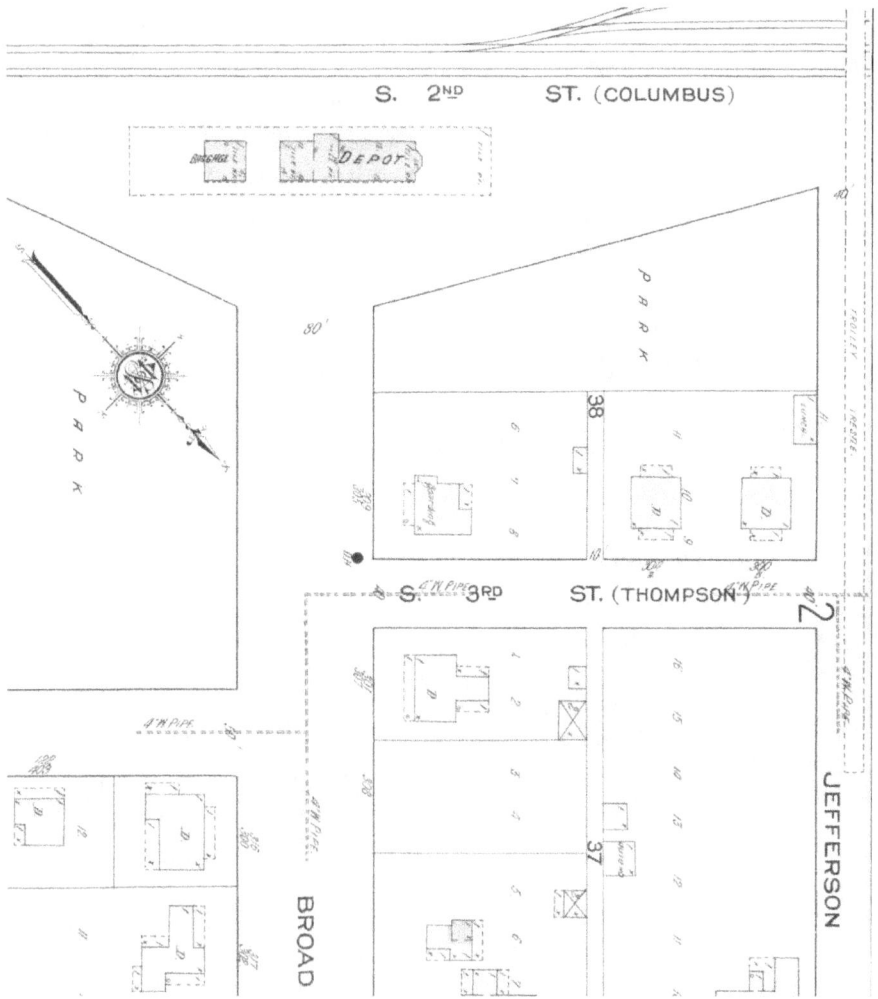

In 1912, Missouri Pacific built a new depot at Van Buren and moved it several blocks to the south at Broad Street, now Broadway. This station was removed when the new Broadway Bridge over the Arkansas River was built in 1969. *Sanborn Fire Insurance Map from Van Buren, Crawford County, Arkansas.* Sanborn Map Company, July 1914. Map. Retrieved from the Library of Congress, https://www.loc.gov/item/sanborn00358_006/.

During February 1910, the St. Louis, Iron Mountain & Southern announced plans for a new station at Van Buren. The depot was to be a pressed brick, two-story building. The first floor would be for passengers with the upper level for the railroad's division officials. Cost of the building was estimated at $29,000. However, the two-story building was built in Fort Smith and

Van Buren received a one-story brick passenger station (24' x 198') with a portico on each end. The new station was built on the east side of the tracks at the end of Broad Street, now Broadway. The old station was moved a short distance and turned into the freight house. In 1925, the depot housed a ticket agency and also served as a coupon ticket station. Located 0.1 miles to the north was the freight agency (carloads and less), also located to the east of the tracks. There was also a Van Buren Dispatcher Office, using the telegraph calls of "DS" and "BN,"

The last Little Rock-Kansas City passenger train served the Van Buren depot on Monday, March 28, 1960. The station continued to be used as a train order and crew change base, but it was torn down by 1969 when the Broadway Bridge was built across the tracks and the Arkansas River. Nothing remains of the station today.

This sand plant of Arkhola Sand & Gravel stands on the river side of the Union Pacific tracks at Van Buren. Northbound trains are often held here for new crews. A unique part of this sand plant is that it is actually worked by the Arkansas & Missouri Railroad. In 2000, the Arkansas & Missouri Railroad began to lease and operate 3.2 miles of rail line from Union Pacific Railroad Company at several locations near UP's Van Buren yard.

Broadway Bridge (U.S. Business Highway 71) crosses the railroad tracks and the Arkansas River at Milepost 498.1. The construction of this bridge required the removal of the brick Missouri Pacific station, which had been built in 1910.

The Jefferson Street Bridge (Missouri Pacific Viaduct) crosses the tracks at Milepost 498.2. This viaduct once connected with the Ft. Smith-Van Buren Free Bridge across the Arkansas River, opened on April 1, 1912. These bridges were used by streetcars, private vehicles, and pedestrians, and was shown as the Trolley Trestle on some maps. This contractor plate from 1936 shows that the structure was rebuilt, and it was then raised in 1943 in response to flooding and the construction of a new levee system along the river. It was replaced by the Broadway Bridge in 1969 as a part of the McClellan-Kerr Arkansas River Navigation System and is now used as an access road to the Van Buren Marina.

Union Pacific often refuels locomotives just south of the Main Street grade crossing at Van Buren.

Centralized Traffic Control – Van Buren to Fort Smith

In 1942, 10.9 miles of single-track centralized traffic control (CTC) signaling was installed on the Van Buren-Greenwood Junction-Fort Smith route, all manufactured by the General Railway Signal Company. The January 1943 issue of *Railway Signaling*, and the June 12, 1943, issue of *Railway Age*, reported on the installation project. The articles stated that because of the number of passenger trains and freight traffic due to "new industries and other activities as a part of the war program... as many as 45 or more moves are being made through this territory daily. If C.T.C. had not been installed, important traffic might be seriously delayed in this area." To explain the work, a diagram of the tracks involved is included in the articles.

Before the installation of the signals, the track from Van Buren to Greenwood Junction (6 miles west of Van Buren) and then south to Fort Smith (about 4 miles) was authorized by timetable and train orders. At the time, all passenger trains operated into and out of Fort Smith via Greenwood Junction, and the need to operate switches by hand and for extra trains to deal with the busy timetable often resulted in long delays. Through freight trains and freight transfer movements were often held at either Van Buren or Greenwood Junction due to this arrangement. As stated by Missouri Pacific, in order to correct these conditions, automatic block signaling and centralized traffic control were installed.

At Van Buren, there was an automatic interlocking crossing with the single-track main line of the St. Louis-San Francisco (Frisco). The interlocking was retained, with the CTC control of Missouri Pacific signals superimposed on the automatic interlocking circuits. At Greenwood Junction, the power switch machines and CTC signals were installed at the three junction switches so that train movements could be authorized on the various routes and without trains stopping to properly line the switches.

An interesting part of the CTC installation was that the CTC control machine was installed in the operators office at Greenwood Junction. The operator actually worked under the direction of the train dispatcher at Coffeyville, Kansas. The machine included "8 levers for the control of 20 signals, 4 levers for the control of 4 power switch machines, and 2 levers for selections required in connection with signal controls over the hand-throw switch and the spring switch at Ft. Smith." The hand-throw switch and the spring switch at Fort Smith were both used by passenger trains to back into the passenger station, located north of the wye at Fort Smith.

498.3 MAIN STREET – Main Street (Milepost 498.260) was first paved in 1908, but it wasn't until 1912 that the Van Buren-Fort Smith Free Bridge was constructed over the Arkansas River. This bridge was several blocks south on Jefferson Street (Milepost 498.155). When built, the bridge hosted private vehicles, pedestrians, and even streetcars. Starting in 1969, a new bridge was built on Broadway (Milepost 498.100), and the old bridge was removed. However, the bridge across the railroad tracks remains. The new Broadway Bridge required that the old Missouri Pacific train station be removed.

For years, the Main Street area was the center of activity on the railroad. While there are only three railroad tracks here today, there were eight in 1897, and nine by 1914. Many of these were used to serve the railroad's freight house, and local warehouses. When the railroad arrived here in 1876, it built down Columbus Street, now known as Second Street. This was one block south of the Crawford County courthouse. By 1892, this was a busy area. One block to the north is Washington Street, where the Van Buren Foundry & Machine Company had their plant west of the tracks and north of Washington. To the east was Van Buren Canning, also west of the tracks.

On the north side of Main Street just west of the tracks was once the W. Q. Haynes plaster factory, which burned during the late 1890s. The lot remained vacant for decades after the plaster factory was removed. On the south side of Main Street was the Home Steam Laundry, located on the corner of Main and Water (today's First) streets. Immediately south of Main Street on the east side of the tracks was the LR&FS station. The Miller & Jones saw and planing mill was located between the tracks and the Arkansas River one-quarter mile south of the courthouse.

By the late 1890s, the railroad had added a number of facilities of their own around Main Street. On the north side of Main Street across from the depot was a Missouri Pacific office with an oil and tool room. A telegraph office was south of the depot. There was a dining hall, boarding and sleeping rooms to the east of the tracks and south of Jefferson Street. At Jefferson Street, there was a spur track that headed to the northeast to serve a salt shed and the Shibley & Wood Grocery Company. Parts of this track still remain.

By 1904, the Missouri Pacific Hotel was located on the south side of Main Street and to the east of the tracks, west of Shibley & Wood. The Missouri Pacific Hotel had both a lunch and a dining room. The Miller & Jones facility was now operated by the Walton & Knox Company, which made fruit and vegetable packaging. The fruit and vegetable industry caused the railroad to build a large icing platform between the tracks between Main and Jefferson, with the Van Buren Ice & Coal Company to the west of the tracks and south of Webster Street. The 1908 *Missouri Pacific Annual Report* stated that fruit shipments were growing heavier each year on the Van Buren District and that the facilities were found to be inadequate for proper handling of the fruit movements. A platform measuring 10 x 460 feet was constructed, with the ice elevated by means of link belt and electric motor.

The Engineering Works, manufacturers of mining equipment, was located near the Walton & Knox Company in 1909. The Fort Smith Compress Company and the Van Buren Ginning Company (cotton gin) were located between Moore and Mary south of the courthouse. Finally, a new Railroad YMCA was built on Helen Gould Avenue, a block south of Ozier Street.

The Railroad YMCA was one of a number of similar projects developed by Helen Gould. Helen Gould was Jay Gould's eldest daughter, and she was involved with making the lives of railroaders more comfortable. Described as "plain, plump, and not interested in society," she became one of the foremost philanthropists and best-loved women of her time. She studied law, championed women's economic equality, helped to finance the Spanish-American War, and became one of the richest and most powerful people in the country. There were few causes that Helen didn't help fund, including libraries, children's homes, colleges, soldier relief, and disaster relief.

In 1914, the railroad office on Main Street was closed and the railroad hotel was used for stores and storage. A new depot had been built and was located on the east side of the tracks at Broad Street. The ice company was owned by the Border City Ice & Coal Company. The cotton gin complex was the Fort Smith Compress Company and The Planters Cotton Gin Company. By the 1920s, The Planters Cotton Gin Company had become the Choctaw Cotton Gin Company. The railroad also served the Van Buren Glass Company which was located east of Virginia & Theodore.

This area today consists of the tracks of Union Pacific's line between Little Rock and Kansas City, as well as the large Simmons poultry processing plant. Simmons Prepared Foods is headquartered in Siloam Springs, Arkansas, but it has plants as far away as Toronto, Canada. The company is a supplier of premium chicken products for the foodservice industry. The firm is also a private-label and contract manufacturer of wet and dry pet food and treats.

The History of Van Buren, Arkansas

The City of Van Buren, one of the oldest cities in Arkansas, traces its history back to 1818 when David Boyd and Thomas Martin settled in the area. Within a year or two, Revolutionary War veteran James Phillips and his two sons, Thomas Phillips and Daniel David Phillips, claimed land here and opened a wood yard to serve the steamboat service on the Arkansas River. The site took the name Phillips Landing and became a shipment point for much of western and northwestern Arkansas, and eastern Oklahoma (Indian Territory). It also became a departure point for traders, explorers, and settlers heading west to places like Santa Fe and California. Van Buren also became the home of whiskey smugglers who hauled their product into Indian Territory.

The Phillips family opened several stores and warehouses at Phillips Landing. The community grew enough that it received a post office in 1831. The post office used the name Van Buren, named for Martin Van Buren, then secretary of state and later the eighth president of the United States (1837-1841). Van Buren was born in 1782 in Kinderhook, New York, the home of many Dutch settlers. This made Martin Van Buren the first president to have been born after the American Revolution, and the only president to have spoken English as a second language. He was a trained attorney and held a seat in the New York State Senate, and then was elected to the United States Senate in 1821. He then served as the ninth governor of New York, the tenth United States secretary of state, and the eighth vice president of the United States before becoming president. He is credited as being a founder of the Democratic Party, the creator of a New York political machine known as the Albany Regency, and a leader of the anti-slavery Free Soil Party. Van Buren passed away in 1862.

Located on the Arkansas River, John Drennen and his brother-in-law David A. Thompson, both from Tennessee, established a ferry service near Van Buren. In 1836, they bought the Phillips site for $11,000, had it surveyed and platted, and officially created the town which became the county seat of Crawford County in 1838. To help with the selection, John Drennen donated the land where the courthouse was built. A notice was published seeking bids for construction of the courthouse on September 8, 1841, Today, the Crawford County courthouse is the oldest functioning courthouse west of the Mississippi River.

This photo from a postcard that dates to about 1900 shows the Crawford County Courthouse at Van Buren, located a block from the tracks of the Little Rock & Fort Smith. Today, the courthouse is surrounded by big trees, but still functions as the head of the county's government.

The Drennen-Scott House, the home of John Drennen, also still stands and is now known as the Drennen-Scott Historic Site and is operated and maintained by the University of Arkansas at Fort Smith. A few blocks away is Fairview Cemetery, established when Drennen donated 10 acres of land to create a public cemetery. Many of those who helped to create the Little Rock & Fort Smith Railroad were buried here.

An effort was made to incorporate the town in 1842 (some sources state that the town was first incorporated on December 24, 1842), but the official date is January 4, 1845. As the town grew, it built a large wood and rock wharf on the river with retired Captain Phillip Pennywitt managing the operation. Pennywitt was a major supporter of the community and operated a riverfront storage warehouse, a busy flourmill, and a popular mineral bathhouse. He was also involved with helping to build the Little Rock & Fort Smith Railway between Little Rock and Van Buren. Van Buren was a major starting point for prospectors of the 1849 California Gold Rush. It was also the site of the first federal district court (created in March 1851), and became a supply point for nearby Indian Territory. In the 1850 census, the population of Van Buren was 549, and then 979 in the 1860 census as the town also developed manufacturing in addition to its mercantile trade.

The home of John Drennen still stands at Van Buren, and is now known as the Drennen-Scott Historic Site. Historic American Buildings Survey, Creator, photograph by Jones, Lester. *Colonel John Drennen House, Van Buren, Crawford County, AR.* Documentation Compiled After. Photograph. Retrieved from the Library of Congress, <www.loc.gov/item/ar0008/>.

In 1853, a company was organized to build a railroad to Fort Smith with John Drennen as the company's first president, and Phillip Pennywitt as its treasurer. The year 1860 was also important as the first construction on the Little Rock & Fort Smith Railroad began in January, but with little success as the funds ran out with just a few miles of clearing and grading completed. The Civil War impacted Van Buren as the river was closed, supplies ran out, guerilla forces roamed the surrounding country, and numerous engagements were fought here. It took several years for the town to recover after the war, with the population basically unchanged in the census of 1870 and 1880. However, the first train arrived in Van Buren from Little Rock on July 24, 1876. The Frisco Railroad arrived from the north a few years later. These railroads allowed Van Buren to grow and made it a thriving shipping hub for farm products. The population more than doubled as it reached 2291 residents in the 1890 census. Strawberries became big business about this time, and both railroads shipped out hundreds of carloads each year.

In 1920, the population of Van Buren was 5224 as it and Fort Smith fought to dominate the Western Arkansas market, a battle that Van Buren soon lost. However, Van Buren was still a thriving community with four bakeries, two bottling works, a newspaper, a photography studio, and water and electric service. The town and railroads also benefitted from a number of manufacturers, including the Nelson Canning Company, Minton Milling Company, Van Buren Flouring Mill Company, and the Fort Smith Compress Company. The timber industry had a number of facilities – L. W. McMaster and Whillock & Perkins (lumber mills) – as did the foundry and casting industry – Ft. Smith Iron & Steel Company, Ketcham Iron Company (manufacturers of steam engines, boilers, saw mills, shafting, pulleys, house castings and mill supplies), James Morrell, Van Buren Foundry Company, and Van Buren Engineering Works. The agriculture business supported the Border City Ice & Cold Storage Company and the Van Buren Ice & Cold Storage Company. Missouri Pacific also had an icing station for their rail cars. Finally, there was the Arkansas Zinc Smelting Corporation, one of three such smelting plants in Arkansas (the other two were in Fort Smith).

During the 1930s, Van Buren and Crawford County received a great deal of attention thanks to Robin "Bob" Burns. Bob Burns was a musical comedian who appeared on radio and in movies from 1930 to 1947. He was born in nearby Greenwood, Arkansas, in 1890, and his family moved to Van Buren when Bob was three. He quickly began to play a number of musical instruments, forming several bands. During this time he created an instrument from pieces of pipe at Hayman's Plumbing Shop, an instrument that he called a "bazooka." The term came from the word "bazoo" which means a windy fellow (from the Dutch bazuin for "trumpet"). During World War I, Burns was in a Marine Corps jazz band at a recruiting station and started to develop a national reputation. He developed several characters for his shows and went to Los Angeles in 1930 to audition for a radio show. He had prepared a 10 minute audition, but was then asked to expand it to 30 minutes. He improvised various stories and tunes and received the job based upon his improvisation. He was promoted from show to show, eventually appearing with Bing Crosby and hosting the 10th Academy Awards held on March 10, 1938. He appeared in about 25 movies, had his own radio show, and ended his performing career on January 30, 1955, appearing on *Toast of the Town*, later known as *The Ed Sullivan Show*. Bob Burns died from kidney cancer on February 2, 1956. A display about his life can be found in the Frisco depot at Van Buren, a collection known as the Bob Burns Museum.

World War II had little direct impact on Van Buren, although Fort Smith benefitted greatly from Camp Chaffee, created in September 1941. Chaffee was used as an army training camp, a prisoner of war camp, and a refugee camp. The property is currently a 66,000-acre Arkansas National Guard training facility, also used as the Razorback Range by the Arkansas Air National Guard for target practice. Van Buren did host the much smaller Camp Jesse Turner, a training facility for military railroaders.

Manufacturing grew after the war, especially for products related to agriculture like canning and poultry production. The city saw a population boom between 1970 (8373 residents) and 1980 (12,020 residents), and the community worked to restore its old downtown area. The Van Buren Historic District along Main Street had almost been abandoned as most businesses had moved north to Interstate 40, and east to Interstate 540. It is now a major tourist attraction, especially with excursion trains operated by the Arkansas & Missouri Railroad.

The city had a reported population of 23,218 in the 2020 census and it is the home of the Van Buren School District and its 6000+ students. Hotels, restaurants, banks, retail stores, and just about any type of business that you are looking for are located at Van Buren. It is the largest city in Crawford County, and in many ways is an active part of the Fort Smith Metropolitan Statistical Area.

On October 5, 1990, a Loram railgrinder was exiting the north siding switch at Van Buren.

Union Pacific 3759 pulls a northbound empty coal train across the Frisco diamond in 1990. This photo was taken before the new connecting track was built on the river side of the crossing.

498.4 CONTROL POINT V498 – Located between Main Street and the former Frisco diamond is the north end of the 10,290-foot-long Van Buren siding. Historically known as North Switch Van Buren, it has been shown to be at Milepost 498 Pole 18.

498.4 ST.L.-S.F. CROSSING – Missouri Pacific (MP) once crossed the Frisco at this location using a diamond of the unusual angle of 32 degrees, 33 minutes. Today, it is Union Pacific (UP) crossing the Arkansas & Missouri Railroad (A&M). The track arrangements here have changed over the years. When the LR&FS started using the Frisco bridge, a loop track was built to the east of the mainline that connected with the Frisco mainline near the diamond. This was shown to be the connection to the Paris Branch for many years. This ended in 1933 when Missouri Pacific moved all traffic to its own Helen Gould Bridge.

A tower was used to control traffic over the diamond, operated by the Missouri Pacific forces. The tower was staffed by three telegrapher-towermen who provided 24-hour service. In 1938, the mechanical system in the tower was replaced by an automatic interlocker. The tower was retired and removed in late 1942 and a telephone booth was installed in 1943, after CTC signaling was placed in service between Van Buren and Greenwood Junction.

After the Corps of Engineers moved the Missouri Pacific trains back to the Frisco bridge in 1970, a connection for northbound MP trains was built on the east side of their tracks that connected with the Frisco route southbound just east of the diamond. The old grade is still visible. Later, a new connection was built to the west of the Missouri Pacific tracks to eliminate these movements across the diamond. Details about the route to Fort Smith can be found in the route guide for the Fort Smith Branch starting on Page 529.

The Arkansas & Missouri now serves the small downtown yard, sand plant, and Van Buren industrial park. The connection on the southwest side of the diamond has again been changed and now connects into the downtown yard. Additionally, a connection was built to the northeast that allows UP grain trains from the north to connect directly with the A&M mainline.

The Frisco Railroad

The St. Louis & San Francisco Railway Co. (StL&SF, or SL-SF), better known as the Frisco, was organized in 1876 in Missouri. The Frisco's first line into Arkansas came south from Monett, Missouri. As was typical at the time, the construction involved a number of paper companies coming together to build and initially operate the railroad. The first of these companies was the St. Louis, Arkansas & Texas Railway Company of Missouri, incorporated June 4, 1880. By summer 1881, the company owned and operated 32 miles of track from Monett to the Missouri-Arkansas state line. The second company involved was incorporated on July 17, 1880. This company, the St. Louis, Arkansas & Texas Railway Company of Arkansas, built approximately 37 miles of track from the Missouri-Arkansas state line to near Fayetteville.

In September 1880, the Frisco created a third railroad subsidiary, the Missouri, Arkansas & Southern Railway of Arkansas. The new subsidiary was authorized "to build in a southerly direction" – likely from Fayetteville (Washington County) – "to some point on the Little Rock & Fort Smith Railway, not east of Clarksville, with total mileage of about 55 miles." Within a year, the railroad had 63 miles of track under construction between Fayetteville and Fort Smith.

On June 28, 1881, these three railroads were merged to create the St. Louis, Arkansas & Texas Railway Company. On January 21, 1882, the St. Louis, Arkansas & Texas Railway Company was sold to the St. Louis & San Francisco Railway Company (which became the St. Louis & San Francisco Railroad Company on June 30, 1896). Later, the Fort Smith & Van Buren Bridge Co., capitalized by the Frisco and incorporated in March 1885, began construction of a bridge over the Arkansas River at Van Buren, finishing it in 1885 and allowing the railway line to continue southwest to Paris, Texas. It was sold to the St. Louis & San Francisco Railroad Company on July 17, 1907.

In 1883, construction continued on south from Fort Smith, through Indian Territory, and on to Paris, Texas (169 miles). The line from Fort Smith to the state line was built by the Ft. Smith & Southern Railway Company. From the state line to Paris, the line was built by the St. Louis & San Francisco Railway Company and the Paris & Great Northern Railroad Company.

The Monett to Paris line was completed on July 1, 1887, connecting with the Texas & Pacific to Dallas and Fort Worth.

After the Frisco's improved mainline was built to the west across Oklahoma during the late 1890s and early 1900s, the line between Monett and Fort Smith, and on south to Paris, Texas, took on the role of a secondary line mostly serving local businesses. The St. Louis & San Francisco Railroad Company became the St. Louis-San Francisco Railway on August 24, 1916. The Frisco became part of the Burlington Northern Railroad on November 21, 1980. Because of the line's slow loss of business, it was determined to be a candidate for a lease-purchase agreement, with the line being turned over to the Arkansas & Missouri Railroad in 1986.

The Henry Wellge & Co. "Perspective Map of Van Buren" also included this scene of the LR&FS-Frisco crossing. Note the Frisco bridge, water tower, and the former depot that guards the crossing. *Perspective map of Van Buren, Ark. county seat of Crawford County.* [Milwaukee, Henry Wellge & Co, 1888] Map. Retrieved from the Library of Congress, https://www.loc.gov/item/75693085/.

498.4 PROPERTY LIMITS BETWEEN LR&FS AND K&AV RAIL-
ROADS – In 1888, the Kansas & Arkansas Valley acquired some of the trackage of the Little Rock & Fort Smith and then "built their own Arkansas trackage, along with 78.2 miles in Oklahoma through Vian and Fort Gibson to Wagoner."

This location was not normally found in timetables, but in 1925 it was shown to be 0.11 miles west (railroad-north) from the Fort Smith Branch Connection, the original connection to the Frisco. The location was also used by the Interstate Commerce Commission and other government agencies to define the property limits between the Little Rock & Fort Smith (to the east) and the Kansas & Arkansas Valley (to the west). In one such report, it was stated that the Kansas & Arkansas Valley started operating "at Van Buren Junction, about 0.27 miles west of Van Buren, in the county of Crawford, in the State of Arkansas, and extending thence westerly through said county of Crawford to the boundary line between the States of Arkansas and Oklahoma, a distance of 5.17 miles, more or less."

The Little Rock & Fort Smith Railway in Oklahoma

The Little Rock & Fort Smith was chartered to connect the cities in its name. Initially to do this, the LR&FS built further west and then looped to the south to the station of Cherokee/Moffett, in what was later Oklahoma. There, it connected to a ferry to Fort Smith. Later, the track was shortened and a ferry was used from nearby Gatlin, Arkansas. Then, when the St. Louis & San Francisco Railroad Company built their bridge across the Arkansas River, the LR&FS began to use that route into Fort Smith. Details about the route to Cherokee/Moffett are included here.

499.5 GATLIN – Gatlin was shown as a station and passenger train stop during the late 1870s and 1880s. Maps showed a small town named Gatlin into the 1890s. The name Gatlin probably came from the Gatlin family who owned land in the area at the time.

This was the area where the Little Rock & Fort Smith built their new incline to reach the Arkansas River transfer boats. Initially, the ferries crossed at Cherokee, despite the operation being illegal due to being in Indian Territory. After several years of delay, the ferry terminal was moved to here. The announcement about the move was published in multiple newspapers, including the September 4, 1878, issue of the *Arkansas Gazette*, which reported that the "Little Rock and Fort Smith Railroad Company proposes to establish a transfer boat at Van Buren and lay a track to Fort Smith from a point opposite Van Buren, so as to run freight through without breaking bulk." As part of the plan, the transfer boat *N.D. Munson* was acquired and moved to Van Buren. This boat could carry a maximum of four freight cars or two passenger cars.

The railroad used a large flat location between the railroad and the river to locate its incline operation. The incline headed geographically southeast to reach the river. Another incline was built on the Fort Smith side of the Arkansas River, climbing to the southwest from the river to the higher ground. Initially, this area was known as South Van Buren and was where construction of a rail line started that would eventually connect with downtown Fort Smith. Once across the river from Van Buren, the railroad was still four miles from the Fort Smith city limits, passing through mostly farm lands.

A report in the January 25, 1879, issue of the *Van Buren Press* reported that the new incline and transfer boat were working "to a charm." It mentioned that the station on the south side of the Arkansas River was being called South Van Buren, and that was where all freight transferred across the river was then shipped by wagon into Fort Smith. The Little Rock & Fort Smith laid rails into the city during late January 1879, ending the use of wagons to move the freight. When the Frisco completed their track from the north into Van Buren, their trains also used the transfer boat *N.D. Munson* to reach Fort Smith. A series of ferries continued to shuttle two to four cars at a time across the river until the Frisco opened their bridge across the Arkansas River in February 1886. Both railroads began to use this bridge to reach their terminals at Fort Smith.

500.1 LEE CREEK BRIDGE – Lee Creek, earlier called Lee's Creek or Lees Creek, is a large stream that essentially marks the west side of Van Buren. The stream forms near West Fork, Arkansas, and flows to the southwest through Devil's Den State Park. The State of Arkansas has declared the stream to be an Extraordinary Resource Waterway. Lee Creek continues into Oklahoma where it is classified as a State Scenic River. The name Lee's Creek is still commonly used in Oklahoma. The stream then flows to the southeast to here and then into the Arkansas River a hundred yards to the south at Van Buren's 104-acre Lee Creek Park. Lee Creek is about 65 miles long and is dammed a few miles north of here, creating Lee Creek Reservoir. This is one of several sources of drinking water in the region.

Union Pacific 5946 heads south across the Lee Creek Bridge in December 2022.

The railroad has had several different bridges over Lee Creek. The current bridge includes 93 feet of concrete pile spans (5 spans on the south end), a 200-foot-long Warren through truss, and 108 feet of concrete pile spans (6 spans on the north end). The Warren through truss span was built in 1907 by the Pennsylvania Steel Company, located in Steelton, Pennsylvania. The steel company was created in 1865 by J. Edgar Thomson (president of the Pennsylvania Railroad) and Samuel Morse Felton Sr. (retired president of the Philadelphia, Wilmington & Baltimore Railroad). Some sources also show Nathaniel Thayer III (American banker and railroad executive) as a founding member, but he would have been only 14 years old at the time. The company built a mill at Steelton, Pennsylvania, starting in 1866, which opened in 1868. The company was acquired by Bethlehem Steel in 1917.

503.5 GREENWOOD JUNCTION – Greenwood Junction was created by the Kansas & Arkansas Valley, but the original mainline of the Little Rock & Fort Smith turned southward in this general area to reach Fort Smith. The south switch to the wye at Greenwood Junction was in Arkansas, while the north switch was located 0.13 miles into Oklahoma. The wye and the Greenwood Branch that headed to the south became necessary in 1891 when the "Helen Gould Bridge" opened across the Arkansas River. This bridge allowed the St. Louis, Iron Mountain & Southern to reach Fort Smith using its own tracks.

These abandoned piles mark where the Greenwood Branch once crossed Garrison Creek at Greenwood Junction.

503.6 ARKANSAS-OKLAHOMA STATE LINE – Heading north, the tracks exit Arkansas and enter Oklahoma at an elevation of 415 feet. The Territory of **Arkansas** was admitted to the Union as the 25th state on June 15, 1836. It is the 29th largest state, and the 32nd most populated. To the north is the Ozark Plateau/ Mountains. This is part of the interior highlands region, the only major mountainous region between the Rocky Mountains and the Appalachian Mountains. Arkansas is also the only state where diamonds are mined, and you can go mine them yourself at the Crater of Diamonds State Park. The former nickname of the state was the Land of Opportunity, but it now uses The Natural State. Little Rock, located near the center of Arkansas, is the capital and largest city in the state.

East of the state line in Arkansas is **Crawford County**, created on October 18, 1820, from part of Pulaski County. When created, it acquired the nickname of "Empire County" since it covered western Arkansas and much of Indian Territory, later part of Oklahoma. Five Arkansas counties were carved out of Crawford County, plus several in Oklahoma. Because of its location on the western border of Arkansas, and between the Arkansas River and the mountains to the north, numerous roads and trails passed through the county, including the Butterfield Overland Mail stage route. The county became known nationwide when radio comedian, newspaper columnist, and movie star Bob Burns would joke about his family and friends back in Crawford County. The county was also the birthplace of former slave Bass Reeves, who later became a noted lawman working out of Fort Smith and covering much of Indian Territory during the late 1800s. The population of the growing county was 60,133 in the 2020 census.

Crawford County was named for William H. Crawford of Georgia, a long-time politician. Crawford was elected to the U.S. Senate in 1807, and was president pro tempore of the Senate when Vice President George Clinton passed away in 1812, essentially making him vice president. During the War of 1812, President James Madison appointed Crawford as the minister to France. He then became Secretary of War, and then the 7th Secretary of the Treasury on October 22, 1816, and held the position until March 6, 1825.

To the west (railroad-north) is **Oklahoma**, once known as Indian Territory (1834-1907), and later partly as Oklahoma Territory (1890-1907). Oklahoma means "red people" in the

Choctaw language, and the name was decided during an 1866 meeting between federal officials and leaders of the five Indian nations who had been moved there. During the late 1800s, the western part of what became Oklahoma was the Oklahoma Territory, while the eastern part was Indian Territory. The two merged and became the 46th state on November 16, 1907. It is the 20th largest state and the 28th most populated, with about four million residents, with two-thirds of Oklahomans living in the Oklahoma City (the state capital) and Tulsa metropolitan areas. The state is known as "The Sooner State" due to the number of white settlers who staked their land claims out before the official opening date in the western Oklahoma Territory.

To the west of the border is **Sequoyah County**. This started as the Skin Bayou District, and became the Sequoyah District of the Cherokee Nation in 1851, named for George Guess (Sequoyah), who invented a Cherokee alphabet. The area was one of the most popular access points into what later became Oklahoma as the federal offices at Fort Smith are just to the east in Arkansas. The county includes the Arkansas River valley, as well as the Ozark Plateau to the north and the Ouachita Mountains to the south. Many of the local names date to French explorers and the Cherokee who started to acquire the land through Lovely's Purchase in 1816. In 1829, the area officially became part of the Western Cherokee Nation. Sallisaw is the county seat and the county's population is about 45,000. The county features mostly farming, ranching and poultry, but tourism and industry also play an important role.

The State Line and the Railroad

The Railroad Act of 1886 opened the way for railroad construction across Indian Territory. The builders of various railroads took advantage of this Act to build across the state, in what was actually a relatively late burst of railroad activity. This is why the Kansas & Arkansas Valley Railway Company was created on November 29, 1885, by the owners of the Little Rock & Fort Smith Railway to build across Oklahoma. The LR&FS did not have permission to build past the Arkansas-Indian Territory border, and a new railroad was created to make the application. On June 1, 1886, the United States Congress granted the Kansas & Arkansas Valley Railway the authority to build in the Indian Territory.

However, this was actually not the first track built across the border near Van Buren. When the Little Rock & Fort Smith built north from Van Buren in 1876, the company built all the way to a terminus known as Cherokee, reportedly also called Moffett, located in Indian Territory. This was basically south of where Greenwood Junction was later located. The station of Cherokee/Moffett was used as a ferry terminal by the railroad. Initially, freight and passengers would have to disembark the train and board ferry boats to cross the Arkansas River to reach Fort Smith. This was later replaced by a transfer boat at Gatlin that could actually carry railroad cars across the river.

The construction of the railroad into Cherokee Nation in Indian Territory resulted in a number of legal petitions, challenges, and rulings. A number of government bodies and officials became involved, including Cherokee Principal Chief Charles Thompson; U.S. Indian Agent S. W. Marston; J. Q. Smith, Commissioner of the Department of Interior's Office of Indian Affairs; and the entire Cherokee National Council. Local newspapers regularly reported on the situation during the last half of 1876.

On June 19, 1876, U.S. Indian Agent S. W. Marston was instructed to "ascertain the facts in this case without delay" and to report them to the Office of Indian Affairs. Meanwhile, the Cherokee National Council was already meeting about the situation. On July 22nd, the *Cherokee Advocate* ("the official organ of the Nation" according to *The Van Buren Press*) reported that representatives had already "entered their solemn protest against the action of the L. R. and Ft. Smith railroad in constructing their road through a portion of the lands belonging to the Cherokee Nation." More details, as well as opinions of the writers, were included.

We learn that the above mentioned Railroad has been completed to a point on the opposite bank of the river from Ft. Smith, which point is, as is well known, about two or three miles west of the Arkansas State line in the Cherokee Nation; and this in direct violation of all treaty stipulation bearing on the subject. The writer of this article was in Ft. Smith when the Delegation returned, who had been sent by the above named Company, to visit Chief Thompson and try to negotiate for the right of way for their road. It is due the Company to say that this Delegation visited Tahlequah but failed to see the Chief. Yet we think it would have been better for all parties interested had the Company deferred further action in the matter until the meeting of the council, instead of continuing the construction of their road through our country in defiance of treaties or other authorities.

Personally we have no objection to the building of this road over this small portion ot our country, and we believe there is no reasonable person who has thought of the matter, but will acknowledge that it would be better for the terminus of this road to be inside of the nation, where our officers could have full control and exert their authority in preventing the introduction of intoxicating liquors – instead of at "Line City" where any amount of liquor would be sold with impunity, and thereby create a hot-bed of drunkenness, debauchery and crime. But we deprecate the principal in any people or company, that prompts them to the violation of law or treaties.

We wish to add in conclusion that we heard a prominent citizen of Ft. Smith, remark that it was the intention of the company, in evidence of their "good faith," to voluntarily pay the Cherokee nation a royalty or tax on the lands over which their road runs.

While on this subject we think it would be well for the Council to consider this last question, as to the expediency of exacting such tax or royalty. We have given the matter careful consideration, and believe that such a precedent would be decidedly legal, beneficial in the future, and in accordance with laws existing in every state and county in the Union – where railroads pass through – which gives the said state or county the right to levy a reasonable tax on the railroad for the privileges they enjoy, and if the Council decides to allow the L. R. & Ft. Smith Railroad the right of way for their road, and accept the Company's offer for the payment of per annum royalty, we hope they (the Council) will not be the least partial, but let such rule or law apply to all railroads that pass through the Cherokee Nation.

On November 17, 1876, the Cherokee National Council stated that the construction of the railroad was in violation of their Treaty of 1866, and passed an Act to react to this "intrusion upon the domain and national sovereignty of the Cherokee Nation."

Principal Chief is hereby authorized and directed to call upon the said Railroad Company to remove said road immediately beyond the limits of the Cherokee Nation.

Be it further enacted, that the Principal Chief, be, and he is hereby authorized to transmit a copy of this act to the President of the United States, the Secretary of the Interior, and the Commissioner of Indian Affairs – with the request that they cause the said railroad to be removed beyond the limits of the Cherokee Nation, without delay.

Within a few days, a report was released that stated that the Little Rock & Fort Smith would have to remove some two miles of track in Indian Territory. The Cherokee Nation had asked the United States government to force the railroad to remove the tracks as the railroad had not obtained permission from the Cherokee Nation for the track-laying. The Cherokee Nation had also ordered the sheriff to arrest any United States citizens who entered in the area. These actions were delayed for several years as multiple solutions were proposed and rejected. Finally, the tracks were removed. The January 23, 1879, issue of the *Cincinnati Enquirer* had an article about the sale of what railroad property remained in the Cherokee Nation of Indian Territory.

> *Today the day for the sale of the depot, stock-yards etc., belonging to the Little Rock and Fort Smith Railroad Company at its terminus at Cherokee, in the Indian Territory, immediately opposite Fort Smith, under an order of confiscation from the Cherokee Council, the Sheriff was on the ground at the appointed hour advertised for the sale to take place, but found nothing to sell but a few rotten ties and seven two-inch planks. The Railroad Company had torn down and moved all its buildings across to Fort Smith, and had taken up its track to the State line. Trains will hereafter come from the north to the south side of the river by transfer boat at this place [Van Buren] and run directly to Fort Smith. The grade is completed from here to Fort Smith and the track is now being laid. All arrangements for through trains to Fort Smith will probably be completed by Monday next.*

The location of Cherokee shows on few maps today, but Moffett is a small community across the river from Fort Smith. It is near what is today called West Fort Smith, the home of the Fort Smith Stockyards. Moffett seems to be the center of the automobile scrap industry as there are several large U-Pick car part yards and repair shops that specialize in using reclaimed parts.

The rail line from Greenwood Junction to Fort Smith was built by the St. Louis, Iron Mountain & Southern as part of a proposed Gurdon to Fort Smith route, later known as the Greenwood Branch, Greenwood Subdivision or the Paris Subdivision. The first section of the line built was from Fort Smith south to the Jenny Lind coal mines near Greenwood, opened in February 1889. About this time, there were announcements that the line would actually be extended to Little Rock, or possibly Morrilton. The line between Greenwood Junction and Fort Smith was completed in 1891 with the opening of the Arkansas

River Bridge. Some court records state that the bridge and line was built by Jay Gould and the Missouri Pacific, but later records cite the Kansas & Arkansas Valley Railway as the owner. Because of this, the line is not covered in detail in this book.

To follow the line, take Oklahoma Highway 640 south from Interstate 40. The old grade can be seen to the east. The railroad once curved across U.S. Highway 64 at Milepost 507.4 before crossing the Arkansas River and into Fort Smith. The remains of this bridge can still be found.

Clarksville Branch
Knoxville Junction to Spadra Junction

The Clarksville Branch, later known as the Clarksville Subdivision, was the original rail route built by the Little Rock & Fort Smith between Knoxville and Spadra. The line served the important community of Clarksville, but at the cost of climbing the ridge near Lamar (Cabin Creek). Because of these grades, a new line was later built along the Arkansas River (1902-1903) with fewer grades, south of what was known as Big Danger Hill. The new line also saved almost five miles of track (6.7 miles versus 11.4 miles), allowing faster speeds and heavier trains.

The new junction near Knoxville became known as Knoxville Junction, or BB Junction. The northern junction became Spadra Junction, or AA Junction. The passenger trains and local freights generally used the original line, while the heavy manifest freights used the new line. However, this changed during late June 1935. The new mainline was washed out during a severe round of flooding, and all trains returned to the line through Clarksville.

During March 1936, officials of Missouri Pacific announced "plans to undertake the construction of 3.71 miles of track" to reopen the new mainline. The first freight train operated over the line at noon on December 16, 1936, ending much of the rail service through Clarksville for the second time. Passenger service didn't return to the new line until early 1937, with some trains still operating via the Clarksville line. After the passenger train service ended in 1960, only a daily local freight served the line, and in 1964 the line between Spadra and Clarksville was abandoned.

With the abandonment, the track between BB Junction and Clarksville became the Clarksville Branch. About the same time, BB Junction was renamed Clarksville Junction. Service on the line became less frequent as freight shippers disappeared. On July 27, 1988, the Interstate Commerce Commission granted Union Pacific the authority to abandon 8.8 miles of railroad between Milepost 435.6 at Clarksville Junction, and Milepost 444.4 at Clarksville. However, a few freight shipments continued until management grew tired of sending a loco-motive and crew up the line and two rails were removed during January 1989 to prevent further movements. Scrapping of what was left of the line started in May 1989 with the rail shipped out and the ties sold wherever possible. The ballast was purchased by the Dardanelle & Russellville Railroad (D&R) and used on their own line rehabilitation. Several of the steel bridges were removed, with one going to the D&R and another to Union Pacific for use elsewhere.

The Clarksville Branch route guide provides information about each former station location, junction, and major bridges. To explain some of the operations, it includes the mileposts, office calls (telegraph call code) from 1925, and any unique train operations at that location.

435.9 KNOXVILLE JUNCTION – In 1923, this was the station name and location of the junction where the new mainline was built westward to avoid the grades on the original mainline via Clarksville. Other names have also been used, including BB Junction and Clarksville Junction. Details about the new mainline between Knoxville Junction and Spadra Junction are found starting on Page 304.

The new route was built about 1903, and train traffic was split between the two lines. During the 1940s, four daily passenger trains and the two local freight trains used the old line via Clarksville, but the through freight trains used the newer route alongside the Arkansas River. To assist with the train movements, a spring switch was installed at BB Junction. After the installation of ABS signals on the new mainline in 1945, the switch was normally set for the new route. Northward passenger trains and local freight trains would have to stop to throw the switch to enter the old line for Clarksville. Meanwhile, southbound trains from Clarksville could spring through the switch without stopping.

Today, Knoxville Junction is known as Clarksville, as shown by this sign at the north switch of the business track.

436.2 SOUTH END OF LAKE DARDANELLE DETOUR – When Dardanelle Dam was completed in 1964, the water level on nearby Cabin Creek became higher. Because of this, a new one-mile line was built to the east of the line to Clarksville on slightly higher ground.

436.8 RED OAK ROAD – This road crosses both the original grade, and the new grade built in the early 1960s. Both crossings can be found southeast of the road's bridge across Cabin Creek.

436.9 INTERSTATE 40 – From Knoxville Junction, the original grade closely followed the new mainline grade until it turned north to follow Cabin Creek through Lamar and towards Clarksville. There are actually two grades in the area immediately west of Exit 64 on Interstate 40. This was because the original grade had to be moved a short distance to the east when Lake Dardanelle was created. In this area, Cabin Creek backed up as part of Lake Dardanelle, so a higher grade was required.

As the railroad left Knoxville Junction, the line dropped down to Cabin Creek and then climbed a stiff uphill grade (maximum of 1.14%) to near Milepost 441. The elevations of the top of rail along the line were 376 feet at Milepost 436, 348 at Milepost 437, 387 at Milepost 438, 414 at Milepost 439, and 435 at Milepost 440. Heading on towards Clarksville, the line dropped using similar grades, with a short grade of 1.56% near

Milepost 443. It was these grades that the new line was built to avoid.

The railroad once passed under Interstate 40 to the northwest of Exit 64. This 2555-mile-long highway connects Wilmington, North Carolina, with Barstow, California, making it the third-longest Interstate Highway in the country. The highway was established by the Federal Aid Highway Act of 1956 and the west end replaced Historic Route 66.

The last part of the rail line between Clarksville Junction and Clarksville was approved for abandonment in 1988. Since then, Interstate 40 has been improved in the area, but the older grade alongside Cabin Creek still can be found below the bridge that still remains.

This marker on the Interstate 40 bridge notes that it is crossing Cabin Creek. The grade of the original Little Rock & Fort Smith can still be seen alongside the stream.

437.2 NORTH END OF LAKE DARDANELLE DETOUR – The two grades come back together in the middle of a large S-curve.

438.2 ROCK QUARRY – A switchback track once headed off to the southwest to serve a local quarry. Rock was one of the primary products shipped from Lamar.

438.5 LAMAR (CB) – This area was near an early military road that connected Little Rock with western Arkansas and further west to what became Indian Territory. In 1835, Samuel Adams established a plantation near here, building one of the first homes in the area that used finished lumber rather than logs. Adams was responsible for the area taking the name Cabin Creek. He built a series of small cabins along the bank of the stream to house his slaves. This led to the stream being called the Stream of Cabins, and later Cabin Creek. Adams became wealthy through farming, land investment, and banking. In 1836, he was elected as a representative from Johnson County to the First Arkansas General Assembly. In 1840, he moved to the Arkansas Senate where he was elected president pro tempore of the Senate in the session of 1842. This led him to be the acting governor of Arkansas after Governor Archibald Yell resigned in April 1844 after being elected to the U.S. House of Representatives. In 1844, Adams was elected as state treasurer. In 1849, he retired and worked on his plantation in Saline County, where he died on February 27, 1850.

Sidney Cazort acquired the Adams plantation in 1850. Cazort cleared land in the area and helped to develop the community of Cabin Creek. One of his major accomplishments was the construction of a lumber mill and a cotton gin, making the community an important market town in Johnson County. Besides the lumber and cotton (3000-4000 bales of cotton a year), local farmers grew hay, corn, oats, berries, and other crops. Several stores, a hotel, and a few other businesses opened to handle the travelers on the military road, as well as farmers across the region.

The Little Rock & Fort Smith arrived at Cabin Creek in 1873 and located a depot and water tower here. William Alexander Cazort, the son of Sidney Cazort, was made the first station agent for the railroad, and then the first postmaster when a post office opened in 1874. As the town grew, a committee of local citizens was organized to incorporate the community. A number of names were suggested, but the committee chose Lamar, naming it for Lucius Quintus Cincinnatus Lamar, Secretary of the Interior in President Grover Cleveland's cabinet. Lamar was born and educated in Georgia and moved to Mississippi to practice law. He held office in both houses of Congress, was an official in the Confederate States of America, served as the U.S. Secretary of the Interior, and as an Associate Justice of the Supreme Court of the United States.

Lamar was incorporated on May 19, 1887, and the post office changed its name from Cabin Creek to Lamar at the same time. However, the railroad kept using the name Cabin Creek until Fall of 1924. Other organizations like The Sanborn Map Company also continued to use the name Cabin Creek until at least 1924.

In the 1900 census, Lamar (Cabin Creek) had a population of 474. As the community grew, the town was divided by the waterway known as Cabin Creek. Most of the town was located to the northeast while the railroad was to the southwest of the stream. The business district covered several blocks along Main Street, today's Cabin Creek Avenue. The first public school didn't open until 1904, but the school building burned in 1914 and school was held in several homes until a new school was built in 1916.

The year 1920 was the peak of the community until after World War II. An experimental peach orchard opened on the property of Lee Cazort, helping to lead to a fruit boom in the region. The book *Centennial History of Arkansas* (1922) described Lamar (Cabin Creek) as "an incorporated banking town on the railroad five miles east of Clarksville. It has a weekly newspaper, sawmills, a large stone quarry, general stores, and a population of 542." The *Arkansas Marketing and Industrial Guide* of 1921 listed several important industries at Lamar. These included the S. G. Cazort quarry (cut stone, crushed stone and rip-rap), the coal mine of the Herring Mining Company, and the two sawmills of J. W. Smith & Company and Ladd & Strong.

The Great Depression of the 1930s hurt the community and many jobs and businesses ended or moved away. Some improvements were made, including a new school gymnasium built in 1938 by the Works Progress Administration (WPA). Lamar slowly grew after World War II, basically as a rural suburb of nearby Clarksville and Russellville. Especially with the construction of Interstate 40, Lamar could be quickly accessed from the two larger cities. The town grew and a new high school opened in 1976, and other nearby schools were consolidated into the Lamar School District. Today, more than 1000 students attend the local school system and the town's population is approaching 2000 residents. The schools are located at the southwest edge of town while most businesses are now located along U.S. Highway 64, today's Main Street, towards the northeast part of Lamar. The old downtown area is now a series of parks and only a few foundations remain of the old businesses.

The name Cabin Creek is still used at Lamar, as shown by this street sign.

The Railroad at Lamar

A depot and water tower, fed by Cabin Creek, were located here soon after the railroad arrived in 1873. There was a difference in names of the post office and railroad station from 1887 until 1924 when the railroad finally changed the station's name to Lamar. In 1900, the railroad built a 176-foot wood spur to serve a local sawmill. Other construction was considered as the steep grade in the area was an early challenge for the railroad.

The challenges of the grades at Cabin Creek sometimes resulted in train issues. One of these occurred during early November 1892, when two freight trains collided near Cabin Creek. Initially an engineer and fireman were reported as dead, and a third death was reported several days later. There were news reports in January 1902 that the Little Rock & Fort Smith was going to double track the road at Lamar. This may have been the construction of a new siding which was shown to be 33-cars long in 1907, and 38-cars long during the 1940s.

The siding passed through Cabin Creek/Lamar with the depot to the southwest of Cabin Creek about where Elberta Street is today. In 1907, there was a daytime telegraph office and a mail crane. A new wooden depot was built in 1910, and then moved to the Elberta Street location and extended in June 1912 when other track improvements were made. In 1925, the depot was located on the west side of the tracks and it housed a ticket and freight agency. The 1932-1933 survey of the railroad stated that the elevation of the top of rail opposite the Lamar station was 405.5 feet. In late 1943, the 21' x 70' depot lost 26 feet of the freight room, and there was work on the 300-foot cinder platform. Because of local truck deliveries, an outside freight platform was added on the rear of the depot in 1947. A train order signal was installed in December 1948. During the 1950s, there was an agent at Lamar who provided train orders as needed on a limited schedule.

The railroad had a cotton platform on the east side of the tracks north of Cumberland Street. The railroad also had a 30' x 55' stock pen that could hold three stock cars of livestock, locat-

ed about 1000 feet north of the depot. In the same area was a 10'
x 100' loading platform with a 20' x 100' shelter.

During the first part of the twentieth century, the railroad
served a number of customers at Lamar, including a lumber
company; three stone quarries; two agricultural implement
dealers; a coal dealer; a feed and flour dealer; a hide, grease and
fur dealer; a cotton gin and two cotton dealers. Today, the railroad is gone and the old grade can barely be made out to the
northeast of Quarry Street.

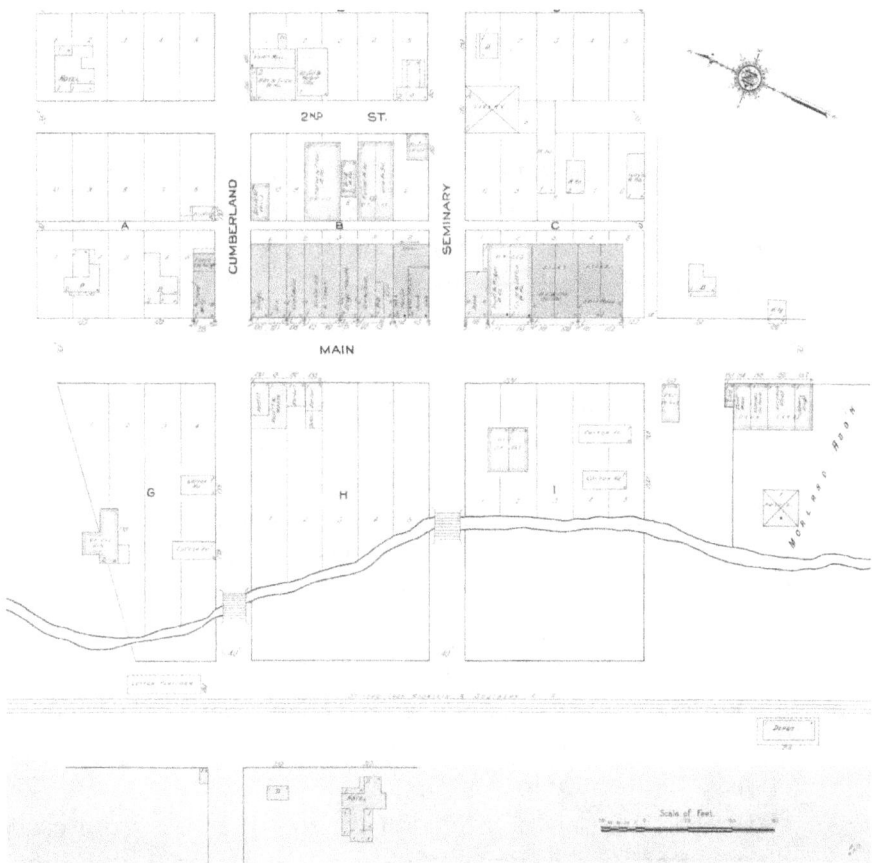

In 1913, the depot at Cabin Creek (Lamar) sat on the west side of the mainline and
siding near where Elberta Street now crosses Cabin Creek. *Sanborn Fire Insurance
Map from Cabin Creek, Johnson County, Arkansas.* Sanborn Map Company, Aug,
1913. Map. Retrieved from the Library of Congress, https://www.loc.gov/item/san-
born00211_001/.

440.7 LAMBRICK SPUR – This 12-car spur track went to the northeast and was located at the grade crossing with Arkansas Highway 23, known locally as Brick Plant Road. It served a brick plant which had its own clay pit to the north. The name Lambrick was officially announced in a General Manager circular dated May 10, 1947.

Lambrick stands for Lamar Brick, but the plant was actually the Eureka Brick & Tile Company. The company was created by Earle K. Johnson, who was born in Clarksville on November 6, 1919. His father was a coal mine owner, and Earle graduated from the University of Arkansas with a degree in civil engineering. He went to work for the U. S. Army Corps of Engineers and was assigned to the Norfolk Dam construction project before serving in World War II. He was promoted to captain and was awarded the Bronze Star and the Silver Star medals for his leadership and actions. After the war, Earle returned to Clarksville and worked with his father to create a brick plant. After a struggle to obtain funding, the Eureka Brick & Tile Company began production in June 1946. By 1955, the company produced 1.5 million bricks per month.

A point of pride for the company was the use of its brick for the exterior of Barnhill Arena at the University of Arkansas. By the mid-1980s, the only Arkansas cities with brick plants were Clarksville, Fort Smith, Hope, Jonesboro, and Malvern. After the death of Earle K. Johnson in 1994, the company remained in the family until sold to the Acme Brick Company during June 1999. By 2009, only four brick plants remained in Arkansas, all owned by Acme Brick, including this one that produced a unique brick in a variety of deep red colors that were prized by residential and commercial builders. Since then, the plant has closed and the property put up for sale.

Lambrick Spur was located at the top of grades from each direction at an elevation of 459 feet. Grades from the south reached 1.34%, while the grade from the north reached as much as 1.56%.

This photo shows the closed Eureka Brick & Tile Company facility.

441.6 SECTION POST – Railroad documents show that this location was the dividing line between Section #46 (towards Clarksville) and Section #46½ (towards Knoxville Junction).

441.9 KING SWITCH – This 36-car track was still in existence up to the abandonment of the Clarksville Branch. In this area were a short industrial siding, a small yard, and several spur tracks on the east side of the mainline, located along East Main Street about the intersection of U.S. Highway 64 and Arkansas Highway 21.

The name came from King & Company, known in the 1950s as the L. H. King Fruit Company. Members of the King family were some of the early leaders of the Clarksville community. W. Ernest King became the postmaster at Clarksville, in place of W. E. King, whose commission expired April 27, 1938. There was also the King & Company mercantile store at 1910 West Main Street.

The north end of the King Switch complex was located about Milepost 442.3.

442.6 WARD'S SPUR – Also known as Ward's Junction by 1887, or simply as Wards during the mid-1900s, this was the switch to a one-mile-long track. In 1925, this was shown to be Ward's Spur, and all freight traffic in and out was to be prepaid.

The name Ward comes from the Ward family, which settled in Arkansas in 1827. Andy F. Ward was known for being engaged in breeding and feeding cattle. He organized the Arkansas Fruit & Farm Company in 1901 and set out three hundred acres of fruit trees. He is often cited as the first man to engage in such pursuits in Johnson County. By 1906, Ward was involved in the coal industry, and became a partner in several firms.

At Ward's Spur were also several tracks, all to the east of the mainline, plus a fruit platform that was removed in 1940.

442.7 MILE 100 – This was once the location of Milepost 100 of the original Little Rock & Fort Smith Railway. The mileposts were later changed when the railroad was acquired by Gould and his St. Louis, Iron Mountain & Southern.

Later, this was the location of Poultry Plant Spur. This track once served the poultry processing plant at Clarksville. While the tracks are gone, the large Tyson processing plant is still active.

442.9 BRIDGE – This bridge, once known as Bridge No. 270, crossed part of an old channel of Spadra Creek. It consisted of a 60-foot deck plate girder span. After the line's scrapping in May 1989, the span was sold to the Dardanelle & Russellville Railroad for use on a proposed line to a new industrial park along the Arkansas River.

In this area, trains heading towards Clarksville were going down a grade of 1.56%. To the south of the old grade is the Clarksville Tyson Processing Plant

443.0 BIG SPADRA CREEK BRIDGE – Spadra Creek starts as a small stream on the east side of Mac Wood Mountain west of

Ozone, Arkansas, and drains parts of the Boston Mountains in northern Johnson County. It flows through downtown Clarksville and then widens as backwaters from the Arkansas River.

Spadra Creek was a challenge for the railroad when it reached Clarksville, and a light bridge was quickly built, later known as Bridge No. 271. In 1875, the LR&FS had a 109-foot covered Howe truss and six frame bent spans over Spadra Creek, shown to be at Milepost 100.3. On May 16, 1891, the *Arkansas Gazette* reported that "A new iron bridge is being built across Spadra Creek at Clarksville by the Little Rock and Fort Smith Railway."

This "new iron bridge" was a 115-foot-long Pratt truss. This bridge became too light by the 1920s and was replaced in 1924 with a 90-foot through plate girder and a 26-foot deck plate girder. The through plate girder span was shown to have limited side clearances. There were timber frame trestle spans as the approaches on each end. After the line was abandoned, the steel spans were removed for use elsewhere by Union Pacific.

443.4 ROBINSON SLOUGH BRIDGE – While Union Pacific records show this to be Robinson Slough, modern maps show the stream to be Craven Branch of Spadra Creek. The stream drains the hills just north of Clarksville and flows into Spadra Creek a short distance south of here. The railroad had a timber pile trestle across the stream that measured 140 feet long. The 11-panel bridge still remains today. At the north end of the bridge, the tracks turned 70 degrees using a 5 degree curve to reach the station at Clarksville.

The name Craven comes from the Cravens family who moved to Clarksville during the 1850s. Several members held political office in Arkansas including Jordan Edgar Cravens, U.S. Representative from Arkansas (1877-1883), and William Ben Cravens, U.S. Representative from Arkansas (1907-1913). In downtown Clarksville, Cravens Street is located on the east side of the old courthouse square.

The Robinson Slough Bridge still stands and essentially marks where the railroad entered downtown Clarksville.

The Spadra Creek Nature Trail uses some of the original Little Rock & Fort Smith railroad grade on the west end of the Robinson Slough Bridge.

Railroad Street can be found on the west side of the Clarksville Depot, one of the reminders that the Little Rock & Fort Smith Railway once passed through downtown Clarksville.

The Clarksville depot is now used by the Clarksville-Johnson County Chamber of Commerce. Despite the track being gone, the station looks like it is ready for train service.

443.7 CLARKSVILLE (P) – Clarksville was an existing community along the planned route of the Little Rock & Fort Smith, and it was often cited in news reports about the railroad, even before the line was completed. In fact, the railroad's charter at one time stated that Clarksville would be the site of the corporate headquarters. In March 1873, the railroad announced that rails were in place as far as the Illinois Bayou and that the railroad would be finished to Clarksville by the 15th of April. However, a report from May 14, 1873, stated that the railroad had built to four miles from Clarksville and that the bridge over Spadra Creek was nearly finished. The railroad was completed to Clarksville in mid-1873, but then construction stopped as the Financial Panic of 1873 made it impossible to borrow money or find investors, and the railroad entered foreclosure because of unpaid mortgage payments.

Because the railroad ended at Clarksville, several stagecoach companies connected here to take passengers and express westward to Fort Smith, and northward to a number of communities. The railroad installed temporary facilities at Clarksville, including a depot, turntable, and locomotive servicing facilities. Construction began again in early 1875, and what later became the Clarksville Subdivision reached Spadra about March 1875. As a part of the new construction, the railroad was reorganized on June 12, 1875, as the Little Rock & Fort Smith Railway.

As the railroad built westward, the facilities at Clarksville became more permanent. In 1874, the temporary depot was replaced by a new one located between Taylor and Fillmore streets. Cotton platforms, a few maintenance sheds, and other railroad structures were built. For example, in 1895 a set of stock pens (two that could hold two carloads of livestock) were constructed at Clarksville. In 1896, the wooden railroad depot was located on the geographical east side of the track south of Taylor Street. There was a cotton platform to the west of the two tracks that passed through town. North of Taylor Street was the J. W. May grain mill, with the I. N. Allbritten flour mill immediately to its north. By 1901, the J. W. May mill was owned by Collier & Johnson, which operated a gin, grist and planing mill on the site.

The next year, Clarksville became concerned as a new route was being built to the south along the Arkansas River. Community leaders were worried that Clarksville was going to be bypassed and left without a railroad, or at least a mainline. Because of this, a proposal was sent to the St. Louis & San Francisco (Frisco) that a financial bonus would be provided if the railroad's St. Paul branch was extended to Clarksville. The Frisco line was never extended to Clarksville and the Missouri Pacific line remained to Clarksville until 1989.

Even with the construction of the new mainline, Clarksville was a daytime telegraph office in 1907. Things continued to change at Clarksville as the Iron Mountain's depot was destroyed by fire on November 16, 1907, along with the nearby Clarksville Steam Bakery where the fire began. A report stated that the depot was a total loss and that it was valued at $500. In response, several boxcars were located at the site and used as the passenger and freight station. Meanwhile the Clarksville Mill & Elevator Company was located south of Sevier Street and east of the tracks by 1908. North of Taylor Street was A. B. Johnson & Sons, which operated a cotton gin and ice plant on the east side of the tracks. The company had part of the ice plant on the south side of Taylor Street. To the south of the depot, the Clarksville Lumber Company had their planing mill south of Fillmore Street.

The use of boxcars for the depot and freight facilities soon wore on the citizens of Clarksville and they filed a petition with the Arkansas Railroad Commission for a new depot in May 1908. On June 16, 1908, the commission held a session in Clarksville, taking up the petition of the residents. *The Daily Picayune* (June 15, 1908) of Prescott, Arkansas, carried news about the hearing.

> *The depot at Clarksville, never an elegant structure, was destroyed by fire many months ago, and since that time the patrons of the Iron Mountain have been forced to wait for trains in box cars provided for the freight. Clarksville is one of the principal shipping points on this railroad between Little Rock and Fort Smith, and the people of Clarksville think it is very poor return on the part of the railroad to leave them without a station at all. While at Clarksville the commission will look after some other complaints from the same vicinity.*

Based upon the hearing, the Arkansas Railroad Commission ordered the St. Louis, Iron Mountain & Southern to build a new depot at Clarksville within 90 days. During October, a new depot opened at the old location at a reported cost of $3000.

During the early 1900s, a number of new businesses opened at Clarksville, many of them located on the railroad. After crossing the bridge over Craven Branch, the railroad curved back to the south as it headed towards Fort Smith. In this area was the Clarksville Electric Plant, located on the southeast corner of Jackson and Railroad (now University) streets. The railroad had a coal spur for the facility, which is now the site of the Clarksville city garage complex. Heading south, there were five industries located to the compass-east of the tracks. They were Laser Grain Company (north of Sevier), A. B. Johnson & Son (cotton gin south of Sevier), A. B. & W. B. Johnson & Son (cotton gin north of Taylor), Crystal Ice (south of Taylor), and Arkansas-Indiana Lumber Company (south of Fillmore). The depot was still to the east south of Taylor, with the cotton platform to the west. The Central Hotel had been built immediately to the east of the depot.

During early 1912, the railroad built several sidetracks and peach sheds, enough to accommodate 75 more cars. This expansion allowed the fruit growers at Clarksville to load about 173 cars a day. By mid-July, a fruit company had already shipped 11 cars of early peaches, plus a few cars of mixed fruit that included peaches, apples and plums.

All the new business at Clarksville soon outgrew the new railroad station's capacity. While the National Register of Historic Places and other documents state that a new brick depot was built at Clarksville in 1910, it was actually completed in 1917. The April 1916 issue of *The Bridgemen's Magazine* reported that the Missouri Pacific Railroad was planning a new depot for Clarksville, while the June 30, 1916, issue of *Railway Age Gazette* had more details on the plans. It stated that the "Missouri Pacific-St. Louis, Iron Mountain & Southern is building a brick passenger station, 24 ft. by 124 ft., at a cost of about $15,000, including the incidental rearrangement of tracks and the construction of necessary platforms." The platform was long enough to handle the longest passenger trains operating over the routes; so long that it crossed nearby Cherry Street.

The new brick depot was built several blocks to the north (actually railroad-south) of the old station, located north of Main

Street and south of Cherry Street, west of Johnson Street and east of Railroad Street. The depot was on the compass-east side of the tracks and just south of the geographical north switch of the siding. The single-story masonry structure was built in the Mediterranean style with a ceramic tile roof that no longer exists. Design comments about the passenger station include that it "is basically rectangular, with a projecting cross-gabled telegrapher's booth on the track side, which is topped by a distinctive parapeted gable. The roof has extended eaves supported by large Italianate brackets."

By 1919, the railroad was lined with factories, mills and warehouses from Main Street to the south end of town. To the north of Sevier Street was the Laser Grain Company, with the lumber yard and planing mill of E. O. Strong & Son to the east. On the south side of Sevier Street was the Johnson County Gin Company (cotton gin to the east) and a series of warehouses for fertilizer, corn, flour, feed, salt, and apples to the west. South of Taylor Street was the Clarksville Ice & Cold Storage to the east. Where the depot once stood was now the railroad's freight house, plus the cotton platform still to the west of the tracks. South of the depot and on both sides of the tracks was a series of freight sheds for lumber and cotton seed. The Arkansas-Indiana Lumber Company was also still located south of Fillmore Street.

In 1925, the Clarksville station featured a coupon ticket station, ticket agency, and a freight agency for carloads and less. In 1932, a survey was conducted and a benchmark was placed "in the front or west wall of the Missouri Pacific Railroad station, 1 foot north of the southwest corner of the operating room, and 5 feet above the platform." The survey reported that the elevation was 379.363 feet.

After the end of passenger service in 1960, a freight agent remained at the depot and the waiting room was leased to Continental Trailways for their bus passengers. After the track was removed in 1964 between Clarksville and Spadra, the line between Clarksville and BB Junction, then known as Clarksville Junction, was operated using yard limits.

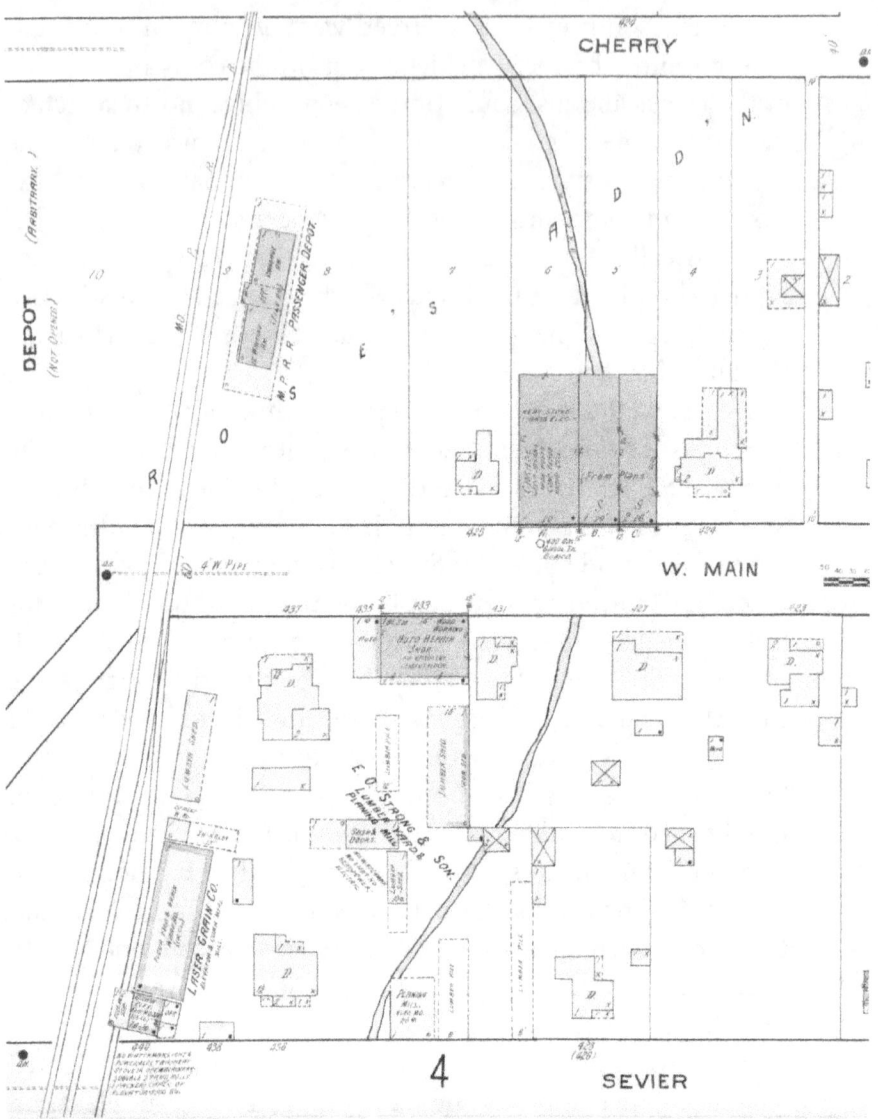

The January 1919 Sanborn map showed that the new Clarksville depot had been completed and was now located between Cherry and Main streets. *Sanborn Fire Insurance Map from Clarksville, Johnson County, Arkansas.* Sanborn Map Company, Jan, 1919. Map. Retrieved from the Library of Congress, https://www.loc.gov/item/sanborn00219_005/.

Until the early 1970s, the Clarksville depot continued to house a train order office that operated on limited hours. A 13-car siding was also located at Clarksville, a relatively flat spot at an elevation of 372 feet on the downhill grade to Spadra. The freight agency was closed in the 1970s and the depot was acquired by the Chamber of Commerce and restored. It was listed on the National Register of Historic Places on June 11, 1992, and the depot still houses the Clarksville-Johnson County Chamber of Commerce.

While the railroad and most of the shippers are gone, a few of their structures remain. This is the May-Marlar Grocer Company, built in 1919 alongside the tracks.

444.0 CLARKSVILLE ENGINE SERVICE FACILITIES – When the Little Rock & Fort Smith was building the railroad, Clarksville was the end of the line for a short time. Because of this, several locomotive and passenger car servicing facilities were built here. Even after the line was completed, the business at Clarksville led to a switch engine often being assigned here. Additionally, during the early 1900s, some passenger and local trains turned here, often requiring basic servicing facilities.

Around Milepost 444, the railroad had a number of these facilities until after World War II. Among the facilities were a tool house, an engine watchman shanty, oil and sand boxes, and a coal dock. Most of these facilities were on the compass-west (railroad-east) side of the Clarksville Branch. Across the tracks and between McKennon and Griffin (now Lucas) were a series of bulk oil facilities. These included Standard Oil Company of Louisiana, Pierce Oil Company (later Pierce Petroleum Corporation), Marland Refining Company, and Magnolia Petroleum Company. At Milepost 444.2 was the end of the siding that started at Cherry Street near the depot.

Just to the north (railroad-south) around Fillmore Street, the railroad had an 18' x 200' fruit shelter, stock pens, a freight house, and several gravel lots and platforms.

This old bulk fuel plant still stands at the former Lucas Street grade crossing and was once served by the railroad.

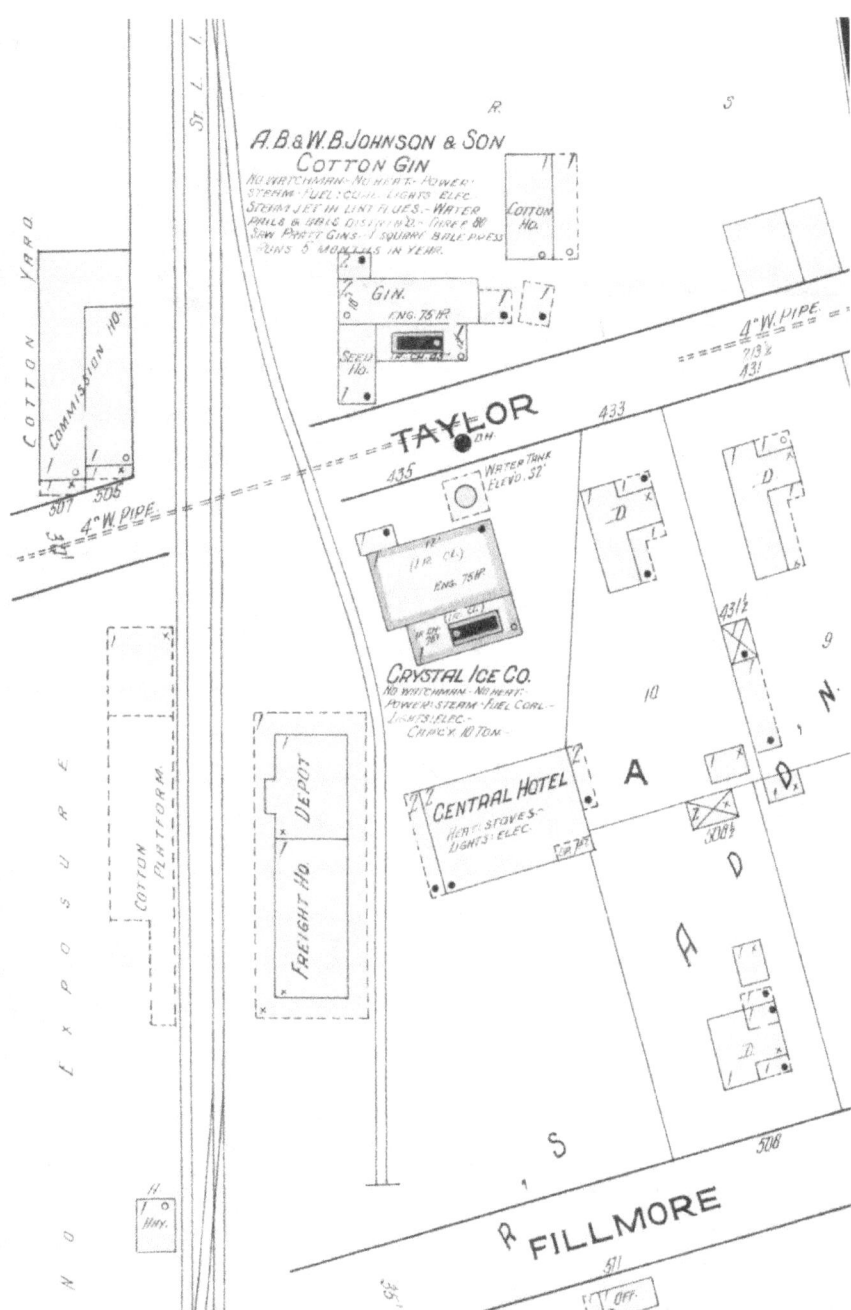

The November 1913 Sanborn map showed that the depot area south of Taylor Street was getting crowded with cotton platforms, the Crystal Ice Company, and the Central Hotel. *Sanborn Fire Insurance Map from Clarksville, Johnson County, Arkansas.* Sanborn Map Company, Nov, 1913. Map. Retrieved from the Library of Congress, https://www.loc.gov/item/sanborn00219_004/.

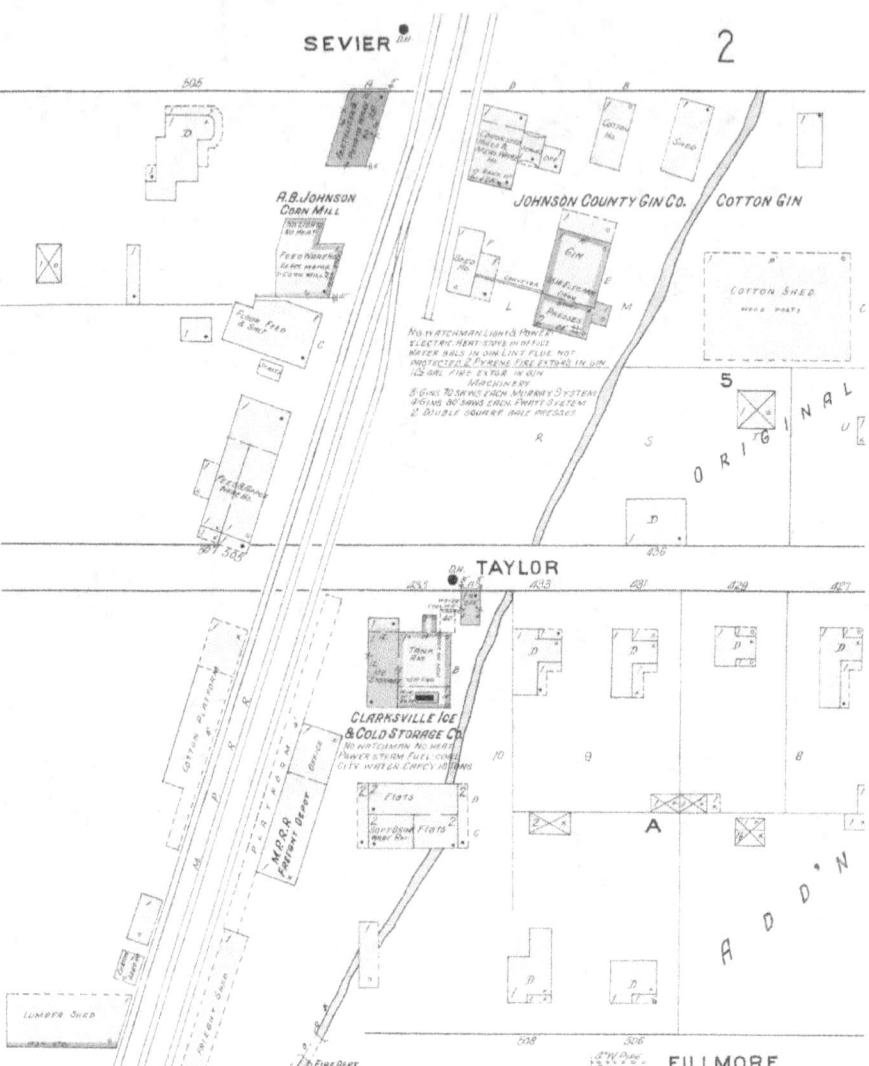

The January 1919 Sanborn map showed that the old Clarksville depot was now the location of the Clarksville freight house. *Sanborn Fire Insurance Map from Clarksville, Johnson County, Arkansas.* Sanborn Map Company, Jan, 1919. Map. Retrieved from the Library of Congress, https://www.loc.gov/item/sanborn00219_005/.

The City of Clarksville

Clarksville came about due to several factors, but most importantly the need for a new county seat when Johnson County was created in November 1836, and the location of an existing road between Little Rock and Fort Smith. A committee was formed to locate the new county seat. The three commissioners involved were Abraham Laster, Elijah B. Alston, and Lorenzo N. Clark. After inspecting several locations, Josiah Cravens donated land that he called Clarksville, named after Lorenzo N. Clark as an attempt to influence the decision. The property was located on Spadra Creek, several miles north of the Arkansas River. The east-west road allowed stagecoach transportation, provided by the Hunter, Hanger and Howell Stage Line, connecting the new county seat with the state capital.

The first court session was held in 1837 in a private building. Being the county seat attracted new settlers, many of them having recently moved from Virginia, Tennessee, and North Carolina. Many were attracted by the Federal Land Office that had located at Clarksville a few years earlier. Coal was discovered to the south of town by 1840, and shipments of tobacco and cotton led to more interest in the community. The growth in population allowed a post office to open at Clarksville in 1841. Later, Clarksville was incorporated on December 21, 1848. The next year Augustus M. Ward established a school for the blind at Clarksville, and then a school for the deaf was founded in 1851.

The population of Clarksville was 398 in the 1850 census. A mix of stores and churches had opened up at Clarksville by this time, and in 1853, the county commissioners authorized the investment of $16,000 in stock of the Little Rock & Fort Smith to ensure that it passed through the county and county seat. During the Civil War, Clarksville was occupied by first one army and then another. During the winter of 1861, many Confederate soldiers died of illness and were buried in unmarked graves in the Oakland Cemetery at Clarksville. Later, Union forces used the town as a rest stop, with the Cumberland Presbyterian Church used as a hospital. When the forces left, they burned the Cumberland Presbyterian Church, other churches, the jail, many of the local businesses, and many of the courthouse records. Several small battles were fought around Clarksville later in the war.

The recovery of Clarksville was helped by the arrival of the Little Rock & Fort Smith Railroad, which allowed local mines to ship their coal to market. The railroad also attracted many German and Austrian families who came to work in the mines, or to farm the nearby hills. The Cumberland Presbyterian Church opened their Arkansas Cumberland College at Clarksville on September 8, 1891, replacing Cane Hill College in Washington County. The college is considered to be the oldest institution of higher education in Arkansas (Cane Hill College opened in 1834), was the first to admit women (1875), and housed the state's first pharmacy school (1946). It became the College of the Ozarks in 1920, and in 1957, was the first predominately white university in Arkansas to integrate, and in 1959 the first to graduate an African-American. It became the University of the Ozarks in 1987. The university has slightly fewer than 1000 students, but they are from as many as 25 countries.

One challenge for Clarksville has been the routine floods of Spadra Creek, and a series of parks as part of a flood control project now reduce the flooding problems. While coal production has dropped greatly, natural gas has taken its place with the Clarksville Gas Field being the largest producing field in the state by the late 1920s. Poultry production and processing has also grown in importance. In 1920, the population of Clarksville reached 2127 and a number of businesses were listed as operating in the community. These included the Clarksville Basket Manufacturing Company, Clarksville Bottling & Manufacturing Company, Laser Grain Company, Clarksville Ice & Cold Storage Company, the A. B. Johnson grist mill, and the lumber mills of Arkansas-Indiana Lumber Company and Strong Lumber Company. Six coal companies were also listed as being based at Clarksville, including the Collier-Dunlap Coal Company, Fernwood Mining Company, Johnson & King Coal Company, North Spadra Coal Company, Sterling Anthracite Coal Company, and the Smokeless Coal Company.

The 1930s saw the growth in the peach industry as a way to meet the challenges of the Great Depression. The effort was so successful that starting in 1938, the town began hosting the annual Johnson County Peach Festival. Today, the population is almost 10,000, and the community features light manufacturing and food production. It also has a large number of restaurants and hotels due to its location near Interstate 40. Numerous retail stores are located around town to serve visitors, college students, and local residents. A full series of public schools are also located in town.

This sign marks the entrance to the manufacturing facility of the Greenville Tube Company, located for many years at the end of the Clarksville Branch.

444.4 END CLARKSVILLE BRANCH – The line from here to Spadra Junction followed along the west side of Spadra Creek, and was abandoned in 1964, leaving the track to the Greenville Tube plant south of Lucas Street. Greenville Tube was founded in 1950 and has a 110,000 square-foot manufacturing facility in Clarksville, which was moved here during the mid-1970s. The company manufactures precision welded tubing and pipe for energy and industrial applications. The company was acquired in 2006 by RathGibson and it still manufactures small-diameter stainless steel and nickel alloy seamless, welded and drawn tubing.

The track headed straight south-southwest from Clarksville to Spadra Junction. Along the three miles of track, the railroad once served at least six different coal mines. These were the Warner Dunlap Coal Company and the Rosson-Rowe Coal Company (both strip mines three miles north of Spadra), Johnson-King Coal Company (a shaft mine three miles north of

Spadra), the Abro Martin Coal Company and Johnson-Cunningham (strip mines two and one-half miles north of Spadra), and the Sterling Anthracite Coal Company (a shaft mine three miles south of Clarksville).

444.8 INTERSTATE 40 – The railroad was abandoned before Interstate 40 was built, and some articles have stated that the track was removed to prevent the need for a highway bridge over the seldom-used tracks. Some of the old grade is used as access roads for gas wells south of here.

445.6 BRIDGE NO. 279 – This was a 71-foot-long, 6-panel timber pile trestle. It was located close to the middle of a long stretch of tangent track between Milepost 443.9 and Milepost 447.0.

446.2 COAL MINES – In this general area were several coal mines during the early 1920s. These included the Sterling mine of the Ellington Coal Company, Mine #1 of the Fernwood Coal Company, and the Joe King mine of the King-Nichols-Lasser Coal Company.

446.6 WATER STATION – Until late 1943, there was a water station here with a pump house and water tower. The pump house (18' x 20') was actually the second one as it had replaced the earlier facility in 1919.

447.1 LITTLE SPADRA CREEK BRIDGE – Little Spadra Creek forms to the west of Clarksville and much of it is now simply a large lake created by backwaters from Lake Dardanelle. In 1963, this was one of a number of Missouri Pacific bridges that were replaced, this one with a new steel span, when Lake Dardanelle was created as part of the Arkansas River navigation system. Other bridges in this area were raised by as much as six feet to stay above the new water level.

This was Bridge No. 282. It was originally a 109-foot covered wooden Howe truss with five wooden pile bents. It was replaced by a 111-foot steel through pin-connected trestle that was replaced with a 113-foot through plate girder span in 1923-24.

This required that the bridge be listed as one with limited side clearances. At the compass-south end of the bridge, the railroad began to curve to the west to junction with the new mainline.

447.3 SPADRA JUNCTION – Also known as AA Junction, this was the north end of the Clarksville Subdivision, the original line of the railroad between Knoxville and Spadra. Because the new line was much shorter (6.72 miles versus 11.40 miles), the location of AA Junction was at Milepost 447.25 via Clarksville, and Milepost 442.57 on the new line. At AA Junction, the line from Clarksville connected into the siding at Spadra. To speed up operations, the north end of the siding was equipped with a spring switch. The switch was lined for the tracks to Clarksville since four daily passenger trains and the two local freight trains used the Clarksville Subdivision. Northbound trains on the new mainline could run through the spring switch without stopping. Only southbound trains using the new route were required to stop and line the switch, saving time for most trains. This changed as more traffic used the new mainline, and especially after the 1945 installation of ABS signals.

In 1919, a two-story frame section house was built at Spadra Junction. Housing both the foreman's family and members of the track gang, the building measured 14 feet by 28 feet with a wing measuring 12 feet by 14 feet.

For more information on the Spadra area, see Page 315.

Altus Branch
Hartman Junction to Ozark Junction

The Altus Branch was the original mainline between Hartman and Ozark. It was a route described as hilly, and when the St. Louis, Iron Mountain & Southern decided to improve the mainline between Little Rock and Fort Smith about 1902, it was a target for improvements. A new line opened in 1903 that went to the south and around a series of ridges, allowing the line to have fewer grades.

The new line was built from Hartman Junction (Milepost 449.43) to Ozark Junction (Milepost 461.70). The original route was 12.27 miles long while the new route was longer at 14.3 miles (the new-line Ozark Junction was at Milepost 463.93). Since the new line served few communities, the passenger trains and a local freight train continued to use the Altus District. Meanwhile, the second class freight trains used the new line, allowing them to haul more freight than on the old line.

By the 1930s, the coal mines along the old mainline were worked out. Little coal actually shipped from Coal Hill, and passenger traffic along the line was minimal. Since almost all of the local coal traffic could be served from the new line, Missouri Pacific applied to the Interstate Commerce Commission for permission to abandon the Altus District on July 3, 1935. The abandonment request stated that "the branch is constructed in a rather rough country, is laid with 75-pound re-lay rail, and is ballasted mostly with cinders or mine waste of various kinds; that there are 209 feet of wooden stringers on masonry abutments, 152 feet of untreated trestles, and one 44-foot deck girder bridge over Pond Creek; that the maximum grade is 2 percent, and there are grades of about 1.5 percent in both directions into Altus." Permission was granted on February 24, 1936, and the last passenger train operated over the line on May 15, 1936. The line was abandoned later that year. The mileposts shown are those that were used when the line was abandoned.

449.4 HARTMAN JUNCTION – Hartman Junction was located immediately west of the depot at Hartman, which explains why there was an agent here for many years. The original route built by the Little Rock & Fort Smith passed through Coal Hill and Altus, traveling over several ridges that required stiff grades on the railroad, a line that was generally called a hilly route. When completed, the new line between Hartman Junction and Ozark Junction became the mainline, hosting most of the freight trains. The original route via Coal Hill and Altus became the Altus District or Altus Branch. This route handled local service and some passenger trains until it was abandoned in 1936. Details about the new route that replaced the Altus District can be found starting on Page 337.

While the new route headed slightly to the southwest at Hartman Junction, the original route curved westward towards Coal Hill. Much of this route can still be found as it winds through a series of small farms. Parts of the route are still used as private farm roads, such as where the railroad once crossed Styles Road a short distance south of U.S. Highway 64. The railroad then came into Coal Hill from the east on a right-of-way south of Alabama Street.

Besides a curvy route, the railroad also had to climb its way to Coal Hill. The elevation of the top of rail at Hartman was 370 feet. At Milepost 451 it had climbed to 422 feet, 467 feet at Milepost 452, and then 471 feet at the Coal Hill station. That was a 100-foot climb in just 3 miles.

450.3 SPUR TRACK – Until 1922, there was a spur track that headed towards the northeast. A number of small coal mines once operated in this area.

452.4 COAL HILL BRANCH JUNCTION – This is the location where the Coal Hill Branch headed to the southwest to Alix. This branch was the original rail line that served the coal mines south of Coal Hill, and was expanded several times to serve new facilities. More details on this branch can be found on Page 517.

The Altus District, sometimes called the Altus Branch, was abandoned in September 1936. However, when the abandonment took place, the Coal Hill Branch remained. Because of this, the Altus District was also saved at Coal Hill starting 226 feet east of here, going all the way to 869 feet west of here. This basically saved a few yard tracks at the town of Coal Hill. After several years of little business on the Coal Hill Branch, the tracks in downtown Coal Hill were abandoned during June 1940.

Welcome to Coal Hill – once reportedly the busiest station on the Little Rock & Fort Smith Railway.

A major challenge with describing the railroad at Coal Hill is that it was once three different small communities, with the original townsite located at the west end of the general area. Each of these communities had their own streets that often used the same names. For example, during the 1930s, the switch for the Coal Hill Branch was located one block west of Second Street, now Seventh Street, which was about three blocks east of the Coal Hill depot. Another major change is Arkansas Street, which once ran north-south on the west end of the community, but now runs east-west on the south side of downtown. Eventually, the three small communities merged into the modern Coal Hill and the streets were renamed and renumbered to eliminate duplication. With the changes, the area where Coal Hill Branch Junction once was is now about Seventh Street.

452.6 COAL HILL (C) – Legend has it that at one time, Coal Hill furnished more business on the LR&FS than any other station due to the coal mines to the south. The town actually started due to the discovery of coal on several farms in the area. A study of the region stated that the coal was found in "a four-foot seam of most excellent quality, either for steam or domestic purposes." A second story about the community states that it was unofficially the largest incorporated city in Johnson County during the late nineteenth century. A third story is true. In 1888, officials from the State of Arkansas investigated the mistreatment of convict labor employed in the mines. At the time, prison labor could be rented to private businesses. While the practice continued for several more decades, tighter regulations from the investigation started the process to end the practice.

The Coal Hill area was settled by the mid-1800s, but it wasn't organized until about 1876 after the railroad was built. The first name used for the community was apparently Whalen's Switch, a name taken from a switch for a track that went into a coal mine. Few explanations about the name Whalen are found, but there was a Whalen Farm near here that the railroad crossed. The coal mine was reportedly operated by the Stewells, and a small worker community formed nearby. After a saloon and a few other stores opened, the town grew and soon developed a reputation as being a wild west community with gambling, gun-fighters, drunken fights, murders, and robberies.

In 1876, an application for a post office was filed. The name Whalen's Switch was rejected by the community as not being professional enough. The name Eureka was suggested but rejected because of the nearby Eureka Springs. The name Moseville was suggested next, designed to honor Mose Butts, an early settler who had surveyed a six-block, ninety-six-lot townsite on

September 26, 1876. Butts turned down the honor and instead suggest Coal Hill, which was accepted. With more coal mines opening, the railroad was soon lined with saloons, hotels and stores. On January 22, 1880, Coal Hill was incorporated and its population was recorded as being 200 in the census that year.

Schools began to open and the Masons arrived, sharing the second school building erected. Coal Hill had problems with their school buildings as several burned, and classes were even held in a saloon until a new school could be built. Soon, Coal Hill was the center of a 170,000-acre coal basin, and other coal towns began to be built around new mines. The Arkansas Improvement Company acquired area land in 1884 and began developing housing. The railroad began to sell their land grant properties, including 500 lots near Coal Hill. In 1887, a brochure stated that Coal Hill had a "a bright future if the proper capital and ability are devoted to the development of its rich natural advantages."

The railroad built branch lines to serve the mines developing in the area. In 1884, a two-and-one-half-mile spur line was built to the Ouita Coal Company mines, leading to the creation of the Coal Hill Branch to the Denning area. The Ouita Coal Company was a modern operation which used cutting machinery in an attempt to compete in the Mississippi Valley market, and quickly became the largest operation in the area. Other operations like the Blue Goose Mine of the Douglas & Son Coal Company also operated in the area. In 1887, Coal Hill shipped 45,998 tons of coal, reportedly ten times as much coal as the rest of the state. In 1888, 67,963 tons were shipped. In 1891, it was estimated that 150,000 tons of coal were shipped on the Little Rock & Fort Smith from Coal Hill. Some reports stated that in just ten years, approximately 47 million tons of coal had been shipped from the entire Coal Hill mining basin. To handle the coal, as many as ten trains occupied the local rail yard at Coal Hill.

There was a record of 1341 residents at Coal Hill in 1900, but the population began to drop as coal mining started to decline or turn to strip mining. In 1913, the community featured six general merchandise stores, two wagon shops, two farm implement shops, two druggists, one bank, one restaurant, one hay dealer, one lumber mill and wholesaler, one movie theater, and two hotels. Also at Coal Hill was the railroad's land office, which sold "timber, coal, and farm lands" in the area.

Reportedly, in 1917, the coal mines in the Coal Hill district produced 26,781 tons of coal per month with average payrolls of $150,000 per mine. However, most of the mines were only worked July to January when the coal was in higher demand. This allowed local farmers to earn extra income during the farming off-season.

During the early 1920s, there were twenty-three coal mines in the county, but it was down to eight less than ten years later. Despite this, Coal Hill was still the second-largest town in Johnson County. Farming, especially fruit and berry production, began to replace the coal industry as the population dropped to a low of 704 in 1960. Over the past 30 years, Coal Hill has begun to grow again, but more as a community that provides a rural style of living. The natural gas industry has grown in the area, and several dozen businesses are now in the town. The Johnson County Westside School complex is located on the northeast side of town. The current population is about 1000 residents.

The Iron Mountain at Coal Hill

The railroad at Coal Hill developed as soon as it arrived due to the coal in the area. In 1885, a track was built to the southwest that eventually became the Coal Hill Branch to Denning. A track scale was located at Coal Hill to weigh coal cars, and other tracks served a cotton gin and cotton dealer, plus several lumber dealers who provided materials for the mines and the construction of homes and barns. A 40-car siding was needed because Coal Hill was the highest point on this part of the railroad, requiring helpers or the doubling of trains. A mail crane also stood near the depot.

With access to cheap coal, the Little Rock & Fort Smith changed from burning wood in its steam locomotives to burning the west Arkansas coal on February 1, 1884. In 1895, a coaling station was built at Coal Hill at a cost of $3,307.08.

During the late 1800s, Coal Hill was a regular stop for passenger trains. These trains generally stopped for 15 to 20 minutes so that passengers could eat at the Central Hotel, located across the street from the depot. Later, when the Coal Hill Branch made the town a busy terminal, the hotel became a favorite eating and rooming house for railroad employees. The depot in 1907 featured a daytime telegraph office and there was a mail crane nearby. There was also a section tool house at Coal Hill.

In January 1910, the Coal Hill depot burned and was quickly replaced by a boxcar. Because of the volume of business, the St. Louis, Iron Mountain & Southern immediately began making plans for a new depot. However, no construction had taken place by an August 16, 1910, hearing of the Arkansas Railroad Commission where the railroad was ordered to build the new structure. At the meeting, the railroad displayed plans for an 86-foot by 26-foot wooden depot. The new depot opened in October and cost $2350. It was located on the north side of the mainline, which ran down the middle of Railroad Street, which is essentially Alabama Street today. During the 1920s, the depot featured a ticket and freight agency (carloads and less). A 1932-1933 survey stated that the elevation of the "top of rail opposite the Missouri Pacific Railroad station" was 470.8 feet.

Coal wasn't the only freight shipped from Coal Hill. On the south side of the mainline and across from the depot was a cotton platform. The platform remained after the Altus Branch was abandoned, but it was finally removed in March 1939. The depot was removed during May 1940.

In 1936, the Altus District was abandoned, but Coal Hill still had rail service due to the Coal Hill Branch from Denning Yard. However, the coal business was mostly on the south end of the line and the branch was retired and abandoned in 1940.

Little remains of the former Little Rock & Fort Smith at Coal Hill except for the old grade and a few culverts like this one.

This old grade, located on the south side of today's Alabama Street, marks the location of the old Coal Hill rail yard.

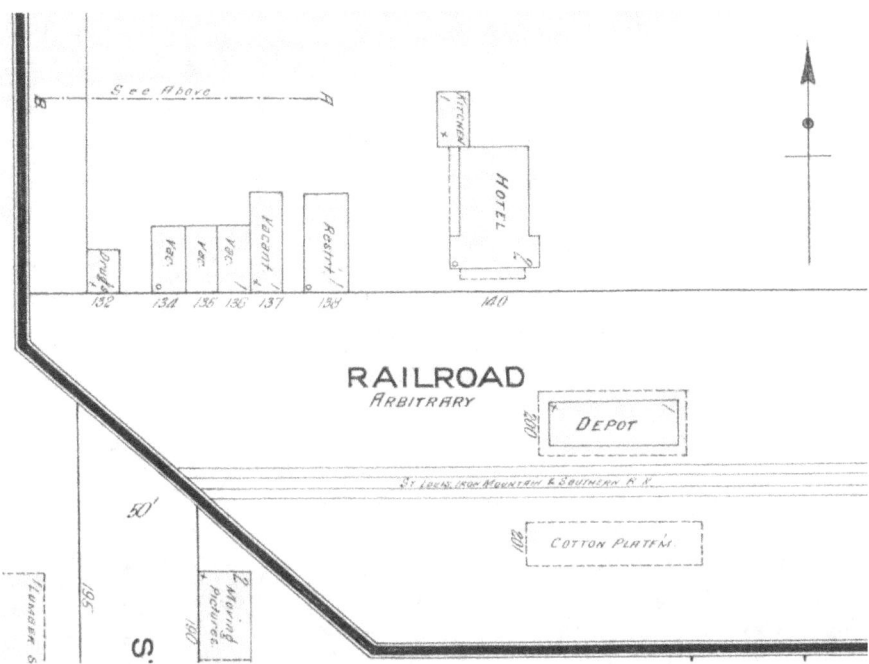

This Sanborn map from August 1913 shows the depot at Coal Hill, located on the north side of the mainline and siding. A cotton platform was located to the south across the tracks. Across the street to the north was a hotel (Taylor Hill Hotel), convenient for traveling coal buyers. *Sanborn Fire Insurance Map from Coal Hill, Johnson County, Arkansas. Sanborn Map Company, Aug, 1913.* Map. Retrieved from the Library of Congress, https://www.loc.gov/item/sanborn00220_001/.

The Taylor Hill Hotel

None of the railroad remains at Coal Hill except for a few grades and culverts. However, one landmark from the days of the railroad still stands – the Taylor Hill Hotel at 409 Alabama Street. This hotel was built sometime between 1884 and 1890, stands facing south, and was located directly across the street from the railroad depot. The structure is a two-story wood-frame building with a gabled roof and weatherboard siding. A two-story ell extends to the rear, giving the building a T shape. A two-story porch extends across much of the front, supported by square columns. The building has a mixture of simple Greek Revival and Folk Victorian details. While the actual date of construction is not known, or the likely first owner, Taylor Hill was the owner and proprietor from the late 1890s until his death on May 13, 1913. The hotel was reportedly the finest in town and was used by many business travelers while in Coal Hill. By the early 1900s, it was one of only two hotels in town.

In 1950, there was no longer the need for a hotel at Coal Hill and the business closed. The structure was converted to a private residence. The Taylor Hill Hotel still stands, and significant repairs were taking place in 2025. The building is often described simply as the yellow house, and was listed on the National Register of Historic Places in 2008. It is the only remaining example of a hotel in Coal Hill.

The Taylor Hill Hotel is an important landmark at Coal Hill. The former LR&FS depot once stood across the street from the old hotel.

453.4 COMMUNITY – A number of early maps show a small community here, but a name is seldom assigned to the location. Some federal government maps from as late as the 1950s show this to be Alix.

454.8 COUNTY LINE – Johnson County, located to the east, is the site of most of the coal mining in Arkansas. The county was created from parts of Pope County on November 16, 1833. Like most of the counties along the railroad, the southern half is in the Arkansas River Valley while the northern part is in the Ozark Mountains. This county was once located in the Cherokee lands, and one of three factories (trading posts) was located at Spadra Bayou, near today's county seat of Clarksville. In 1840, the county's population was 3433. Some coal was shipped on the Arkansas River, but with the construction of the railroad, large volumes began to be mined. Almost 20 different mines operated in the county at the peak of coal mining. Timber, cotton, fruit (apples, pears, and peaches), poultry, and natural gas all are major sources of business in the county. In particular, the Missouri Pacific Railroad heavily promoted the Johnson County peaches across the country.

The population temporarily peaked in 1920 with the county having 21,062 residents. With the end of manual labor in farming, coal mining and timber production, the population dropped to 12,421 in the 1960 census. Since then, retail and light manufacturing have moved to the county. A Walmart Distribution Center has brought fame as being the first Walmart grocery distribution center in the nation, and it has been awarded the Walmart "DC Grocery of the Year" award for four straight years. Since 1938, Johnson County has hosted an annual Peach Festival, and outdoor activities have brought many visitors to the county. Even the notorious bandit Bill Doolin, the founder of the Wild Bunch, is an attraction as he was born in Johnson County in 1858. The population in the 2020 census was 25,749.

To the west is **Franklin County**, created on December 19, 1837, from part of Crawford County. Franklin County covers mostly very rural and rugged country on both sides of the Arkansas River, each with its own county seat – Ozark north of the river and Charleston to the south. When created, the county was named for Benjamin Franklin, and the population was shown to be 2665 in 1840. Forestry, mining (coal, clay, iron, shale and other minerals) and farming have traditionally been the largest economic activities, especially after Swiss-German immigrants moved to the area, settling in the mountains that reminded them of home. Wine grapes soon became a major crop grown and were shipped out on the railroad for decades. The first oil strike in Arkansas happened in Franklin County and natural gas is still produced. Poultry has become a major activity, and the wine industry and its annual Winefest makes the county a major tourist attraction. One interesting feature about the county is that because of the wine, the north part of the county is "wet" and alcohol is sold almost everywhere. Meanwhile, south of the Arkansas River the county is "dry" with no alcohol sales. The current population is 17,097 and the county is still very rural.

457.6 SOUTH SWITCH ALTUS – This was once the south switch of the siding at Altus, located railroad-west of the main track. There was also a short spur track off of the siding that was built in 1923, and then extended in 1926. The north switch of the siding was located at the Milepost 458 sign.

458.0 ALTUS (G) – Altus was the highest point on the original railroad line between Fort Smith and Little Rock. The Latin word for high is often stated to be altus, and thus the name was given to this location. In July 1875, Altus was the temporary end of the railroad. The railroad bragged that the first carload of wheat ever shipped from Franklin County was moved for "Messrs. Williamson and Harmon." The movements became routine, and in September it was reported that "Six car loads of wheat shipped at Altus yesterday for Little Rock, three hundred bushels per car." Lumber (Tom Ross mill) and coal (Altus Black Coal Company, Blanscet Coal Company, B. H. S. Coal Company, and Liberty Coal Company) were also shipped over the railroad over the next fifty years.

The first depot at what was called Altus was actually located about a quarter-mile to the south of where the last station was located. It moved to the north when Uriah J. Nichols established the Altus townsite, creating lots that were offered to the railroad on an alternating basis. The plan also included a 300-foot by 300-foot depot square surrounded by four streets. The new board and batten depot was supported by a board and batten freight house across the tracks. There was also a fruit (especially grapes) and cotton platform with shelter nearby, and a stock pen (31' x 48') that could hold two carloads of livestock. A 30-

car siding passed through the town at the depot. In 1907, the St. Louis, Iron Mountain & Southern showed that there was a daytime telegraph office at Altus and a mail crane. There was also a tool house and oil house for the local track forces.

South of the current Altus depot and located at the northwest corner of the intersection of Franklin and Main was reportedly a water supply well for the railroad. The history of the well is poorly documented, but legend states that the well was dug sometime during the 1870s or 1880s for the railroad, and was also used to provide "water for the horses and mules used for hauling cotton from the ferry on the Arkansas River to the railroad for shipment." Sometime about 1920, the well was capped and a concrete and wood octagonal gazebo was built on top of it. The gazebo now sits at the southeast corner of the Altus City Park. It was listed on the National Register of Historic Places on September 12, 1996.

In the 1921 Arkansas General Assembly, a bill entitled "An Act to require Missouri Pacific Railroad Company to build, erect and maintain a depot at Altus, Arkansas, and for other purposes" was presented and voted upon. At the time, residents of Altus felt that a larger and more modern depot was needed at Altus, much like those built at other area communities. During the early 1920s (dates cited include 1920, 1921 and 1924), a new single-story wood frame structure depot, finished in stucco, was built. The new depot handled both passengers and local freight, and has been described as being "largely devoid of significant exterior detail, relying upon the broad, spreading eaves and the rough texture of the stucco finish on the exterior to lend it a somewhat Mediterranean appearance that was common to the depots of this railroad line."

This gazebo at Altus reportedly covers the original railroad well.

Missouri Pacific records use a date of September 1924 for the opening of the new depot. This is supported by a 1923 Arkansas Railroad Commission report on a hearing about building the structure. The depot was later extended 41 feet, and the platform was extended also. About the time the new station was built, the freight house was moved. In 1925, the Altus depot was shown to be a coupon ticket station, capable of selling interline tickets. Besides the ticket agency, there was a freight agency for carload volumes and less. During the early 1930s, a survey reported that the top of the rail opposite the Altus station was at an elevation of 537.7 feet. The last passenger train passed through Altus on May 15, 1936, and the rail line was abandoned.

Even after the Altus Branch was abandoned in 1936, the depot remained. It was finally sold in June 1947 and acquired by the City of Altus, which used the building as a community center, with some small alterations. With the tracks abandoned, the depot became a fixture next to U.S. Highway 64 on the north side of Altus City Park, located between Franklin and Hendrix streets. Today, the old depot is used as a liquor store and was placed on the National Register of Historic Places on July 8, 1992.

Although the tracks through Altus were abandoned in 1936, the railroad depot still exists, used as a liquor store.

Heading west, the old grade followed U.S. 64 for a short distance before turning to the northwest on a right-of-way now used by Breezeway Lane. At the Nichols Cemetery, the route becomes a tree-lined grade for a short distance before becoming Shady Lane. Shady Lane, County Road 540, uses the grade to the southeast side of Reed Mountain. Lock and Dam Road then uses the grade to near Ozark Junction at Milepost 461.7. Along these almost four miles of track, the railroad grade drops approximately 150 feet back down to the Arkansas River.

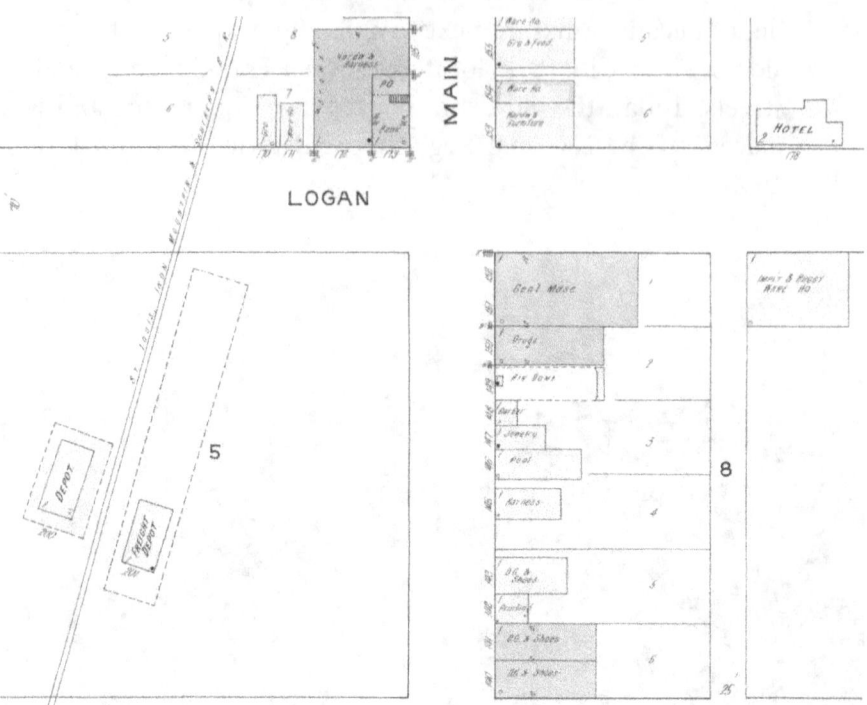

In 1913, the Altus passenger depot was to the north of the tracks, and the freight house was located to the south. At the time, they were located between Logan (today's Franklin) and Ozark (today's Hendrix) streets. *Sanborn Fire Insurance Map from Altus, Franklin County, Arkansas. Sanborn Map Company, Aug, 1913.* Map. Retrieved from the Library of Congress, https://www.loc.gov/item/sanborn00190_001/.

The City of Altus

As stated by numerous sources, the community of Altus was founded after the Little Rock & Fort Smith Railroad laid its tracks through the hills to the north of the Arkansas River in the 1870s. Some reports state that the station was originally known as Summit. Like other communities in the area, the first settlers were early traders and farmers located along the Arkansas River. For example, Jean Baptiste Dardenne claimed almost 550 acres in the area in June 1814. The first settlers often traded with the Osage and other tribes that moved through the area. In 1818, Cherokees moved into the area and many Europeans were removed from the lands. However, in 1828, the Cherokees were moved from northwest Arkansas and white settlers returned to the region. When the railroad was built, it received large amounts of land through the area and then encouraged European immigrants, especially those from Germany, Austria and Switzerland, to settle here. Some of these new residents worked for the railroad, while others started farms and businesses. Many of the new settlers located on Pond Creek Mountain to the north of Altus, and began growing grapes. These grapes were used to make wine, and were also sold in bulk to fruit and vegetable dealers.

With the initial construction of a railroad depot near Altus, and then the creation of a small townsite by Uriah J. Nichols, a post office opened using the name Altus on July 6, 1875. By this time, Nichols and several others had opened stores at Altus, and a grist mill and cotton gin were operating by the mid-1880s. The population of Altus was shown to be 224 in the 1880 census. This was when a significant number of German and Swiss immigrants started arriving at Altus, and the start of the vineyard and wine-making industry in the area, generally credited to families like Wiederkehr and Post. Even today, this is still the center of the wine industry in Arkansas.

Altus was incorporated on August 31, 1888. Beside the local farming and grape industries, coal and education were also helping Altus to grow. On October 31, 1876, the Central Institute was founded at Altus by Methodist Minister Isham L. Burrow, and then renamed Central Collegiate Institute in 1881. The Institute included a main school building and several boarding houses. The school was acquired by three conferences of the Methodist Episcopal Church, South, in 1884. In 1889, the school was renamed Hendrix College and then was moved to Conway, Arkansas, in 1890. Reverend Burrow retained the property at Altus and opened the Hiram & Lydia College during the fall of 1890. In 1906, the college closed and the school buildings were sold to the Altus School District, and the boarding houses to several local residents.

Coal was located to the south of Altus, often known as the low coal field. Many miners lived in or around Altus, and Local 2121 of the United Mine Workers was based here. The coal mines played out by World War II, but they are marked by the Altus Coal Miner's Memorial, located on the east side of Altus City Park. The memorial includes a statue of a coal miner, lunch bucket in hand, and five granite pillars with the names of hundreds of local coal miners.

The Altus Area Coal Miners Memorial is a noted monument found at Altus, located in the Altus City Park.

Hotels, theaters, general stores, grocery and meat stores, confectionary and drug stores, shoe and millinery stores, stationery and office supply stores, nurseries, and fruit dealerships, and an icehouse also opened and operated at Altus at the time. Schools and churches also were organized at Altus. One of these churches was started by Father Beatus Maria Ziswyler, who organized the Altus Catholic Church on November 21, 1879. The church is sometimes known as Our Lady of Perpetual Help, but more properly Our Lady, Help of Christians. It is more commonly known as St. Mary's Catholic Church. A native stone church building was erected north of town on Pond Creek Mountain, dedicated on September 2, 1902. The church is visited by thousands of tourists yearly and was placed on the National Register of Historic Places on May 3, 1976.

The population of Altus peaked in the 1920 census with 709 residents. A tornado (March 18, 1918) and a fire (July 10, 1922) destroyed much of the business community, but the German-American Bank and its two-story red brick masonry structure survived, and it was listed on the National Register of Historic Places on September 13, 1990. The building is now the home of the Altus Heritage House Museum. Several new brick buildings were built over the next few years. During the late 1920s, J. H. Jacobson, a Chicago millionaire, bought large amounts of land on Pond Creek Mountain and began building summer cabins for his wealthy friends and business associates. However, the Great Depression ruined Jacobson and stopped most of the community's improvements. The population of Altus started to drop and reached a low of 392 in 1960. With the continued growth in the nearby wine industry, the population grew back to 817 in the 2000 census. It has dropped since then to the 665 residents reported in the 2020 census. In 2004, the Altus-Denning School District closed and was consolidated with the Ozark School District.

The German-American Bank Building at Altus, located on the city square south of the depot, now houses the Altus Heritage House Museum.

The annual Altus Grape Festival (Grapefest), the Wiederkehr Village Weinfest, and the many Oktoberfest events make Altus a busy town during parts of the year. Visitors are still coming to Altus because of the 2001 show *The Simple Life*, which covered the adventures of Paris Hilton and Nicole Richie as they spent time on a local farm and tried to handle regular jobs in the community. Other famous people from Altus include Janice Holt Giles, an author of historical fiction, and Charles "Boss" Schmidt, a miner who played six seasons with the Detroit Tigers (1906 to 1911) and then returned to Altus as a coal miner before becoming a coach and manager in the minor leagues.

459.0 DOUBLING SPUR – A mile west of Altus was a track that was used by trains that needed to double the hill between Ozark and Altus. The station was listed for several decades, but no siding was noted. However, track maps showed a track to the south (railroad-west) that was shown to handle prepaid freight, carload in and out, in 1925. The track was removed in May 1931.

The elevation of the top of the rail at Doubling Spur was 509.9 feet in 1933. Heading north, the elevation at Milepost 460 was 454.7 feet. The grade averaged more than one percent for trains climbing towards Altus.

The old grade is now used as Breezeway Lane from U.S. Highway 64 northward to near here, marked by Nichols Cemetery. The grade is used as a driveway for a short distance, and then is simply a fill across a pasture.

Nichols Cemetery stands on the east side of the old LR&FS grade near where Doubling Spur once was.

459.6 POND CREEK BRIDGE – Immediately east of West Creek Road, County Road 93, a high fill was once used to cross Pond Creek and a low pasture. Over Pond Creek, the railroad had a 44-foot deck plate girder bridge, officially known as Bridge #330. This short distance between Breezeway Lane and Shady Lane is the only part of the Altus District grade north of Altus not currently used as a road. This is because the deck plate girder span was removed and there is now a deep hole in this fill. The large stone headwalls also still stand.

459.7 WEST CREEK ROAD – The grade crosses this road, which is also County Road 93. Heading west, the old railroad grade is now Shady Lane, County Road 540.

This large stone headwall is about all that remains of the bridge that once crossed Pond Creek.

North of West Creek Road, the former LR&FS grade is now Shady Lane.

460.4 STONE ARCH – A large stone arch or culvert can be found under Shady Lane at this location. The stone arch is only ten feet long, but is 59 feet high. The culvert has been updated with concrete headwalls and wings. To the east, the railroad fill and stone arch have created a small lake.

461.3 BRIDGE #337 – Immediately south of the grade crossing to reach Lock & Dam 12, also known as Ozark-Jetta Taylor Lock & Dam, are the stone remains of Bridge #337. This bridge consisted of masonry headwalls, with the track set on 11-foot-long wooden stringers. A number of similar structures existed through here to allow water to flow off of Reed Mountain and west to the Arkansas River.

Some of the stone headwall of Bridge #337 still remains near the tracks at Lock & Dam 12 near Ozark. The original grade can also be found alongside the road to the south of the bridge.

461.4 BRIDGE #338 – The masonry remains of this bridge are located a short distance north of the grade crossing for Lock & Dam 12. This bridge used 14-foot-long wooden stringers. The masonry structure is still used as part of the current culvert.

The remains of Bridge #338 can still be found near the road entrance to Lock & Dam 12 near Ozark.

461.7 OZARK JUNCTION – This was the north junction between the original mainline through Coal Hill and Altus, and the new rail line that was built through Denning. Lock and Dam Road from Shady Lane is the old railroad grade and the junction was a short distance north of the lock and dam on the Arkansas River. The mainline milepost here is 463.93 and details about the junction and mainline can be found on Page 363.

Coal Hill Branch
Coal Hill to Denning

The area to the south of Coal Hill and Altus was identified to have beds of high-grade semi-anthracite coal. Some drift, shaft and open pit mines opened alongside the original Little Rock & Fort Smith route, but most of the coal lands were to the south. The LR&FS couldn't build in that direction as its charter did not provide such a branchline. Therefore, on December 26, 1884, the Coal Hill Branch of the Little Rock & Fort Smith Railway was chartered in Arkansas. The road had a capital stock of $10,000, and it was announced that the new railroad would build from Coal Hill to Allister's coal mine. On January 12, 1885, the Coal Hill Branch charter was sold to the Little Rock & Fort Smith, which announced plans to build a coal branch southwest from Coal Hill.

The valuation report of Missouri Pacific, created by the Interstate Commerce Commission in 1932-33, provided a brief description of the Coal Hill Branch of the Little Rock & Fort Smith Railway, a "predecessor of the Little Rock and Fort Smith Railway." It stated that the "company was organized by officials of The Little Rock and Fort Smith Railway for the purpose of constructing about 3 miles of road extending from Coal Hill to the Allister Coal Mine, Ark. It was in existence less than a month and to the date of its sale, January 12, 1885, had constructed no property."

In July 1885, there was an announcement that the Coal Hill Branch would build the line to the coal fields of Logan and Sebastian counties. This plan included a bridge across the Arkansas River (never built), and actual construction on the Coal Hill Branch started on July 9, 1885. In 1887, *Poor's Manual* reported that the Coal Hill Branch was 2.0 miles long, and other reports stated that it was built with 56-pound rail. Besides the Allister coal mine, the Douglas & Son Coal Company had their Blue Goose Mine (shaft mine) located on the Coal Hill Branch, one and one-quarter miles southwest of Coal Hill. In 1892, the St. Louis, Iron Mountain & Southern reported that it had leased the Coal Hill Branch, 2.66 miles from Coal Hill to Lloyd's (end of track).

At the time, Lloyds, or Lloyd's, was a small community built around a coal mine located a short distance west of the Johnson-Franklin county line. The railroad reported that the track actually extended 242 feet west of the mine.

A geology report about the Arkansas coal fields included information about the Coal Hill field. It stated that the Coal Hill field, located 15 miles west of the Spadra field, "produce a coal from a four-foot seam of most excellent quality, either for steam or domestic purposes. A branch road has been built from Coal Hill to the mines of the Ouita Coal Company, where coal cutting machinery has been introduced, and it is hoped that this will enable these coals to be marketed in the Mississippi Valley in competition with Pittsburgh and other coals."

In January 1893, the stockholders of the Little Rock & Fort Smith Railway met to authorize the construction of a three-mile extension of the Coal Hill Branch. Approval was received and the railroad extended the line 2.67 miles, and built 1.5 miles of sidings, to reach a new coal mine in Franklin County. This area was several miles east of the community of Denning. Within a few years, the Joe Hoeing Coal Company and their slope mile, located one and three-quarter miles northeast of Alix, was advertising that they had railroad connections with the Iron Mountain's Coal Hill Branch. Over the next several years, the branch was extended westward to serve more coal mines, passing through Alix and reaching the mining community of Denning.

In 1903, approximately 1.21 miles of the very end of the Coal Hill Branch became part of the new mainline when a grade reduction program included a new line to the south of the original Altus line. The line connected with the Coal Hill Branch near Alix and used the branch's track to near Denning, where the new line was built westward towards Ozark. Most freight service moved to this new route and the old mainline became the Altus District. This also impacted the Coal Hill Branch as coal now moved south to the new Denning Yard (Alix) instead of north to Coal Hill.

In a 1917 report by the Missouri Pacific Railroad Company, the company included the Coal Hill Branch in its listing of spurs and branches. It described the line as being "from a point near Coal Hill, in the County of Johnson, Arkansas, through the Counties of Johnson and Franklin, Arkansas, to a connection with Double Track Spur, about 9.24 miles southeast of Ozark Junction, in said County of Franklin, about 4.18 miles." At the time, the State of Arkansas still showed that the Coal Hill Branch of the Little Rock & Fort Smith Railway was an incorporated organization. On April 23, 1923, the line's incorporation was revoked by order of Arkansas Governor Thomas McRae.

In 1936, the Altus District was abandoned, leaving the Coal Hill Branch to serve the carload freight business at Coal Hill, with Coal Hill functioning as a non-agency station. However, the Missouri Pacific was also interested in abandoning most of the Coal Branch. During 1934-1938, no regular freight service was provided on the line, with a switch engine being operated from Alix (Denning Yard) as required. Because of this, the entire Coal Hill branch was operated under yard limit rules.

As reported in an Interstate Commerce Commission hearing, "no freight was handled on the line in 1939, and only 59 carloads (36 of which were coal) were handled in the four preceding years, 1934-1938." The peak revenue during this time was apparently $1358 in 1935, with only $475 in 1938. The line also still had its original 56-pound rail which needed replacing. On January 2, 1940, Missouri Pacific applied for permission to abandon the Coal Hill Branch. It was received and became effective on April 19, 1940. The track was removed by the end of the year.

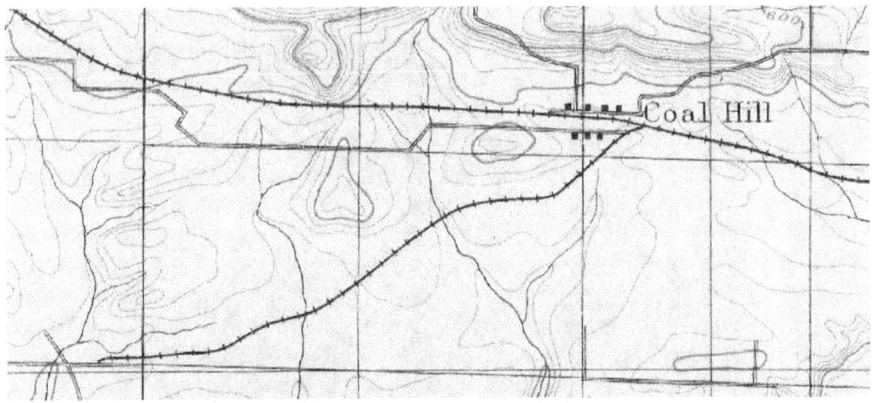

This topographic map from 1887 shows the Coal Hill Branch as it existed at that time, ending about the current location of Alix, Arkansas. *N.E. Part of Magazine Mountain (AR) Quadrangle*, 1887. U.S. Geological Survey, Geological Survey of Arkansas.

0.0   **COAL HILL BRANCH JUNCTION** – Some timetables showed this location to be simply Junction, but most referred to it as Coal Hill or Coal Hill Branch Junction. This was the origin of the Coal Hill Branch. During the 1930s, the switch for the Coal Hill Branch was located one block west of Second Street, Later, many of the streets were renamed and the area where Coal Hill Branch Junction once was is now about Seventh Street. Details about Coal Hill can be found on Page 494.

The Coal Hill Branch headed south along Fourth Street where there was a 41' x 82' stock pen on the east side of the tracks at Milepost 0.15. There was a spur track to the east, located south of the stock pen (Milepost 0.4). The branch line then curved to the southwest near Arkansas Street. It then crossed Main (Milepost 0.5) and Bell (Milepost 0.6) streets before passing through the intersection of West Railroad and Quaile streets. There were several tracks in this area including a track to the west that ran alongside the Coal Hill Branch northward (Milepost 0.7) and a private track to the east (Milepost 0.9).

Heading towards Denning Yard, much of the old grade is now a thin line of woods, generally passing through pasture and hay fields. The grade then turns to the west, running a short distance north of Nortontown Road, County Road 539.

The Coal Hill Branch once passed through the intersection of Railroad and Quail streets, heading northeast to southwest. The short street to the southwest uses the grade of the old branchline.

1.3 **BLUE GOOSE MINE** – During the 1890s, the Douglas & Son Coal Company had their Blue Goose Mine, a shaft mine, located on the Coal Hill Branch here. In the June 30, 1924, *Annual Report of the State Inspector of Coal Mines – State of Arkansas*, the Douglas & Son Coal Company was shown to have their Mine #1 located just 1/4 mile south of Coal Hill on the Coal Hill Branch. The 90-foot-deep shaft mine employed about 15 workers and produced more than 3000 tons of coal in 1924. The Denning Branch Coal Company also had a mine 1/4 mile south of Coal Hill in 1924.

The mines in this area seemed to have been sold and traded among the many companies involved in the industry. In 1924, the Franklin Coal Company had a strip mine 1.5 miles southwest of Coal Hill, and the Hoeing Coal Company had their shaft mine #1 in the same area.

1.4 **PERSIMMON SWITCH** – This was the name given to a track and small community at this location. The persimmon tree, along with blackjack, white and red oak and hickory trees, were noted as growing along the hillsides in the region. The tree is known for its large orange-brown fleshy fruits that are edible after the first frost.

1.5 **FRANKLIN COAL** – To the east were several tracks that served the Franklin Coal Company, reportedly a strip mine. These tracks were extended and relocated several times while the mine was worked.

2.1 **SNODDY, KARR, AND DOUGLASS COAL COMPANY** – A track went to the east to serve this coal company.

2.5 **BRIDGE NO. 14** – When this branch was built, there were a number of small timber pile trestles installed over small streams. Many of them were later filled or shortened. At 81 feet long and consisting of six panels, this was one of the longest on the line. It crossed a small stream that flowed off of the hills to the north.

2.6   **COUNTY LINE** – By 1924, the Rafter Mine of the Western Coal Mining Company operated in this area, shipping 11,891 tons of coal (July 1923-June 1924) out on the railroad. The shipping point was actually shown to be in Johnson County.

Shady Brook Road is generally on the county line in this area. This is the line between Johnson and Franklin counties, the home of a large number of coal mines, which explains the initial construction of the Coal Hill Branch. In 1924, the *Annual Report of the State Inspector of Coal Mines – State of Arkansas* reported that there were 27 coal mines on the former Little Rock & Fort Smith in Johnson County, and 35 coal mines in Franklin County.

Johnson County, located to the east, was the site of most of the coal mining in Arkansas. The county was created from parts of Pope County on November 16, 1833. Like most of the counties along the railroad, the southern half is in the Arkansas River Valley while the northern part is in the Ozark Mountains. This county was once located in the Cherokee lands, and one of three factories (trading posts) was located at Spadra Bayou, near today's county seat of Clarksville. In 1840, the county's population was 3433. Some coal was shipped on the Arkansas River, but with the construction of the railroad, large volumes began to be mined. Almost 20 different mine companies operated in the county at the peak of coal mining. Timber, cotton, fruit (apples, pears, and peaches), poultry, and natural gas all were major sources of business in the county. In particular, the Missouri Pacific Railroad heavily promoted the Johnson County peaches across the country.

The population temporarily peaked in 1920 with the county having 21,062 residents. With the end of manual labor in farming, coal and timber production, the population dropped to 12,421 in the 1960 census. Since then, retail and light manufacturing have moved to the county, and even a Walmart Distribution Center has brought fame after it earned the "Grocery Distribution Center of the Year" award for three straight years. Since 1938, Johnson County has hosted an annual Peach Festival, and outdoor activities have brought many visitors to the county. Even the notorious bandit Bill Doolin, the founder of the Wild Bunch, is an attraction as he was born in Johnson County in 1858. The population in the 2020 census was 25,749.

To the west is **Franklin County**, created on December 19, 1837, from part of Crawford County. Franklin County covers mostly very rural and rugged country on both sides of the Arkansas River, each with its own county seat – Ozark north of the river and Charleston to the south. When created, the county was named for Benjamin Franklin, and the population was shown to be 2665 in 1840. Forestry, mining (coal, clay, iron, shale and other minerals) and farming have traditionally been the largest economic activities, especially after Swiss-German immigrants moved to the area, settling in the mountains that reminded them of home. Wine grapes soon became a major crop grown and were shipped out on the railroad for decades. The first oil strike in Arkansas happened in Franklin County and natural gas is still produced. Poultry has become a major activity, and the wine industry and its annual Winefest makes the county a major tourist attraction. One interesting feature about the county is that because of the wine, the north part of the county is "wet" and alcohol is sold almost everywhere. Meanwhile, south of the Arkansas River the county is "dry" with no alcohol sales. The current population is 17,097 and the county is still very rural.

2.6   **OUITA COAL MINES** – South of the intersection between Wandering Way (County Road 539) and Highgate Road was once a series of coal mines operated by the Ouita Coal Company, but owned by David and James Allister. The Allister brothers had once mined the area, but then leased their mines to the Ouita Coal Company for the term of twenty years on June 13, 1885. During this lease, the Little Rock & Fort Smith built their Coal Hill Branch across the Allister property, leading to legal challenges by the property owners. The complaint by David and James Allister was that the "line of railway recently built over the lands described in its complaint runs where our tipple stood when we were working what is known as the Free Labor Slope." The brothers stated that they had designed the tipple so that most coal moved downhill, allowing a mule to be used to fill the coal tipple. The case, *Little Rock & Fort Smith Railway Company* *v. Alister et al*, went to the Supreme Court of Arkansas for settlement, with an opinion delivered on February 8, 1896.

The trial provided some interesting information about the Coal Hill Branch and some of the mines that it served. In particular, two mines were owned by the Allister brothers. The Coal Hill Branch ran "about midway between the two slopes, leaving the Convict Slope in Johnson county, and the Free Slope in Franklin county, formerly so called, because the convicts were once worked in the Johnson county slope, while the Franklin county slope was worked by free labor." There were comments that when convict labor was no longer used in the Coal Hill mines, that the Ouita Coal Company stopped working both mines during the early 1890s.

Maps from the 1880s and 1890s show a town named Allister located a short distance west of the county line between Johnson and Franklin counties. However, no post office was ever assigned to the community and only a few coal spoil piles mark the location today.

2.7　**LLOYDS** – *Poor's Manual of Railroads of 1892* stated the Coal Hill Branch was constructed 2.66 miles southwest of Coal Hill to Lloyds, Arkansas. Lloyds was described as a small community built around a coal mine located a short distance west of the Johnson-Franklin county line. After the line was extended, a private track was built to the west at Milepost 2.8.

3.3　**BIG SIX COAL COMPANY** – In 1924, there were two mines in this area. The northernmost mine was the Dodson Mine of the Big Six Coal Company. This mine operated into the mid-1930s. To the south was the Sambo Mine of the Semi-Anthracite Coal Company.

Railroad documents showed a tipple and two tracks to the east used by the New Alix Coal Company. To help switch the facility, there was a siding on the west side of the mainline. These tracks were built in 1923 and were removed a decade later. They were then installed again in 1944 when a track was extended from Alix Yard to serve a new coal operation.

3.4   **ALIX WYE** – The improved 1903 mainline towards Fort Smith headed straight, while the line towards Little Rock curved to the southeast and became the south yard lead. When the Coal Hill Branch was abandoned in 1940, a short stub was left to allow locomotives to turn on the wye. Later, the stub track was extended during World War II to serve a coal mine. The west end of Nortontown Road uses part of this old grade.

Little remains of the Coal Hill Branch – abandoned in 1940. Some of the line near Alix was used during World War II to serve a local coal mine. This old grade can still be seen from Nortontown Road at Alix.

3.5   **BRIDGE NO. 17** – At 82 feet long, this 6-panel timber pile trestle was the longest bridge on the Coal Hill Branch.

3.7   **CROSSOVER** – A switch was once located here to allow trains to enter the yard from the Coal Hill Branch. The track was used often enough that a switchman shanty was located here, built from a carbody that measured 9 feet by 33 feet.

A report about the Coal Hill Branch stated that after additional branchline construction in 1893, the branch reached 3.87 miles from Coal Hill to serve coal mines east of Denning.

3.9   **OVERHEAD BRIDGE** – With the busy Alix Yard to the south, a highway bridge was built over all of the tracks. The main span consisted of a 134-foot-long steel Pratt truss set on timber bents. The north approach was 118 feet long and consisted of an eight-panel frame trestle and 30 feet of rubble. The south approach had the same 30 feet of rubble approach, plus 211 feet of frame trestle consisting of 13 panels. There were tell-tales 200 feet on either side of the bridge to warn anyone riding the tops of trains.

    There were other structures in this area that were used by the train crews and maintenance forces at Alix. One of these was a tool house located at Milepost 4.0.

4.2   **ALIX** – The Coal Hill Branch reached this location first. A small yard was built here, and then it was greatly expanded when the new mainline was built. After the new route was built, the Coal Hill Branch Connection at Denning Yard (Alix) was identified as being at Milepost 456.9. The railroad called this location Denning Yard, although Denning was almost two miles to the west. The locals called the town Alix. Details about Alix and Denning Yard can be found on Page 346.

    The grade of the Coal Hill Branch can still be found as it comes in from the east. Heading east on Northtown Road from Arkansas Highway 186, the railroad grade continues to the east where the roadway curves to the southeast. A set of livestock corrals mark the location, and a line of trees identify the route of the old Coal Hill Branch.

    When the new mainline was built through Denning Yard, the Coal Hill Branch officially connected to the Double Track Spur at the new terminal. In early 1912, the tracks were rearranged and there was a change of connections with the Double Track Spur and with the Main Line that added 0.31 miles of track to the branch. Eventually this location in Denning Yard became known as Coal Hill Branch Junction and Coal Hill was shown to be at the end of the line. By this time, almost all traffic from the branch moved to Denning Yard (Alix) instead of Coal Hill.

5.3 **DENNING** – This was shown to be the end of the branch in 1894 through 1902. Several coal mines were reported to be in the area just east of Denning. In 1892, the railroad purchased about 4000 acres of the Denning property, including coal and mining rights. This purchase provided room for tracks and allowed the railroad to support the growing coal mining industry.

With planning for the various line improvements, the railroad produced several reports on the route. Some of the terms seemed to have been incorrect. For example, even in 1902, this location was shown to be "End of Track, Lloyd's." The track between Alix and Denning was converted from being the Coal Hill Branch to the new mainline, built about 1903. Details about Denning can be found on Page 353.

Fort Smith Branch
Van Buren to Fort Smith

This route completed the line between Little Rock and Fort Smith, even though it originally used several transfer boats to cross the Arkansas River, and then the bridge of the Frisco Railroad. Initially, the railroad used a ferry to transfer passengers and freight across the Arkansas River to reach Fort Smith. The first service was from the end of track in Cherokee Territory, near what is today known as West Fort Smith, or Moffet. At the time, the Little Rock & Fort Smith Railway called the location Cherokee.

During late 1878, the Little Rock & Fort Smith announced that it was moving its Fort Smith ferry from Cherokee (Moffet) to Gatlin, a short distance west of Van Buren. As a part of the move, inclines were built on each side of the river for the transfer boat *N.D. Munson*. The railroad then built a rail line from the south shore of the Arkansas River into downtown Fort Smith. The newspaper *Fort Smith New Era* (February 5, 1879) reported on the news when it was all completed. "At 4 p.m. Thursday, the laying of the last rail of the Little Rock & Fort Smith Railway was completed, establishing the Fort Smith's first rail link." The first through movement was reportedly one passenger car and one baggage car. Several years later, the trains of the Frisco also began to use the transfer boat service.

Note the 1879 date for the establishment of a railroad into Fort Smith. This date conflicts some with the book and movie *True Grit*, an adventure story about a young girl undertaking a quest to avenge her father's murder. The route of the adventure is celebrated today as the True Grit Trail in Arkansas and Oklahoma. One issue with the story, which takes place in 1878, is the use of a train by Mattie Ross between Dardanelle, Arkansas, and Fort Smith. The train she would have ridden was the Little Rock & Fort Smith Railway, but the line into Fort Smith wasn't yet completed.

In 1886, the Fort Smith & Van Buren Bridge Company, a Frisco subsidiary, finished building their bridge across the Arkansas River. Trains of the Little Rock & Fort Smith quickly obtained trackage rights over the bridge and some Frisco trackage to reach their existing tracks to Fort Smith. It didn't take long for the tracks to be lined with new industries and even new communities.

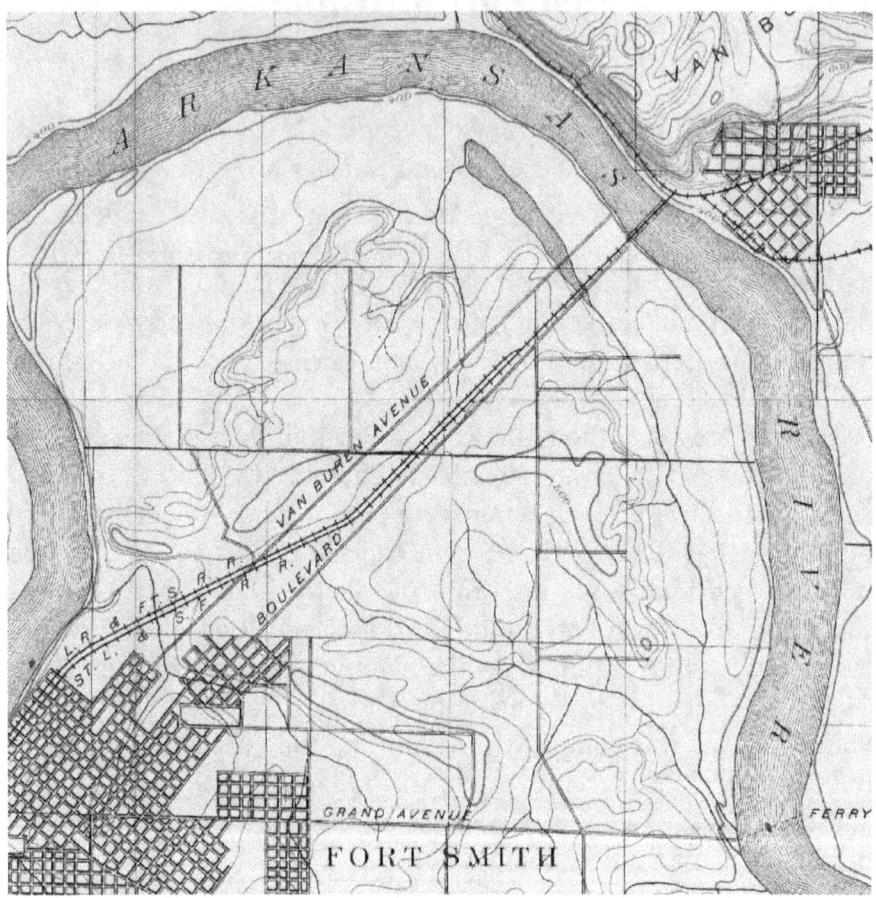

This topographic map from 1887 shows the Fort Smith Branch, a year after the Arkansas River bridge was built by the Fort Smith & Van Buren Bridge Company (St. Louis & San Francisco – Frisco). *Northwest Part of Fort Smith (AR) Quadrangle, 1887.* U.S. Geological Survey, Geological Survey of Arkansas.

Most of the LR&FS traffic moved to the new Iron Mountain-owned Helen Gould Bridge when it opened in 1891. This bridge was on the west side of downtown Fort Smith and crossed the Arkansas River near where the original Cherokee ferry once operated. The Interstate Commerce Commission described these routes in a 1929 report.

> *A branch line of applicant's railroad [Missouri Pacif-*
> *ic] extends from Greenwood Junction on the main line*
> *mentioned south through Fort Smith to Greenwood and*
> *another branch extends from Fort Smith northeastward*
> *to Van Buren. This branch, over which much of the traf-*
> *fic on applicant's line between Little Rock and Coffeyville*
> *passes, uses Frisco trackage for about 1 mile near Van*
> *Buren.*

As stated, some Missouri Pacific passenger and freight trains still used the Frisco's bridge until 1933 when Missouri Pacific moved all traffic to its own Helen Gould Bridge. This made the old Fort Smith Branch simply an industrial switching line. In 1970, the Corps of Engineers moved the Missouri Pacific trains back to the Frisco bridge and this line as part of the navigation project on the Arkansas River. This move allowed the Corps of Engineers to remove the Helen Gould Bridge, which restricted traffic in a series of curves on the river.

By the 1980s, Union Pacific called the route the Paris Branch, but stopped using the line a decade later and let the Arkansas & Missouri move any traffic to the Fort Smith Railroad, which had leased much of the Paris Branch in 1991. This means that Union Pacific trains almost never travel over the former Little Rock & Fort Smith Railway to downtown Fort Smith. The Fort Smith Railroad, which technically operates the line, uses it to reach several rail shippers. The Arkansas & Missouri Railroad operates over the line most weekdays to handle interchange traffic between the Fort Smith Railroad and Union Pacific.

It should be noted that over the years, the mileposts used on the Fort Smith Branch have changed several times. The ones used here are from recent Union Pacific track charts, but with older St. Louis, Iron Mountain & Southern mileposts also cited. Also, even though Missouri Pacific showed their mileposts in their employee timetables, the actual mileposts on the tracks owned by the Arkansas & Missouri are the ones assigned by the Frisco. All are shown in this route guide.

Fort Smith Railroad

The Little Rock & Fort Smith trackage from the Arkansas River Bridge to downtown Fort Smith is now operated by the Fort Smith Railroad. It also operates trackage to the southeast of town, and to the east to the Fort Chaffee area, for a total of almost 24 miles. When the railroad was created in 1991, it actually went further east to Paris, Arkansas, but that track was abandoned in 1995.

The Fort Smith Railroad was originally owned by Pioneer Railcorp, which leased the tracks on July 7, 1991. The railroad was known for its fleet of former Santa Fe Railroad EMD GP20 locomotives, plus power from other Pioneer operations. The railroad was sold to the Patriot Rail Company in August 2022. This company has begun to move some of their more modern locomotives to the property.

This sign on the railroad's office near Garrison Avenue, photographed in February 2025, shows that the Patriot Rail Company now controls the company.

502.5 VAN BUREN TRACKAGE RIGHTS BEGIN – This was the location where a loop track was built to the east of the LR&FS mainline that connected with the Frisco mainline near the diamond. This was shown to be the connection to the Paris Branch for many years. For the first several miles of the Paris Branch, trains operated via Frisco timetable instructions. This area has changed greatly over the years, and more details about the ST.L.-S.F. CROSSING area are available on Page 448.

Reports about the trackage rights during the late 1800s stated that the agreement was dated November 24, 1885, and was updated on November 2, 1891. The trackage rights covered 1.39 miles of track from the "STL&SF north connection [29 feet north of SLSF crossing at Van Buren] to StL&SF south connection, located between Ark. River bridge and Ft. Smith." The charges were clearly stated as being $2.00 for each engine or passenger car, and $1.50 for each freight car. There was a yearly minimum charge of $12,000.

502.6 FRISCO AND LR&FS CROSSING – Little Rock & Fort Smith trains heading towards Fort Smith actually crossed their own mainline using the tracks of the Frisco (St. Louis & San Francisco, later St. Louis-San Francisco). This is Milepost 410.5 on the Frisco, and the line was signaled between their Milepost 410 Pole 21 and Milepost 411 by Automatic Block Signaling (ABS). This signal system was designed to protect trains at the Missouri Pacific diamond in Van Buren and on the Arkansas River bridge.

502.7 ARKANSAS RIVER BRIDGE – The Frisco showed this bridge to be at their Milepost 410.6. At 1460 miles long, the Arkansas River is the longest tributary in the Mississippi-Missouri River system. From its source near Leadville, Colorado, the river drops 10,000 feet in 125 miles, travels through Kansas, and then through northeastern Oklahoma. There, it is joined by the Canadian, Cimarron, Neosho-Grand, and Verdigris rivers. It then crosses Arkansas, emptying into the Mississippi River 600 miles north of New Orleans, Louisiana.

The railroad crosses from Crawford County into Sebastian County while crossing the Arkansas River. Located on the north side of the river, **Crawford County** was created on October 18, 1820, from part of Pulaski County. When created, it acquired the nickname of "Empire County" since it covered western Arkansas and much of Indian Territory, later part of Oklahoma. Crawford County was named for William H. Crawford of Georgia, a long-time politician. Crawford was elected to the U.S. Senate in 1807, appointed as the minister to France during the War of 1812, then Secretary of War, and then the 7th Secretary of the Treasury on October 22, 1816, and he held the position until March 6, 1825. Van Buren is its county seat.

Sebastian County was created in 1851 and named after William K. Sebastian, a judge for the U.S. Circuit Court. The county seat was first located at Greenwood, then moved to the second-largest community in Arkansas, Fort Smith, before being relocated back to Greenwood in 1852. In 1861, it was decided that the county would have two seats of government: one at Fort Smith and the other at Greenwood.

Building the Bridge

The St Louis, Iron Mountain & Southern once had trackage rights over the Fort Smith & Van Buren Bridge Company from the SLSF north connection (29 feet north of SLSF Crossing at Van Buren) to the SLSF south connection, located between the Arkansas River bridge and Fort Smith. The total trackage rights mileage was 1.39 miles. The agreement lasted from November 24, 1885, to November 2, 1891, and was then extended until 1931. However, this does not tell the full story about the bridge.

The Arkansas River was a major challenge for the growing Frisco Railroad. In November 1882, the St. Louis & San Francisco Railway Company (SLSF) arrived in Van Buren and regular service between Monett and Fort Smith began in January 1883. To cross the river, the railroad used the Little Rock & Fort Smith's transfer boat *Harold B* (a double-ended side wheeler which had replaced the transfer boat *N.D. Munson*) until 1886.

Congress authorized the Frisco railroad bridge at Van Buren on July 3, 1882. However, the authorization was subject to approval of the company's plans by the Chief of Engineers, United States Army. The railroad's plans were submitted on November 6, 1882, but were rejected on November 24th. After more than a year of arguments, the Frisco agreed to a number of changes and received permission to build the bridge on January 26, 1884.

In 1885, the Union Bridge Company began to build a wrought iron and steel bridge (1,794,247 pounds of iron and 1,153,191 pounds of steel) to cross the river. Construction was first slowed by high water during 1885 and then by a shortage of iron. The original bridge rested on 10 piers numbered from the Van Buren bank southward. The piers were made of white limestone, mainly from a quarry near Beaver, with lesser amounts coming from quarries in Mountainburg and Garfield, all in Arkansas. The construction of this bridge, technically owned by the Frisco's Fort Smith & Van Buren Bridge Company subsidiary, took two lives. The first train to cross the bridge was southbound Frisco No. 17, on February 9, 1886.

The bridge superstructure consisted of 4 fixed spans of 165' length on the south end and 3 fixed spans of 256'-9" length, separated by a pivot span of 366' length, on the north end. Total length of the original bridge was 1798 feet. The pivot span, which rotated to allow river navigation traffic when necessary, rested on a circular 30-foot diameter rock pier and rotated on a 27-foot diameter cast and wrought-iron turntable.

Due to heavier locomotives and railcars, the Frisco announced plans in 1912 to rebuild the bridge. The plans included replacing the metal superstructure of the original Van Buren bridge with new trusses which were more than twice as heavy, to handle axle loads which had also doubled by that time. As the rebuilding was underway in December 1913, high water caused a collapse of the false work used to support the bridge.

Numerous other problems occurred as the Frisco attempted to rebuild the bridge. Local newspapers dubbed the new bridge the "Jonah Bridge" as parts kept collapsing into the river. Although much of the preliminary work had been at least partially finished, a large amount of money had been spent and the bridge now had a large gap in it over the deepest part of the river channel. Additionally, the railroad's only 106-ton derrick had gone swimming in the river along with its three-man crew. The Frisco had to detour via the Missouri Pacific bridge to enter Fort Smith for more than a month.

On January 1, 1914, reconstruction of the bridge was turned over to the Kansas City Bridge Company. By January 11th, trains were again using the bridge, although it was many months before everything was completed. On April 7, 1915, newspapers announced that the steel work was finally finished. The bridge project was formally finished April 27, 1915.

In May 1943, major flooding again took out numerous spans of the bridge, closing it for several months. During the repairs, a 300-foot through truss span and a 50-foot through plate girder span were added to the south end and four deck girder spans were used to replace the lost Span 1 on the north end.

The McClellan-Kerr Arkansas River Navigation System navigation project resulted in the removal of the nearby Missouri Pacific (Iron Mountain's Helen Gould Bridge) bridge. The Missouri Pacific then returned to using the Frisco bridge from Van Buren to reach Fort Smith. As part of the McClellan-Kerr Arkansas River Navigation System, a new vertical lift span was installed in 1976 in the location of the new channel. This required removal of three of the old spans and replacement by the lift span and a short span.

Heading south, trains face a short grade of 1.47% coming off the Arkansas River Bridge as the tracks cross a low ridge. The track then drops briefly before encountering a short 1.20% grade at Milepost 503.8. It then drops and climbs before a 1.42% grade at Milepost 505.1 as the line peaks at 461 feet above sea level. The rail line then slowly drops downhill as it passes through Fort Smith.

This post card, printed in Germany shortly before World War I, shows the Frisco Bridge across the Arkansas River from the Van Buren side. At the time, the bridge was used by some Iron Mountain trains. This post card can still be found in antique markets and is a popular collector's item. Similar photos from the time can also be found.

504.3 ST. L. & S. F. JUNCTION – This location, at Frisco Milepost 411.9, was known as Missouri Pacific Paris Branch Switch in many Frisco documents. Early Iron Mountain timetables showed it to be at Milepost 502.7. After the McClellan-Kerr Arkansas River Navigation System project, the Missouri Pacific (MP) bridge into Fort Smith was abandoned and MP reacquired trackage rights to use the Frisco bridge. This is where the Missouri Pacific entered their own trackage in the Fort Smith area, located just to the west of the Frisco. At one time, the tracks followed the Frisco through town and then turned eastward to reach a number of coal mines and a large poultry feed mill at Paris, Arkansas. The line was leased to the Fort Smith Railroad in 1991 and eventually was abandoned between Fort Chaffee and Paris after the feed mill closed and moved to near Russellville, Arkansas. However, there is still a great deal of local rail business in the Fort Smith area and tracks wind around each other, often with several railroads serving each customer.

The junction between the Frisco and Missouri Pacific actually began many years earlier. First, the Frisco used the transfer boat of the Little Rock & Fort Smith Railway. Later, when the Frisco originally opened their Arkansas River bridge, the Little Rock & Fort Smith gained rights into Fort Smith over the Frisco, and a junction was built here for the LR&FS to get back onto their own tracks. At one time this was known as SLIM&S Junction, and it later became known as MoP Junction. For many years, this area was known as Race Track Prairie. It was named for the generally flat and straight route that roads, and later railroads, took through the open fields. The name became very appropriate when the two railroads were built side-by-side.

Just north of the junction are a number of rail shippers. To the west is the large freezer plant of OK Foods. OK Foods is now a part of Bachoco USA, a Mexican poultry producer which acquired the Arkansas company in 2011. While once served by both Missouri Pacific and Frisco, only tracks off the Frisco mainline remain. To the east is the large Georgia Pacific Dixie Products pulpboard plant. The Dixie plant was one of the first manufacturing operations to move to Fort Smith after World War II. Once the Dixie Cup Division of the American Can Company, the plant started by producing soda fountain paper cups. The plant is today known for manufacturing paper plates. Other rail-served industries are to the west, including Gerber Products and Covia. While you might not have heard of Covia (a provider of diversified mineral solutions to the oil and gas, glass, ceramics, coatings, metals, foundry, polymers, construction, water filtration, and sport sand recreation markets), many have heard of Gerber (this plant opened in 1964 to produce various baby food purees).

504.4 OAK PARK – Oak Park is a neighborhood in Fort Smith that is currently the home of facilities operated by OK Foods, Gerber Products, International Paper, and Georgia Pacific. A rail line off of the former LR&FS line serves several of these shippers.

Oak Park features a number of small homes, many built for workers at nearby manufacturing facilities. Many have a similar look, very reminiscent of a company town.

504.6 KCS CONNECTION – The three main railroads at Fort Smith – Missouri Pacific, Frisco, and Kansas City Southern – all had tracks at one time throughout the industrial and manufacturing areas of Fort Smith. These railroads often had trackage rights over each other to reach these spur tracks. In this case, the Kansas City Southern had a line to the west during much of the 1900s.

504.8 TRUSTY SPUR – This location was found in the 1925 list of Missouri Pacific stations on the Central Division, and it was earlier shown as Potato Spur. It would have been located a short distance north of the Spradling Avenue grade crossing, and the 278-foot-long spur was shown to be on the west side of the mainline. There was also a 1933-foot-long siding to the west, located south of Spradling Avenue.

Trusty Spur also had a mail crane and was served for both inbound and outbound carload freight. The area still is often called Trusty, as shown by the name assigned to a local elementary school.

The Arkansas & Missouri is handling interchange between Union Pacific and the Fort Smith Railroad in this May 2021 scene at Mathews. Both trains (A&M 50 southbound and PREX 2031 northbound) are on the tracks of the former Little Rock & Fort Smith.

506.0 MATHEWS – Located at the old Iron Mountain Milepost of 504.4 was a station using the name Mathews. This station from the 1925 listing of Missouri Pacific stations was located a short distance north of the North 6th Street grade crossing. It was shown to have a mail crane and was served for both inbound and outbound carload freight.

This was once a small community that was full of furniture factories. These included the facilities of Ballman Cummings Furniture Company, Fort Smith Folding Bed & Table Company, and the Ward Furniture Manufacturing Company. All were served by the railroad.

This area currently includes a short siding and two spur tracks, used as a RIP (repair in place) and transload facility by the Fort Smith Railroad.

This crossing sign at North 27th Street shows that the Fort Smith Branch is now operated by the Fort Smith Railroad Company.

Where Mathews once was located, the Fort Smith Railroad now has a RIP (repair in place) and transload facility.

PREX 2031, handling the Fort Smith Railroad switching duties on the north side of Fort Smith, is shown heading northbound near the former Fort Smith Suburban Railway connection.

506.3 FORT SMITH SUBURBAN RAILWAY COMPANY CONNECTION – To the east was the Fort Smith Suburban Railway Company, a railroad incorporated on July 29, 1902. It came under the control of Missouri Pacific on May 4, 1903, when George Gould was elected president. The original proposal for

the company was to build and operate an electric belt railroad around Fort Smith, connecting the city with outlying towns. A total of 20 to 30 miles of track was planned. Announcements later stated that the 6.3-mile Fort Smith Suburban Railway was completed in February 1904 and was built to attract new industry to the city. Interstate Commerce Commission reports stated that the railway was a subsidiary of the St. Louis, Iron Mountain & Southern, which was a subsidiary of the Missouri Pacific. The Suburban Railway was operated under trackage rights by the St. Louis, Iron Mountain & Southern, and it was controlled through ownership of all the company's stock. On December 1, 1937, the railroad entered receivership, and was then merged into the Missouri Pacific Railroad on March 1, 1956. The trackage is basically all now abandoned.

The Fort Smith Suburban Railway was originally built from the south and ended near the north side of the rail yard of the Frisco. The route was described in a 1929 Interstate Commerce Commission (ICC) report. It stated that the railroad extended from a connection with the Missouri Pacific line about 3 miles south of the Missouri Pacific depot "in Fort Smith eastward about 1.5 miles, then northward about 3 miles and then westward through the city of Fort Smith about 2 miles, the last mile of the line being roughly parallel with and a little to the south of the line of the Frisco." The purpose of the ICC report was an application by Missouri Pacific to build a short piece of track here across the Frisco to connect to the north end of the Fort Smith Suburban Railway. At the time, almost all of the industries on the line, which shipped or received 2499 cars in 1928, were at the north end of the railroad. These included the Fort Smith Couch & Bedding Company (150 cars inbound and 450 cars outbound per year) and the Kelly-Evans Rock Crusher plant (600 cars of stone shipped in 1928 with an expected 1800 cars in 1929).

Missouri Pacific had determined that the new connection would cut in half the time it took to serve the customers, and would allow more frequent service of the busiest shippers. The ICC approved the plan of connecting the Missouri Pacific line with the Fort Smith Suburban Railway about "1 mile from the westerly end of the northerly part of the Suburban line" where it came within a few feet of the line of the Frisco. The new connection had to cross the Frisco, and a series of gates would be used to control the train movements. This connection was located south of North 22nd Street. A few of the old railroad grades still remain and can be found in the brush.

While the Fort Smith Suburban Railway has been abandoned, a few signs of the line can still be found to the east of the Fort Smith Railroad near North P Street.

506.9 KCS RAILWAY CROSSING – At one time, Kansas City Southern had a spur track off of the Frisco line that curved to the north, crossing the Little Rock & Fort Smith Railway/Missouri Pacific. It closely followed a spur track operated by Missouri Pacific, and actually crossed it at grade three times. Some of these tracks still remain, located north of the Arkansas & Missouri rail yard.

The Fort Smith Branch once served a number of industries, requiring frequent spur tracks. Additionally, tracks of Kansas City Southern and St. Louis-San Francisco (Frisco) once also crossed the Iron Mountain to reach rail shippers. Most are now gone. This diamond at Milepost 506.9 is one of the few left in the area.

A week before Christmas in 2022, ARMN refrigerated railcar 110150 was spotted at the Arkansas Refrigerated Services near North E Street in Fort Smith.

507.5 NORTH E STREET – South of this crossing, the Fort Smith Railroad serves Arkansas Refrigerated Services, a firm that specializes in storing and moving frozen products. The firm can blast freeze 960,000 pounds of product a day and has 3.6 million cubic feet of fully-racked freezer space in its various facilities. The firm also operates a refrigerated trucking business.

507.8 FORT SMITH – When the Little Rock & Fort Smith originally built its line, their one-story wooden depot was located to the east on the south side of Mulberry (2 blocks north of Garrison and now known as North B Street). A "lunch room" was located alongside Mulberry Street north of the depot. A coal trestle, water tank, and tool house were to the west of the tracks. The freight house of the LR&FS was located south of the depot. The tracks went as far south as Garrison Avenue to serve the Philipp Mehlburger Vulcan Foundry. Three blocks to the north was the Border City Ice & Coal Company, to the east of the tracks between Hickory (North D Street) and Ash (North E Street). Another block to the north was the Fort Smith Oil & Cotton Compress Company (advertised as being the largest in the world), located between Ash and Vine (North G Street) and to the east of the LR&FS. Throughout this area, the Frisco mainline was a block to the east running down Ozark Street. Most of the industries were served by both railroads.

Garrison Avenue was laid out by city founder John Rogers in 1838, using the parade garrison of the original Fort Smith military installation. It became the major east-west thoroughfare in the city, and the street was lined with stores, warehouses, hotels, bars, and other businesses that served those traveling on the Santa Fe Trail and Butterfield Overland Stage route. Cattle drives, settlers, and many of those who headed west for the California Gold Rush passed down Garrison Avenue, supporting these businesses. When the railroad was built, serving Garrison Avenue became the goal of the passenger station and freight house.

Note that multiple names are given for many of the streets at Fort Smith. Initially, the streets north of Garrison were named for various types of trees. By 1892, these had been renamed using the alphabet, with Walnut becoming North A, Mulberry becoming North B, and so on. To the south of Garrison, the streets were named after early leaders of Arkansas and a few nearby cities. Those streets south of the National Cemetery were also renamed. For example, Powell Street became South A and Sullivan became South B.

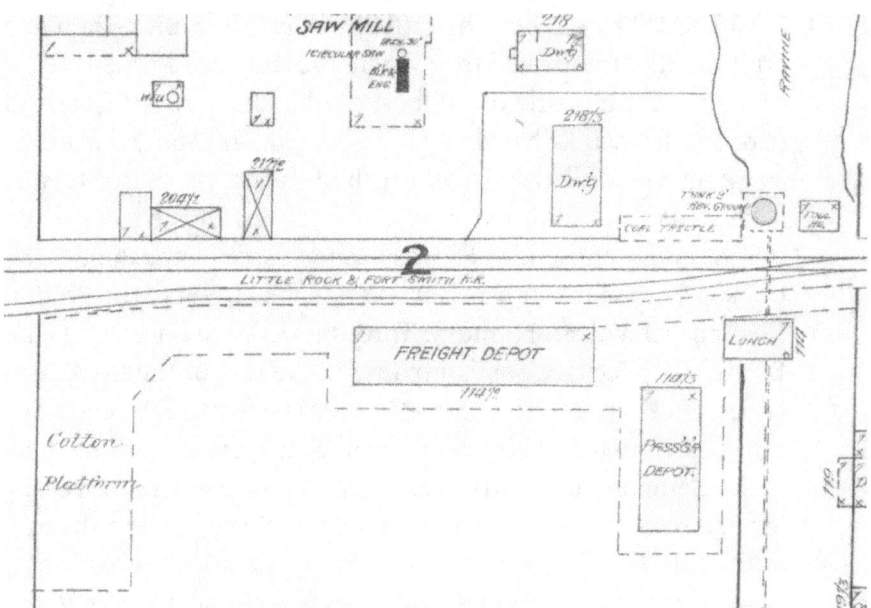

This Sanborn map shows the depot, freight house and other Little Rock & Fort Smith facilities in Fort Smith in 1886. *Sanborn Fire Insurance Map from Fort Smith, Sebastian County, Arkansas.* Sanborn Map Company, May, 1886. Map. Retrieved from the Library of Congress, https://www.loc.gov/item/sanborn00247_001/.

In 1887, Missouri Pacific had its subsidiaries expand their operations in Fort Smith and build to the coal fields to the south. Grading south from the Garrison Avenue area started in September of 1887. As a part of this effort, the Helen Gould Bridge over the Arkansas River and into downtown Fort Smith opened in 1891. The bridge was reported on in *The Missouri Pacific Railway Company Eleventh Annual Report – Year Ending December 31, 1891.*

The bridge across the Arkansas river at Ft. Smith, Ark., the construction of which was commenced in 1890, was completed during the year and opened for traffic on May 25, 1891. This bridge consists of ten fixed spans, each 200 feet long, and one draw span 370 feet long, a total length of 2,370 feet. The superstructure is of iron on piers of concrete founded on rock. The opening of the bridge for foot and wagon traffic has been delayed by litigation, concerning the right of the Company to use its right-of-way for approaches, which has recently been decided in the United States courts favorably to the Kansas and Arkansas Valley Railway.

At the Fort Smith end of the bridge was a wye, with the north leg serving the Garrison Avenue station. The south leg connected to the Greenwood Branch and the coal fields to the south. In the middle of the wye was a water tank to service steam locomotives. When the Helen Gould Bridge was built, the Fort Smith Wye was actually in Oklahoma. At the time, the line between Arkansas and Indian Territory was east of the Arkansas and Poteau rivers in this area. On February 10, 1905, an Act of the United States Congress moved the line to the center of the two rivers, moving the wye into Arkansas.

About the same time as the bridge was built, a new brick passenger station was erected on the south side of Garrison Avenue along the river. This new station was needed due to the additional traffic from the Greenwood Branch to the coal fields, the Arkansas Central line to Paris, and the growth of Fort Smith. The old wooden depot was turned into a tool room. A new brick freight house was also built, located immediately north of Garrison Avenue. These new facilities were essentially located at the end of the Helen Gould Bridge. In the 1907 St. Louis, Iron Mountain & Southern employee timetable, Fort Smith was shown to feature a day and night telegraph office, water, and a wye.

Business was good, and the new passenger station was renovated in 1910 for $26,000, connecting the passenger and baggage sections of the building, expanding the northern portion of the station, and adding steam heat and a hot water system. The station was again expanded after World War I, adding a building on the west side for the growing Railway Express Agency business.

All of these buildings are now gone. The office of the Fort Smith Railroad, which leases the remaining Fort Smith-area tracks of Missouri Pacific, now sits where the original wooden depot was built. Modern distribution centers for Belle Point Beverages sit where the passenger station and freight house once stood. To the east where the Fort Smith Pavilion now stands was once the site of the St. Louis & San Francisco's passenger depot, restaurant, and freight depot.

The tracks of the Fort Smith Railroad pass some of the facilities of Arkansas Refrigerated Services and cross North B Street, entering the shop area of the railroad.

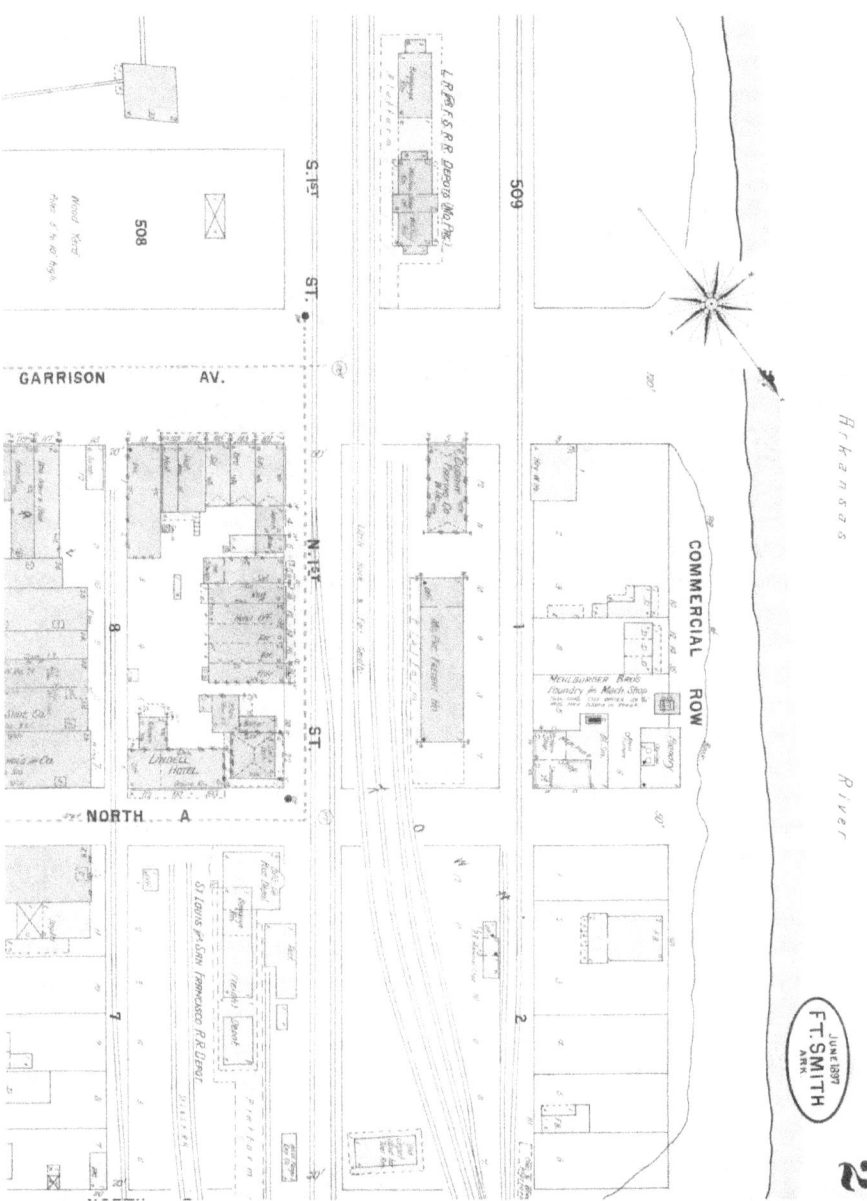

This Sanborn map from 1897 shows the new LR&FS (Mo Pac) passenger station and freight house located on Garrison Avenue. A map from 1892 showed that the station was the M. P. R. R. Passenger Depot. *Sanborn Fire Insurance Map from Fort Smith, Sebastian County, Arkansas.* Sanborn Map Company, Jun, 1897. Map. Retrieved from the Library of Congress, https://www.loc.gov/item/sanborn00247_004/.

For years, the Fort Smith Railroad was a subsidiary of Pioneer Railcorp, and locomotives from almost any of its operations could be found operating on the line. In 2022, this included Alabama & Florida 1612.

The Federal Government at Fort Smith

Fort Smith, as can be imagined, has an early military history. The first Fort Smith was established at the confluence of the Arkansas and Poteau rivers in 1817 at a place called Belle Point. It was the highest navigable point on the Arkansas River at the time the site was chosen by the U.S. Army. Soldiers arrived in 1817 and named the site Fort Smith after their commanding officer, Thomas A. Smith. The army abandoned the fort in 1824. Foundations from this original construction are visible to visitors today.

A second fort was built here in 1838, located a bit higher above the rivers. Major buildings included two officer's quarters, a barracks, commissary, and quartermaster storehouse, all enclosed by a stone wall. The former military barracks and the commissary storehouse, the oldest buildings still standing in Fort Smith, are part of the Fort Smith National Historic Site. General Zachary Taylor, later President Taylor, lived here 1846-1848 while he was Commander of the Western Military District. Remains of his home still exist.

This "First Fort" was necessary to prevent a war between the local Osage Indians and a band of Cherokee who had migrated west to lands in western Arkansas. The "Second Fort" came about due to white encroachment into the Indian Territory after the Indian Removal Act of 1830. Being located on the Arkansas River, the fort became a supply point for other military facilities within the region. It also later housed the United States District Court for the Western District of Arkansas, which presided over the western half of Arkansas and all of Indian Territory.

For many people, the name Fort Smith might sound familiar. For anyone who has seen the movies, or read the book, Fort Smith is the base of action for the story of *True Grit*. It was here at the court of Judge Parker that Mattie Ross first heard of, and saw, Rooster Cogburn. While much of the story is fiction, Fort Smith was a base of the legal system for this area and into Indian Territory, now Oklahoma. While Rooster Cogburn wasn't real, there are enough stories about the real marshals to fill many books. One of the most famous was Bass Reeves, a Black U.S. marshal who worked for Judge Parker out of Fort Smith. He often rode into Indian Territory with his friend, an Indian policeman. Some have alleged that stories about Reeves could have been the inspiration for the Lone Ranger stories.

In 1872, the former military barracks were converted into the federal courthouse. When the military barracks were used as a courthouse the basement was turned into a jail. In 1888, a new jail wing was constructed. The federal courthouse, which originally was a 1½ story structure with full porches, was changed to its present appearance in 1890.

From 1873 through 1896, a total of 86 men were executed on the gallows at Fort Smith. All the men executed were convicted of rape or murder. After the Civil War, there was a mandatory federal death sentence in cases of rape or murder. Of the 86 men executed here, 29 were sentenced to death by Judge Parker. During Judge Parker's 21-year tenure, a total of 160 death sentences were handed down. Of that number, 43 were commuted to life in prison or lesser terms; 2 were pardoned by the President; 31 had appeals that resulted in acquittals or convictions overturned; 2 were granted new trials and discharged; 1 was shot and killed while attempting to escape; and 2 died in jail while awaiting execution. During his years on the bench, Parker handled more than 13,000 cases with more than 9000 of the defendants being convicted or pleading guilty. A reproduction of the 1886 gallows stands on its original site and is a reminder of "the chaotic social conditions that existed in Indian Territory during Judge Parker's time."

Building of Judge Isaac C. Parker. The barracks were built by the U. S. Army in 1851 and converted into a courthouse and jail (built in the former mess halls in the basement and known as "Hell on the Border") in 1872 by the Federal Court for the Western District of Arkansas. In 1888 a new jail building was built adjacent to the barracks/courthouse. In 1889, a new federal courthouse and post office opened, replaced in 1937 with what is now the Judge Isaac C. Parker Federal Building. Today, the former barracks building houses the visitor center of the Fort Smith National Historic Site. *Federal Court Building, South Third Street & Rogers Avenue, Fort Smith, Sebastian County, AR.* Photograph. Historic American Buildings Survey, Creator. Retrieved from the Library of Congress, https://www.loc.gov/item/ar0116/.

The federal court for the Western District of Arkansas still exists, holding court in the Judge Isaac C. Parker Federal Building, three blocks from the National Historic Site. The court currently has federal jurisdiction over the western counties of the State of Arkansas. The Indian Territory jurisdiction of the court came to an end on September 1, 1896, thus ending the unique nature of the court.

The City of Fort Smith

The second Fort Smith was built here in 1838, and a community began to grow around it that served the Indian Territory, western Arkansas, and the many explorers who were heading west. The 1840 census showed a population of 144, and the city was incorporated on December 24, 1842. The town remained a supply point until the Civil War, when federal troops left the area, then fought their way back a few years later. The area was heavily impacted by guerilla forces fighting for both sides, and federal forces spent several years after the war working to restore order to the countryside and rural areas around Fort Smith. Fort Smith was considered to be a relatively safe place and saw its population grow from 1532 people in 1860 to 2226 residents in 1870.

Fort Smith is one of two county seats of Sebastian County, which bounced back and forth with Greenwood until 1861 when a decision was made to have two seats of county government. The federal government helped to reestablish Fort Smith by creating places for war refugees to live. The city was restored as a center of government and was used as a meeting location to negotiate new treaties with the former Confederate Indian nations.

When railroads reached Fort Smith, local industry grew to handle regional and even national demand. Fort Smith quickly became known as a furniture town with almost a dozen factories turning out chairs, tables, beds and other wooden furniture. During the 1880s, the population grew from 3099 to 11,311 residents as factory jobs attracted many workers, and then local retail businesses were created to handle the needs of the residents.

By 1910, the population had reached 23,975, it was 31,429 in 1930, and 47,942 in 1950. In fact, the population of Fort Smith has increased in every census since the city's founding. Several major industrial firms like the Norge Company (later Whirlpool), Baldor Electric, Georgia-Pacific, Gerber, Planters Peanuts, and many others have protected the reputation of Fort Smith being an industrial and manufacturing town. The population in the 2020 census was 89,142 and the city also features schools, hospitals, plenty of retail shopping, the Fort Smith National Historic Site, and the Belle Grove Historic District.

About the Author

Barton Jennings grew up in Arkansas, spending years exploring the various railroad lines throughout the state. He has written numerous articles for magazines like *Trains*, *Railfan & Railroad*, and *Pacific Rail News*. He has also written books about area railroads such as the De-Queen & Eastern, Arkansas & Missouri, the Missouri & North Arkansas, and the Rock Island's Choctaw Route.

Additionally, for almost three decades, Barton Jennings has been organizing charter passenger trains and writing the route descriptions, both for planning purposes and for the enjoyment of the passengers. These trips have been in all areas of the United States, often covering operations that haven't seen a passenger train in decades. He has also had the pleasure of riding the trips of other organizations, where some of the material for this book was collected.

Bart currently lives within earshot of the former Little Rock & Fort Smith Railway, often heading out the door at the sound of a horn. This has allowed him to explore the route as he follows trains to and from Little Rock and Van Buren.

His house has several rooms full of books, timetables and other documents about this and other railroads – important research items from a time long before today's internet. Today, Bart Jennings, after years working in the railroad industry, is a professor emeritus of supply chain management and teaches transportation operations. He also still teaches regulatory issues for the railroad industry, a way to stay in touch with the industry he loves.

The author holding a proof copy of this book alongside the line of the old Little Rock & Fort Smith Railway at Atkins, Arkansas. Photo by Sarah Jennings.

www.ingramcontent.com/pod-product-compliance
Lightning Source LLC
Chambersburg PA
CBHW070902130626
46555CB00001B/4